Text and Act

TEXT

and

ACT

Essays on Music and Performance

RICHARD TARUSKIN

New York   Oxford
OXFORD UNIVERSITY PRESS
1995

Oxford University Press

Oxford   New York
Athens   Auckland   Bangkok   Bombay
Calcutta   Cape Town   Dar es Salaam   Delhi
Florence   Hong Kong   Istanbul   Karachi
Kuala Lumpur   Madras   Madrid   Melbourne
Mexico City   Nairobi   Paris   Singapore
Taipei   Tokyo   Toronto

and associated companies in
Berlin   Ibadan

Library of Congress Cataloging-in-Publication Data
Taruskin, Richard.
    Text and act : essays on music and performance /
    Richard Taruskin.
        p.   cm.
    Includes bibliographical references and index.
    ISBN 0-19-509437-9. — ISBN 0-19-509458-1 (pbk.)
    1. Performance practice (Music)
    2. Style, Musical.
    I. Title.
    ML457.T37   1995   781.4'3 — dc20   94-24903

9 8 7 6 5 4 3 2 1
Printed in the United States of America
on acid-free paper

Contents

Bach

Antiquarian Innocence

Full Circle

Author's Note

Every piece in this collection has been thoroughly reedited—to expunge redundancies, to correct the style, to refine or enrich the argument. If I am asking my readers to reread me, the least I can do is to offer them an improved text. Those encountering these pieces for the first time need never know what they have been spared.

INTRODUCTION

Last Thoughts First: Wherein the Author Gently Replies to a Few of His Critics and Takes Tender Leave of the Topic

Some years after I had moved away from New York City and left my performing activities behind, I learned that a fable lived on there about a self-serving choir director who used to give dreadfully unauthentic performances of Renaissance music and who, when this was pointed out to him, resolved not to reform but instead to wreck the whole idea of authenticity. "And that," the fable concludes, "is why we can no longer use the word."

That is flattering, but not what I remember. What I remember is that in 1981 I was asked by Professor D. Kern Holoman on behalf of the American Musicological Society to participate in a panel at that year's national meeting to be called "The Musicologist Today and in the Future," in which a group of "younger" spokesmen for the profession would assess prospects for music scholarship from various "applied" perspectives. I was chosen to represent musicology as applied to performance because three years earlier the choir I directed, Cappella Nova, had received the Society's first Noah Greenberg Award ("for a distinguished contribution to the study and performance of early music," as the guidelines then read), which had financed our recording of Ockeghem's *Missa Prolationum*. I was nobody's idea of a maverick or an iconoclast, least of all my own. Had I been so regarded, I would never have been honored with an invitation to address the Society in those days. (Nowadays it may be a different story; but, then, my contemporaries and I are no longer "younger" scholars . . .)

The talk I gave, somewhat expanded and adapted, is the opening essay in this book. It is pretty tame. But well do I remember the mounting dread I felt while drafting it, and the consternation with which it was received by some members of the audience at the Boston Park Plaza Hotel. Partly as a result of my having immersed myself in a study of Stravinsky, I had begun to notice parallels between aspects of the academic performance-practice ideal (we did not yet call it an ideology) and aspects of neoclassical modernism. Performance-practice orthodoxy, to which I still felt loyal albeit uneasily so, was fast crystallizing, with the help of the record companies, around the notion of authenticity. Some influential reviewers like John Rockwell and Andrew Porter were on the bandwagon. Musicologists naturally felt a certain triumph at this, since their (our) ideas seemed to be making an impact in the wider world. At the same Boston meeting of the AMS, Joshua Rifkin unveiled the "B Minor Madrigal," as a few recusants were heard to mutter, his trendsetting "one-on-a-part" realization of Bach's Mass in B Minor. ("First performance of the original version," the promotional leaflet proclaimed, promising "an unprecedented experience—one of the greatest masterworks of Western music heard truly for the first time.") It did not go unchallenged—the conductor's face-off with Professor Robert Marshall on the subject of "Bach's Choir" (did he have one? did he want one?) was mobbed and memorable—but it was an indubitable benchmark. Bach-and-Handel was the extent of Early Music's reach in those days, though it would soon travel further, and fast. If Rifkin was right, truth was on the march.

And here I was relativizing the whole business. If I was right, not truth but taste was on the march. And authenticity was headed, at best, for nervous scare quote status, doomed forever to be surrounded by those pesky diacritics that "appear to take back what is advanced between them, while they oddly also insist on the necessity of advancing it."[1] My little talk, I was pleased later to reflect, was willy-nilly kin to Ruth Solie's pithily subversive, nearly coetaneous piece entitled "The Living Work: Organicism and Musical Analysis,"[2] which, by situating Schenkerian analysis in intellectual history, had relativized the claims of another hegemonic discourse (as we have learned to say)—one that had purported to furnish the means by which "the greatest masterworks of Western music" were in another sense "heard truly for the first time."

If all that Early Music was was taste, why then we could take it or leave it. (Later we discovered that we could take or leave historical

[1]Peter Kivy (quoting Gregg Horowitz) in "Composers and 'Composers': A Response to David Rosen," *Cambridge Opera Journal* 4 (1992): 179.
[2]*19th-Century Music* 4 (1980–81): 147–56.

facts as well.) Some, as I say, were quicker than I was to recognize the threat. A notably exercised Verdian, for example, rose up in Boston to denounce me for wishing to "throw out" all evidence of historical performance practice. The charge surprised me. I had called for no such thing; but I *had* come out against accepting historical evidence uncritically, and this, it seemed, was heresy enough. I began then and there to see to what an extent nominally positivistic scholarship had in fact invested in systems of belief that discouraged or disallowed independent thinking; which is to say, I began to see how heavily our discipline, which prided itself on its freedom from "ideology" (that is, of course, from Marxism), had bought into ideologies of other (not unrelated and equally dogmatic) kinds. Rose Rosengard Subotnik's presentation at the same Boston symposium—she, not I, being the designated iconoclast of the afternoon—also did much to open my eyes to this state of affairs, both at the time (especially during the acrimonious debate that followed it) and when our essays later appeared side by side in print.[3]

So if I shook things up in Boston, I got as good as I gave. I learned a lot that day. I left the meeting not only strengthened in my skepticism of historical performance practice and its hegemonic designs, but newly skeptical about the claims of "disinterested" scholarship tout court. My continuing work with Stravinsky and his intellectual environment brought me into contact with many more texts that corroborated the parallels I had noted before, and began to prompt a theory. What we had been accustomed to regard as historically authentic performances, I began to see, represented neither any determinable historical prototype nor any coherent revival of practices coeval with the repertories they addressed. Rather, they embodied a whole wish list of modern(ist) values, validated in the academy and the marketplace alike by an eclectic, opportunistic reading of historical evidence.

When I began to look at things in this way, a far-reaching pattern began to take shape in my mind, one that touched on and linked many other aspects of modernism and academic practice, and suggested many unforeseen points of congruence with the emerging postmodernist critique of knowledge and its politics. At the same time, Early Music was rampaging demurely through the historical epochs, making ever more sweeping, ever more blustery claims on behalf of prim

---

[3]See R. Subotnik, "Musicology and Criticism," in D. Kern Holoman and Claude V. Palisca (eds.), *Musicology in the 1980s: Methods, Goals, Opportunities* (New York: Da Capo Press, 1982), pp. 145–60; reprinted in Subotnik, *Developing Variations: Style and Ideology in Western Music* (Minneapolis: University of Minnesota Press, 1991), 87–97; also idem, "The Role of Ideology in the Study of Western Music," *Journal of Musicology* 2 (1983): 1–12; reprt. *Developing Variations*, 3–14.

correctness, winning souls away from the "modern" style in ever greater numbers and in ever more "mainstream" repertories, surrounding its apostles of impersonalism with potent personality cults, exposing ever more flagrantly the brute modernist bias and the totalizing assumptions that underlay its civilizing, sanitizing, miniaturizing project. No one was calling the bluff; so all at once, I found, I was a man with a mission. I was morally engaged. I seized every opportunity to continue developing and promoting my ideas, and was fortunate that new and unexpected opportunities for reaching wider audiences presented themselves as the success of historical performance practice exacerbated the tenor of the surrounding debate.

Nicholas Kenyon, on assuming the reins as editor of *Early Music* magazine, sought to launch his tenure with a splash of sensationalism and commissioned the symposium, "The Limits of Authenticity," that furnished the pretext for writing essay 2. The wide notice that discussion received led Sir William Glock, then of Eulenburg Books, to ask Kenyon to put together a full-dress exposition of *Authenticity in Early Music*, as the book was eventually called on publication by another house. Asked by the editor to summarize my position, I took the occasion to expand my critique of "the authenticity movement" (O antic oxymoron!) into its most fully developed formulation. This is essay 4, the longest in this book (and in Kenyon's; I am much obliged to him for his indulgence). Yet despite its amplitude, the statement did not prove definitive. It couldn't, for the terms of the debate were in constant flux.

Between the two Kenyon commissions, in 1984, a common acquaintance put me in touch with James R. Oestreich just as the latter was starting up that wonderful short-lived venture known as *Opus* magazine. Originating as a bolt from *High Fidelity* by its disenfranchised classical staff, *Opus* was no ordinary record collector's forum. It filled the gap between the music-biz and fan mags, on the one hand, and the scholarly journals on the other. Though its audience was nonprofessional, and its contributors had for the most part to avoid technical lingo and musical notation, it offered writers space and scope such as I have never enjoyed anywhere else, and an editor more devoted to airing serious, qualified opinion than any other with whom I have had the pleasure of working. It still seems a miracle that Jim Oestreich took my big Beethoven review (essay 8) without asking for a single cut. That piece would have been turned down by any scholarly journal as too topical, by any Early Music forum as too impious, and by any record magazine as too detailed (not to mention long), but for *Opus*, or for Jim, it was just right. I believe it to be perhaps the most valuable piece in the present book because of how it immediately applies theoretical premises to the exercise of "practical criticism." I would like to think it exemplary in its way, but there is no magazine in the world today that would print it.

Opus was too good to last. It folded in March 1988—not (as widely assumed) because of a financial crisis but because its parent company got hostilely taken over. A couple of years later, after a stint as program annotator for the Cleveland Orchestra, Jim Oestreich benignly took over the classical music page for the Sunday *New York Times* and began mustering his old "troops." The same editor—the same umpire, so to speak—but this was a new ball game. My first piece for the *Times* was essay 6 in this collection, based on some off-the-cuff remarks I made at a smug and humdrum symposium at Berkeley to which I had been invited, it seemed, as the local curmudgeon.[4] The complacency of the other participants, and the way in which I felt my position was being demeaned, no doubt account in part for the rhetorical temperature in the version I sent the *Times*. It is the strongest, most belligerent statement I ever hope to make. That, of course, was very much to the taste of the *Times*. But whereas at *Opus* Jim Oestreich was the very caring boss, at the *Times* he could be no more than an advocate for his writers; and just as often he had to work the other side of the street, conveying to his writers and helping them meet the paper's demands. He was not even a successful intercessor in every case, and sometimes things went out of his control altogether. Life became dangerous. (In essay 7 I have sketched some of the noisome if retrospectively comical vicissitudes that befell essay 6 on its way to print.)

Where *Opus* had a cozy coterie readership and space to burn, the *Times* has a circulation beyond a musicologist's maddest imagining and no room at all. That was the trade-off. One's pieces there are shaved to the bone, and then some; often Jim Oestreich and I would spend an hour on the transcontinental phone looking for ten words to cut, or even, when things became excessively "format-specific," a single one. I did not mind. For me it was a school. Harder to get used to was the response. People actually read (and, I found, virtuosically misread) the *New York Times*. And there was this rule: if they loved your work they wanted you to know, and wrote you; if they hated your work they wanted the world to know, and wrote the *Times*. On two occasions, harsh backlash to something I had written filled the Arts & Leisure mail column. One such column concerned essay 6, and it will be sampled in situ. One's hide is toughened by such treatment; one loses one's inhibitions and becomes truthful. This, too, was

---

[4]The original remarks were taken down stenographically and published, belatedly and rather pointlessly, in Joseph Kerman et al., "The Early Music Debate: Ancients, Moderns, Postmoderns," *Journal of Musicology* 10 (1992): 113–30. It was like seeing the egg return after the chicken had hatched.

school. And if intensity of backlash is a measure of an issue's sensitivity, there would seem to be no issue more sensitive right now than Early Music. (It must be because, as everyone is obscurely aware, the issue is much, much more important than by rights it ought to be.)

At any rate, thanks at first to sheer persistence, and later to the fortuities of opportunity, my painstakingly worked-out thesis on the matter of historical performance and its cultural meaning is no longer an academic secret. It has passed into folklore and become one of the standard positions on the subject, to which many now subscribe (it delights me to say) without knowing its source. The essays and reviews in this book collectively lay out the argument, trace its development, support it with practical applications, and illustrate it with many examples.

Those who persist in taking the claims of Early Music or "historical" performance at face value now do so under an onus. Consciousness has been raised. The claims cannot be merely asserted; they must be defended. The scare quotes now de rigueur for certain words (as in this paragraph's opening sentence) testify to the general loss of innocence. Lewis Lockwood's nostalgic address to the Lincoln Center Mozart conference in May 1991 was called "Performance and 'Authenticity.' "[5] A few years ago it would have been called "Performance and Authenticity." To risk a title like that now—as in Peter Le Huray's recent *Authenticity in Performance*—is to court "a raised eyebrow" from reviewers.[6] John Rockwell, reviewing the work of some suitably scare-quoted " 'authentic' early-music conductors," still wants to believe (or wants us to believe) that "the early-music movement's preference for brisk tempos, light textures and no-nonsense forward momentum represents an honest effort to re-imagine what concerts actually sounded like 200 years ago"; and yet, feeling the breath upon his neck, he pays lip service to my claim—made, he says, "with insight and bile"—that the movement "merely reflects modernist assumptions about how all music should sound."[7]

Readers of these collected essays can assess the ratio of insight to bile for themselves, but right up front I want to disavow—and contest— Mr. Rockwell's "merely." It shows he has not understood me at all. Not only does the word imply that I have sought to belittle the Early Music movement, it also suggests that restoration—"re-imagining" some-

    [5]See *Early Music* 19 (1991): 501–8.

    [6]Cambridge: Cambridge University Press, 1990; for the raised eyebrow see David Montgomery, "Views, Reviews, and Nonviews: Two Studies in Historical Performance Practice," *Musical Quarterly* 76 (1992): 265. It should be noted that although the title lacks them, the scare quotes are generally in place throughout Dr. Le Huray's text.

    [7]"Early Musicker Arrives Late But Catches Up in a Big Way," *New York Times*, Arts and Leisure, 24 May 1992.

thing old—is ideally a better accomplishment than participating in the creation of something new. I believe the opposite to be true, and have said so as loudly as I can (loudest perhaps in essay 6); that is why I so admire the best of the "Early Musickers," whose work I find to be, in a sense most music critics seem to have forgotten or repressed, quite profoundly authentic (no scare quotes here) because it truly reflects our times and our tastes and gives us a sense not only of who we truly are but of how we have come to be that way—and how we might be changed. What deserves to be called "mere" is the chimerical historical accuracy so many performers wish (or think they wish) to achieve. That is the most overrated of all possible aims.

So only half the battle is won. The false authenticity has been exposed, but the true authenticity—a necessary pleonasm, alas—remains hidden. Indeed, to the extent that musicians sincerely believe in the lie of restoration—to the extent to which they have, in effect, bought their own hype—it has been a brake on authenticity. The matter is worth one more go.

HOW WORKS WORK

My general thesis has received several fresh challenges since my last opportunity to defend it. One of them, more a complement than a clash, can be easily harmonized with my viewpoint, opening it out onto a fresh and promising terrain. In a dissertation in progress at Stanford as of the present writing, but surely destined to be a book, José Antonio Bowen points out that the "modernist" stance I have identified with Early Music had a considerable prior history. "My research makes it clear," he writes,

> that the ideology of authenticity (as well as many of the specific performance practices associated with it) originated in the nineteenth century. This study contributes to the current authenticity debate by (1) showing how the fidelity to the spirit of the composer's intentions came to be understood as "authenticity" and (2) by demonstrating how and why fast strict tempos (among other performance practices) became necessarily associated with fidelity to the musical work.[8]

[8]*Abstracts of Papers Read at the Fifty-Eighth Annual Meeting of the American Musicological Society*, ed. Laurence Dreyfus (Madison: A-R Editions, 1992), 22. Bowen's paper, drawn from the dissertation, was entitled "The Origins of the Ideology of Authenticity in Interpretation: Mendelssohn, Berlioz and Wagner as Conductors." A version of it has been published as "Mendelssohn, Berlioz, and Wagner as Conductors: the Origins of the Ideal of 'Fidelity to the Composer,' " *Historical Performance* 6 (1993): 77–88.

So, Bowen argues, authenticity is not "modern" but "romantic." Well of course it is. That is just what I have been implying all along. Modernism, as Leonard B. Meyer memorably puts it, is "the late, late Romantic ideology."[9] Its beliefs and practices, as enunciated and implemented whether by Schoenberg or Stravinsky, whether by John Cage or Roger Norrington, are all maximalizations of a nineteenth-century inheritance. The specific move Bowen traces is that associated with the emergence of the concept known as *Werktreue* ("fidelity to the musical work," as he translates it), which, as explicitly confirmed in essay 11, is the best possible access to the nebulous cluster of concepts intended by the tainted A-word when contemporary musicians use it. But before there could be a notion of *Werktreue* there had to be a notion of the reified *Werk* — the objectified musical work-thing to which fidelity is owed. The emergence of that concept was the crucial philosophical move, coeval with musical romanticism and virtually defining it. Without it there could be no notion of "classical music." The "museum ideology" which I identify and deplore in essay 4 (and again in essay 6) as the main prop to our modern concept of authenticity could never have arisen until there was something to store in the museum.

The "work-concept," as Lydia Goehr so excellently shows in her recent treatise on the philosophy of musical museum-culture,[10] regulates not only our musical attitudes but also our social practices. It dictates the behavior of all members of the classical music community, whether composers, performers, or listeners. It imposes a strict etiquette, for instance, on audiences.[11] On performers it inflicts a truly stifling regimen by radically hardening and patrolling what had formerly been a fluid, easily crossed boundary between the performing and composing roles.

The Romantic notion of the autonomous transcendent artwork entailed a hierarchized, strictly enforced split between emancipated creators, beholden (in theory) to no one but the muse, and selfless curators, sworn to submission. The producers of timeless works are the gods, exulting in their liberation from the world of social ("extramusical") obligation and issuing peremptory commands. The recipients of the commands are the Nibelungs, bound scrupulously to carry out the masters' intentions for the sake of their glory, their own lives pledged to a sterile humdrum of preservation and handing-on. That is the mythol-

---

[9]"A Pride of Prejudices; Or, Delight in Diversity," *Music Theory Spectrum* 13 (1991): 241.

[10]*The Imaginary Museum of Musical Works: An Essay in the Philosophy of Music* (Oxford: Clarendon Press, 1992).

[11]The epigraph to Goehr's book is an abridgment of Byron Belt's familiar set of concert-going shalt-nots, reprinted from *Stagebill.*

ogy of our concert life. There is also a class of Alberichs, of course, Nibelungs (chiefly of the podium, the keyboard, and the larynx) who aspire to godlike power, and who are dependably crushed for their hubris by critics and pedagogues, the priests of the *Werktreue* faith, though their fellow Nibelungs secretly egg them on and they enjoy wide sympathy among the mortals in the outer darkness of the hall.[12]

Precisely due to its internalization as a superego by generations of classical musicians and music lovers, the work-concept is hard to bring up to the surface of consciousness. Normally, since we do not consider alternatives, we operate without a working definition of this our most central musical concept. Its very identity, and the manner in which it may be specified, constitute a notorious philosophical "problem." Books have been devoted to its exploration, such as those by Roman Ingarden and Nelson Goodman that are briefly discussed in essay 8, and (most successfully) the new one by Goehr, which I warmly recommend. Although easily distinguished from performance, which is ephemeral and contingent, the notion of "the (timeless) work," as it has been called (see below), is not easily disengaged from that of the (permanent) text through which it is transmitted. And yet the distinction is a crucial one if we are to understand the precise nature of modern "authenticity," which, though both conceptually and historically dependent on the Romantic notion of *Werktreue,* is nevertheless not precisely coterminous with it. (All parties to the classical music esthetic have been imbued with loyalty to the notion of the "musical work" whether or not they profess allegiance to the "authenticity" ideal as currently proclaimed.)

Even Carl Dahlhaus, whose historical discussions of the rise of the work-concept are widely regarded as definitive,[13] fails to draw the crucial distinction between work and text. Dahlhaus properly identifies the work-concept as "the strong concept of art, without which music would be unable to stand on a par with literature and the visual arts." That was the reason for its institution. But then he identifies musical works in this strong sense with "inviolable musical 'texts' whose meaning is to be deciphered with 'exegetical' interpretations."[14] That is, he identifies the musical work with the score, the physical

---

[12]For a keen analysis of the way in which this set of practices is inculcated and enforced, see Henry Kingsbury, *Music, Talent, and Performance: A Conservatory Cultural System* (Philadelphia: Temple University Press, 1988), an ethnography à clef of an unnamed but easily recognized American conservatory.

[13]In *Nineteenth-Century Music,* trans. J. Bradford Robinson (Berkeley and Los Angeles: University of California Press, 1990); *Esthetics of Music,* trans. William Austin (Cambridge: Cambridge University Press, 1982); and *The Idea of Absolute Music,* trans. Roger Lustig (Chicago: University of Chicago Press, 1989).

[14]*Nineteenth-Century Music,* 9.

object produced by the composer, as the writer produces the book or
the painter the colored canvas. Whereas up to the eighteenth century,
he notes, musical texts were "mere 'scenarios' " for ephemeral performance occasions, from the nineteenth century onward the performance was regarded, contrariwise, as "a function of a text which it
attempted to interpret."[15]

How, then, if this is so, can we square the performances of Wilhelm
Furtwängler, which so freely interpret the "inviolable" text (adding a
wealth of unnotated nuances and perpetually varying the tempo), with
the notion of *Werktreue*? Furtwängler, after all, was just as committed
to *Werktreue* as any of the modern textualists with whose performances his are minutely contrasted in essays 4 and 9. Indeed, in his day
Furtwängler was regarded as the concept's very paragon (as, in an earlier
day, was Wagner). The difference between his performance of Beethoven's Ninth and Roger Norrington's, set out in great detail in essay 9,
illustrates the way in which the notion of the work, and of fidelity to it,
has narrowed over the course of the twentieth century, squeezing the
spiritual or metaphysical dimension out of the work-concept until
work-fidelity did finally become coextensive with text-fidelity.

This positivistic "progress," paralleling the progression from
nineteenth-century "absolute music" to twentieth-century formalism, not only exposes the anachronism in any formulation of the
work-concept that invokes the text as final arbiter, but also pinpoints
the difference between the "Romantic" and the "modern" within the
big tent of *Werktreue*. It has been the particular contribution—or
fallacy, or sin—of modernists (including Early Music modernists) to
cut the philosophical Gordian knot by finally identifying the Romantic work-concept purely and simply with the text. It is precisely this
move that I have tried to unmask in essays 7 and 11.

Not only Beethoven's symphonies, the original musical site of the
"strong concept of art," but all classical music has been assimilated by
now to the work-concept in this strict textualist construction. The
operas of Rossini and the concertos of Paganini, composers once (and,
by Dahlhausians, forever) regarded as Beethoven's dialectical adver-
saries, have been reified and sacralized (in a word, Beethovenized),
made "solid and durable, like the museum masters," as Cézanne once
put it of his own modernist project. I have seen a review of a recording
of Liszt's keyboard arrangements of Beethoven symphonies in which
the pianist is reproached for violating the letter of the score; and even
one in which an authentically Ivesian performer of the *Concord*
Sonata (that is, one who attempted to capture something of the
perpetually evolving and contingent character the composer prized as

---

[15]Ibid., 138.

the very essence of that *work*) was dourly enjoined "to learn humility in the face of the *text*."[16] Opera divas and virtuoso fiddlers have joined the ranks of museum curators, with disastrous results—disastrous, that is, for the people who pay to hear them. But what theorist of performance practice ever pays the audience any heed? And what better indication do we need that performance practice is a branch office of modernism?

The whole trouble with Early Music as a "movement" (as I have emphasized repeatedly; see essays 6, 7, and 11) is the way it has uncritically accepted the post-Romantic work-concept and imposed it anachronistically on pre-Romantic repertories. What is troubling, of course, is not the anachronism but the uncritical acceptance—and the imposition. A movement that might, in the name of history, have shown the way back to a truly creative performance practice has only furthered the stifling of creativity in the name of normative controls. Here Early Music actively colludes with the so-called "mainstream" it externally impugns.

Does this sound paranoiac, as some have suggested? Do I exaggerate the evil? Consider the article on "Performing Practice" (per British usage) in the *New Grove Dictionary of Music and Musicians*. The central position—and the central anachronism—is announced in the very first paragraph (14:370), which posits the problem performance practice addresses as that of ascertaining "the amount and kind of deviation from a precisely determined ideal tolerated (or even encouraged) by composers" at various times and in various places. In this deconstructive age one need hardly point out the prejudicial work accomplished by the words "deviation" and even "even." The whole situation is cast at once in ethical, adversarial, and resolutely hierarchical terms that project a set of cherished modernist desiderata on the whole historical panoply. Performers are *essentially* corrupters—deviants, in fact. Composers and their musicological champions are the preservers of abiding values. Toleration of deviance is better than encouragement (and intransigence, one must surmise, is best of all), but in any case it is the composer, or his scholarly surrogate, who must grant any indulgence. The "precisely determined ideal" is presupposed a universal given, exempt from the historical flux.

The history of the composer/performer relationship is represented as a steady progress whereby a master race has managed by degrees to subjugate an inferior population. It is precisely the gods versus the Nibelungs as sketched (fancifully, it may have seemed)

---

[16]*Musical America* 110/3 (May 1990): 78 (italics added); compare (*re* Ives's attitudes) Sondra Rae Clark, "The Element of Choice in Ives's *Concord Sonata*," *Musical Quarterly* 60 (1974): 167–86.

above. The paragraph under scrutiny ends with this stunning sentence: "The principle that the performers should be allowed some scope to 'interpret' [scare quotes!] the notation subjectively has been challenged successfully for the first time in the 20th century, with the advent of recordings and electronic means of fixing a composition in its definitive form once and for all." Anyone who has worked with Stravinsky's many recordings (about which details will be found in several of the essays collected here, beginning with the first) will know that the advent of recordings has only exacerbated the difficulty of determining the ontological status of musical works. The only solution to the problem is the one referred to up above as the Gordian knot solution: to privilege the text over anyone's performance of it, including the composer's, who when performing is demoted to the inferior rank. Essay 7 ends with a piquant example of this privileging process, inferred from recordings of a piano piece by Prokofiev.

But all this, while bemusing enough, is secondary. The main theme is broached in the allusion to "successful" challenge, which not only celebrates victory over the Nibelungs but also presumes that there had been previous unsuccessful skirmishes between preservers and defilers of culture. It should be obvious that this is yet another fanciful projection of present values on the past. The premise, central to performance-practice orthodoxy, that composers inherently suspect and wish to control their natural enemies presupposes as a historical constant the hard and fast distinction between the creative and re-creative roles that has only existed since the nineteenth century. The mistrust that is at the heart of performance practice as a discipline can scarcely be documented for any creative figure earlier than the "neoclassical" Stravinsky. Counterexamples, both earlier and later, are notoriously thick on the ground.

Even writers more sensitive to the contingency of relationships the *New Grove* takes as timelessly stable nevertheless manage to insinuate ahistorical hierarchies and anachronistic snobberies into their accounts of performance practice. David Fuller's otherwise very sophisticated discussion of Baroque performance practice, suggestively titled "The Performer as Composer," undermines its own enlightened premises by an unguarded use of figurative language—a too-telling metaphor here, an almost surely unconscious oxymoron there: "A large part of the music of the whole era was sketched rather than fully realized," Fuller writes, "and the performer had something of the *responsibility of a child* with a colouring book, to turn these sketches into rounded art-works."[17]

[17] *Performance Practice: Music after 1600*, ed. Howard M. Brown and Stanley Sadie (London: Macmillan Press, 1989), 117; italics added.

The ideology informing the *New Grove* account of performance practice is perhaps most vividly displayed in a passage evidently meant as a timely sop to pluralism:

> Reproducing as closely as one can the techniques and timbres known to be appropriate to a given period can never replace performances that are musically convincing to the audience; and yet the means and style of performance imagined by a composer are so indissolubly bound up with the whole musical fabric that he has set down, that the communication and impact of the composition are seriously impaired if the sounds he imagined are not at least kept in mind when preparing modern performances (14:371).

The oppositional hierarchy introduced here—between producer (composer) and consumer (audience), with the performer occupying the position of shady broker—is wholly derived from the rhetoric of mandarin modernism, as Paul Griffiths, best known as a new-music advocate, confirms when he attempts to collapse the distinction between the works of Mozart and those of Milton Babbitt as sites of interpretive contest:

> Whereas a performer of Mozart might justifiably assume a hierarchy of intentions, so that liberties with accent, dynamic level, phrasing and tempo would be more allowable than liberties with rhythm, and liberties with rhythm more allowable than liberties with pitch, in Babbitt there is no such hierarchy: . . . a tiny distinction in dynamic may be at the same level of meaning as a choice of pitch. A performer might argue that the "meaning" here is more theoretical than practical, but such a view would be informed by an experience of Mozart rather than Babbitt: it would be a perpetuation of attitudes that may no longer be relevant. And again, the whole message of such a book as this [i.e., an encyclopedia of performance practice] is that the old view of a hierarchy of intention may not be justified in any music, that matters previously left to personal choice or tradition must be subjected to scrutiny in the light of documentary research, that the timbres of Mozart are indeed as important as the harmonies.[18]

If they are, it will only be by fiat, as it is only by fiat (or by faith) that the *New Grove*'s dictum holds true concerning the unquestionable (therefore unquestioned) relevance of bygone performance habits to "the communication and impact of the composition" to or on today's audiences. This is not a truth but a truism. It can neither be demonstrated nor effectively confuted, only believed or disbelieved. It is, in short, not a scholarly but a pious verity.

[18]Ibid., 488.

Now pieties can be tolerated, even encouraged as a spur to good works, but a characteristic inconsistency should not pass unnoticed: while demanding strict documentary accountability from performers, the performance-practice movement insulates its own major premises from any comparable scrutiny. The confident identification or equation of what is intended (by the composer) with what is communicated (to the audience) under conditions "appropriate to a given period" is a utopian assumption that our daily experience in our own period manifestly contradicts. (Just ask Milton Babbitt.) It is absolutely necessary, however, to the maintenance of the arbitrary hierarchies and power relations on which the performance-practice movement rests. And it betrays the link, in this as in any coercive practice, between utopian vision and authoritarian fulfillment. Will we ever get over our wishful unwillingness to recognize this fatal (or, at least, fated) conjunction? At the end of the twentieth century, a century ruined by authoritarian utopias of many kinds, the answer seems a depressing no—unless postmodernism, as I fervently hope, signals precisely such a recognition.

Timeless or Taboo?

Because the current practice of "authenticity" entails so many anachronisms, a mere account of its origins (in romanticism, in *Werktreue*) can neither explain it nor even adequately characterize it. The fact that the *Werktreue* ideal is roomy enough to house both the Furt-wänglers and the Norringtons (as, in the nineteenth century, it housed both the Mendelssohns and the Wagners) shows that in itself it cannot shed light on the current authenticity debate, in which a hundred schools of thought, each with a fully legitimate claim of descent from the parent concept, loudly contend.

Hence the incompleteness of an account of "the ideology of authenticity" that focuses on its nineteenth-century manifestations. Such an account describes the common origin of all the factions in our current debate but provides no model by which their differences can be rationalized or explained. Besides, the task is not just to explain the world, as someone once said, but to change it. Without an accurate model of contemporary practice there can be no critique of its shortcomings, nor can alternative models be convincingly advanced. Concerned as I am not only with the historical background to the desperate straits in which "classical music" now finds itself, but with their alleviation, I regard as futile any account that fails to propose alternatives. My most positive statement of this kind is in essay 7. It is nothing new, certainly nothing radical. It could even be called reactionary, with its seeming advocacy of a premodernist esthetic. Here, however, premodernism and postmodernism coincide. *Torniamo all'antico*, as someone else once said: *sarà un progresso*.

"Serious, classical, and 'work' music have come to be equated and, together, have come to be accorded the highest status possible if not in Western then at least in European musical culture," writes Lydia Goehr.[19] The postmodern project for music, as I take it, is to dismantle this triple nexus, and to revoke its privileged status. Such dismantling must further entail the undoing of the two primary moves by which the work-concept was instituted at the turn of the nineteenth century: "the *transcendent* move from the worldly and particular to the spiritual and universal; [and] the *formalist* move which brought meaning from music's outside into its inside."[20] A tremendous amount of critical activity is now devoted to refuting the claims of formalism and transcendentalism: to showing that the music regarded as set off from the world is still in the world, doing worldly work; to showing that musical meaning continues, as before, to arise out of the relations between the musical artwork and its many contexts, pharisaically stigmatized as "extramusical"; to showing that artistic seriousness is not incompatible with social function (which even Goehr, misleadingly as I think, calls "extramusical" function); hence, in fine, to showing that the myth of transcendence has necessarily entailed manifold repressions, giving rise (as repressions inevitably do) to a multifarious malaise. The dismantling of the utopian lie, runs the postmodernist argument, will be as much a cathartic and a therapeutic for art as it has proved of late to be for the body politic and economic.

I certainly believe this to be the case, and in essay 7 I have said so quite explicitly. To guardians of Valhalla that essay has seemed little more than a defense of Alberich. I would not necessarily deny it. I may yet be provoked into attempting a cultural interpretation of the systematic belittling one of the great musical geniuses of the twentieth-century, Vladimir Horowitz, has suffered at the hands of critics committed to norm-seeking modernist values like performance practice and reified "structure." The situation is complicated, though; there would have to be a companion piece called "Horowitz Defended against His Devotees." And there would have to be a concomitant study of Glenn Gould reception, to discover why this equally arrogant Alberich has enjoyed modernist adulation. (Short answer: He epitomized unworldliness [transcendence] and abstraction [formalism], whereas Horowitz particularized and concretized; and he upgraded

[19] *The Imaginary Museum of Musical Works*, 121.
[20] Ibid., 153.

modernist indifference to the audience to the point of anhedonia while Horowitz aimed to please; all of which is to say that of the two, Gould was by far the truer romantic.)

But if I seem to be Alberich's advocate it is only out of general principles. My first commitment is to the mortals—that is, the audience—and to their interests, since I am one of them. Persistent propaganda notwithstanding, these interests are not served except incidentally and fortuitously by "performance practice." It should be obvious that nomothetic investigation of group performer-behavior is primarily intended for the benefit of the gods and, secondarily, for the prestige of their prophets, the lawgivers.

Performance-practice research, ideally, is an attempt, on the basis of documentary or statistical evidence, to bridge the gap between what is written in the old musical texts that survive and what was actually heard in typical contemporary performances. The information uncovered by such study can be no end absorbing and useful (nor, as a committed scholar, do I believe that anyone is ever too well informed). The enthusiastic reviews I have entered on behalf of many "historical" performers, of which several are reprinted herein, should offer sufficient testimony to my esteem for first-rate performance practice research, for the inferences it has allowed imaginative minds to draw, and for the benefits that have on occasion accrued therefrom to listeners. Yet because I have been forthright about the incidental or haphazard nature of those benefits, and because I have pointed out the biases that have informed the practice of performance practice, I stand accused of having "spearheaded the anti-performance-practice movement."[21]

I reject the charge not merely as a point of honor, but because my own work fits the performance-practice paradigm my accusers uphold. Throughout my career as spearhead I have been defining and, what is more, explaining historical styles of performance—viz., the group performer-behavior that distinguishes the present historical moment. Like any other performance-practice researcher, I have been attempting, on the basis of documentary and statistical evidence, to bridge the gap between what is written in the old texts we have and what we actually hear today in typical contemporary performances. I have done this, moreover, not merely in a debunking spirit, but because I believe that the most important task of the contemporary historian is to write the history of the present. To give the present a past is to situate the present (that is, specify its exact location) in the Heraclitean flux, rather than accept its premises as transcendental givens.

    21"Editorial: Performance Practice and Its Critics—The Debate Goes On," Performance Practice Review 4 (1991): 113.

It is fashionable, and very easy, to deride such a project as folly, "an impossible task to which most academic work in the humanities is now devoted."[22] But the impossibility of final achievement is something it shares with all other epistemological endeavors. (Try making a *complete* description of the book you are now holding in your hands.) Such a trivial objection can in no way impugn the necessity or the urgency of any task. In this, as Joseph Kerman reminded us a long time ago (though with quite another project in mind), a project like mine does not differ from "all our other ultimate pursuits."[23]

What I am after, in a word, is liberation: only when we know something about the sources of our contemporary practices and beliefs, when we know something about the reasons why we do as we do and think as we think, and when we are aware of alternatives, can we in any sense claim to be free in our choice of action and creed, and responsible for it. As essay 2 attests, such a claim is the most basic prerequisite to authenticity in its non-cant, post-Kant meaning.

Such knowledge, like anything liberating, is subversive of dogma. If I have been read out of the "performance-practice movement" and stigmatized as its Antichrist or its Trotsky, it is because the movement, as distinct from the research field, has never been quite the disinterested pursuit it has made itself out to be. It has interests aplenty, and protects them. Where performance-practice research is descriptive, the performance-practice movement is aggressively prescriptive and territorial, dispensing or conferring the status of authenticity as oxymoronical reward for conformity, claiming a specious moral authority, and laying guilt trips on those who fail to endorse its goals. (Altogether typical was Neal Zaslaw's answer to an interviewer who asked him where "the early music approach," which as of the Mozart year had been applied to composers as late as Wagner and Brahms, might end. "If by 'the early music approach' you mean doing your homework before you perform music or write about it," Prof. Zaslaw opined, "then it need never end!"[24]) My research has been dredging up the movement's reactionary subtexts and its coercive strategies, and (by its own lights even worse) exposing its anachronistic position vis-à-vis the actual performance practices and ideologies of old.

These contradictions come out especially clearly in Roland Jackson's unsigned rebuttal to essay 7 — or rather to the precis of essay 7 I

[22]Roger Scruton, "In Inverted Commas," *Times Literary Supplement* (18 December 1992): 3.

[23]"A Profile for American Musicology," *Journal of the American Musicological Society* (*JAMS*) 18 (1965): 63 (paraphrasing Allan Tate, to whose New Critical mantle Kerman then aspired).

[24]"Editorial," *Early Music* 20 (1992): 195.

delivered orally at the end of the Lincoln Center Mozart conference in
May 1991. What provoked the "spearhead" label was a bit of spontaneous by-play with Neal Zaslaw, the conference organizer, which did
not survive into the published version of the essay. Actually, I confess,
it was not quite spontaneous. I had been saving up for five days a
rejoinder to Prof. Zaslaw's keynote remarks, in which he asserted that
"a historically informed performance will take into consideration
both a piece's documentary tradition and its oral tradition."[25] When it
came my turn to mount the rostrum, I remonstrated that "documentary tradition" was a tendentious misnomer; rather, and more simply,
there were the documents—the weapons with which those committed to "historical performance" attack tradition ("oral" by definition—
see essay 7). (Documents in themselves can constitute no tradition,
for tradition requires agency, and documents do not talk to documents.) Prof. Jackson found this formulation "surprising," but it really
amounts to nothing more than the ordinary hermeneutic posture as
set forth at length not only in essay 7 but also in essay 10, more
narrowly focused on Mozart. The reader can compare my actual
arguments with Prof. Jackson's representation of them. His paraphrase can stand as a perfect specimen of the Wagnerian mythology of
the concert hall I set out (not at all hyperbolically, it turns out) near
the beginning of this introduction.

   My views, Prof. Jackson contends, are

> typical of the swing towards subjectivism in current critical thought, of
> a movement away from the single work, from the search for objective
> reality, to pluralism and individuality of interpretation, away from the
> notion of the "timeless" work (or "timeless" performance) to a considera-
> tion of the personal responses of those who at various times have
> experienced (or will experience) the work. Implicit in the new scepti-
> cism and subjectivity are its anti-textuality (did the work exist in a
> single form? did the composer have only one performance in mind?), its
> refunctioning (the work is simply adapted to new situations), its con-
> ceptualism (works are as we perceive them), and its historicism (history
> and its manifestations "exist" only in accordance with our view of
> them).[26]

Although I thought it necessary to quote the whole paragraph in
order to give a context to the points I will single out for discussion
(and also so that the reader can judge whether my remarks on interpretive tradition as a social phenomenon really amount to "subjectivism"), what seems of greatest moment here is the notion of "the

[25]I quote from James M. Keller's summary: see "Talking Mozart," *Historical Performance* 4 (1991): 133.
[26]*Performance Practice Review* 4 (1991): 113.

'timeless' work (or 'timeless' performance)." As the recurrent scare quotes squirmingly attest, this is the most mystifying contradiction of all. It is quite literally paradoxical to assert that applying the documented performance practices of a stipulated historical time and place to a musical document of similarly determinate historical provenance will lift the latter out of history into a condition of timelessness, which is to say a condition outside of subjective human experience. (Not for nothing does Prof. Jackson, unwittingly assuming T. S. Eliot's voice, exhort the performer to behave "selflessly.")[27] Prof. Jackson's "timeless" is a familiar euphemism for "inviolate" or "sacred," perhaps taboo. Performance practice, on this account, is a sacrament that aims at something akin to transubstantiation. The reality it seeks is not objective but transcendent. The singleness toward which it aspires is to be found not in the untidy world we all inhabit (still less the one Bach or Mozart inhabited) but in the realm of romance. I cannot see what it has to do with scholarship.

Cannon to the Right of Me, Cannon to the Left of Me

Prof. Jackson's strictures are emblematic of the confusion that must ensue when the line between the scholarly and the artistic is blurred. Many would like to erase that line. My insistence that it should be respected has met with a great deal of opposition. What assures me that I must be right is the fact that opposition comes from both extremes—from those who, like Prof. Jackson, would like to assimilate the artistic to the scholarly in the name of accountability or "objectivity," and also from the trendier faction that would like to assimilate the scholarly to the artistic in the name of imagination or "subjectivity." Both sides in this case are wrong, not only because both invest morally neutral concepts with spurious moral values, but because the rigid subject/object antithesis that both arguments invoke, and on which both utterly depend, is an intellectually impoverishing illusion to begin with. Neither side can admit the pragmatic flexibility that alone can take adequate account of differing contexts and purposes; hence neither side can contribute usefully to any dialogue between scholars and artists.

The former stance, the customary premise of the performance-practice discipline, is the position I have ordinarily addressed, and is therefore addressed repeatedly in the pages that follow. It needs no special attention up front. Here I will single out only one recent,

[27]Ibid., 114.

especially radical formulation, because it was enunciated, interestingly, not from the performance-practice perspective, but from
what seems a distinct if not altogether unrelated field. In the course of
a debate on the relevance of historical research to the objectives and
methodology of musical analysis, Douglas Dempster and Matthew
Brown declare a fatal inconsistency in what they are pleased to call
my "bitter campaign against scientific . . . paradigms not only in music theory but also in other branches of musicology, such as historically informed performance practice."[28] Where on the one hand my
critiques of certain analytical methods[29] have seemed to embody "a
strong endorsement of [naive] historicism," in my "strident attacks on
'authentic' performance practice" (and not even Dempster and Brown
can dodge the scare-quotes), I "actually denounc[e] naive historicism."[30] "Taken at face value," they claim, characteristically distorting
what they purport to paraphrase,

> Taruskin's appeals to history for corroborating music analyses/theories
> plainly contradict his skepticism about historical reconstruction for
> performance practice. After all, why should we accept that a per-
> former's or critic's interpretation of a piece is bound to the present, but
> insist that a theorist's interpretation be bound to the past, as revealed
> through historical studies of the composer's theoretical and musical
> background? Why are historians [observe the switch] any less bound to
> present day aesthetics than performers or critics?[31]

My answer to this familiar, hardly ingenuous challenge is already
given in essay 1. It is not a theoretical but a pragmatic answer. To
summarize briefly, and to sharpen it: the demand that performers be
subject to ordinary scholarly or scientific standards of accountability
places not only onerous but irrelevant limitations on their freedom
(limitations having to do not with anybody's intentions or "aesthetics"
but merely with the state of research), and places arbitrary obstacles

---

[28]Douglas Dempster and Matthew Brown, "Evaluating Musical Analyses and Theories: Five Perspectives," *Journal of Music Theory* 34 (1990): 260. This article was a
follow-up to a previous exchange: see Matthew Brown and Douglas Dempster, "The
Scientific Image of Music Theory," *Journal of Music Theory* 33 (1989): 65–106, and my
"Reply" on pp. 155–63.

[29]In particular, my critiques of Stravinsky and Scriabin analyses employing the "set
theoretic" method: see R. Taruskin, review of Allen Forte, *The Harmonic Organization
of "The Rite of Spring,"* *Current Musicology* 28 (1979): 114–29; idem, "Letter to the
Editor," *Music Analysis* 5 (1986): 313–20; idem, "Reply to [Pieter] Van den Toorn," *In
Theory Only* 10/3 (October 1987): 47–57; idem, review of James M. Baker, *The Music of
Alexander Scriabin* and Boris de Schloezer, *Scriabin: Artist and Mystic,* in *Music
Theory Spectrum* 10 (1988): 143–69.

[30]Dempster and Brown, 262; "naive" in this philosophical usage means not artless
or callow but "without preconceptions."

[31]Ibid., 263.

in the performer's path that can frustrate the goal of performance, which I define pre- or postmodernly (take your pick) as that of pleasing or moving an audience in the here and now. Dempster and Brown very precisely exemplify a definition altogether opposed to mine, one quite specifically associated with modernism.

The expressive or communicative purpose of musical performance, like that of art in general, has been discredited under modernism in the name of dehumanization, which is transcendence in its maximal phase. (To accompany the citations from Eliot, Ortega, and Pound adduced and analyzed in essays 1 and 4, here is an even more pungent pronouncement by Cage: "One of us is not trying to put his emotions into someone else. That way you 'rouse rabbles'; it seems on the surface humane, but it animalizes, and we're not doing it.")[32] To the communication model of art modernism has long opposed a research model, most commonly associated with Milton Babbitt of "Who Cares if You Listen?" fame.[33] But Babbitt is only one of the research model's extreme enunciators. Cage, superficially Babbitt's antipode, is another. And the proponents of "historical" performance, like Roland Jackson and Brown & Dempster, are collectively a third. Their fundamental collective enterprise, obscured by their surface differences, is the perpetual reenactment of the myth of transcendence. Like all utopian paradigms, this kind of "research model" is primarily if tacitly a means of exclusion, and what it excludes is the very thing that motivates performance in the first place. (Nor, as I will argue, does it serve scholarship any better.)

Modernist performance ethics, serving the idealization of the objectified work and seeking by the proscriptive use of research evidence to keep the threateningly contingent subjectivity of the performer at bay, has received a great boost from modern technology. In broadcast and recording situations, where the physical presence of the audience has been (or can be) removed from the scene, the audience, and any responsibility owed it, can be all the more easily forgotten. (Isn't that why Glenn Gould made his retreat from the concert hall to the studio?) The illusion of dehumanization is facilitated. One can really believe, when committing a performance to records, that "no one is speaking" (cf. essay 4).

[32]"Where Are We Going? And What Are We Doing?," in *Silence* (Cambridge, Mass.: MIT Press, 1966), 250.

[33]"Who Cares if You Listen?" first appeared in *High Fidelity* 8/2 (February 1958), and has been very widely anthologized, e.g., in Piero Weiss and Richard Taruskin, *Music in the Western World: A History in Documents* (New York: Schirmer Books, 1984), 529–34. The famous title was editorial; Babbitt's original title was "The Composer as Specialist."

But these are pseudo-ethics, born of a misplaced sense of obligation. A performer cannot please or move the ancient dead and owes
them no such effort. There is no way that we can harm Bach or Mozart
any more, nor any way that we can earn their gratitude. Our obliga-
tions are to the living. Still less can a performer please or move an
inanimate object or an abstract idea. We owe them even less obligation. Turning ideas into objects, and putting objects in place of people,
is the essential modernist fallacy—the fallacy of reification, as it is
called. It fosters the further fallacy of forgetting that performances,
even canned performances, are not things but acts. The pernicious
consequences are hinted at the end of essay 4.

As for musical analysis, if it is not to be merely another reinforcement of transcendentalist myths—if, that is, it is going to tell us
something we don't already "know"—it should provide us with information (yes, historical information) about composing techniques.
The history of music, we postmodernly realize, is more than the
history of composition. But the history of composition is still of
interest; much about it remains to be learned; and if analysis still has
a place in musicology, it should be our discovery tool. What we want
to discover is not "how the music works" (that is, how the work is a
work). That is no discovery; that is just a constitutive premise endlessly and circularly confirmed. What we want to know is how composers worked. If we are not interested in learning that (and many
have by now so declared themselves) then analysis has nothing to tell
us but comforting or inspiring bedtime stories, for which just as many
retain a seemingly insatiable appetite.

More engaging are the objections of Leo Treitler, who comes at
me from the other direction. In the course of a generally welcoming
response to essay 1, he worries about what I then called the "accountability we rightly demand of any scholar," noting somewhat ruefully
that "only historical performance, not scholarship, is let off the hook
of accountability" ("and opened to intuition," he appends; I'll come
back to that). "I don't know whether Taruskin would make a principled defense of the differentiation," he writes, adding, "I hope not."[34]

He could have called me up. But I suspect he knew what I'd say. I
must and do defend the distinction, again for pragmatic reasons, and
for ethical ones as well. It makes a difference.

But first, let's dispose of a false distinction of Treitler's. There is,
or should be, no contradiction between accountability and intuition. I
certainly do not want to see scholarship closed off to the latter. Most
of our best ideas, surely most of the best connections we draw, occur

---

[34]"The Power of Positivist Thinking" (review of Joseph Kerman, *Contemplating
Music: Challenges to Musicology*), *JAMS* 42 (1989): 399.

to us as intuitions. I only say that scholarly intuitions deserve to be tested by scholarly methods. That is all I mean by accountability. Shouldn't intuitive performances also be tested? Of course, and I never said otherwise (if not, there would be no need for critics—now *there's* a thought). But for performances there are other, more appropriate tests. Such tests are mooted in the essays that follow; here I will address the scholarly side of the coin.

(For a teaser, though, consider, on the one hand, the standards a treatise on performance practice—let us say, on *notes inégales* or mensural proportions—ought to meet, and, on the other, those to which a performance of a Couperin suite or a Busnoys Mass should be held accountable. Are they the same? Both treatise and performance ought to be "convincing," all right, but does the word mean the same thing in both applications? Nor is there any reason why both should not be "correct"—but again, what does that mean? Is the difference in standards simply that one is "objective" and the other is "subjective"? To say so is to court woe from philosophical terrorists, as we have seen and will see again. Is not the difference simply that the criteria for the treatise do not begin to suffice for the performance? Yes indeed—but no, there is nothing "simple" about that . . .)

Treitler is properly wary of "testing by scholarly methods"—or rather, he is wary of the kind of narrow, exclusionary tests musicologists habitually apply. Some of Treitler's most salutary writing has been devoted to exposing the peremptory limits neopositivistic methods have set on musicological inquiry, particularly critical inquiry. And yet when he calls for an end to accountability I side with stern old Nabokov, who wrote that his scholarly output (unlike his novels and his other literary performances) "possesses an ethical side, moral and human elements. It reflects the compiler's honesty or dishonesty, skill or sloppiness. If told I am a bad poet, I smile; but if told I am a poor scholar, I reach for my heaviest dictionary."[35]

That, of course, is only the short answer—and, its lofty source notwithstanding, a crude answer that will have to be refined if it is to meet a sophisticated argument like Treitler's. Treitler's quarrel with accountability is only the superficies of a general onslaught against the notion of objectivity, and particularly against the high value musicology has persisted in placing on scholarly detachment, an attack Treitler has been mounting on and off for some time. Its conceptual source lies in the historicism of R. G. Collingwood, who opposed the positivist insistence on "right answers" (that is,

---

[35]"Reply to My Critics" (concerning his annotated translation of Pushkin's *Eugene Onegin*), in *The Portable Nabokov*, ed. Page Stegner (Harmondsworth: Penguin Books, 1977), 300.

knowledge that can be verified, or, more properly, refuted) with a model of historical knowledge that substituted certainty—a subjective criterion—for veracity, and hence admitted critical interpretation into the realm of learning.[36]

I'm all for that result, and I even agree that scholarly hypotheses as well as critical interpretations are performances in their way, and can only be more or less persuasive (which is where testing comes in).[37] Nothing convinces like conviction, accountable or not. But certainty troubles me, especially when it is radically opposed to, and exalted above, mere truth. Treitler, untroubled, presses on back from Collingwood to Giambattista Vico, whose "brilliant insight" about truth vs. certainty (in *Principi di una Scienza Nuova*, 1725) he appropriates and paraphrases as follows (he calls it "an interpretive reduction"; fair enough):

> It is not at all necessarily the same to be certain of something as it is to regard something as being true. There are all sorts of things—matters of fact or feeling or action—about which we may be certain although they may not be judged either true or false. That is mainly because our judgements about them are contingent upon our experience and present circumstance, while true propositions are those that we expect to hold in all circumstances.[38]

Do we always know the difference? Do we not, on the contrary, constantly confuse contingent experience with "common sense"? Have we not all falsely generalized from our own limited perspectives? (And if we do not think we have done this, doesn't everybody else we know?) Is not precisely this confusion the root of all belief in astrology, flat earth, occultism, quack medicine—as well as every unshakeable dogma and prejudice? And does this confusion at the heart of Vico's "new science" have nothing to do with the fact that Vico, ignored by his enlightened contemporaries, became the object of a cult in the heyday of nineteenth-century unreason, rehabilitated by Nietzsche and revered by Mme. Blavatsky, the theosophist, thence by race theorists like Joseph-Arthur de Gobineau and Houston Stewart Chamberlain?

It is easy enough to say that "an integrated study that aims for both truth and certainty . . . would be not at all a bad program for musical studies"[39]—or, indeed, for studies of any other kind. But given the ease with which one mistakes one's certainties for truths, Treitler's

---

[36]See "The Power of Positivist Thinking," 381.

[37]See R. Taruskin, "She Do the Ring in Different Voices" (review of *Unsung Voices* by Carolyn Abbate), *Cambridge Opera Journal* 4 (1992): 187–97, esp. 192–94.

[38]"The Power of Positivist Thinking," 389.

[39]Ibid.

confidence in "integration" seems more than a little rosy. How, precisely, can the difference between the two be successfully maintained and conveyed? If it is not, what will safeguard "integration"? What will prevent its degenerating into assimilation—that is, a forgetting of the crucial difference? And what could be more pernicious, more lethal to scholarship?

I see no such safeguard in Treitler's formulation, nor even any honest evaluation of the risk. Confronted with such a potential moral confusion, I'll take bourgeois, democratic positivism any day. As their criterion of "falsifiability" implies, positivists actively despise certainty. They hold on to their right answers only until righter ones come along. Indeed, Karl Popper keeps assuring us, they look forward to that eventuality.[40] Well, on their best behavior they do, perhaps—but at least they have a standard of good behavior. Even convictions can be overturned. But certainty is something else again. It is the stock-in-trade of zealots and bigots. It despises rational constraint. Its primary products are propaganda . . . and inspired artistry. Certainty is the artist's sine qua non and the scholar's mortal enemy. I believe we should be wary of a scholar who thinks he is an artist.

The problem gets worse when Treitler goes from carping against objectivity to actively promoting subjectivity. He wants to cast the split as one between dehumanization ("history without names") and human empathy ("the I to I contact between historian and subject"). "The sharp edge dividing the two ways of thinking," he writes, "is the attitude toward the relation between subject and object in scholarship, between the knower and the known. On one side, knowledge depends on the maintenance of a strict separation between subject and object. On the other it entails a bonding between the two." More grandly yet, he casts the difference as "a difference about the nature of the self," between a pathologically divided consciousness—the great Western disease—and the healthfully integrated personality, "whose disciplined subjectivity is welcomed as a factor in judgement."[41]

That Treitler's thinking here is uncharacteristically cloudy is evident from his confusion of the categories he wants to "bond": what is "subject" in one quote ("the I to I contact . . .") is "object" in the next. He celebrates the letting loose of "the play of the subjective self,"[42] the legitimizing within the scholarly process of "human desires, ambitions, needs, emotions—those of the historian and of the historical

---

[40]See, for a particularly clear articulation, "Truth, Rationality, and the Growth of Scientific Knowledge," in Karl Popper, *Conjectures and Refutations* (London: Routledge and Kegan Paul, 1963), 215–50.

[41]Quotations in this paragraph from "The Power of Positivist Thinking," 389–91.

[42]Leo Treitler, *Music and the Historical Imagination* (Cambridge, Mass.: Harvard University Press, 1989), 9.

subject,"[43] but, as in the case of "certainty," he does not pause to take stock of the danger, or even to take stock of those human needs and ambitions. Everything is papered over with bland reference to "disciplined subjectivity." But what mysteriously disciplines it? What, if not those dowdy old Nabokovian virtues of ethics and honesty, or my own more accommodating "accountability"? Why does Treitler resist that word, even as (later) he solemnly warns us of the dark power relationships implicit in such other words as "control" and "discipline" (the latter a word he will appropriate gladly enough when it suits his immediate purpose) with which scholars routinely ratify their enterprise and dole out their approbation?[44] What, one cannot help wondering, are his own needs, his ambitions? And why is he so keen to have them all hang out?

Where Treitler goes as wrong as Roland Jackson is in his radical dichotomization of objectivity and subjectivity—an extreme position he has uncritically accepted from the discourses he means to oppose. He turns it on its head, but does not escape its consequences. In the introduction to *Music and the Historical Imagination*, his collected essays, he elaborates this central opposition with a congeries of other familiar binarisms. *Objectivity vs. subjectivity*::the West vs. the East, via a shallow description, cribbed from the work of an anthropologist acquaintance, of a Laotian concept of knowledge based on "a bonding of the knower with the known rather than a separation" (pp. 10–11). *Objectivity vs. subjectivity*::the artificially ordered Cartesian worldview versus the premodern organic universe, via a nostalgic passage quoted from Owen Barfield and a militant one from Susan Bordo (p. 16). In back of this, *Objectivity vs. subjectivity*::male vs. female, via the widely disseminated feminist contention that girls develop psychologically by bonding with their mothers and boys by separating from them (p. 15). In every instance Treitler identifies strongly with the "other," lending the argument a troubling tinge of vainglory or exhibitionism—the need to see himself and the ambition to display himself, in contradistinction to the scholarly (and Western, and modern, and male) majority, as a member of a morally sensitive elite.

But, as always, he fails to reckon with the dark side. Nostalgia for a prelapsarian organic sensibility is no feminist invention. It is an ancient Romantic cliche. Treitler's whole set of binarisms, in fact, is a Romantic-cum-modernist bromide, aspects of which have continually surfaced and resurfaced, sometimes horribly, in the recent history of Western thought. The same nostalgia informed the cultural debates

[43]"The Power of Positivist Thinking," 390.
[44]Ibid., 401; see also *Music and the Historical Imagination*, 17.

within the Russian intelligentsia that contributed an important part of the background to Stravinsky's *Sacre du Printemps*: then it took the form of a contest between proponents of *kul'tura*, the fragmented rationalistic modern sensibility, and *stikhiya*, primitive organic wholeness of experience.[45] Treitler's side was most eloquently argued then by the poet Alexander Blok. A century earlier, that side had been argued by Schelling and Herder, who laid the foundation in Germany for interminable debate concerning *Kultur* versus *Zivilisation*, where *Kultur*, despite its being a superficial cognate to the Russian *kul'tura*, stood for the opposite category, the property of organic oneness and authenticity by which many Germans have ever since defined their special nature, their special role, and their special mission. Let's not forget where that mission led them. The politics of identification, of subjective bonding, like the politics of certainty, can be a pretty hairy politics. It underwrites all tribalisms, every mindless group identity, every petty or bloody nationalism. Its essence is intolerance.

Leo Treitler means to be tolerant. He ends his essay in binary stereotypes with a plea "to take the still more radical step of purging our conception about understanding of the ancient and harmful idea that it has two modes, and of their underlying identification as genderized epistemological styles."[46] But bland lip service to Pollyanna paradise can do little to offset the force of the whole argument that has led up to it, in which the hoariest binarisms are resurrected and invested with very up-to-date notions of right thinking. The dualisms, presented in such essential terms, effectively subvert any casually asserted happy ending. How can one spend the bulk of an essay indulging in an intransigent and totalizing rhetoric of oppositions, ruthlessly sacrificing thinking on the altar of feeling, demonizing ordinary rational discourse (I do not say rationalism) with hyperbolic reference to Lorca's nightmare visions and Herman Kahn's "nukespeak,"[47] and then hope to take it all back at the end with a grin? Treitler may ultimately see the danger in his oppositional thinking, but he is trapped in it. He cannot offer a way out, he can only ask that we find one.

Better never to enter this intellectual cul-de-sac. Better to keep away from primitive binarisms. They shackle thought, and they are ineluctably prejudicial. Treitler's method, first invoking them, then attempting to fuse (or "bond") them, is an especially futile move, as his

[45]For a summary of the debate in its maximalized, postrevolutionary phase, see Vyacheslav Ivanov and Mikhail Gershenzon, "A Corner-to-Corner Correspondence," in Marc Raeff (ed.), *Russian Intellectual History: An Anthology* (New York: Harcourt, Brace & World, 1966), 373–401.

[46]*Music and the Historical Imagination*, 18.

[47]Ibid., 13.

discussions of both certainty and subjectivity attest. So when I propose to distinguish performance from scholarship I do not mean crudely to oppose performance to scholarship. As a performer I used to help myself greedily from the scholar's table. Indeed, essay 1, where all the trouble started, is cast in the form of an interior dialogue between the performer and the scholar within me (or better, a dialectic, since both subjects are transformed by it). Is that just an example of what Treitler would call "divided consciousness"? No, it was an example of pragmatism, of adapting method to purpose. The purpose of scholarship, including scholarly criticism, is to instruct. That of performance is to delight. Instruction can be delightful. Delight can be instructive. But instruction can require actions that are not always conducive to delight, and delight can "merely" divert.

As essay 1 gratefully affirms, the fruits of scholarship can mightily assist the performer's purposes; but to insist that the performer obey the scholar is just as tyrannically limiting as it would be to insist that the scholar pursue no project that cannot be turned to the performer's immediate advantage. Especially is this the case in light of positivism's reminder that the fruits of scholarship, however rigorously tested, are only to be held provisionally true. "Good" positivists have known all along that they do not leave their subjective selves at home when they set out in pursuit of truth. Why else demand "accountability" in the first place? Treitler's position could all too easily degenerate into a plea for privilege or (at worst) a license to lie. Good faith should be assumed, but also safeguarded. As Gorbachev told Reagan and Reagan told Gorbachev, *doveryai, no proveryai* (trust but check).

Interestingly enough, in light of this discussion, the one time Treitler addresses the matter of performance practice in his published work, he comes down hard (if not for all the usual reasons) on the side of exigent "authenticity." Bonding intersubjectively with Mozart (Hildesheimer's Mozart, that is),[48] he finds in the "historical" approach to the Symphony No. 39 in E-flat (viz., the 1983 recording by the Academy of Ancient Music under Jaap Schroeder and Christopher Hogwood) a truer reflection of its content (which Treitler, following the recent hermeneutic revival, interprets as a psychological self-portrait) than the more familiar, traditionally "expressive" style represented by Bruno Walter's bicentennial recording of 1956. With reference to the slow movement, he writes:

> The lively *andante* of the Academy of Ancient Music, characteristic of their Mozart performances in general, is an aspect of their efforts to

---

[48]I.e., the subject of the Swiss writer and painter Wolfgang Hildesheimer's debunking bestseller of 1977, published in English five years later: see *Mozart*, trans. Marion Faber (New York: Farrar Straus Giroux, 1982).

follow eighteenth-century performance practices. Evidence for the historical authenticity of such a tempo has been published by Neal Zaslaw, who was a consultant for the recordings. The interpretation that is offered here [that is, Treitler's hermeneutic reading of the music] constitutes evidence of another sort, but to the same effect. At Walter's tempo the frivolity and eccentricity, the contrasts and deceptions and shifts of character and playfulness and high seriousness, and manipulations of harmonic and instrumental color, and the play of register and roles, and the thematic transformations and ironies—all that fades into a uniformly benign "expressivity," a realization of the Apollonian Mozart image that Hildesheimer was concerned to pull down. It requires a livelier tempo to bring out the immense range and fluency of expression in the movement, and to give us a glimpse of what the writers around 1800 might have heard in this music, to write as they did.[49]

I do not propose to make the relative merits of the performances an issue here; for that sort of thing, the reader can turn to essay 4. Nor will I point out for the umpteenth time that a modern construction of Mozart (Hildesheimer's; often enough it is Peter Schaffer's) is yet again being put forth, just as Hogwood and Schroeder have done, as a historical "original." But to call one's critical reaction historical evidence (even corroborating evidence)—that is obviously dirty pool. It is not even a question of subjectivity (though clearly we have an example here of Treitler's "certainty"). It is a question of a familiar sort of authoritarianism. (Who is "let off the hook of accountability" here, and "opened to intuition"? Not even the performers, it would seem.) Treitler wants to speak with Mozart's own voice—or at the least to appropriate the voices of Mozart's romantic contemporaries like Hoffmann and Wackenroder, whose works are extensively glossed in the essay from which the extract comes, and to whom the last sentence in the extract alludes. The critic thinks his empathy entitles him to do these things. It is not even a case of "cheating at telephone," as I call a related self-aggrandizing move in essay 7. It is more as if Edgar Bergen had made himself very small and tried to sit on Charlie McCarthy's lap. Treitler here seats himself on Hildesheimer, who is sitting on Hoffmann, who is sitting on poor Mozart, by now altogether crushed under the weight of three ventriloquists. And this is called hermeneutics.

Back to Bork

Treitler was far closer to the mark on the very first page of *Music and the Historical Imagination*, where he wrote that "the meaning of a

---

[49]"Mozart and the Idea of Absolute Music," *Music and the Historical Imagination*, 214.

text is not fixed within its boundaries but is ever contingent upon the interests and the circumstances of the community of readers or listeners." The urge to claim access to original intention is the need or ambition to elevate oneself above the community of one's peers. In his startlingly uncommunitarian discussion of Mozart, Treitler finds himself in the unexpected company of Robert Bork, who, since the media exposure given his debacle before the Senate Judiciary Committee in 1987, has been the exemplary practitioner of what has been defined as legal modernism.[50]

Modernism, according to this special definition, is rationalism stiffened into pessimistic intransigence under threat to its prerational assumptions. Although deprived of any easy faith in consensus,

> modernism does not break entirely with the hopes of the Enlightenment. Instead, modernism seeks to deepen Enlightenment projects by acquainting them with the dark side of reason. Yet, in the holistic concept of totality—be it *Geist*, class relations, will to power or id/ego/superego [i.e., whether it takes its bearings from (or in reaction to) Hegel, Marx, Nietzsche, or Freud]—modernism retains some hope for epistemological or even ontological coherence. As modernism is the first to recognize, however, this hope is usually ruthlessly denied. The modernist thus understands the present as a period of anguish, estrangement, and alienation.[51]

Similarly (I have argued), "historical" performance, sensing the fragility of the idealized ("timeless") work, seeks to salvage it by warding off all the contingent readings the work has received over time, and by adopting a characteristically anguished modern stance of estrangement against any subjectivity but its own. In its attempt to bond with the original intentions that produced the work, it excludes all other intentions. Under cover of hermeneutics it resists hermeneutics (cf. essay 10). And a familiar entropy sets in: "modernism usually precipitates in rationalist solutions; rationalism degenerates into prerationalist prejudice."[52]

At the root of it all is fear. Just as legal modernists fear that "subjective" legal interpretation will ultimately discredit the law and subvert its power to undergird the social fabric, so performance-practice fundamentalists fear that the refusal of the Nibelungs duly to submit to the will of the gods as revealed by their academic prophets

[50]See Pierre Schlag, "Missing Pieces: A Cognitive Approach to Law," *Texas Law Review* 67 (1989): 1213–17.

[51]Ibid., 1219; see also Levinson and Balkin (note 59), who argue that the "difference between the modernist and the premodernist is precisely that the modernist feels that there is something that has been lost" (1646).

[52]Schlag, 1238.

will undermine the authority of the canonical repertory and eat away its power to validate contemporary practice. Both projects require that we repudiate the proliferation of possibilities, since both have accepted (with certainty!) the prerational belief that "a culture that engages itself to the interminable opening of possibility issues its own death warrant."[53] Both projects, though indentifying themselves with tradition, in fact deny the role of tradition in supporting culture (as I elaborate in essay 7), because, as Charles Rosen puts it of music, "[m]ultiple possibilities of realizing a musical text are a basic tradition of Western music."[54] But both projects, though they may enjoy momentary advantages, are chimerical. Legal modernism has not and will not put an end to divisive debate about social policy (say, the constitutionality of abortion rights), and if something is going to save the classical canon from sliding into the margins of our culture, it is not going to be historical performance.

The congruence between legal modernism and authentistic performance practice has been widely observed from both the legal and the musical perspectives. Essays 8 and 9, on Beethoven performance, both allude to it (though at the time No. 8 was written Judge Bork had not yet become a media celebrity and the posture in question is associated with Edwin Meese, Ronald Reagan's contentious attorney general). Acknowledgement of the parallel from the legal side has given my reading of authenticity-as-modernism a most powerful confirmation (I'd say the most powerful it has received). The first such explicit remarks known to me are in a whimsical piece by Judge Richard A. Posner called "Bork and Beethoven," in which the author affects wonder that Samuel Lipman, the music critic for *Commentary* and a dependable opponent of "historical" performance, could be so out of step with his magazine's neoconservative editorial policy.[55] A remarkable antimodernist harbinger is "Words and Music: Some

---

[53]Philip Rieff, *Fellow Teachers: Of Culture and Its Second Death* (Chicago: University of Chicago Press, 1972), 70. For this quote, and for several of its surrounding formulations, I am beholden to Danielle M. Lussier, a member of a seminar I conducted at the University of California at Berkeley in the fall of 1992, and her paper, "Ruminations on Modernism, Authority, and Interpretation."

[54]The *New York Review of Books*, 14 February 1991, 50 (responding to a letter to the editor from Neal Zaslaw). Sanford Levinson and J. M. Balkin offer some deft amplification to the concept of tradition (and how musical authenticists misunderstand it) as advanced implicitly here by Rosen and explicitly in essay 7: "What allows one . . . to consider him or herself a 'traditional' Jew is surely not some fantasy that one is doing exactly what was done 3,000 years ago in ancient Israel, but rather a felt confidence that one is participating as the latest member of a recognizable way of life whose transhistorical identity has endured whatever the surface changes. Few traditions assume stasis as the operative condition of life." ("Law, Music, and Other Performing Arts" [see note 59], p. 1623]).

[55]*Stanford Law Review* 42 (1990): 1365–82.

Remarks on Statutory Interpretation," by Jerome Frank, a speech delivered nearly half a century ago, before musical authenticity had become
more than an academic issue.[56] Taking off from some remarks of Ernst
Krenek skeptical of *Werktreue*,[57] the author reached the conclusion
that "[t]he legislature is like a composer. It cannot help itself: It must
leave interpretation to others, principally to the courts."[58]

The most extensive such discussion, offering a veritable gold
mine to anyone interested in pursuing fresh approaches to our ongoing disciplinary debates, is "Law, Music, and Other Performing Arts,"
by Sanford Levinson and J. M. Balkin.[59] This substantial article is
ostensibly a review of *Authenticity and Early Music*, the collection in
which essay 4 first appeared, and is by far the widest-ranging, most
searching review that much-reviewed volume has received. The authors locate the crux of the argument precisely where it ought to be
located: "What," they ask, "explains the development at this juncture
of our culture of a movement organized around the notion of authenticity in musical performance?" (p. 1628). The answer to that question, whatever the particular perspective from which it is posed, will
radiate onto "central aspects of the experience of modernity in Western culture as a whole" (pp. 1628–29). The question itself, betokening
distance from the modern condition, implies "its gradual transformation into what is now called the postmodern" (p. 1658).

The authors begin by taking stock of the "real" stakes in the
authenticity game, the issues that lie behind or beneath the deco-
rously abstract matters (responsibility vs. freedom, truth vs. taste)
that play on the surface of discussion. What drives debate are basic
drives indeed: "great sums of money and great professional power and
prestige" (p. 1602). It's a matter not of esthetics but of economics, not

---

[56]*Columbia Law Review* 47 (1947): 1259–78.

[57]Quoted is an article, "The Composer and the Interpreter," that appeared in the
Black Mountain College Bulletin in 1934; the author also cites Krenek's well-known
collection of essays, *Music Here and Now* (trans. Barthold Fles, New York: W. W.
Norton, 1939), in which the earlier piece seems to have been absorbed (see the remarks
on "The Role of the Conductor," on "Work-Fidelity," and on "The Schooling of Interpreters" on pp. 224–31).

[58]"Words and Music," 1264. Most pertinent, with respect to the political implications of modernism, are Prof. Frank's obiter dicta about the tendency of despots (he
names Frederick the Great and Napoleon) to forbid judges from interpreting statutes.
Closer to home, he notes that "in the decades preceding fascism, even the so-called
liberals on the European continent had a similar aim. When in charge of a democratic
government, they had . . . out of distrust of the discretion of judges, engaged in the
pursuit of that legal blue bird, the perfect statute that would foresee, classify and
judicially regulate in advance every possible case. In so doing . . . they had paved the
way for fascism" (1268).

[59]*University of Pennsylvania Law Review* 139 (1991): 1597–1658; further references
will be made in the text.

truth or even taste but politics. That is already enough to justify an interdisciplinary analysis of musical performance issues. The authors handily dismiss two familiar objections to such an enterprise: first, that "[l]egal interpretation affects people's lives and fortunes, whereas nothing of consequence flows from what literary [or musical] interpreters do"; and, second, that "unlike artistic interpretation, [legal] adjudication is distinctively an act of power" (p. 1609). "To be sure, Roger Norrington does not have the same power that the Supreme Court does," they allow. "But even if Norrington has less power to enforce conformity with his views than an appellate court, it is a mistake to view him as having no power at all, especially to the extent that his devotees gain control and influence over institutions that shape our musical tastes and preferences" (p. 1610).[60]

They back up these contentions with clever recourse to a very homely source: the *Penguin Stereo Record Guide,* a "record collector's bible" issued under the auspices of the *Gramophone Magazine,* a widely circulated British monthly.

> In the second edition, published in 1975, the authors speak paternalistically but often approvingly of the very small number of authentic performances of Baroque music then recorded; in their view, it's quite all right if you like that sort of thing. But traditional performances constitute virtually all recommended albums of Baroque music. As the Eighties progressed, more and more authentic performances, first of Baroque, and then of Classical music appeared. In the 1984 successor volume, *The Complete Penguin Stereo Record and Cassette Guide,* the authors express their approval of many individual "authentic" performances, tempered with occasional distress at the new fundamentalism that appears to inform them. "Traditional," rather than "authentic," performances, however, constitute the lion's share of recommendations. In the work's latest incarnation, *The Penguin Guide to Compact Discs,* published this past year [1990], the field of Baroque music has been largely ceded to authentic performers. It is assumed that most listeners will want such performances, although recommendations are still offered for those who insist on more traditional versions. With millions of classical music discs sold each year on the recommendations of *Gramophone* and similar magazines, it is clear that interpretive debates are hardly exclusively about matters of expression (pp. 1610–11, footnotes omitted).

"The monetary interest alone, a cynic might suggest, is enough to attract the attention of lawyers," the authors affably concede;

---

[60]To this the authors add two pertinent observations: first, that acts of musical interpretation can be not just performances but "performative utterances which simultaneously constitute acts of power," and, second, that "the legal act of interpretation, which clothes power through an act of cognition, is the normal, paradigmatic act of interpretation" (1613).

but, they say, "that is not quite the reason we became interested in these matters. Our interest is in the theory of interpreting commands" (p. 1602). That seems to locate with excellent economy the genuine point of intersection between theories of musical and legal interpretation, and to clarify both the reason why the musical authenticity movement is such a producer of ferment within its own manifest domain and why it has opened out so resonantly onto wider intellectual and political arenas. That is the best proof of its cultural importance and vitality. It crystallizes microscopically matters of virtually infinite urgency and ramification. "Just as the music of the *Eroica* is not identical with its score," the authors write (perhaps without realizing how controversial an assertion they are making within the intersecting fields of music and philosophy: see above and also essay 8), "so too the social practice of law is not fully identical with its written texts, but needs the activity of those entrusted with its performance to be realized" (p. 1609). The contradiction—the problem, the debate—arises in both fields because all we have today are the score and the statute; and both score and statute, Levinson and Balkin emphasize, are "designed to structure other people's behavior" (p. 1627).[61]

These legal scholars, pushing farther many of the arguments to be found in this book, associate both legal modernism and authentic performance practice with such symptoms of the "crisis of modernity" as "the bureaucratization and rationalization of society," and "the eventual collapse of the concept of reason into a barren instrumentalism" (p. 1629).[62] Yet they refrain from indictment (and also from celebration), identifying with the postmodern stance of "rejection either of applause or of dejection, which are themselves . . . the products of specific cultural moments, in favor of a somewhat more detached acceptance of the inevitability of change and our inability to place such changes as occur within any master narrative" (p. 1631). Failure to reckon with this inevitability leads to what the authors call the "paradox of authenticity" (adumbrated in essay 2): "The more one self-consciously tries to be authentic to a tradition, the less authentic

---

[61]The word "structure," they comment, is "purposely elusive, leaving open the possibility that the particular passions (and, dare we say, political commitments) of the gifted performer might have as much to do with the performance possibilities she chooses as some impossible fidelity to purportedly timeless and acontextual commands contained in the texts."

[62]The latter position, of course, is a tenet of the Frankfurt School, which sought to ward off that threatened entropy with "negative dialectics"; sure enough, many of Levinson's and Balkin's points about historical performance ideology were anticipated in Adorno's Bach bicentennial harangue, "Bach Defended against His Devotees" (1950): see T. W. Adorno, *Prisms*, trans. Samuel and Shierry Weber (Cambridge, Mass.: MIT Press, 1981), 133–46.

one's practice becomes" (p. 1632). *But*: "the modernist will both invariably fail at regaining this lost authenticity and invariably succeed in epitomizing an authentic experience—the authentic experience of separation from the past, which is the authentic experience of modernity" (p. 1634). And that is why—see essays 4, 6, and 7—Early Music, while never historical, is at all times authentic if not "authentic."

In the end, of course, one circles back to Bork, the twentieth-century Hobbes, authentistic legal performer par excellence, in whom, the authors say (their language recalling Leo Treitler's), one encounters the same "modernist anxiety and detachment" from the sentient self, the same "quest to regain 'objective' indicia of performance and the invention of sacralized 'traditions'" (p. 1644). Faced with an opinion by Justice John Marshall Harlan appealing to tradition as a "living thing," concerned "both [with] continuity [and] with alterations of previous traditions," Bork scoffs that such a notion is "entirely legislative."[63] This not only recalls Neal Zaslaw's appeal to an invented and sacralized "documentary tradition," but also resonates with Jerome Frank's musical analogy, in terms of which Bork sees a (judicial) performer attempting to usurp the (legislative) composer's role: Alberich again. Levinson and Balkin make no bones about what they take to be the repressive political motives of any quest to regain paradise: "Faced with this Heraclitian whirl of flux and discontinuity . . . , some may be tempted to form authentic performance-of-legal-scholarship movements with a concomitant attempt to delegitimize those they now perceive as contributing to the flux" (p. 1653).

In the Aftermath of the Great Trauma

It is evident that the issue of performance practice cuts very near to the cultural quick, and that debate about it will be exceptionally revealing of cultural attitudes. So let us return in closing to the debates within musicology and focus a bit more intensely on their intradisciplinary implications.

Where Prof. Jackson in his editorial[64] opposes "the search for objective reality" to my "subjectivism," he might seem to be committing the ancient error Adorno debunked so long ago in his dear old screed against the dogmatic performance practitioners of yore: "Objectivity," he scolded, "is not left over after the subject is extracted."[65] What

---

[63]Robert H. Bork, *The Tempting of America: The Political Seduction of Law* (1990), quoted in Levinson and Balkin, 165f.

[64]See note 21.

[65]"Bach Defended against His Devotees," 144.

is left over in that case is nonsense, since all sense requires an interaction of subject and object.

But if I read Prof. Jackson aright, he has something else on his mind: the old-fashioned Anglo-American prejudice against the speculative or the conjectural. Further down the page, in fact, Prof. Jackson adds "speculation" to the list of my sins, and explicitly links it with "subjectivism."[66] While a conjecture or a speculation is by definition an opinion that cannot (yet) be empirically confirmed, such an opinion need not be just a hunch. A conjecture can as easily be arrived at by strict reasoning as by caprice (or "intuition," to recall what Leo Treitler prefers to accountability). There is no reason to assume that a conjecture is "merely subjective," still less is there any reason to stigmatize it a priori.

But that is the habit among scholars in England and America, where the performance-practice movement chiefly thrives. To understand it we must look around the corner at a closely related scholarly practice, textual criticism, where authenticity is also (and in this case quite properly) the central concern. It was on textual criticism, on its methods, and on its special musicological vices that the field of performance practice was modeled (rather than on art restoration, as more commonly advertised). That is why I have included a couple of discussions of textual criticism in this volume (essays 3 and 5), and why I want to take a quick look at it up front.

The aim of textual criticism is the recovery of original texts, a project that has received enhanced prestige in music as the concepts of "text" and "work" have merged. The text critic is a purifier—and a prophet. By spotting and removing errors and interpolations that have accreted to a text in the course of its transmission, the critic restores the author's intentions, allowing him like a good modernist to "speak to us in his own language."[67] The process is ideally concerned with letter only, about which one need merely make knowledgeable decisions; but meaning (and with it, the onus of judgment) enters the purview of text criticism when an error, having been spotted, cannot be corrected on a purely mechanical basis. (And that is why A. E. Housman, one of the great text critics, called his discipline "the science of discovering error in texts and the art of removing it."[68])

To say this, of course, is vastly to oversimplify. "Art" and "science," the latest stand-ins for subject and object, are as interdependent in

[66]*Performance Practice Review* 4 (1991): 113.

[67]Philip Gossett, review of Rossini, *The Siege of Corinth* (Angel SCLX 3819, cond. Schippers), *Musical Quarterly* 61 (1975): 626–38.

[68]A. E. Housman, "The Application of Thought to Textual Criticism" (1921), in R. Gottesman and S. Bennett, ed., *Art and Error: Modern Textual Editing* (London: Methuen, 1970), 2.

textual criticism as everywhere else. One often needs more than just technical knowledge (of grammar, say, or paleography) to spot an error, and all the taste in the world will not help an ignorant critic (or performer—see essay 17) to correct it. But I have given enough of an account of textual criticism to establish two things. First, the superficial parallels should be evident whereby textual criticism could be at once the model for performance research and the means of its straying into literalistic error: as several of the essays that follow will illustrate, the source of error is the confusion of a physical object (text) with an act (performance) and an idea (work). Second, it should be clear that conjecture plays an important part in any fully responsible—that is, scientific—job of textual criticism.

This second, possibly surprising, point is true because the product of textual criticism (the critical edition or recension) should be a text that is better than any of its extant sources and therefore different from all of them. This is the goal even when holograph sources are available; for no text, not even the one you are now holding in your hands (and not even the best critical edition, alas), is ever wholly free of error. But the need for conjecture becomes ever greater as we go back in time and sources become scarcer, to the point where centuries may intervene between the date of a composition and that of its earliest extant physical embodiment. Since all sources are corrupt, a truly critical edition will be by definition conflationary—that is, it will incorporate readings from various sources that in the editor's informed judgment (i.e., according to the editor's best conjecture) represent what the author wrote. It may well need to incorporate readings that cannot be found in any extant source, but had to be supplied by the editor on the basis of an informed conjecture as to what the author meant to write.[69]

These are the assumptions under which the legacy of classical literature has been edited since the time of the Renaissance, and also the assumptions under which modern biblical scholarship proceeds (though the case of biblical recension is complicated by fundamentalist opposition). No literary scholar believes in any source enough to give it unqualified loyalty. Loyalty is owed to the author, not to the sources.

---

[69]See essay 3; for a more technical discussion leading to the same conclusion see Margaret Bent, "Some Criteria for Establishing Relationships between Sources of Late-Medieval Polyphony," in *Music in Medieval and Early Modern Europe*, ed. Iain Fenlon (Cambridge: Cambridge University Press, 1981), 295–317. Bent remarks: "[T]he editor's duty goes beyond respect for manuscripts. Even more respect, surely, is owed to the original intentions of the composer" (313—I would say, simply, "the original text"); and, "the modern editor is just as fallible as the medieval scribe, a condition from which he can no more escape by taking the 'safe' course of literal copying than by exercising his mind and judgment" (316).

By conflating the sources—that is, by disrespecting their individual integrity—one aims to restore the integrity of the original text.

But try to sell this method to a musicologist! With honorable exceptions like Bent (quoted in note 69), musical scholars have remained wedded to the so-called "copy-text," an idea that was tried out in literary studies a century ago and discarded.[70] It was a by-product of that nineteenth-century innovation in textual studies whereby sources were grouped genealogically ("filiated") so as to assess their relative authority. While this was a great gain in mechanical rigor and efficiency, there was the danger that once a source was proclaimed the "best text," that is, the most authoritative surviving transmitter, it would then begin to claim the loyalty properly due the author; its integrity would become an issue, and all of its readings would be followed uncritically unless (reluctantly) adjudged impossible. (But as Housman observed, "Chance and the common course of nature will not bring it to pass that the readings of a MS are right wherever they are possible and impossible wherever they are wrong."[71] Whatever doubts scholars may have had about the truth of that formula a century ago have surely been dispelled since the advent of computer spell-checkers.) The gain in efficiency quickly metamorphosed into a patent loss of sense as chance redactions were elevated to an unearned but unquestioned authority, and where good pedigree could weigh in favor of bad readings.[72]

Timorous editors defended the method not as a means of establishing an authentic text but merely as the lesser of two evils; "what they believed," in the words of W. W. Greg, "was that from it less harm would result than from opening the door to individual choice among variants, since it substituted an objective for a subjective method of determination" (p. 24). This begins to resemble Roland Jackson's language. But as Greg further noted:

> it is impossible to exclude individual judgement from editorial procedure: it operates of necessity in the all-important matter of the choice of copy-text and in the minor one of deciding what readings are possible

[70]See W. W. Greg, "The Rationale of Copy-Text" (1950), in Art and Error, 17–36. The last major literary exponent of the method was Ronald McKerrow, a Shakespeare scholar, who died in 1940; and even he abandoned it, in the radical formulation that is common among musicologists, in his later work.

[71]Introduction to Manilius (1903), xxxii; quoted by Greg, 18. Further citations from Greg will be made in the text.

[72]Current practice varies, but most literary editors save time by relying on copy-texts for what are known as "accidentals" (details of spelling, punctuation, and other matters of formal presentation) while conflating with regard to "substantives" (i.e., that which affects meaning, as even punctuation may sometimes do). The more idiosyncratic an author, of course, the less can be classified as "accidental."

and what not; why, therefore, should the choice between possible readings be withdrawn from its competence? Uniformity of result at
the hands of different editors is worth little if it means only uniformity
in error; and it may not be too optimistic a belief that the judgement
of an editor, fallible as it must necessarily be, is likely to bring us closer
to what the author wrote than the enforcement of an arbitrary rule.
(Ibid.)

These words were written over forty years ago, and they represent
what was even then pretty much the consensus among critical editors
of literary texts. But now compare what the *New Grove Dictionary of
Music and Musicians* advised its readers as recently as 1980: "Most
modern editors agree that it is better to base a new edition on one
good source than to publish a conflation resembling nothing that
existed at or soon after the period of the work itself."[73]

If they agree, it is because they have all misunderstood the purpose of textual criticism as completely as the *New Grove* has misunderstood it; for the aim of conflation is precisely to produce the text
that existed at the period of the work itself, indeed at the moment of
the work's completion. That this text no longer exists as a physical
object should not alter its status as intentional object or as editorial
goal. But since it can exist for us only in the realm of conjecture it
cannot claim authority in the minds of the idolatrous, who need some
old piece of paper or parchment to worship — or to wave hypnotically
at performers. Precisely because music, unlike literature, is a performing art whose sources (as the lawyers put it) issue commands, its
scholarly wing still relies on "aura" and "mana" rather than on rational
argument to secure obedience.

The copy-text method is not abandoned by musicologists even
when the source thus privileged is objectively known to be corrupt.
Known wrongness is preferred to conjectural rightness. We can live
with error, in effect, so long as it is not our error. What we as
musicologists cannot live with, it seems, is uncertainty. But if that is
so, we are not critics and we are not scholars, and we have no business
advising performers.

In the book reviewed in essay 3, John Caldwell defends the copy-
text method as "a legitimate method in itself where the object is
to illustrate a repertory or a scribal choice."[74] By "illustrating a
repertory" he refers euphemistically to the now lamentably widespread practice of transcribing manuscript anthologies of renaissance songs or motets in toto, and calling the resultant hodgepodge
of untested redactions a "critical edition" of the given source — a

[73]"Editing," *New Grove*, vol. 5, 840.
[74]*Editing Early Music* (Oxford: Clarendon Press, 1985), 2.

manifest contradiction in terms, not mitigated by the inclusion of voluminous collations with other sources, among whose readings the editor has not ventured to choose. (The real editorial work, under such a dispensation, is effectively passed on to the consumer.) By "illustrating a scribal choice" Mr. Caldwell evidently refers to the occasional practice of deliberately choosing inferior readings to transcribe and publish (one cannot say edit) if superior ones are already available in print.[75]

What can be the use of this practice, in which one editor monumentalizes the work of another, less competent editor? I have no idea. How did we reach such a pass? That, I think, can be explained. Once again (with apologies to Mel Brooks and his two-thousand-year-old man), fear has been the main propulsion.

It is conventional to assert about music that while its style and its structure are "facts," its sense is "merely" subjective, without any decent epistemological footing. Until quite recently (and what has happened recently is a story for another day), this view fairly circumscribed the field of musicology: style and structure were its objects of study (the former being the province of music history, the latter of theory), whereas musical meaning was off-limits to properly musicological investigation (though it kept a little toehold on the margins of philosophy). Manfred Bukofzer summed things up neatly from the historian's standpoint when he wrote, "If the history of music is to have more than an antiquarian interest and significance, it must be seen as a history of musical styles, and the history of *styles* in turn as a history of *ideas*."[76] So style is already idea. "Extramusical" ideas could only cloud the musicological vision. Musicology studied "the music itself" (a notion critiqued in essay 14).

Several years after Bukofzer wrote, the musicological world suffered a great trauma when Philipp Spitta's chronology of the works of J. S. Bach, a landmark of what Bukofzer called "factual stylistic analysis," turned out not to be factual at all. A team of German researchers in the early 1950s succeeded in falsifying it in good positivist fashion by using more refined philological methods, meanwhile proving that Spitta's work had been prejudiced all along by "ideas" about the "mean-

---

[75]For one avowed instance of this policy see W. Thomas Marrocco, *The Music of Jacopo da Bologna* (Berkeley and Los Angeles: University of California Press, 1954); for evidence of its damaging effect on performance see Alexander Blachly's review of two recordings of trecento music in *The Musical Quarterly* 57 (1971): 340.

[76]*Music in the Baroque Era* (New York: Norton, 1947), xiii. He went on from there, famously, to assert: "The ideas that underlie musical styles can only be shown in a factual stylistic analysis that takes music apart as a mechanic does a motor and shows how musical elements are combined, how they achieve their specific effect, and what constitutes the difference between externally similar factors."

ing" of Bach's life and work.[77] The man who brought the sad tidings to the English-speaking world was Arthur Mendel, a Bach scholar and (significantly enough) a performance-practice historian at Princeton University who figures prominently in essays 4, 7 and 16.[78] Reeling from the impact of the great trauma, Mendel became susceptible to the influence of neopositivist philosophers of science like Carl Hempel, who then dominated the Princeton philosophy department (and who had already made a musical convert in Milton Babbitt, Mendel's colleague, who was just then refashioning music theory on a neopositivist basis). Taking his cue from them, Mendel tried to insulate musicology from error. In an extraordinarily brash manifesto he delivered before an international congress of musicologists in 1961 (it was also extraordinarily conflicted, but that was not noticed till later), Mendel launched what became a virtual era of documentary fetishism in Anglo-American musicology.[79] It was precisely during this this reign of scientistic intellectual terror that the performance-practice movement was born.

Under neopositivism, what you cannot see or hear or touch or taste cannot be said to exist, and cannot provide "evidence" to support belief. To believe or to imagine what could not be verified by observation and strict rules of inference was stigmatized as mysticism. (And the strain of living under such neurotically stringent conditions of intellectual accountability easily explains, and goes far toward excusing, such immoderate reactions to them as we have observed in Leo Treitler.) Traumatized by the Spitta debacle, musicologists learned better than any other group of humanistic scholars to distrust conjecture, indeed to deride it, and to regard as real only what can be seen and touched. Josquin des Prez's motets cannot be seen or touched, but a manuscript containing them, regardless of who actually may have inscribed it, is present to our senses. The manuscript, not the text, became the focus of study, fusing with the text in the mind of the

[77]For a general report on the new Bach chronology see Gerhard Herz, "Preface" and "The Historical Background," in J. S. Bach, *Cantata No. 140* (Norton Critical Scores; New York: W. W. Norton, 1972), vii–viii, 3–50; and idem, "Toward a New Image of Bach," *Bach: Quarterly Journal of the Riemenschneider Bach Institute* 1/4 (1970): 9–27; 2/1 (1971): 7–28. For a radical reassessment in its wake see Friedrich Blume, "Outlines of a New Picture of Bach," *Music & Letters* 44 (1963): 214–27.

[78]See Arthur Mendel, "Recent Developments in Bach Chronology," *Musical Quarterly* 46 (1960): 283–300.

[79]See "Evidence and Explanation," *Report of the Eighth Congress of the International Musicological Society, New York, 1961* (Kassel: Barenreiter Verlag, 1962), vol. 2, 2–18. This paper has been extensively commented on in the "metamusicological" literature. See Joseph Kerman, *Contemplating Music* (Cambridge, Mass.: Harvard University Press, 1985), pp. 55–59; Leo Treitler, "The Power of Positivist Thinking," 391–94.

scholar even as the text fused with the work. To edit and annotate the
readings in a physically present manuscript was to accomplish something real. To restore an original text—or even, often enough, to alter
impossible readings—was to engage in mystique.

Now just as the prejudice against conjecture prevents musical
text critics from indulging in the luxury of a truly critical method, it
also inhibits students of performance practice from exercising critical judgment when implementing their factual findings. Just as surviving sources are treated as inviolable authorities (in preference to
what the author may actually have written or what makes subjective
sense), so any fortuitously surviving documentary evidence is granted
automatic authority over performance decisions (again in preference
to what the author may have wanted or what pleases us now). In both
cases, "what is (or was)" is tacitly allowed to supplant the question of
"what should be" (or is even equated with it) precisely so as to circum-
vent considerations of value and judgment, assimilating everything to
questions of observed data—limiting questions, in short, to those that
can have unequivocal "right answers."[80]

Sometimes the equation of fact and value is not even tacit. David
Schulenberg, in a recent article, has tried to rescue the word *authenticity* from the scare quotes to which I have consigned it.[81] "In considering expression in Bach's keyboard music," he begins by acknowledging,
"we face two rather different questions: the historical one of how this
music might have been understood in his own time, and the philosophical and practical one of how we are to comprehend it today"
(p. 450). By the end of the article, though, he is ready to discard (or
forget) the distinction, implying now that historical understanding
guarantees the other. Defending his notion of authenticity as an

---

[80]Where autograph sources do exist, the fusing process can turn altogether maudlin, the manuscript actually becoming the person. Thus Lewis Lockwood, exhorting
performers to substitute detailed knowledge of Mozart's autograph scores for "impas-
sioned guesswork," calls attention to the fact that the return of the opening theme to
close the slow movement of the "Jupiter" Symphony was an apparent afterthought,
added after another ending had already been entered in the manuscript, and recom-
mends that the performer somehow try to convey in sound the way the manuscript
looks: "This may or may not be possible, but if it were, the spirit behind it would convey
the sense that what is being accomplished is truly Mozart's—and therefore truly
authentic" ("Performance and 'Authenticity,' " 512.) We may enliven the music with a
show of spontaneity, in other words, only so long as the spontaneity thus accomplished
is not merely spontaneous—merely, if truly, ours, that is, and guesswork—but an
impersonation of a spontaneous decision that left a positive trace on paper a couple of
centuries ago. To Professor Lockwood I would address precisely the same question
directed in essay 7 at Jacob Lateiner, who propounded a similar tautology.

[81]"Expression and Authenticity in the Harpsichord Music of J. S. Bach," *Journal of
Musicology* 8 (1990): 449–76. Further page references to this article will be made in the
text.

ontological privilege arising out of superior historical knowledge, he writes: "[W]e *know* that we know more now about some music than we used to. We *do* have a better idea of how a Bach sarabande should sound—of what it *is*—than we [sic] did a century ago" (pp. 474–75; on the matter of "what it *is*" see essay 8).

The italics are his. Were I doing the italicizing, I would single out the phrase *should sound*, which stands so blatantly in lieu of "sounded." No one, I trust, will deny that today we know more about how Bach sarabandes sounded in Bach's day than people knew a hundred years ago; just think of all the effort we've expended in quest of that knowledge. The difference is that a hundred years ago such knowledge would less likely have been confused (or deliberately equated) with knowledge of how the piece should sound—something that, after all, is for *us* to decide (or rather, for us to *decide*).

Recent debate surrounding the Bach performances of Andrew Parrott, Joshua Rifkin, and some others, moreover, has clarified the nature of the privileged knowledge ("what it *is*") to which Schulenberg aspires, and the belief system that underwrites the privilege. Conventional assumptions notwithstanding, performance practice ideology is not to be equated with mere "intentionalism." We now think, for example, that we possess knowledge both of how Bach performed his concerted vocal music and of how he wished to have it performed. The two are not the same. Which one gets the privilege? The one represented by the surviving performance parts, of course, because (we think) they tell us what Bach did, not what he "intended" to do. Bach's unrealized (and therefore unheard) wishes are treated by performance practitioners exactly the way musical text critics treat the conjectural products of classical text editing: they are despised as representing (in the words of the *New Grove*) "nothing that existed at or soon after the period of the work itself." Documents outrank people, no matter who.

When we do not have contemporary documents we gladly settle for anachronistic or even hypothetical ones, just so long as they provide us with what we are looking for—namely, an authority that will save us from the onus of conjecture, for which read the onus of personal choice and responsibility. "If Obrecht's motet was still sung in the 1530s," writes Alejandro Planchart, "it is not unlikely that it was sung at the pitch suggested here."[82] Or if not, perhaps we can find the permission we need in the 1550s, or the 1670s, or the 1920s. Any port in a storm! But the storm rages only in frightened minds.

---

[82]A. Planchart, "On Singing and the Vocal Ensemble II," in Jeffery T. Kite-Powell (ed.), *A Practical Guide to Historical Performance: The Renaissance* (New York: Early Music America, 1989), 24.

At times the prejudice can take an even more brazenly tautological turn. Schulenberg reminds us that "[c]omposers like Bach did, *presumably*, know what they were doing." (We don't have to discern his meaning; it is enough to know it's there.) "Inasmuch as *we believe* that most of the details of a successful composition have been integrated into a coherent whole, then *we should expect* an inauthentic performance to be incoherent in some degree." Thus bigotry is openly promoted. All that Schulenberg can instance in support of this defamatory assertion are sitting ducks like Peter Sellar's pastiche opera productions—knowing anachronisms that play deliberately on the tension that arises out of stylistic rupture. Yet Schulenberg does not hesitate to hit and run, suggesting with no basis save bias that "perhaps any 'inauthentic' performance is incoherent in roughly the same way" as Sellar's (adding, of course, that "that cannot be demonstrated here").[83] Even Judge Bork could tell him where the burden of proof ought to lie.

What Schulenberg, Lockwood, Jackson, and the others simply cannot tolerate is the sense that they are personally involved and implicated in their practices. And this gives rise to the greatest tautology of all. Discussing his own manner of performing a Bach sarabande, Schulenberg complains that "Taruskin seems to argue [in essay 4] that the determining factor in the type of performance decisions I have been describing is what the performer or the audience *likes*" (p. 473; italics original). After squirming a bit he finds that he must grant the point, but there's a "but": "In fact, I would not deny liking what I would term the more 'authentic' tempo for this piece. But I do not think that this has been my reason for calling it authentic." Of course not; quite the contrary: your determination that the tempo was authentic was what gave you permission to like it. "I might add that the type of process I have described for determining the tempo of a Bach sarabande is one that responsible performers of all types carry out repeatedly in arriving at their decisions about how to play all manner of pieces" (Ibid.).

Responsible performers of all types? But "responsible performers" are a single type—the modernist type, the type with the punitive *Werktreulich* superego, the type eager to be controlled by the composer and by the composer's surrogates both animate and inanimate, the type Stravinsky liked and the *New Grove* approves, who does not "interpret" but "transmits." Such performers have no lock on historical practice. As I try to point out in essays 6, 7, 11, and elsewhere, such performers are more likely than any others to repress the manifold authenticated historical practices that demand creative departures

---

[83]"Expression and Authenticity," 475; italics added passim.

from the text. And as essay 2 will show, they certainly have no lock on authenticity.

So whereas the essays in this book have been widely interpreted (by their more sympathetic readers, anyway) as cheerfully pluralistic,[84] and whereas I realize (and try to show) that "responsible performers" have important virtues (one being the way they give reflection to salient aspects of our contemporary culture and bring them to consciousness), in the end I hope to foster alternative models of authentic performance, which I would prefer not to call "irresponsible" but "postauthoritarian," a term that chimes with some of the more encouraging symptoms of the postmodern attitude.

As essay 7 avers, I take some comfort in the increasing pluralism to be observed in the contemporary concert scene. The "multiculturalism" that many now misprize and deride is a welcome and necessary (if temporarily exorbitant) corrective to a sterile purism. I am glad to see that pop culture has been recognized by many classically trained musicians as a livelier site of activity and innovation than today's (or, hopefully, yesterday's) version of classical composition, and that the artificial, discommoding walls between the "high" and the "low" are beginning to yield. I am glad to see increasing impatience with an excessively production-oriented system of values in classical music and the proper reassertion of consumer values (yes, audience response) as a stylistic regulator. These are signs of critical systemic change—healthy change—in our culture that betoken the weakening of an increasingly irrelevant, pointlessly self-denying esthetic.

Postmodernist performance values, I would like to think, have to do with the opening-up of borders, in particular that border between the creative and the re-creative that began closing two long centuries ago. The postmodern attitude challenges the "strong concept of art," and its exclusive claim to seriousness. It is attempting to undo those life-transcending formalist commitments that have stifled musical creativity and recreativity alike. I dedicate this book to the furtherance of these objectives, trusting that as historical performers free themselves to become more truly historical, they will contribute vitally to the renewal of our musical life.

---

[84]For some, far too cheerful: see Robert Garis, "The Academy in Pretty Good Form" (review of Kenyon [ed.], *Authenticity and Early Music*) *Historical Performance*, 2/1 (Spring 1989): 31–34. I happily confess that I am less happy now with some aspects of the current scene than I was in 1986 when I wrote essay 4, and that the later pieces in this volume do reflect an increasing discomfort that will no doubt comfort Prof. Garis.

IN THEORY

I

On Letting the Music Speak for Itself

The title of today's panel may suggest that I will give a state-of-the-art report on the relationship between musicology and performance or else outline a program for the future development of that relationship. But neither would be worth my while to prepare nor yours to hear. Things are going well. Never, it seems, have scholars and performers worked so closely and happily together or learned more from each other, nor have so many ever before combined the roles as successfully as now. Musicologically trained performers are proliferating in graduate programs around the country. Historical performance practice is now a recognized subdiscipline both of academic musicology and of conservatory curricula. When Mr. Henahan of the *New York Times* can devote a Sunday column to the merits of historical instruments, or when Mr. Rockwell of the same paper, in a glowing review of Pomerium Musices, can actually list among the group's assets that its director is a musicologist, we may all take some justifiable satisfaction in going at last off the defensive vis-à-vis the press and, let us hope, the public. May this trend of recognition continue. We've all worked hard for it, we deserve it, and everything I say here is meant to abet it.

But at the same time I should like, as it were among friends, to examine what Charles Rosen has recently called the "peculiar metaphysical and ontological assumptions"[1] that underlie much current

---

[1]Charles Rosen, "The Musicological Marvel" (Review of the *New Grove Dictionary of Music and Musicians*), *New York Review of Books* (28 May 1981): 36.

Originally read as part of a panel discussion entitled "The Musicologist Today and in the Future," at the national meeting of the American Musicological Society in Boston, 13 November 1981. First published in the *Journal of Musicology* 1:3 (1982): 338–49. Copyright © 1982 by the Imperial Printing Company, Inc. Later published under the title "The Musicologist and the Performer" in the panel proceedings, *Musicology in the 1980s*, ed. D. Kern Holoman and Claude V. Palisca (New York: Da Capo, 1982), 101–18.

thinking about musicology and performance, or musicology-cum-performance, or even musicology *versus* performance. And if much of what follows sounds like an *apologia pro vita sua*, and therefore immodest, it is because I feel that the only way for me, as a musicologist performer, honestly to approach the question of musicology and performance, is to look within.

So let me take as my point of departure a little colloquy I had some time ago with a graduate student at Columbia. He claimed that performances of Renaissance sacred music by Cappella Nova, the choral group I direct, were arbitrary and overly personal, and that I would be better advised to "let the music speak for itself." Well, I can tell you that his remarks rankled in their implication of irresponsibility. I do my homework. I edit the music we perform from its original sources, or at least from pedigreed *Gesamtausgaben*, I have read up on musica ficta, on text underlay, on proportions, and we do not gussy up the music with instruments. Yet I knew just what the fellow meant, and knew also that his view of our work was widely shared among scholars, or at least among graduate students. Debating the matter with him did me good. It made me examine my own premises with greater detachment than before, and made me attempt to separate my own musicological attitudes from my performer's attitudes—something I rarely do consciously, any more than I am separately aware of inhaling and exhaling.

It seems a curious request to make of a performer, to "let the music speak for itself." If a performer did not have the urge to participate in the music and, yes, to contribute to it, why then he wouldn't have become a performer in the first place. The only time I could recall being told previously to "let the music speak for itself" was when I played the opening movement of Bach's B minor French Suite to my piano teacher many years ago and ventured a few ornaments. Most of the time the idea of letting the music speak for itself implies hostility, contempt, or at least mistrust of performers. It is what Brahms had in mind, for example, when he declined an invitation to the opera saying that if he sat at home with the score he'd hear a better performance. Or think of Stravinsky, with all his raillery against "interpretation," or Milton Babbitt, when describing his motives for adopting electronic media as a way of compensating for what he called the "low redundancy" of his music.[2] All three composers seem to share a view of performers as undesirable middle men, whose

---

[2]Cf. "Who Cares if You Listen?," *High Fidelity* 8/2 (February 1958) and widely anthologized thereafter, e.g., in Elliott Schwartz and Barney Childs (eds.), *Contemporary Composers on Contemporary Music* (New York: Holt Rinehart Winston, 1967), 244–50.

elimination would only improve communication between composer and audience. But only in Babbitt's case was letting the music speak for itself in this way a practicable alternative. Stravinsky, for his part, was moved by his mistrust of performers to become one himself, so as to document his music first in piano rolls and then in recordings and thus achieve the inviolable musical "object" he sought. The trouble was that whenever Stravinsky documented his performances more than once he created quite different objects, particularly with regard to tempo, which was always the main object of documentation to begin with. Moreover, Stravinsky's recorded tempi were almost always faster than his indications in the score, sometimes by a truly bewildering margin, as in the case of *Zvezdoliki*, which I single out because Stravinsky referred to his recording of that piece as a particularly successful documentation.[3] So Stravinsky, sitting at home with the score like Brahms, heard a performance that was if not better, then at least consistently slower than the ones he himself produced in actual sound. His efforts at documentation have only produced a confusing problem for those who would obey his wishes. But the problems he created are as nothing next to those created by such pianist composers as Debussy or Prokofiev, whose performances on rolls and records are so at variance with their notation that no one could get away with copying them (as I found out when I took a Gavotte by Prokofiev to another piano teacher). As for Brahms himself, even if we allow that his remark amounted to no more than persiflage, we may ask nonetheless whether the better performance he heard was better because it was more faithful to the music in some obscure way, or because it perfectly suited his tastes and interests as another's rendition could not?

In short, music can never under any circumstances but electronic speak for itself. In the case of notated music there is always a middle man, even if it is only ourselves as we contemplate the written symbols. And if anyone still doubts this, let him drop in on any analysis symposium.

But even if impossible to realize absolutely, "letting the music speak for itself" may still be a worthy ideal to aspire toward. What does it mean, though? For the moment, let us assume it means realizing the composer's intentions as far as our knowledge of them permits. What we are really being told, then, is to let the composer speak for himself. I will not rehearse here the familiar epistemological impediments to learning what the composer's intentions were, especially a

---

[3]"Contemporary Music and Recording," in Igor Stravinsky and Robert Craft, *Dialogues and a Diary* (New York: Doubleday, 1963), 33. Reprinted in Schwartz and Childs, 56.

composer as remote from us as Ockeghem, whose music it was that I
was enjoined to let speak for itself. I wish to go a bit further and
suggest that in many if not most instances composers do not even
have the intentions we would like to ascertain. And I am not even
talking about what are sometimes called "high level" versus "low
level" intentions, that is, specific intentions with regard to individual
pieces as opposed to assumptions based on prevailing conditions the
composer took for granted.[4] No, I mean something even more fundamental: that composing concerns are different from performing concerns, and that once the piece is finished, the composer regards it and
relates to it either as a performer if he is one, or else simply as a
listener. I'll give a few examples. One is Irving Berlin, who once said of
Fred Astaire, "I like him because he doesn't change my songs, or if he
does, he changes them for the better." Another is Debussy again. He
said to George Copeland on their first meeting that he never thought
he'd hear his piano music played so well during his lifetime. No
question then that Copeland's playing realized the composer's intentions to the latter's satisfaction. On another occasion, though, Debussy asked Copeland why he played the opening of *Reflets dans l'eau*
the way he did. Copeland's response was that old performer's standby,
calculated to make any musicologist see red: "Because I feel it that
way." To which Debussy replied that as for himself he felt it differently, but that Copeland must go on playing it as he, Copeland, felt it.[5]
So once the pianist's credentials as a Debussy performer were established, his performances were accepted by the composer as being no
less authoritative than his own. Debussy, as pianist, was in his own
eyes only one interpreter among others.

My next example stems from personal experience. I once sat in as
page turner at a rehearsal of Elliott Carter's *Duo* for violin and piano
under the composer's supervision. He couldn't have been less helpful.
Whenever the performers sought guidance on matters of balance or
tempo, his reply was invariably, "I don't know, let's see . . . ," and then
he would join them in seeking solutions, as often asking their advice
as they his. At one point, when the performers were having some
difficulty with his very finicky rhythmic notation, Carter said (so
help me), "For heaven's sake don't count—just feel it." At the end of the
rehearsal he commented that every performance of the *Duo* was very
different from every other one, but that "whichever one I'm hearing
always seems the best." So much for intentions. If that was Carter's

[4]Cf. Randall R. Dipert, "The Composer's Intentions: An Examination of their
Relevance for Performance," *Musical Quarterly* 66 (1980): 205–18.
[5]Cf. George Copeland, "The First—and Last—Times I Saw Debussy," *Music*, Preview Issue (November 1944): 6–9.

attitude, what do you suppose Ockeghem would have cared about Cappella Nova's ficta? We seem to be committing another "intentional fallacy" here, trying, just as Wimsatt and Beardsley said we should never do, to solve our problems by "consulting the oracle."[6]

It seems to me that much of what I will make bold to characterize as the "musicological" attitude toward performance is based on consulting the oracle in an even more spurious, because roundabout, way. We tend to assume that if we can re-create all the external conditions that obtained in the original performance of a piece we will thus recreate the composer's inner experience of the piece and thus allow him to speak for himself. In a lecture I recently attended on the staging of one of Verdi's operas in Paris, a great deal of fascinating detail was recounted on all of the vicissitudes encountered in the course of mounting the work and in making it conform to the special demands of the Paris Opera. The point was constantly reiterated that every aspect of the production was completely documented in surviving records, so that one could revive the work tomorrow just as it was being described. I ventured to ask at the end of the lecture why this would be desirable, and I was told, with eyebrows raised and voice pitched high to show how obvious the answer was, that in this way the composer's intentions would be realized. And this after a lecture in which it had just been demonstrated that the intentions realized in the original production had belonged to many, not just Verdi, and that in a large number of instances the composer's intentions had been overruled and frustrated.

So why *do* we consult the oracle? A simple answer, the usual answer, is that we want our performances to be authentic. But that is no answer. What *is* this thing called authenticity and why do we want it? While most of us would by now agree with the premise, so elegantly and humorously set forth by Michael Morrow in *Early Music* a few years ago,[7] that authenticity of the kind we usually have in mind when talking musicologically about performance practice is a chimaera, most of us are nevertheless no more deterred by this realization from seeking it than was Bellerophon himself. Again I ask, why?

We usually trace the origins of modern musicology to romantic historicism. But it seems to me that musicological ideals of performance style owe as much if not more to the modernist esthetic that rose to dominance out of the ashes of the First World War. We in music usually think of it as the "Stravinskian" esthetic, though it had been

[6]W. K. Wimsatt, Jr., and Monroe C. Beardsley, "The Intentional Fallacy," *Sewanee Review* (1946): 468–88.

[7]Michael Morrow, "Musical Performance and Authenticity," *Early Music* 6/2 (1978): 233–46.

anticipated with astonishing, if cranky, completeness as early as Hanslick's *The Beautiful in Music*. It is often described, after Ortega y Gasset, as "dehumanization,"[8] but since that word (though meant by Ortega with approval) carries such unpleasant overtones, I prefer to use T. S. Eliot's term, depersonalization, defined as "the surrender of [the artist] as he is at the moment to something much more valuable," that thing being Tradition, which, as Eliot warns us, "cannot be inherited, and if you want it you must obtain it by great labour."[9] And why do we in music want it? So that our performances may capture something of what the folklorist Jeffrey Mark so percipiently described half a century ago in an article entitled "The Fundamental Qualities of Folk Music," but which is actually the best characterization I know of the modernist esthetic as applied to music:

> The performer, whether as singer, dancer, or player, does his part without giving any or much impression that he is participating in the act. And his native wood notes wild, far from giving the popularly conceived effect of a free and careless improvisation, show him definitely to be in the grip of a remorseless and comparatively inelastic tradition which gives him little or no scope for personal expression (again as popularly conceived). *Through him the culture speaks*, and he has neither the desire nor the specific comprehension to mutilate what he has received. His whole attitude and manner [is] one of profound gravity and cool, inevitable intention. There [is] not the faintest suggestion of the flushed cheek and the sparkling eye. And [the performance] is ten times the more impressive because of it.[10]

So here at last is the real challenge my critic issued me in the encounter I began by describing: "Let the culture speak for itself." Ah, would that we could, for this is what real authenticity is, the kind Eliot wrote about, not what Michael Morrow called the "contemporary cult meaning" of the word, which really amounts to little more than time-travel nostalgia. The trouble is that the artifacts of past culture with which Eliot dealt are still intact and available in a way that musical artifacts obviously can never be. Music has to be imaginatively re-created in order to be retrieved, and here is where conflicts are likely to arise between the performer's imagination and the scholar's conscience, even (or especially) when the two are housed in a single mind.

[8]Cf. José Ortega y Gasset, "The Dehumanization of Art" (1925), in *The Dehumanization of Art and Other Essays on Art, Culture, and Literature* trans. Helene Weyl (Princeton: Princeton University Press, 1968), 3–56.

[9]"Tradition and the Individual Talent (1917)" in Frank Kermode (ed.), *Selected Prose of T. S. Eliot* (New York: Harcourt Brace Jovanovich/Farrar, Straus and Giroux, 1975), 40, 38.

[10]Jeffrey Mark, "The Fundamental Qualities of Folk Music," *Music and Letters* 10/3 (1929): 287–90, passim. Italics mine.

Verdi, speaking ironically about the aims of verismo, said, "it's fine to reproduce reality, but how much better to create it." In a similar spirit I would say, "it's fine to assemble the shards of a lost performance tradition, but how much better to reinvent it." Research alone has never given, and is never likely to give (again for obvious reasons), enough information to achieve that wholeness of conception and that sureness of style—in a word, that fearlessness—any authentic, which is to say authoritative, performance must embody. Here is a paradox: which is more "authentic," an historical reconstruction of, say, *Messiah*, or a Three Choirs Festival performance? Which, in other words, enjoys the commonality of work, performer, and (lest we forget) audience, the certainty of experience and of expectation that lends the proceedings the "cool, inevitable intention" Jeffrey Mark described? The Three Choirs performance surely speaks for a culture, not Handel's perhaps, but that of the performers and their audience, certainly. It gives what Eliot called a sense "not only of the pastness of the past, but its presence."[11] The modernist, avant-garde, historical reconstruction of *Messiah* can only evoke the pastness of the past, and will therefore appeal not to the esthetic sense but merely to antiquarian curiosity—unless it derives its sustenance not only from whatever evidence musicological research may provide, but from imaginative leaps that will fill in the gaps research by its very nature must leave. Otherwise we will have not a performance but a documentation of the state of knowledge. As long as the reconstructionist performer holds himself to the same strict standards of accountability we rightly demand of any scholar, his efforts will be bent not on doing what the music was meant to do, but on simply "getting it right," that is, on achieving what the mainstream performer takes for granted. He will end up, if he is lucky, with what the mainstream performer starts out with.

The most authoritative and compelling reconstructionist performances of old music, as well as the most controversial, have always been those that have proceeded from a vividly imagined—that is frankly to say imaginary—but coherent performance style. They provide themselves with Tradition, in the Eliot sense, and bestow authenticity upon themselves. Where such performers do not know the composer's intentions they are unafraid to have intentions of their own, and to treat them with a comparable respect. I suppose I am thinking now of the performances of the Early Music Quartet and some recent ones by the Concentus Musicus among those I have heard, and among those I have not, of the radical reconstructionist performance of *Messiah* given in Ann Arbor under Edward Parmentier

[11]Eliot, "Tradition," 38.

last year, which I know only by enthusiastic rumor, and by reports of the uproar it created among some of the scholars in attendance.

In this light, let me return now to the criticisms of Cappella Nova. What was mainly under attack was our approach to phrasing and dynamics, both of which are very sharply profiled in our performances, and which from the very beginning have always been singled out by our hearers either for praise or for blame. The origins of the approach lie, I have no hesitation in admitting, in my own subjective response to the nature of the lines in complex, melismatic, and polyphonic textures. I know of no specific historical sanction for it, except insofar as subjective responses of contemporary hearers have been occasionally and vaguely recorded. In the absence of hard evidence I felt not only free but duty-bound to invent an approach. Or, to put things as they really happened, it was because this approach to phrasing and dynamics evolved in me during my period as director of the Columbia University Collegium Musicum, that I felt I had a stake in this music and was moved to form Cappella Nova to begin with. Although its origins lay not in certain knowledge but in imagination, the approach is very much an objective feature of Cappella Nova's style. It is an element of what we take to be, and present as, the authentic sound of the music, and its presence is, far from an intrusion, quite necessary if for us the music is, yes, to "speak for itself." Those whose scholar's conscience equates silence with prohibition must inevitably regard our performances as arbitrary. But what is arbitrary in my view is the flat dynamic and the lack of phrasing, that is, of molding lines to their high points, which characterize so many so-called "objective" performances of Renaissance music. For these derive not from any demonstrable condition or feature of the music or of its historical context, but merely from the state of evidence, over which the performer can exercise no control. Strict accountability thus reduces performance practice to a lottery. It has nothing to do with authenticity. Authenticity stems from conviction. Conviction in turn stems as much from belief as it does from knowledge. Our beliefs—naive or sophisticated, to be sure, depending on the state of our knowledge—are what alone can give us the sense of assurance and of style possessed by those fortunate enough to have behind them an unbroken tradition of performance.

This brings me to a perhaps even more fundamental caveat. What, after all, is historical method, and to what kind of knowledge does it lead? If we were to reduce it all to a single word, that word would have to be generalization. Style criticism, often held up as the ultimate goal of historical scholarship in music, is above all the abstraction of contexts from cases, the establishment of generalizing criteria. Think of Riemann, for example, of whom we read in the *New*

Grove that "he was not interested in the individual case as such, but rather in discerning its typicality and its place in the entire system."[12] And of course most properly historical musicological work is either that or it is a preparation for that. But this is as far from the performer's mentality as it is possible to be. *His* concern is *only* with individual cases, taken one at a time. As George Perle remarked admiringly abut Seiji Ozawa, who was performing one of his works at Tanglewood, "When he's playing it his whole repertoire consists of one piece—mine." And here is what Erich Leinsdorf has to say in a recent book which was actually meant as a polemic against interpretive excess: "Every great work is first and last a meaningful musical utterance unlike any other. If it did not have its own unique meaning it would have come and gone and would not be part of our living repertoire." Leinsdorf's words are fighting words, and what he is fighting is what he calls the "sacrifice of the sense of music to a simplistic notion of period style."[13] For him, then, historical reconstruction is just another variety of interpretive excess. But one needn't accept his belligerent equation of style consciousness with simplemindedness to note the real enough danger of our sense of style becoming reductive owing to an insufficient appreciation or response to the uniqueness of individual compositions.

This is a very easy trap to fall into. Our training as scholars gives us very precise and efficient ways of dealing with generalities. We have a vocabulary for them, and the process of framing them invokes reassuringly scientific methods and criteria, many of them quantitative and exact. We have no such aids in dealing with uniqueness. We have no vocabulary: words can no more give an exact representation of an individual piece of music than they can render an individual face. We have to draw the face and play the piece. But a scholar is never so insecure as when he is at a loss for words. And nothing is less scientific than the evaluation not of quantities but of artistic qualities, the specific details, the "divine details" as Nabokov would say. These must be apprehended by imaginative response, empathic identification, artistic insight—all euphemisms, of course, for intuition, which word embarrasses and antagonizes the scholar in us. Unwilling to claim intuition as a guide, both for the reason just given and for the reason given a while ago—that it violates our scholarly principles of accountability—we often tend to flee from characterizing the uniqueness of a piece in performance, and seek

---

[12]Mark Hoffman, "Riemann, Hugo," in Stanley Sadie (ed.), *The New Grove Dictionary*, vol. 16, 5.

[13]Erich Leinsdorf, *The Composer's Advocate: A Radical Orthodoxy for Musicians* (New Haven: Yale University Press, 1981), 88–89.

our refuge in our objective knowledge, which is in all cases a generalized one. Since it is never possible to talk about the unique with the
same objectivity as one can about the typical, we are tempted to
ignore distinguishing characteristics and instead parade our basic
knowledge of style as if it were specific insight. The results are
familiar, typified, if you will, by performances of choral masterpieces
by Bach or Handel that reduce them to demonstrations of dance
tempi, A-415, and (pace Prof. Neumann!) notes inégales. There is a
corollary to this in the form of reliance upon authentic editions,
authentic instruments, or authentic performance practices learned
from authentic treatises, in place of critical consideration of the
music. An actual, if extreme, recent example was an advertising flyer
sent out by a New York harpsichordist announcing that his would be
the first New York performance of the "Goldberg" Variations from the
Neue Bach-Ausgabe. This kind of thing is the performer's analogue to
what is regrettably becoming a pair of recognizable types among
scholarly papers—the kind that merely lists variants between versions or sources, and the kind that makes an exhaustive physical
description of a sketch, both kinds purporting meanwhile to describe
"compositional process." This is preparatory work offered as the substance of scholarship. Similarly, a performance that merely sets out to
demonstrate that Bach was Baroque represents preparatory work, not
the substance of performance.

But even at their best and most successful—or especially at their
best and most successful—historical reconstructionist performances
are in no sense re-creations of the past. They are quintessentially
modern performances, modernist performances in fact, the product
of an esthetic wholly of our own era, no less time-bound than the
performance styles they would supplant. Like all other modernist
philosophies, historical reconstructionism views the work of art,
including performing art, as an autonomous object, not as a process or
an activity. It views the internal relationships of the art work as
synonymous with its content, and in the case of music it renounces
all distinction between sound and substance: to realize the sound is in
fact to realize the substance, hence the enormous and, be it said,
ofttimes exaggerated concern today for the use of authentic period
instruments for all periods. The aim of historical reconstruction is, as
Ortega put it, "a scrupulous realization,"[14] and as Eliot put it, "not a
turning loose of emotion, but an escape from emotion; . . . not the
expression of personality, but an escape from personality,"[15] the emotions and the personality escaped from being, of course, those of the

[14]"The Dehumanization of Art," 14.
[15]"Tradition and the Individual Talent," 43.

performer "as he is at the moment."[16] The artist trades in objective, factual knowledge, not subjective feeling. His aim is not communication with his audience, but something he sees as a much higher, in Eliot's words "much more valuable" goal, communion with Art itself and with its history, and he enlists musicology's aid in achieving it. To return once more to the starting point, this is what is meant today by "letting the music speak for itself."

I am describing no monstrosity, no straw man, but an ideal of beauty that inspired many of the greatest creative minds of our century. And it is only in the nature of things that what dominated advanced creative minds half a century ago should be dominating advanced recreative minds today. The paradox and the problem—or is it just my problem?—is that this way of thinking about art and performance has no demonstrable relevance to the ways people thought about art and performance before the twentieth century. Applied to the music of the Renaissance and the Baroque, to say nothing of the nineteenth century, it all seems exquisitely anachronistic. And what seems to prove my point is that with the possible exception of the rather ambiguous case of continuo realization, the modern reconstructionist movement has produced many scrupulous realizers of musical notation but has yet to produce a single genuine master of improvisation, which we all know to have been nine-tenths of the Renaissance and Baroque musical icebergs.

Some may be wondering now who it is I'm really thinking of. But I am thinking of no individual; I am thinking of a little bit of each of us. We all share these attitudes to some extent if we are at all alive to our own time. Do I seem then to be generally skeptical of historical reconstructionism or of musicology as an ally of performance? Nothing could be further from the truth, as I hope my own activities testify. But I am skeptical of the complacency with which difficult issues are often addressed, and I do deplore the equation of modernist objectivity with scientific truth.[17]

---

[16]The invention of sound recording has obviously been a tremendous spur to this tendency, since it offers the possibility of permanence to a medium that had formerly existed only "at the moment." Most historical reconstructionist performances aspire at least tacitly to the status of document, if not that of Denkmal. When the performance is recorded, the aim usually becomes explicit (witness the slogan of the SEON series of historical recordings: "Document & Masterwork"). No less than the score, the performance is regarded as a "text" rather than as an activity, and this creates another pressure toward the elimination from it of anything spontaneous or "merely" personal, let alone idiosyncratic.

[17]Having used the word, I feel I must say a thing or two about "scientific" attitudes, though I fear they will be the most controversial of all (perhaps that is why I am seeking the sanctuary of a footnote). Empirical science, as all the world knows, claims to be "value-free." But art is not, and performance must not be. The adoption of the doc-

To even the score now, and to return to a more personal note, let me attempt to list the assets my musicological training has given me as a performer. At the very top of the list goes curiosity, with its implications, so far as human nature allows, of open-mindedness, receptivity to new ideas, and love of experiment. It is in this spirit that I believe investigations of past performance practices should be conducted. Let us indeed try out everything we may learn about in every treatise, every archival document, every picture, every literary description, and the more adventurously the better. But let us not do it in a spirit of dutiful self-denial or with illusions that the more knowledge one garners, the fewer decisions one will have to make. Let us accept from the scholar in us only that which genuinely excites the performer in us, if for no other reason than because both the attractive and the unattractive finding are equally likely to be wrong. Above all, let us not be afraid, as Rose Rosengard Subotnik recently put it with respect to criticism,[18] to "acknowledge our own presence" in our work and to accept it, if for no other reason than because it is in the final analysis inescapable. The suspension of personality in a modernist performance immediately stamps the performance as such, and is therefore paradoxically tantamount to an assertion of personality. We impose our esthetic on Bach no less than did Liszt, Busoni, or even Stokowski.

The second great advantage musicological training confers is knowledge of what there is and where to find it. When one has mastered a scholar's bibliographical and paleographical skills, one need not be limited by the vagaries of editors and publishers. But here too there is an attendant pitfall in the form of an overly bibliographical approach to programming. I have in mind the kind of program that starts off with sixteen settings of *J'ay pris amours*, followed by one

trinaire empiricist, positivist, and unprincipled stance of scientific research when investigating performance practice can be pernicious, leading in extreme cases to an evasion of responsibility, something distressingly close to a musical Eichmann defense. I have in mind the perpetration of musical results the performer himself regards as unattractive, in the belief that that's how it was done, like it or not ("I was just following orders"). There have been notable recent instances of this in Bach performance, where the situation is exacerbated by the knowledge that Bach himself did not like certain aspects of his own performance practice, notably involving the size and quality of his choir in Leipzig. Still more disturbing is the "scientific" pressure to keep up with the state of research, whatever one's personal predilections. I know of more than one instance in which performers of Renaissance and Baroque music have followed practices of which they were not personally convinced either historically or esthetically for fear that otherwise they might be suspected of ignorance.

[18]"Musicology, Analysis, and Criticism," a paper read at the same panel discussion as the present one, published (as "Musicology and Criticism") in *Musicology in the 1980s*, 145–60, and reprinted in Rose Rosengard Subotnik, *Developing Variations* (Minneapolis: University of Minnesota Press, 1991), 87–97.

bassadanza from each of five collections, and finally a Machaut ballade performed with two voices, then three voices, then four voices, as it is transmitted in three different sources. These are seminar reports in sound, not concert programs. And another didactic programming pitfall is the practice, once far more widespread than it is now (as those who attended the Josquin Festival-Conference ten years ago may recall),[19] of presenting a kind of analysis of a piece in lieu of a performance of it—for example, changing the scoring of an isorhythmic motet on each talea, or bringing out by hook or crook the cantus firmus of any mass or motet. In either event, the performer takes it upon himself to throw into relief something the composer in many cases took elaborate pains to conceal, and is being the very opposite of authentic, however the term is construed. We tend, many of us, particularly those of us who teach music history for our daily bread, to turn our concerts into classrooms, and I know from personal experience that no bad habit born of musicology is more difficult to break. It is a case of the scholar's conscience once more, this time actually masquerading as the performer's imagination.

Speaking of teaching and of classrooms reminds me that when thinking of the relationship between the musicologist and the performer we usually assume that the former teaches and the latter learns. But good performers can teach receptive scholars a great deal, and communication both ways is needed if a real symbiosis of musicology and performance is to occur. Sometimes one is lucky enough to have it happen within oneself if one combines the roles. It was the performer in me that taught the scholar in me the extent to which *modus*, the division of longas into breves, continues, though not explicit in the notation, to operate throughout the Renaissance period, at least in church music, as an organizer of rhythm. This is a feature totally obscured by modern editions which base their barring on the tactus—a feature of modern editorial practice which, as Lowinsky demonstrated over twenty years ago,[20] is perfectly authentic, but, for a final paradox, no less a falsification for that. For *modus* is, as I have come to believe, *the* operative factor in projecting the rhythmic life of much of Isaac, for example, or of Josquin. It is a matter I intend to pursue in the context of "pure research," but it was a discovery I made purely serendipitously as a performer.

---

[19]See the transcripts of the "Workshops on Performance and Interpretation" published along with the rest of the proceedings of the Festival-Conference in Edward Lowinsky, ed., *Josquin des Prez* (London: Oxford University Press, 1976), 645–719, and most especially, Ludwig Finscher's paper, "Historical Reconstruction versus Structural Interpretation in the Performance of Josquin's Motets" in the same volume, 627–32.

[20]Edward Lowinsky, "Early Scores in Manuscript," *Journal of the American Musicological Society* 13 (1960), 126–73.

I began this little essay by noting that musicologists and performers are on better terms now than ever before, and I wish to reaffirm this heartening fact in conclusion. It might not be amiss to recall that it was not always so. Dmitri Shostakovich once had a good laugh over a definition of a musicologist he heard at breakfast one day from his piano teacher, and repeated it all his life. "What's a musicologist? I'll tell you. Our cook, Pasha, prepared the scrambled eggs for us and we are eating them. Now imagine a person who did not cook the eggs and does not eat them, but talks about them—*that* is a musicologist."[21] Well, we're eating them now, and even cook up a few on occasion, as when we do a little discreet composing to make a fragmentary piece performable. Now, if we could only sell them . . .

POSTSCRIPT, 1994

Renewed attack on this harmless piece unexpectedly surfaced after a full decade's lag in a volume entitled *Companion to Contemporary* [sic] *Musical Thought*.[1] The trouble with "artistic conviction," writes Peter Williams, a British organist on the faculty of Duke University, "is, of course, that under such a flag would be collected a terrible army of misunderstandings, vanities, speciousnesses, irresponsibilities, all masquerading as artistic conviction!"[2] The finger-in-the-dike mentality dies hard. In Britain it may never die. I would only ask Mr. Williams how he would distinguish the terrible army he imagines from the wonderful army I can just as easily imagine of fresh understandings and responsible reinterpretations, and also why we should trust him, of all people, to stand sentry at the gate of the admissible?

"Good 'mainstream' performance is less and less satisfying even in the music for which it assumed to be correct," he writes, as if "mainstream performance" were not itself undergoing perpetual change (under the influence of, among other things, Early Music). Like other musicological Tories, Mr. Williams does not understand what tradition is, or what it does (see essay 7). As to goals, he wants—purely and very, very simply—to revive the first performance, with that touching faith, entertained by those who have never attended a new music concert, that first is always best:

---

[21]Nikolai Malko, *A Certain Art* (New York: William Morrow, 1966), 180.

[1]Ed. John Paynter et al. (London and New York: Routledge, 1992).

[2]"Performance Practice Studies: Some Current Approaches to the Early Music Phenomenon," 931–47. The passages cited are on pp. 937–38.

> We are still some way from hearing Brahms's Violin Concerto played as
> Joachim played it for its premiere—with all gut strings and at a slightly
> lower pitch than today's—and the greatest artistic conviction of a per-
> formance with partly steel strings at a higher pitch today will never
> satisfy those wanting to know what Brahms heard, at least as to timbre.
> Timbre is admittedly a first stage, and the violinist must admittedly be
> a great artist, but it is Brahms himself who is the goal here, our
> legitimate aim being to hear what he heard. As a matter of fact, this may
> totally change our sense of what "artistic conviction" *is.*

I couldn't hope for a better illustration of the Wellsian time-travel
fantasies I describe in essay 4, nor a better specimen of the happy
naïvete that envisions the meaning of a musical work as completely
vested and timelessly immanent, there to be "recovered." (This latter
is also in its way a sci-fi fantasy; cf. *The Day the Earth Stood Still.)*
Such follies are harmless enough. What I must object to in all seriousness is Mr. William's evocation of "Brahms himself" (let alone "what
he heard") as goal—or what Mr. Williams, protesting a bit too much,
calls "our legitimate aim." That goal has been unavailable since
3 April 1897. What is available is not Brahms, but only "Brahms,"
something Mr. Williams and like thinkers construct as the covert
locus of their own authority. (Essay 7 includes a detailed elaboration
of this point.)

Finally, Mr. Williams insists that "for a performer merely to
'document the state of present knowledge' is by no means a ridiculous
idea." Indeed, he claims,

> perhaps "documenting present knowledge" is no more and no less than
> what any performance ever does, a necessary limitation but one seldom
> problematic in the past simply because in less discerning ages listeners
> were less experienced or sophisticated, and performers were more eas-
> ily found convincing and effective. As music-studies learn to avoid the
> quick performance practice answers, it will become a high ideal to use
> the concert area [*recte* "arena"?] as a place to "document the state of
> knowledge," for true knowledge might increasingly be seen as a better
> goal than concert-hall entertainment.

Complacent authoritarianism speaks for itself, and Mr. Williams
is more honest than most performance-practice authoritarians when
he implies what the evasive deny, viz., that there is a single right
interpretation arising out of omniscience, the single goal toward
which all must iteratively aspire.

This, I am happy to report, no longer represents contemporary
musical thought, even in Britain, even in the academy. Even in those
august places, the question is no longer "How did the music sound to
Brahms?" or even "What did the music mean to Brahms?" Many have

seen by now that preoccupation with these questions, wholly blink-
ered by the production-centered viewpoint of high modernism, can
only lead to an obsession with trivialities (strings, pitch). The important questions, to which the matters Mr. Williams likes to address
can indeed contribute if placed in perspective, are "What does this
music mean to us?" and, even more important, "What can it mean to
us?" These questions, being critical questions, do not have trivially
right answers, and so of course Mr. Williams will never ask them.

2

The Limits of Authenticity:
A Contribution

I was struck, recently, to read what Sylvia Townsend Warner told Vaughan Williams when he asked her, "a little sternly," why she had given up composing for a literary career. "I didn't do it authentically enough," she explained, "whereas when I turned to writing I never had a doubt as to what I meant to say." Here, though very casually put, was an exigent conception of authenticity indeed—one with a long, illustrious history, but very much with us still in many areas of life. Woody Allen, for example, in one of his covertly moralizing comedies, observes (in character) that when one is confronting death, one's life all at once assumes an authenticity it might have lacked before. His obvious meaning—that one's values and priorities take on a previously unacknowledged and compelling clarity—strikes a responsive chord in each of us, whether or not we know that we have been given a satirical crash course in existentialism.

Authenticity, in this sense, is more than just saying what you mean. That is mere sincerity, what Stravinsky called "a *sine qua non* that at the same time guarantees nothing." It carries little or no moral weight. In fact, to acknowledge someone's sincerity is generally a patronizing prelude to dismissal. Authenticity, on the other hand, is knowing what you mean and whence comes that knowledge. And more than that, even, authenticity is knowing what you are, and acting in accordance with that knowledge. It is having what Rousseau called a "sentiment of being" that is independent of the values, opinions, and demands of others.

But nowadays, in the area of musical performance, it sometimes seems as if authenticity, as word and as concept, had been stood on its

First published, alongside contributions by Nicholas Temperley, Daniel Leech-Wilkinson, and Robert Winter, in *Early Music* 12 (February 1984): 3–12. Reprinted by permission of Oxford University Press.

head. In a recent favorable review of an Early Music performance, a
critic for the *New York Times* who prides himself on his philosophical training praised the performers' "conviction," noting that because
of it their performances were "more than just authentic," they were
"passionate contemporary statements." In other words, by transcending authenticity they had achieved authenticity. Elsewhere in the
review he made reference to what he called the " 'authenticity' movement," implying by the use of quotes a kind of conformism that is
quite contrary to anything Rousseau (or even Woody Allen) could have
had in mind. Clearly, an authenticity that needs ironical quotation
marks, one that arises from the observance of pieties and unreflective
adherence to fashion, is no authenticity. The word needs either to
be rescued from its current purveyors or to be dropped by those who
would aspire to the values it properly signifies. A thicket of mis-
perceptions has grown up around it as applied to musical performance, obstructing the view not only of the public and its appointed
spokesmen, but of many practitioners, too. Some fresh perspectives,
partly drawn from other fields, may help to clear away some of
the underbrush.

Let us, to begin with, recognize that the word "authentic" is used
in many areas other than moral philosophy, and in some perfectly
legitimate senses that are quite unrelated to those outlined above.
With reference to works of art, the most common meaning is simply
"genuine," that is, traceable to a stipulated origin. The first task that
confronts the discoverer of a "new" painting by an old master, after all,
is that of authentication. It must be ascertained that the painting is
not by a lesser master, let alone a forger. And one important reason
why this must be done, and hence why art "connoisseurship" is such
an exacting and well-remunerated skill, is obvious. Of course, huge
sums are not usually involved in authentications made in the field of
music (except in the borderline case of violins): when a "new" Mozart
symphony was discovered in Denmark no one's fortune was made.
Nor was anyone impoverished when Mozart's "37th Symphony" was
exposed as unauthentic apart from its slow introduction. And yet the
material value placed on authorship in Western society is such that
the cultural value of a work of art, as much as its pecuniary value, can
be crucially affected by it. Just try, for example, to get a record company to issue a collection of anonymi! And whatever happened to
"Josquin's" *Missa "Da pacem"* since Edgar Sparks gave it to Baulde-
weyn? It used to be regarded as one of the exemplary Netherlands
masses, and, in particular, as a paradigm of Josquin's mature style. It
has, in effect, become a lesser work since it was attributed to a lesser
man. In a clever study in the realm of musical sociology, John Spitzer
has shown how the critical assessments of Mozart's Sinfonia Concer-

tante in E-flat K. 297*b* have varied depending on received opinion as to its authenticity. Knowledge of authorship, it would seem, relieves a critic of the need to make his own evaluation. In extreme cases it paralyses critical evaluation altogether. We already have a small but pernicious paradox involving two meanings of authenticity. The establishment of a work as authentic can take the place of authentic critical judgement of it.

Nor is the value we attach to this kind of authenticity solely material. When the Renaissance discovered the classics, the precious ancient heritage was immediately seen to have been transmitted through a haze of imperfect documents. So textual criticism, the art or science (opinions differ) of establishing authentic texts, was born. Sophisticated techniques have been developed over centuries, and are still being developed, to rid texts of errors and accretions, and these have been well codified and taught to generations of scholars, first in classics, then in biblical studies, and latterly in the realm of modern literature. Only in the last 150 years or so have modern techniques of textual criticism been applied to musical texts: first to Gregorian chant by the monks of Solesmes, then to medieval and Renaissance polyphony, and now to everything—Rossini's operas, Gilbert and Sullivan, Scott Joplin, Bob Dylan.

Criticism presupposes a critic, and a critic is one who judges and chooses. But we often encounter a curious reluctance on the part of textual editors to exercise these functions. Instead there has been a quixotic quest for mechanistically infallible techniques. The ostensible motive is to eliminate human error, but the underlying motive is the wish to eliminate the responsibility of applying judgment. In place of a multitude of small arbitrary decisions, many textual critics prefer to make a few big arbitrary decisions they then call "laws": for example, that printed editions are in principle more trustworthy than manuscripts, or that manuscripts are in principle more trustworthy than printed editions. Or, to cite one classic debate, that "sincere" sources are more trustworthy than "interpolated" ones, however otherwise corrupt they may be. Lately there has been a tendency (and this has been especially true of musicologists) to renounce choice among available variants altogether, even though this perverts the whole aim of textual criticism as originally conceived. Since the Renaissance, the aim of a critical edition has always been precisely to be critical: that is, to subject all sources to scrutiny and to arrive at a text that is more correct (i.e., more authentic) than any extant source. But as that requires the courage of commitment and choice, and the multifarious exercise of personal judgment, editors today more typically aim lower: they fasten on a single extant source (arriving at their choice by methods that are not always very critical) and elevate it to the status of authority. The assumption seems to be that the errors or accretions of old are preferable to the errors and accretions of today: let us grant them authority and thus be spared the risk of making our own mistakes. A spurious "authenticity," this, further reflected in the current fashion of editing and publishing sources rather than works; of issuing transcriptions and even recordings of individual chansonniers and codices, tacitly raising what are, after all, mere redactions to the status of authentic texts.

Many, if not most, of us who concern ourselves with "authentic" interpretation of music approach musical performance with the attitudes of textual critics, and fail to make the fundamental distinction between music as tones-in-motion and music as notes-on-page. This may be simply because we are, on the whole, textual critics by trade, not performers. How else explain the strange case of the Rossini expert who informs us that "an Italian opera in the first half of the nineteenth century . . . was treated as a collection of individual units that could be rearranged, substituted or omitted depending on local conditions of performance, local taste or, on many occasions, whim" and then excoriates the conductor of a revival of one such opera for treating it precisely as he described, for the reason that the version thus arrived at did not conform to any that could be documented from Rossini's own lifetime and therefore lacked "authenticity"? How Rossini, of all composers, would laugh at the zeal with which the sanctity of his "intentions" is defended!

Sometimes a scholar who engages professionally in textual criticism and authentication also performs, and may bring his scholarly rectitude excessively to bear on his attitude toward performance. This, at least, is how I choose to understand the categorical assertion made recently in print by a well-known performing scholar that all performers labor under "an absolute injunction to try to find out all that can be known about the performance traditions and the sound-world of any piece that is to be performed and to try to duplicate these as faithfully as possible." Without laboring the point that literally to do so would spell the immediate end of the Early Music concert as we know it, and probably of the Early Music boom as well, it must be obvious that to invoke absolute injunctions in a field so hedged around and booby-trapped with variables of all kinds as musical performance (or textual criticism, for that matter) can only represent once more that eagerness we have already noted to evade the responsibility of judgment and choice. Why is one never told to duplicate those traditions and that sound-world "as faithfully as one sees fit"? That, after all, is what we do. The line we draw between our idea of the historical realities and our present-day performance practices is never determined solely by feasibility. There is always an element of choice and taste involved; but that is often, indeed usually, left unmentioned or even hidden behind a smoke screen of musicological rationalization, in the name of "authenticity."

There are, conversely, performers who sometimes find themselves cast willy-nilly in the role of textual critics. One excellent gambist, who recently brought out a lavish edition of the first book of viol pieces by Marais, performed a really first-class, indeed Herculean job of textual collation in ascertaining what he described as the "terminal state" of the printing plates, reflecting the composer's latest intentions with regard to the secondary aspects of the text: bowing, ornamentation, fingering, etc. But is not the term misleading? If the second printing (1689) of the book shows that in the three years since the first printing Marais's way of playing the pieces had changed, why should we not assume that another three years later there were yet more changes in his performances, and so on to the end of his life? To call the edition of 1689 "terminal" is to impute the attitudes of a twentieth-century textual critic to an eighteenth-century performing musician. It changes what the editor's own research has shown to have been a descriptive notation of the composer's own fluid performance practice into a prescriptive one, by implication binding and setting limits on performers today.

One more pertinent example of this need to establish the Urtext comes to mind from my own performing experience. Recording some fifteenth-century chansons under the direction of a scholar-performer with exacting standards of textual authenticity, my instrumentalist colleagues and I ornamented the cadences in a manner derived from variations observed in the sources transmitting this repertory. The director, who had made his own transcriptions from the sources he preferred, insisted that we refrain from tampering with them. The ensuing quarrel was resolved by a compromise: the director made a collation of all the sources for the pieces we were to record, and supplied us with embellishments drawn from alternative sources for the passages we wished to decorate. In this way he could be satisfied that our ornaments were "authentic." From that moment, I should say, date my doubts about the way musical scholars understand the nature of authenticity.

Since then I have continued to be dismayed at the extent to which it is the textual critic's, rather than the moral philosopher's, definition of authenticity that has set the tone for our movement, that is, the definition that equates it with mere freedom from error or anachronism. Modern performers seem to regard their performances as texts rather than acts, and to prepare for them with the same goal as present-day textual editors: to clear away accretions. Not that this is not a laudable and necessary step; but what is an ultimate step for an editor should be only a first step for a performer, as the very temporal relationship between the functions of editing and performing already suggests. Once the accretions have been removed, what is to take their place? All too often the answer is: nothing. All too often the sound of a modern "authentic" performance of old music presents the aural equivalent of an Urtext score: the notes and rests are presented with complete accuracy and an equally complete neutrality (and this seems to be most characteristic—dare I say it?—of English performances). Nothing is allowed to intrude into the performance that cannot be "authenticated." And this means nothing can be allowed that will give the performance, in the sense in which we first defined the word, the authenticity of conviction. For the first thing that must go in a critical edition, as in the kind of "authentic" performance I am describing, is any sense of the editor's or performer's own presence; any sentiment, as Rousseau would have said, of his being.

We seem to have paid a heavy price indeed for the literacy that sets Western musical culture so much apart and makes its past available in the first place, if the text must be so venerated. Is the text only an exacting responsibility? And if so, to what or whom is the responsibility due? Can the text not be an opportunity—for the exercise of imagination, the communication of delight, even the sharing of emotion? Can there be no reconciliation between the two authenticities, that is, the authenticity of the object performed and the authenticity of the subject performing? And is a musical performance to be regarded as an "object" at all?

This is a complex and daunting set of questions. And needless to say, the situation that gives rise to them is not so simply determined as I seem to have made out. In essay 1, I attempted to set the authenticity movement within a broader context of modernist objectivity and impersonalism. Some thought my thesis harsh and pessimistic, but for real pessimism we might turn to Lionel Trilling's beautiful and disquieting set of lectures, *Sincerity and Authenticity* (Cambridge, Mass.: Harvard University Press, 1972), a book with many insights to offer any musician in this field. For Trilling, authenticity is "a word of ominous import . . . part of the moral slang of our day, [which] points to the peculiar nature of our fallen condition, our anxiety over the credibility of existence and of individual existences." What started as the first impulse toward Romantic egoism—Rousseau's happily self-validating sentiment of being—has become a stick we use (with considerable assistance from Freud and the existentialists) to beat our psyches into submission. The artist today is in a tough predicament. He is heir to what Trilling calls "two centuries of aesthetic theory and artistic practice which have been less and less willing to take account of the habitual preferences of the audience"—and virtually all important artistic movements since Romanticism (including, of course, our authenticity movement) have shared in this contempt for the public as arbiter of taste, whatever their differences may otherwise have been—and yet he no longer has the cast-iron Romantic stomach it takes to proclaim that (in Trilling's words) "his reference is to himself only." For, as any popular cultural historian will tell you, the Romantic sense of self seems irrevocably lost to modern man. So instead he appeals (we appeal) "to some transcendent power which—or who—has decreed his enterprise and alone is worthy to judge it." We are back, in other words, to a sort of pre-Renaissance abjectness of spirit in which the authenticating function once exercised by religion with regard to the creations of man has been arrogated to impersonal secular gods.

What—or who—are they? Surely the most exigent has been the sense of history, a god whose manifestations have been extremely various. So much of what has happened since the nineteenth century has been motivated, or at least justified, by appeal to "historical necessity," and this applies to the arts no less than to mass murder. Schoenberg tended to explain what he had done in terms practically borrowed from Hegel, casting himself in the role of reluctant "world-historical individual" compelled to satisfy the demands of history. But at the opposite pole, Stravinsky, too, justified himself in terms not dissimilar. His neoclassicism was a *reprise de contact* with the healthy historical mainstream after the unfortunate neurotic vagaries of Romanticism. There is scarcely an artist at work today who has not the kind of precise consciousness of his place in history described by T. S. Eliot in "Tradition and the Individual Talent," and a heavy attendant sense of responsibility to that place, and this applies as well to radicals as to conservatives. Even performers tend to see themselves and to be seen in historical terms. The more intellectual critics of today like to describe the performances they review as part of the history of the music performed. History is something "bigger than both of us"—creator (or performer) and audience—and therefore not to be fought. The past has never been so much with us, whatever our relationship or attitude to "musicology."

And never have we judged it less. Our historical outlook is totally relativistic. Every age is regarded, Spinoza-fashion, as its own perfect embodiment. We are trained not to look for teleologies, and especially not to regard our own age as any kind of summit. How smugly naive Burney and Hawkins look to us now (to say nothing of Parry or Wooldridge). We all take our bearings from the German historicists who sought to discover and empathically comprehend the historical "Ding an sich." We are enjoined to call no composer "transitional," nor any period "pre" or "post." Haydn's symphonies are not more "advanced" than Stamitz's, nor Bach's fugues more advanced than Böhm's. And for some of us, it seems, they are no more valuable. We are taught, in short, not to discriminate, not to interpolate our own judgment, if we are to have an "authentic" sense of the past. It is the same wish to apprehend the past directly and without the distorting lens of modern values that leads us to the old instruments and old performance practices we prize so highly.

But it is nonetheless an error to assume that the self-evident heuristic value of this approach translates ipso facto into a self-evident aesthetic value. Old instruments and old performance practices are in themselves of no aesthetic value. The claim of self-evidence for the value of old instruments, like the claim of self-evidence for the virtue of adhering to a composer's "intentions," is really nothing but a mystique, and more often than one can tell, that is the only justification offered. Consequently, though he is happily less in evidence than before, the naked emperor still parades through halls where "authentic" performances are heard.

To understand this presumed self-evidence, we must look to another modern god to which artists have sacrificed their egos in the name of authenticity: the autonomous work of art. "New criticism" crystallized in literary studies half a century ago, and after a few decades of hegemony it was challenged and demoted from its position of preeminence. Undaunted, it brushed itself off and went to music, where, under the rubrics "theory" and "analysis," it reigns supreme. This profoundly modernist viewpoint decrees that the work of art is not to be described or valued for its effects (e.g., on an audience) or its human interest (e.g., with respect to its creator), but strictly on its own formal, quasi-mechanistic or quasi-organic terms. And further, that all of the arts aspire to the purity of their respective media. In music, whose "absoluteness" as a medium has always been the envy of the other arts (at least in the modernist view), we can observe best the translation, once again, of what started out as a heuristic principle into an aesthetic one. Moreover, there is a noticeable split among musical autonomists between those who regard the absolute "meaning" of a work of art as a matter of abstract internal relationships, and those who would limit the meaning (or rather, perhaps, the essence) quite simply and stringently to the physical reality, that is, to the sounds themselves. The split is perhaps most evident in the realm of composition (the Babbitts on the one hand and the Cages on the other). But it profoundly affects performance values as well.

The "relationist" viewpoint is well exemplified by the once so fashionable performances of, say, Bach on the Moog synthesizer. We may look back on this fad as a mere commercial venture or a bastard child of pop culture, but in its short-lived heyday it was seen quite otherwise by many. Walter (now Wendy) Carlos, its driving force, was a serious electronic composer whose motives in recomposing Bach for the synthesizer were as pure (at the outset, anyway) as Milton Babbitt's in composing directly for that instrument: to achieve the utter impersonality and freedom from "human" intrusion their view of music as autonomous structure demanded. And the early "Switched-on Bach" records were greeted enthusiastically by Glenn Gould, whose unconventional pianism (as unrelated to normal piano technique in his performances of Bach as it was to that of "historical" instruments) was similarly motivated: to strip away the veneer of medium and reveal the message.

Well, that approach has given way to the even more stringently modernist one that the medium is the message, a position that owes everything to the spirit of positivism, that rosy-eyed philosophy which holds, as one writer has put it, "that the world is reflected with perfect literalness in the will-less mind of the observer." The relationship between positivist thinking and musical interpretation cannot be better summarized than in the words of the hermeneuticist E.D. Hirsch, whose *Aims of Interpretation* (Chicago: University of Chicago Press, 1976) is one of the most stimulating books anyone interested in current interpretative issues (in any medium) could read. "Under positivism," writes Hirsch:

> the mystical distinction between the letter and the spirit is repudiated. The interpreter should ignore the ghost in the verbal machine and simply explain how the verbal machine actually functions. If the rules and canons are made precise, and if the tools of linguistic analysis are sharpened and refined, the problems of interpretation will be resolved into operational procedures. . . . The spirit killeth, but the letter giveth life. Hence, for positivism, meaning is an epiphenomenon, a secondary quality of linguistic forms themselves. Positivism assumes a congruence of the signified with the signifier; of that which is represented with the vehicle of its representation. Thence comes the doctrine that style is itself part of the meaning it represents. . . . Within its context, a particular style requires a particular meaning. The letter compelleth the spirit.

Hirsch is talking about literary hermeneutics; but *mutatis mutandis* his description fits the authenticity movement like a glove. We can begin to understand what seemed the unaccountably pugnacious assertion set forth a few years ago by an excellent fortepianist in no need whatever of special pleading: "Perhaps it is wrong to put the instrument before the artist, but I have begun to feel that it must be done." For if what is represented is congruent with the vehicle of its representation, then the "right instrument," yielding the "right sound," holds an automatic key to the music, while the difference between one artist and another is but an ephemeral one between two personalities. And the difference between their interpretations is a mere "epiphenomenon" compared with the essential matter of the actual sound of the instrument. Hirsch's brilliant encapsulation of the positivist promise, "the problems of interpretation will be resolved into operational procedures," encapsulates one of the chief claims—perhaps the major claim—of the authenticity movement as well. The instrument compelleth the music.

Sometimes the assumption that the sense of the music is identical with the sound of the medium can go to bemusing lengths, and not only in early music, though the attitude is obviously most pervasive there. In reviewing a recent New York concert at which a new work by Milton Babbitt was played on a new Bösendorfer grand, one critic (a well-known enthusiast of period pianos) remarked that at last he was hearing a piano piece as it was meant to be heard, whereas even performances of Brahms or Debussy on such an instrument involved some degree of distorting "transcription." Now if I know Babbitt, that piece, insofar as it was conceived for any piano at all, was conceived in terms of some battered old upright in his Princeton office. The equation of sound and sense is by no means the self-evident proposition positivists think it to be, except maybe in the case of orchestral pieces by Rimsky-Korsakov or Respighi. Sometimes one wants to exclaim with Charles Ives, "My God, what has sound got to do with music!"

Anyone who can appreciate what Ives meant will understand what sometimes depresses me about the authenticity movement. When followed unreflectively it can become a positivistic purgatory, literalistic and dehumanizing, a thing of taboos and shalt-nots instead of the liberating expansion of horizons and opportunities it could be and was meant to be. At its worst, authenticity is just another name for purism. Trilling caught well the special oxymoronic irony that is implied by the very term "authenticity movement" (though the term is ours, not his): "The concerted effort of a culture or of a segment of a culture to achieve authenticity generates its own conventions, its generalities, its commonplaces, its maxims, what Sartre, taking the word from Heidegger, calls the 'gabble.'" He went on to note drily that Sartre himself contributed more to the gabble than practically anyone else. But that was not necessarily Sartre's fault. Gabble is the creation of followers, not leaders. The gabble that now surrounds the concept of authenticity in musical performance is not to be laid at the door of the movement's inspirers, but rather at the door of those who have heard the sounds but not the music. And it is only in the nature of things that as the movement gathers momentum the gabble will increase, for even as the authenticity movement has begun to achieve the technical proficiency that is at last gaining it credibility and acceptance in the music world at large, it is unfortunately taking on some of the less attractive characteristics of that world. We now have our own star system, our personality cults and fan magazines, our hype machines and our beautiful people. And above all one encounters self-congratulation and the heaping of scorn upon the mainstream artists from whom we still have many lessons—and some of the most basic ones, at that—to learn. What entitles us to our airs of moral superiority? Our commitment to authenticity? Not if our authenticity is as spurious as I have come to believe, in many ways, it is.

It seems to me that the special opportunity, and the special task, of a movement in musical interpretation that aspires to authenticity is to foster an approach to performance that is founded to an unprecedented degree on personal conviction and on individual response to individual pieces. Such an approach will seek to bring to consciousness and thereby to transcend the constraints that are variously imposed by fashion, by conventional training, by historical evidence, and even, or especially, by our intuition. And this means, ultimately, cultivating an essentially sceptical frame of mind that will allow no "truth" to pass unexamined.

No one who reads these lines will need to be persuaded to regard modern mainstream performance styles with a jaundiced eye. But the reason for doing so ought not to be that they are anachronistic. They are not anachronistic for everything, after all, and we will all differ as to where the line of anachronism is to be drawn. The reason, rather, is that a performer schooled in the mainstream (any mainstream) receives his basic training before he has reached the age of consent, and that therefore his musical responses and tastes will have been formed at a preconscious level—will be vested, so to speak, in his spinal column. And there would be nothing wrong with that if our musical culture were the kind of homogeneous thing it remained, say, until World War 1. In fact it would be the best possible thing, as we may still observe in performances of new music, and especially in folk and pop music, where there is a tacit, wholly internalized, integrated and implicit identification of the performer's habits with the demands of the music performed and the expectations of the audience. But now that our classical musical culture has become so wildly pluralistic (which, after all, is in large part the reason why authenticity ever became an issue), the conditioned reflexes of our mainstream performers give rise to a uniformity of performance style (manifested in, for example, those perennial bugbears, vibrato and seamless phrasing) that has seemed ever more essentially and disconcertingly at variance with the enormous stylistic diversity encompassed by their (our) repertory.

But simple rejection of the mainstream will only produce a vacuum, and it will not suffice to fill it by merely inferring what can be inferred from the documentary remains of the past. Such evidence, being as fragmentary and ambiguous as our modern mainstream is oceanic and generalized, is just as suspect, just as needful of being judged and tested. Those who follow the evidence whither it leads will never achieve authenticity in any meaningful sense. Everyone by now agrees (if only for the sake of argument) that we will never really know "what was." But that is not what we want to find out, anyway. We want to find out what was, or rather, *is* good for the music—and for ourselves. And of course by that I mean ourselves in the actual here and now, not some projection of ourselves into an imaginary past. For as Trilling wrote in his essay "The Sense of the Past" over forty years ago, "to suppose that we can think like men of another time is as much an illusion as to suppose that we can think in a wholly different way." We need values of our own and the courage to live up to them, whatever the music we perform.

And we won't get them by intuition, either, at least at the outset. For our intuitions are not the fine, free, feral things we may think they are. They are thoroughly domesticated beasts, trained to run along narrow paths by long years of unconscious conditioning, endowed with vast reserves of cliché, naive posture, and nonsense. If you are a trained musician, what you will find if you scratch your intuition will be the unexamined mainstream, your most ingrained responses, treacherously masquerading as imagination. This was most comically demonstrated a couple of decades ago, when the conductor of a famous American orchestra took it into his head to have his men concoct an aleatory composition extempore, and was faced with Kreutzer etudes from the fiddles, *Rite of Spring* arpeggios from the wind, and military fanfares from the brass. And it is demonstrated, too, when most early musicians apply embellishments.

So where does one begin? Surely with the music, with one's love for it, with endless study of it, and with the determination to challenge one's every assumption about it, especially the assumptions we do not know we are making because, to quote Whitehead, "no other way of putting things has ever occurred" to us. Many of our most excellent performers of nonmainstream music have gone far out of their way to devise stratagems to challenge themselves in this way. One musician whom I particularly admire, a lutenist, once told me that when he began to experiment with improvisatory practices to accompany medieval song, he deliberately mistuned his instrument so that his fingers would not be able to run along familiar paths.

And here, in my view, is where the "old instruments" are valuable and perhaps indispensable in achieving truly authentic performances:

as part of the mental process I am describing. The unfamiliarity of the instrument forces mind, hand, and ear out of their familiar routines and into more direct confrontation with the music. It has a kind of *Entfremdungseffekt*, which serves the same purpose as in modernist literature. The presentation of a familiar object (the music) in an unfamiliar context (the instrument and the new problems it poses) forces one to see it freshly, more immediately, more observantly—in a word, more authentically. Notice, though, that this is primarily a heuristic benefit to the player, and only secondarily an aesthetic benefit to the listener. The common claim, which I quote from a recent record review in the very magazine in which this essay first appeared, that "Baroque instruments, played in an appropriate manner, have a greater expressive range than their modern equivalents" is the purest gabble. If played in an appropriate manner, modern instruments too would be capable of anything the player wished to produce on them. But they are not played in that way, and, for reasons outlined above, they probably never will be. For players of modern instruments have neither the impulse nor the means to free their minds from their habits in the way the old instruments compel one to do.

Experiments based on historical research serve the same purpose for performers: they open their minds and ears to new experiences, and enable them to transcend their habitual, and therefore unconsidered, ways of hearing and thinking about the music. We do have an "absolute injunction" to take history into account, since it offers us another potent challenge. But the object is not to duplicate the sounds of the past, for if that were our aim we would never know whether we had succeeded. What we are aiming at, rather, is the startling shock of newness, of immediacy, the sense of rightness that occurs when after countless frustrating experiments we feel as though we have achieved the identification of performance style with the demands of the music mentioned above as the hallmark of a living tradition. Obviously any and all information we can gather as to contemporary conventions, particularly unwritten conventions, will help us toward that result. But to limit oneself to positive data is nothing but literalism, leading at best to an impersonation of what Thurston Dart would call the "dull dogs" of the past. And impersonation of anything, after all, is the opposite of authentic.

So whence comes the verification that our sense of rightness is right? The whole point of my argument (and, if you like, the rub) is that it can come only from within. The idea of objective, external verifiability, attractive as it is to some, is only one of the many false promises of positivism. It is based on what Hirsch has dubbed the "fallacy of the homogeneous past" (not that he is by any means alone in having identified it). "To assume," he writes, "that *any* cultural environment is homogeneous, even on the very abstract level at which literary history [or performance research] is conducted, is to make an assumption about human communities which experience contradicts." Human characters, personality types, likes and dislikes differ now, and they just as surely (but tell it not at the *Aufführungspraxis* seminar!) differed then. The fifteenth century must have had its Toscaninis and its Furtwänglers, the sixteenth its Horowitzes and its Schnabels, the seventeenth its Hogwoods and its Leppards. There have always been those who, given *a* and *c*, will hesitate to infer *b*, and those who, given *a* and *b*, are ready to infer *x*, *y*, and *z*. Performance styles in the past, no less than in the present, had their proponents and their detractors, and many of the practical and theoretical problems that bedevil us today were bedevilments then too, the subject of often acrimonious debate (as we need only read Tinctoris to learn).

Mention of Tinctoris brings a convenient example to mind: that of mensural proportions, surely an unsettled issue if ever there was one, as Arthur Mendel so forcefully pointed out a decade ago. In the time that has since elapsed, musicological opinion has divided rather neatly into two extreme camps: those who insist that successive proportions did possess an unambiguous uniformity in the Renaissance, even if the theorists disagree chaotically and we have therefore not been able to recover it (there have even been one or two misguided attempts to legislate it for the present), and those who have not only despaired of ascertaining it, but have convinced themselves on the basis of the theorists' lack of agreement that they were all talking through their hats and that successive proportions were not arithmetically coordinated at all. The scholarship on both sides of the issue has been ample. What few seem willing to grant is the only answer that I find plausible: that preferences and practices were multifarious, varying not only over time and from place to place, but also according to personalities. I have long since found that my own preferences call for arithmetical coordination of successive tempos (what I call gear shifts)—and not only for Renaissance music but for French overtures, too—if my own performances are to give me the sense of rightness I seek. (I have even worked out the numbers for myself.) I do not claim that such relationships have more historical validity than the rough *più* or *meno mosso* others prefer, only that I must observe them if my own performances are to have authenticity.

In the course of over fifteen years' experience in conducting Renaissance choral music, in fact, I seem to have built up quite a collection of specific performance practices, as I learnt recently when some members of my choir Cappella Nova presented me with a treatise they had compiled from our week-to-week doings in rehearsal. Hardly a one of them is historically sanctioned; but, taken as a whole, they are what give our performances authenticity, of a type that is not a thing achieved but a perpetually self-renewing challenge. For as our own discoveries have changed us, they have given rise to new dissatisfactions and new ideals. Ours is a constantly evolving style of performance that, in the words of one reviewer, "requires great conviction, and it will not be to everyone's taste." That is certainly true; indeed, I would have added "therefore" before the last clause, for that is the nature of convictions. But what else are we (or should we be) talking about when we talk about authenticity?

An authenticity of this type has tremendous moral force and is, regardless of the gabble, what keeps our movement alive and gaining ground. The performances of artists who have, at great personal cost, stripped themselves down and then laboriously built themselves up again in their dedication to their chosen repertory, are, in the words of Sartre's Roquentin, "beautiful and hard as steel and make people ashamed of their existence." Many of us who have devoted ourselves to the ideal of authentic interpretation of music can probably trace our first impulse to do so to a shaming experience of this kind. But it matters little if we now use the most accurate instruments, tune to the lowest pitch, or read from the most original notation. Unless we put ourselves through that crucible, our performances will never possess an authenticity that matters.

POSTSCRIPT, 1994

The reason why this essay was cast (despite the editor's entreaties) as something of a critique à clef, sans footnotes, was not only to spare friends and colleagues, but because the *New York Times* comment quoted in the preamble was from a review of one of my own performances with Cappella Nova, and I felt squeamish lest there be the appearance of a puff. Ten years after the group in question has ceased to exist, the secret no longer seems worth keeping.

The "new" Mozart symphony (a.k.a. the "Odense" symphony, K. Anh. 220) was very much in the news in 1984, but its claims to authenticity were soon dismissed.[1] The latest if not last word on the Sinfonia Concertante in E-flat, K. 297b, is a four-hundred-page book

---

[1]See Neal Zaslaw, *Mozart's Symphonies: Context, Performance Practice, Reception* (Oxford: Clarendon Press, 1989), 265–81.

by Robert Levin.[2] Levin's answer—Mozart, all right, but for a different combination of soloists and with very different tuttis—has been widely if not universally accepted,[3] and his published reconstruction of the "original" has been recorded several times. The author, by the way, is the same Robert Levin whose pioneering revival at the keyboard of eighteenth-century improvisatory practices forces some modification of a major point in essay 1. His work will figure again in essays 7 and 11.

[2]*Who Wrote the Mozart Four-Wind Concertante?* (Stuyvesant, NY: Pendragon Press, 1988), incorporating findings previously reported in the *Mozart-Jahrbuch* in collaboration with Daniel Leeson.

[3]For resistant arguments see reviews by William Drabkin (*Musical Times* [March 1990]: 142–45) and Richard Maunder (*Journal of the Royal Musical Association* 116 [1991]: 136–39). Both are careful not to judge the quality of the work in weighing its authenticity.

3

Down with the Fence

Times have certainly changed since this book's like-named predecessor—a 22-page booklet jointly authored by Thurston Dart, Walter Emery, and Christopher Morris—was jointly published by Stainer & Bell, Novello, and the Oxford University Press in 1963. For one thing, the booklet carried the Arcadian legend, so widely remarked in its time, that "The Publishers do not claim copyright in this book, and it may be freely quoted without acknowledgment," while the 125-page replacement has the standard businesslike warnings against infringements. For another, the flighty, avuncular, jocularly dogmatic obiter dicta of the earlier publication have been replaced by Mr. Caldwell's serious, thorough, at times weighty discussions-in-the-round of sundry issues, which chiefly account for the fivefold increase in the volume's girth. Both booklet and book are symptomatic of their respective times. What was once an essentially amateur activity has become solidly academicized and professionalized. It is taken seriously. John Caldwell's treatment of his subject does honor to its new-won status. At a time when some writers have seen fit conspicuously to downgrade the editorial function in the scheme of things musicological, it is good to see a book that upholds it so ardently. No musicological activity is more important than editing, for it is competent editing that makes most of the rest possible.

The book opens with a disclaimer: "There is no attempt to instruct in the detailed technicalities of palaeography, notation, and source studies. . . . It is intended rather for the guidance of those who have acquired a good knowledge of their chosen field, but who may not have thought very deeply about the problems of presentation in

Originally published as a review of *Editing Early Music* by John Caldwell (Oxford: Oxford University Press, 1985). Reprinted from *Notes: Quarterly Journal of the Music Library Association* 42 (1985–86): 775–79, by permission of the Music Library Association.

the form of an edition" (p. 4). As one who has taught paleography, notation, and source studies, I do welcome a book that covers the myriad practical editorial details there never seems to be time to address adequately in the classroom. But I hasten to point out that the disclaimer, in fact, is not entirely justified, since Caldwell at times backs up his arguments for his preferred editorial practices with quite detailed considerations of paleographical, theoretical, and source-critical issues. As a result, the book has a rich scholarly texture. It is by no means the kind of peremptory "how-to" manual the reader might expect.

The author wisely recognizes the futility of trying to reduce the whole multifarious business of textual editing to a set of universally applicable rules. All the same, he does take a definite and responsible stand on all matters within his purview, as indeed he must. No one will agree with every one of them. Since, obviously, this book is going to be very influential, a certain amount of public discussion of its premises is clearly called for, if only to signal the fact (lest unwary novices be tempted to let Caldwell do all their thinking for them) that the water is still full of sharks, and that practically any act of practical edition-making will raise problems neither this nor any primer can solve. The following discussion, then, is intended as a contribution to that airing of fundamental issues. Though it will emphasize points of difference rather than agreement, it is offered not in a spirit of recusancy or disputatiousness, but in recognition of the book's serious purpose. For every carp and cavil shortly to be raised, the reader may rest assured that there are a dozen points on which I find Caldwell's proposals sane, just, and eminently worth adopting.

Most of the discussion will focus on late Medieval and Renaissance music, although the scope of the book extends from plainchant through the age of Mozart and even Beethoven (soon, no doubt, "Early Music" will be taking in everything through middle-period Babbitt). It is not only that the problems loom larger in this repertoire than in others (though I believe that this is so), but I am freshly battle-scarred by a major editorial project involving the Latin-texted works of Busnoys, which has left me not only sharply aware of certain technical issues, but also more aware than I have ever been of the irreducibly sui generis nature of editorial problems, ergo the necessarily provisional and tentative nature of all editorial precepts, and hence (my most basic point of difference with the author) the necessarily personal nature of editorial decisions. The tacit aim of most editorial guidelines is to build a fence around a text that will exclude the editor's person. My experience is that the only way of achieving this is indiscriminately to photograph and publish all the sources. Otherwise, even the best-intentioned, most puritanical editor will find himself willy-nilly inside the fence, not out. For editing is interpretation. Period.

On page 1 Caldwell writes, "there are really only two fundamental requirements for an edition of music: clarity and consistency." My God, what a minefield lurks in that last innocuous word! Consistency with what? I have found even internal consistency (that is, within the edition—presumably what Caldwell has in mind) to be chimerical. In order to edit one of Busnoys's Masses to my own satisfaction for example, I had to interpret a single mensuration sign in two different ways within the work. And what should one do with repeat signs when one finds (as in the binary *pièces de viole* of Marais) that the composer's (or his engraver's) practice seems capricious? Routinely bring them all into conformity with what one has been taught (on what authority?) to regard as the standard practice for the period? Leave them exactly as they are in the source (which source?) and effectively pass the buck to the performers? Caldwell blandly advises, "analysis should be employed to test the authenticity of repeat signs (or their lack)" (p. 89). Easy enough to say, but does he have a method in mind? If so, let's have it, please.

On page 2, Caldwell deals with a vexing question indeed: whether to base an edition on a single extant source, or to conflate. The "classical" tradition of textual criticism was virtually by definition conflationary. Few editors of music espouse that method today. Caldwell writes:

> In earlier music, [the composer's] intentions may simply not be ascertainable, owing to the lack of sources sufficiently close to the composer in time or cultural milieu, or to lack of precision in the notation of those which have come down to us. An acceptable substitute may be to reproduce a version which can be shown to have been current at some particular time and place. For such a purpose, the reproduction of a single representative source may be the best method. The objective value of such a procedure may in any case commend it as being preferable to a more fanciful solution.

Appeal to intentions will get us nowhere, for it can be demonstrated on any number of grounds that the intentions of Medieval and Renaissance composers were not congruent with those of modern editors—that is, they were not concerned with the fixing of a definitive, prescriptive text. That's our problem, not theirs. And it will not do to stigmatize the alternative to a single-source edition (which can in effect spuriously elevate a single chance redaction to the status of authority) as "fanciful." Where Caldwell has "fanciful" I would put "critical," and in so doing, identify the chief failing of most modern editors of early music: a failure of nerve.

Where is the courage of that doughty textual critic of old, quoted by Housman in his immortal tirade on "The Application of Thought to Textual Criticism," who proclaimed, "If the sense requires it, I am prepared to write *Constantinopolitanus* where the MSS. have the monosyllabic interjection o"? Not, by and large, among the editors of Early Music, who tend to be, by Housmanian standards, quite pusillanimous. "Sense" is something *we* have to determine, and we seem to be happier hunting down "intentions" (that is, authority) where sense (that is, judgment) is what is required.

Of course authority is preferable to guesswork. Housman would have agreed, as would Haupt, whom he quotes. But where we have not got a real authority, we have to become authorities, and not bestow authority upon some undeserving source that has merely chanced to survive. In editing the work of Busnoys I was fortunate that some of his motets apparently survive in autographs (the earliest such from the hand of any major Western composer). But when there was no autograph I felt not merely free but duty-bound to interpolate time signatures and text placement at variance with the extant sources if I had good reason to believe that the sources were wrong. I reject the characterization of such a procedure as "fanciful." Caldwell writes, "a haphazard conflation based on pragmatic or subjective criteria is to be avoided" (p. 4), and, "the most objective method of presentation is likely to be that which takes a single source as its point of reference" (p. 5). Haphazardness, certainly, is to be avoided. But (informed) subjectivity is the essence of judgment (that is, criticism), while "pragmatic" methods—which to Caldwell seem to imply arbitrary or irresponsible ones—are in proper parlance simply those best geared to practical results. Are the latter not both necessary and desirable? "Objectivity"—desirable to the extent that it means "impartiality," and a sine qua non, to be sure, in a court of law—is useless when it means (as at times it seems to mean to Caldwell) the uncritical acceptance—or worse, the craven conferral—of factitious authority.

It so happens that one of the examples given by Caldwell of model editorial practice—the "Christe eleyson" from Busnoys's *Missa O crux lignum triumphale* (p. 25)—by a strange coincidence involves a passage in which I found it desirable to make one of the interpolations alluded to above. It can serve the present discussion as a perfect test case. There is only one source for the Mass, and at the spot in question it gives the mensuration signature for *tempus imperfectum diminutum* (₵). Accordingly, the model transcription presented by Caldwell (actually prepared by Donald W. Shipley) bars (or rather, "mensurstrichs") the music in a modern $\frac{4}{4}$ meter. This is because modern editors tend to assume that the old mensuration signatures are the obsolete equivalents of our modern meter signatures. Indeed, defending the drawing of modern bars through the whole system of the modern score to coincide with the original tactus count, Caldwell refers (p. 48) to the "capacity of barring to . . . point to underlying metre." This is a potentially mischievous misapprehension. Although meter could and did exist in Renaissance music, it was a function of recurrent rhythmic patterns or points of alignment explicitly expressed in the note values. It was not implicit in the mensuration signs as such. All the latter established was the way in which the durations expressed by the written note values related to one another.

One has to be especially careful in interpreting the sign ₵, because of its special properties and history. Over the course of the sixteenth century, ₵ gradually usurped the place of all the other mensural signs, to the point where it became practically the only mensuration sign employed. This process had nothing to do with meters, but with the fact that, like modern notation, ₵ specified unambiguous binary divisions at all mensural levels. Musicians singing or playing from parts notated under ₵ never had to worry about "imperfection" or "alteration" of durations; the sign took the guesswork out of sightreading (and paved the way toward modern rhythmic notation). It was used to notate music in all meters, including mid–sixteenth-century ensemble dances that were unambiguously in triple time (as expressed by the actual rhythmic patterns).

Therefore, to assume that ₵ is the fifteenth- or sixteenth-century equivalent of our modern $\frac{4}{4}$ meter is just plain wrong; to transcribe music under the sign in duple meter, without considering whether the actual rhythmic character of the music justifies the choice, is uncritical; and to draw up charts prescribing modern *metrical* equivalents for fifteenth-century *mensural* signatures (as Caldwell has done on pp. 20–21) is both misguided and misleading. In the present case, if the editor of the Busnoys Christe had scanned the music in advance, he would have noticed that its note values are grouped in ternary *tempora* (measures), that the whole piece adds up to an integral number of (ternary) measures (when ₵ is treated as a "duple meter," the final cadence occurs "off the beat"), and that when the meter is counted as ternary, the suspension-resolution cadences fall much more frequently at the beginnings of tempus units. This is a persuasive prima facie case, in my opinion, further testable by comparing the mensural practice of the *Missa O crux lignum triumphale* with that of the same composer's *Missa L'Homme armé,* and by comparing the mensural usages of the former's single surviving source (a Sistine Chapel manuscript) with those found in other sources of its ilk, as well as those found in more centrally positioned Busnoys sources.

All the evidence, both internal and external, leads in one direction—to wit, that the sign ₵ as found in the one surviving source for the *Missa O crux lignum triumphale* is probably a corruption of the sign O2 as habitually employed by Busnoys. This means not only that the measures shown in the model transcription on page 25 are the wrong length (they should contain six quarter notes, not four), but that the tempo equivalency indicated (by Caldwell, as a supplement to Shipley's transcription) between the Christe and the preceding Kyrie is also incorrect. In Busnoys's usage a breve under O2 equals a semibreve under O, so that the correct equivalency (allowing for the differing reduction schemes) ought not to have been "half equals dotted half" but "half equals half." The matter of tempo equivalence is a particularly crucial one for performers, of course, and one that most editors, pleading convenient ignorance, tend to shirk. I contend that secure directions can be given only after a review of the specific situation for the individual piece. Yes, I mean that they must be "ad hoc" and subject to the editor's informed "interpretation."

Even at best, moreover, the use of modern meter signatures is bound to falsify the music and lead to bad performances of it unless the editor writes the caveats very large indeed. Meters to us mean *a priori* stress patterns, and our modern notation takes this into account not only in matters of barring but also in matters of ties and beams. Here confusion is rampant among editors and those who attempt to guide them. On ties and beams, Caldwell offers the following advice, which I find astonishing (p. 25):

> The reduction of time-values increases the extent to which the editor must take responsibility for translating the separate notes of his sources into cross-beamed groups. . . . [T]here will remain many instances in which he will have to decide how much interpretation to offer through patterns of beaming suggestive of accentuation and articulation. . . . It is important to guard against over-interpretation. If there is any doubt, it is best to stick to standard patternings, limiting the cross-beam to simple subdivisions of the bar (e.g. ♫♫ ♫♫ rather than ♫ ♫♫).

But the "standard patterning" is itself an interpretation, and an especially insidious one, since it wears the sheep's clothing of accepted (and for Renaissance music, irrelevant and anachronistic) convention. It invites the performer to apply all kinds of assumptions he makes about "music in general" to a specific repertoire with which he is probably not very familiar—assumptions especially difficult to shed because one is generally unaware that one entertains them. Let the reader—without reflecting on the matter in advance!—"sing" the two notations in the extract above—preferably into a tape recorder, so that it can be played back—and see whether the two renditions in fact came out the same. Has he not "squeezed" the tie in the first instance, in accordance with an implicitly felt beat? What has that got to do with Renaissance rhythm?

If an editor, after much study and reflection, feels he knows how the music he is editing ought to be accented and articulated, he is *bound*, if he takes his responsibilities seriously, to offer his interpretation to his reader. This will appear to many a radical and willful idea. But of the two alternatives offered by Caldwell, I prefer to regard as "overinterpreted" the version that covertly enlists the performer's unconscious prejudices, rather than the one that, by virtue of an unconventional appearance, calls attention to itself and may enlist the performer's critical faculties through the old, familiar device of defamiliarization.

End of sermon. The very fact that Caldwell's book provoked it should show its value. To me it is seriously marred by the prejudice against interpretation that is such an old story in twentieth-century intellectual history by now, a viewpoint that discourages ventursomeness and counsels contentment with small gains. At times it even veers off into what might be termed "editorial formalism," as where, rather incredibly, the author holds up William Waite's thoroughly discredited transcriptions of *organum duplum* as "com[ing] near to editorial perfection" because of its exemplary handling of certain details of formal presentation. But withal, the book is an excellent and, obviously, highly stimulating introduction to the issues. It is *not* a self-tutor. A student using it would need to be exposed to the other side of many stories by an experienced teacher (and would have to be cautioned in particular that the author's grasp of editorial accidentals is unsophisticated). As a basis for properly directed discussion *Editing Early Music* has no current peer. All the same, I would hate to see even its own publisher turn it into a style manual.

4

The Pastness of the Present and the Presence of the Past

I

Do we really want to talk about "authenticity" any more? I had hoped a consensus was forming that to use the word in connection with the performance of music—and especially to define a particular style, manner, or philosophy of performance—is neither description nor critique, but commercial propaganda, the stock-in-trade of press agents and promoters. I note with some satisfaction that John Spitzer's entry under "authenticity" in *the New Harvard Dictionary of Music* does not even mention performance.[1] It deals, rather, with "the nature of the link between a composer and a work that bears his or her name," that is, with texts and transmission, the traditional and proper domain of scholarly authentication.

Satisfaction is somewhat diminished as the eye wanders up to the entry preceding Spitzer's, where we find, as the third of five definitions of the adjective "authentic," the following: "In performance practice, instruments or styles of playing that are historically appropriate to the music being performed." There it is at last in all its purloined majesty, this word that simply cannot be rid of its moral and ethical overtones (and which always carries its invidious antonym in tow), being used to privilege one philosophy of performance over all others. While one certainly cannot fault a dictionary for

[1]Don Michael Randel (ed.), *The New Harvard Dictionary of Music* (Cambridge, Mass.: Harvard University Press, 1986), 60–61.

Originally published in *Authenticity and Early Music*, ed. Nicholas Kenyon (Oxford: Oxford University Press, 1988), 137–210. Reprinted by permission of Oxford University Press.

reporting current usage—and the currency of the usage in question, alas, cannot be denied—there does seem to be some (perhaps unwitting) complicity in the perpetuation of the propaganda here, since the operative synonym, "appropriate," is also an ineluctably value-laden term. One simply cannot dissent from the concept when it is defined in this way. One is hardly free to say, "I prefer inauthenticity to authenticity," or, "I prefer inappropriateness to appropriateness"—at least if one is interested in maintaining respectability with the crowd that swears by the *Harvard Dictionary*. Once the terms have been equated in this way, commitment to the values they assign and the privileges they grant must necessarily follow.

The mischief is compounded when we turn to the article on "performance practice," to which the definition of "authentic" refers us. On its face the article is quite reasonable and sophisticated, especially when compared with its notorious predecessor in the "old" *Harvard Dictionary*. Where the earlier entry began by defining the term as "the study of how early music, from the Middle Ages to Bach, was performed and the many problems connected with attempts to restore its original sound in modern performance," and ended with what seems now the incredibly provincial observation that "in the period after Bach the problems of performance practice largely disappear, owing to the more specific directions of composers for clearly indicating their intentions,"[2] its replacement starts out with a minor masterpiece of sweeping yet cautious generalization, defining performance practice as "the conventions and knowledge that enable a performer to create a performance." Very pointedly, the article goes on to emphasize the fact that although "historically, the study of performance practice has concentrated on periods and repertories in which the gap between what was notated and what was thought necessary for a performance (especially a historically authentic performance) was greatest," nevertheless "the recent history of this study has seen the extent and importance of this gap recognized in repertories ever closer to the present."[3]

What we have here is a rather subtle—and again, in all likelihood, benign and unwitting—Socratic bait and switch in which, first, the very recent concept of historical authenticity is implicitly projected back into historical periods that never knew it (this by the use of the past tense in the first of the quoted sentences for both of the phrases in apposition: "what *was* notated and what *was* thought necessary for a . . . historically authentic performance," instead of "what *is* thought necessary . . ." or simply, "what was performed"), and, second, the

[2]Willi Apel (ed.), *Harvard Dictionary of Music*, 2nd edn. (Cambridge, Mass.: Harvard University Press, 1969), 658–9.
[3]*New Harvard Dictionary*, 624.

application of the loaded term to a virtually unlimited musical and historical terrain (effected by carrying over the word "gap," which has been invested both with the notion of the problem and with that of its approved solution, into the second sentence). The definition has become authoritarian, and it signifies a definite encroachment of "historically authentic performance" beyond areas of traditional historical concern into areas where it now threatens the status of artists not trained in "historically appropriate instruments or styles of playing." Which is why the "classical music scene"—in the view of the editor who put the headline to Will Crutchfield's discussion of the so-called "authentic performance movement" in the Sunday *New York Times*—has lately taken on the appearance of a "battlefield,"[4] and why we are fighting it out, in this book and elsewhere.

Many have realized that the battle is bloodier than it ought to be precisely because of that dread yet hollow shibboleth with which one of the armies insists on scourging the other. So some writers, myself among them, have proposed that talk of authenticity might better be left to moral philosophers, textual critics, and luthiers. Gary Tomlinson wants to reserve it to historians such as himself: by his lights an "authentic" performance would seem to be a performance accompanied by a good set of program notes.[5] Joseph Kerman calls "authentic" a "baleful term which has caused endless acrimony," for it "resonates with unearned good vibrations."[6] A retreat into euphemism can be observed. The American Musicological Society, in its guidelines to the Noah Greenberg Award, now uses the term "historically-aware."[7] The New York concert series "Music Before 1800" has used "historically accurate" in its promotional literature.[8] At the Oberlin conference at which this essay was in part delivered as a lecture in March

---

[4]Will Crutchfield, "A Report From the Battlefield," *New York Times* (Sunday, 28 July 1985), sec. 2, 1. The headline on the article's continuation (p. 8) reads "Musicians Are at War over the 'Right' Way to Play."

[5]"The Historian, the Performer, and Authentic Meaning in Music, in *Authenticity in Early Music*, 115–36.

[6]*Contemplating Music: Challenges to Musicology* (Cambridge, Mass.: Harvard University Press, 1985), 192.

[7]*AMS Newsletter* 16/2 (Aug. 1986): 5, 14.

[8]This phrase was also used as an interchangeable equivalent with "historically authentic" (though not explicitly identified as such) by Donald J. Grout in his essay, "On Historical Authenticity in the Performance of Old Music," in *Essays on Music in Honor of Archibald Thompson Davison* (Cambridge, Mass.: Harvard University Press, 1957), 341–47. This forty-year-old piece, the title of which seems to contain one of the earliest uses of the word "authenticity" in the sense that has since become so widespread and cultish, can serve as a convenient benchmark by which to measure the subsequent progress of the field. Much that Grout wrote off as pipe-dreaming in 1957, particularly as regards mastering old instruments and singing techniques, is taken for granted as a fact of musical life today.

1987, "historically informed" was the going phrase. But these ersatz shibboleths will not achieve a cease-fire, if that is their intent, for they still imply invidious comparison with what is unaware, inaccurate, and un- or misinformed. Whether we even have a right to use the word "accurate" is grounds for a battle in itself; and I doubt whether history has much to do with it, as you will see.

Kerman proposes the Tomlinsonesque word "contextual" as a "value-free substitute," and while the word does pass the invidious-antonym test, it raises problems of its own. It seems to validate what is often cited as a major shortcoming of "historical" performance, that it places the chief emphasis on factors external to the music performed and can actually subvert real interpretation, the value Kerman sets above all others. At the very least it seems to encourage what seems to me the naive assumption that re-creating all the external conditions that obtained in the original performance of a piece will thus re-create the composer's inner experience of the piece and allow him to "speak for himself," that is, unimpeded by that base intruder, the performer's subjectivity. Doubtless Kerman would not construe contexts so narrowly as I fear, but others certainly have. Christopher Hogwood's recording of the "Eroica" Symphony, for example, is an express attempt to re-create the conditions that obtained at the first performance of that piece, at a private house, by "a very powerful company (consisting almost entirely of amateurs)."[9] These factors are cited to justify a performance practice that lacks the "wider variety of nuance and tempo modification which were later to be considered the hallmarks of a conductor's interpretation," but instead features the "uncomplicated, rhythmical" approach typical of amateur performances to this day.[10] I would like to think that Kerman would recoil along with me from such an abject and literalistic rejection of interpretive responsibilities, which arises not so much out of serious artistic conviction as out of Wellsian time-travel fantasies. But such performances do follow logically from the premises his word implies. The concept of contextuality seems especially paradoxical when you consider that practically all music composed before 1800, and a great deal composed since, is almost invariably heard out of context today—that is, in that most anachronistic of all settings, the concert hall. But what am I saying? Now we can hear *Aida* on the patio and the St. Matthew Passion in the shower—in anybody's performance. No, clearly, "contextual" will not do.

---

[9]Christopher Hogwood, "Hogwood's Beethoven," *Gramophone* (Mar. 1986): 1136. For details of this performance at the Vienna palace of Prince von Lobkowitz, and the rehearsals that led up to it, see Tomislar Volek and Jaroslav Macek, "Beethoven's Rehearsals at the Lobkowitz's," *Musical Times* 127 (1986): 75–80.

[10]Clive Brown, notes to Oiseau-Lyre 414 338.

How about "verisimilar," then? Can we fairly say, without introducing spurious moral issues, that performances of a type described
in days of yore as "authentic" are actually aiming at nothing more
controversial than historical verisimilitude? I'm afraid not. For one
thing, it *is* controversial, and has been so from the beginning. Why
should this be our aim? What does such an aim say about us? If,
Donald Grout wrote some forty years ago, a composer of "old music"

> could by some miracle be brought to life in the twentieth century to be
> quizzed about the methods of performance in his own times, his first
> reaction would certainly be one of astonishment at our interest in such
> matters. Have we no living tradition of music, that we must be seeking
> to revive a dead one? The question might be embarrassing. Musical
> archaism may be a symptom of a disintegrating civilization.[11]

Besides, our conception of historical verisimilitude, despite all
the strides that have been made in the decades since Grout wrote, and
despite any strides we are likely to make in the future, remains just as
speculative and contingent—and hence, just as specious—as it was in
1957. It is true that some performance styles that have arisen in the
last quarter century under the banner of historical verisimilitude
have proven extremely persuasive, influential, and (with the passage
of time) authoritative—at least within the world of performance. One
is the, shall we call it, "Mediterranean" style of rendering the songs of
the troubadours, pioneered in the 1960s by Thomas Binkley, Andrea
von Ramm, and their colleagues in the Studio der frühen Musik in
Munich. Another is the Netherlandish style of baroque string playing
associated with names such as Jaap Schröder, Anner Bylsma, and the
brothers Kuijken. An earlier example would be the style of Gregorian
chant singing evolved at the Benedictine Abbey of Solesmes by Pothier
and Mocquereau. The fact is, however, that in not one of these cases
can the historicity of the style in question withstand the slightest
scrutiny on any positive documentary basis. Does that invalidate
them? Only from the point of view of historical data. Whatever the
case a scholarly prosecutor might choose to bring against them, they
will remain as persuasive and authoritative as ever, until a more
persuasive style, as is inevitable, comes along to supersede them.
What makes for persuasion, I want to emphasize—and hence, what
makes for authority and authenticity, in a sense I would approve—has
to do both with the persuaders and with the persuaded.

Those whose scholarly superego insists that everything they do
must survive a trial-by-document are doomed to a marginal existence
as performers. As I have argued before, strict accountability reduces

---

[11]"On Historical Authenticity," 346.

performance practice to a lottery, for the performer can exercise no control over the state of evidence. If you construe your fragmentary evidence the way religious fundamentalists construe scripture—that is, if you believe that what is not permitted is prohibited—then you will find yourself in the position of the Early Music performer who happily averred that, when making records (which are themselves "documents" of a special narcissistic kind), "I personally try to restrain all the people who work with me. . . . I think it's best to be minimal about your additions," lest the recording "embarrass us for another twenty years."[12] There is logic in this position, but it is the logic of certain death. There is nothing you can do, after all, and be sure that someone will not say, "Hey, you can't do that!" If you want no one to say it, you must do nothing—as many do in the name of "authenticity." Such an authenticity is worthy neither of the name nor of serious discussion.

The inadequacy of "historical verisimilitude" as an umbrella concept to account for the style of performance we are trying to name is especially poignant in the case of certain performers and groups that explicitly eschew verisimilitude as a performance ideal yet are clearly within the pale of the so-called "authenticity movement." Peter Phillips, the director of the Tallis Scholars, one of the young English choirs whose work has set a new standard in the performance of Renaissance sacred polyphony, has come right out and said that "we can guess at the type of sound produced by sixteenth-century choirs, and the evidence suggests that imitation of them would be highly undesirable." Even more forthrightly, he continued: "It is unlikely that any choir in the sixteenth century had at any one time a group of singers who were sufficiently young to perform in a manner which we should consider to be ideal—conditions then were not so favourable to experiment and choice as they are now, and it is for that very reason that we can be so bold as to say that we think we can do better."[13] I dare say we ought to do better than the band of amateurs who thrashed their uncomplicated rhythmical way through the first performance of the "Eroica," too.

The difference between the new English choirs and their sixteenth-century prototypes was a matter not only of age, but of gender as well. The new choirs use women rather than boys on the stratospheric treble parts in Tudor music. This was a decision consciously taken in the mid-1960s by David Wulstan, the founder and director of the

[12]James Badal, "On Record: Christopher Hogwood," *Fanfare* (Nov.–Dec. 1985): 90–91.

[13]"Performance Practice in 16th-Century English Choral Music," *Early Music* 6 (1978): 195.

Clerkes of Oxenford, the first of the new choirs, after five years in which the group had worked as a traditional men-and-boys choir. It is curiously revealing that Wulstan and his spokesmen were at first not so straightforward as Phillips about methods and aims. "The primary object [was] to obtain as nearly as possible the sound of the great English Sixteenth Century Choirs," we may read in the programme notes to one of Wulstan's early recordings. "Because boys' voices now break early, they tend to find the high vocal parts of the period overtaxing: with proper training, however, girls' voices can produce exactly the right sound."[14] Now Wulstan, obviously, had never heard a "great English Sixteenth Century Choir." He knew what he wanted, though, and knew he would never get it from boys as young as English choirboys now are. Since he had never heard a seventeen-year-old sixteenth-century choirboy, the sound to which his "girls' " voices came "as nearly as possible" was one he had imagined, not heard. It was, in short, a creation of the twentieth century, not the sixteenth. And yet it somehow had to be passed off as a historical reconstruction.

Why? To placate ol' debbil musicology, I guess. Wulstan is an academic musicologist, Phillips is not. Their differing perspectives on what they were doing (or what they wanted to present themselves as doing) points up the ambivalences in the relationship between musical scholarship and musical performance. Scholars tend to assume it is they who have furnished the major impetus for historical performance. Grout put this in terms of a rather unattractive joke: "Historical Musicology, like Original Sin, has given everybody a bad conscience," he wrote, putting an end to the "days of innocence" when "people did not bother about the original tradition, but simply assumed that the practice of their own nineteenth century was the universal rule and proceeded to apply it accordingly."[15] While some performers do seem to be motivated by a bad conscience — and Grout's choice of simile accords well with what was said earlier about "religious fundamentalism" — I believe he was dead wrong about the origins of the kind of performance we are considering today, and about what sustains it. A glance at the historical record will show that musicology has been a Johnny-come-lately to the authentic performance movement,[16] and I will make bold to assert that musicology has been responsible for more of what has gone wrong with "authen-

[14]W. A. Chislett, notes to Seraphim LP 60256 (works of Tallis).

[15]"On Historical Authenticity," 342.

[16]The two most reliable historical surveys (though we could still use a more comprehensive one) are Howard Mayer Brown, "Pedantry or Liberation? A Sketch of the Historical Performance Movement," in *Authenticity and Early Music*, 27–56; and Harry Haskell, *The Early Music Revival: A History* (London: Thames and Hudson, 1988).

tic" performance than what has gone right with it—though there are welcome signs that this may be changing.

It is the academic mind, not the performer's, that is trained to generalize and to seek normative procedures—even when this means elbowing off the table the difficulties and ambiguities that surround, for a notable example, the Renaissance mensural system.[17] Edgard Varèse once gloomily predicted that "it will not be long before some musical mortician begins embalming electronic music in rules."[18] Compare that with Christopher Hogwood, who looks forward to the day when we will be able, after digesting "sufficient data," to make "rules and regulations" to govern performances of nineteenth-century music.[19] The academic mentality tends to operate on the basis of authority ("objectivity") not identification ("subjectivity").

Let us consider in this light the vexed matter of the composer's intentions vis-à-vis the performer's responsibilities. Musicologists have characteristically assumed, to quote Donald Grout in 1957, that "an ideal performance is one that perfectly realizes the composer's intentions,"[20] or, to quote Howard Mayer Brown, that "the central question can be formulated very simply: should we play music in the way the composer intended it?"[21] I have already had occasion to express my scepticism about such an ideal from standpoints both practical and philosophical. We cannot know intentions, for many reasons—or rather, we cannot know we know them. Composers do not always express them. If they do express them, they may do so disingenuously. Or they may be honestly mistaken, owing to the passage of time or a not necessarily consciously experienced change of taste. If anyone doubts this, let him listen to the five recordings Stravinsky made of *The Rite of Spring*, and try to decide how the composer intended it to go.[22] (For "help," one may consult his published reviews of five other performances.)[23] The decision will have to

[17]Cf. Philip Gossett, "The Mensural System and the *Choralis Constantinus*," in Robert Marshall (ed.), *Studies in Renaissance and Baroque Music in Honor of Arthur Mendel* (Kassel and Hackensack: Bärenreiter Verlag and Joseph Boonin, 1974), 71–107.

[18]Edgard Varèse, "The Liberation of Sound," in Benjamin Boretz and Edward T. Cone (eds.), *Perspectives on American Composers* (New York: W.W. Norton, 1971), 32.

[19]"On Record: Christopher Hogwood," 89.

[20]"On Historical Authenticity," 341.

[21]"Pedantry or Liberation," 27.

[22]They include three studio recordings: 1928 (with a Paris pickup ensemble), 1940 (with the Philharmonic-Symphony Orchestra of New York), 1960 (with the Columbia Symphony Orchestra); a piano roll (Paris: Pleyela, c. 1925); and a live performance (the last he would ever conduct of this work) with the Swedish Radio Symphony Orchestra, recorded on 24 September 1961 and issued on Discocorp RR-224 (with rehearsal sequences).

[23]"Three Types of Spring Fever (Stravinsky Reviews *The Rite*)," in Igor Stravinsky and Robert Craft, *Retrospectives and Conclusions* (New York: Alfred A. Knopf, 1969),

be made either on the basis of one's preferences (in which case the recourse to authority has been entirely spurious), or on the basis of some arbitrary rule (the "Fassung letzter Aufnahme?"), which comes down anyway to an appeal to an authority higher than the composer's. But all that is really beside the point. I continue to maintain that composers do not usually have intentions such as we would like to ascertain, and that the need obliquely to gain the composer's approval for what we do bespeaks a failure of nerve, not to say an infantile dependency. The appeal to intentions is an evasion of the performer's obligation to understand what he is performing. It is what Wimsatt and Beardsley, at the conclusion of their immortal (if usually misunderstood) "Intentional Fallacy," called "consulting the oracle."[24]

Now compare Wanda Landowska: "If Rameau himself would rise from his grave to demand of me some changes in my interpretation of his *Dauphine*, I would answer, "You gave birth to it; it is beautiful. But now leave me alone with it. You have nothing more to say; go away!"[25] No consulting the oracle for her! But would the oracle demand to be consulted? In essay 1 I gave copious examples from the literature and from my own experience to show that "once the piece is finished, the composer regards it and relates to it either as a performer if he is one, or else simply as a listener." To the examples cited there from Irving Berlin, Debussy, and Elliott Carter, I should like to add some comments George Perle voiced in private conversation. After recalling occasions on which he had edited or modified his compositions to reflect some of the better performances of them that he had heard, he reflected that the relationship between composer and performer is "a complicated business" that performers who do not work directly with composers are unlikely to understand. The greatest single source of bad performance, he averred, is literalism, adding, "It's what you expect nowadays."

But whatever we may make of these examples, the fact remains that the whole matter of intentions is just a red herring, and cannot be used as a way of characterizing "authenticity." For adherents to the point of view we are dissecting here have no unique claim in the matter of fidelity to the composer's intentions. Everyone claims it.

123–30 (performances by Karajan, Boulez, Craft); "Spring Fever: A Review of Three Recent Recordings of *The Rite of Spring*," in Igor Stravinsky, *Themes and Conclusions* (Berkeley and Los Angeles: University of California Press, 1982), 234–41 (performances by Boulez, Mehta, and his own of 1960).

[24]W. K. Wimsatt, Jr., and Monroe C. Beardsley, "The Intentional Fallacy," *Sewanee Review* (1946): 468–88; very widely anthologized, e.g., in Hazard Adams (ed.), *Critical Theory Since Plato* (New York: Harcourt Brace Jovanovich 1971), 1015–22; Frank A. Tillman and Steven M. Cahn (eds.), *Philosophy of Art and Aesthetics* (New York: Harper and Row, 1969), 657–69.

[25]*Landowska On Music*, ed. Denise Restout (New York: Stein and Day, 1981), 407.

Landowska, in the very same essay that contains her defiant retort to Rameau, gave the following as her answer to the rhetorical question, "On what do I base my interpretations?"

> By living intimately with the works of a composer I endeavor to pene-
> trate his spirit, to move with an increasing ease in the world of his
> thoughts, and to know them "by heart" so that I may recognize imme-
> diately when Mozart is in good humor or when Handel wants to express
> triumphant joy. I want to know when Bach is raging and throwing a
> handful of sixteenths at the face of some imaginary adversary or a
> flaming spray of arpeggios, as he does in *The Chromatic Fantasy*. The
> goal is to attain such an identification with the composer that no more
> effort has to be made *to understand the slightest of his intentions* or to
> follow the subtlest fluctuations of his mind.[26]

Bruno Walter, in his "Notes on Bach's *St. Matthew Passion*," continually emphasizes his "endeavors to be faithful to Bach's inten-tions"[27] — often as a justification for his departures from eighteenth-century performance practice. More recently, the harpsichordist Ken-neth Cooper, representing the Chamber Music Society of Lincoln Center in its much-advertised joint appearance with Christopher Hogwood's Academy of Ancient Music in September 1984, admon-ished an interviewer in a televised intermission feature with the remark that "We're no less concerned with Bach's intentions than Chris is."

The difference between the point of view represented here by Landowska, Walter, and Cooper, and what from here on I shall in desperation call the "authentistic" point of view (authentistic being to authentic as Hellenistic was to Hellenic), is that the former con-strues intentions "internally," that is, in spiritual, metaphysical, or emotional terms, and sees their realization in terms of the "effect" of a performance, while the latter construes intentions in terms of empirically ascertainable — and hence, though tacitly, external — facts, and sees their realization purely in terms of sound. Walter speaks explicitly of the performer's responsibility to gain "intimate knowledge of the spiritual content of Bach's compositions," while Landowska said, "Little do I care if, to attain the proper effect, I use means that were not exactly those available to Bach."[28] The difference, to put matters in historical perspective, is that between idealism on the one hand, which recognizes a sharp distinction be-tween content and form and between spirit and letter, and positivism

---

[26]*Landowska On Music*, 406 (italics added).
[27]Bruno Walter, *Of Music and Music-Making*, trans. Paul Hamburger (New York: W.W. Norton, 1961), 183.
[28]*Landowska On Music*, 356.

on the other, which denies the existence of any but sensory experience, and hence any knowledge not based on sensory data. To a positivist content is a function of form, spirit a function of letter. Content and spirit as concepts in themselves are illusions born of reifying subjective sensation.

Both of these viewpoints go back to the nineteenth century—under different names, of course, they go back to the Greeks—and both are still with us today, though clearly the positivists are wielding the bigger guns. There seems to be a wall of misunderstanding between them. Howard Mayer Brown surely misconstrues Landowska when he says, with reference to the passage just cited, that she "believed more strongly in her own personal understanding of the music and her commitment to it than in any more dispassionate quest for what the composer would have wanted or expected."[29] As we have seen, she believed she had reached a point of identification with the composers she played that was so close that she could divine what they wanted and expected, though she did not think of these desires and expectations primarily ("merely," she would have said) in terms of sound. When she says "the proper effect," she means "the effect intended by Bach," pure if not so simple.

Early in her career Landowska wrote an essay on transcriptions as intransigent as any modern textualist or authenticist might be today. And just like today's writers, she began by taking aim at her predecessors. She quoted Hans von Bülow: "The harpsichord works of Bach are the Old Testament; Beethoven's Sonatas the New. We must believe in both." And then she commented: "While saying that, he added several bars to the Chromatic Fantasy, changed the answer of the Fugue, and doubled the basses; thus he impregnated this work with an emphatic and theatrical character. A true believer must not change anything in the New or the Old Testament."[30] Yet if we compare her recorded performance of the Chromatic Fantasy (see Appendix, Recording No. 1) with one by a present-day authenticist, we shall, many of us, be tempted to level the same strictures at her as she leveled at von Bülow (listen, particularly, to her renditions of the passages in block chords that carry the laconic instruction, "arpeggio"). But if this means we misunderstand her now, she would have had a hard time understanding us as well. She would have wondered, for one thing, what anything "dispassionate" had to do with art.

The wall of misunderstanding was evident in the Kenneth Cooper–Christopher Hogwood TV exchange, too, even though the participants affected comradely agreement. Cooper, responding to the inter-

[29]"Pedantry or Liberation," 39.
[30]Landowska on Music, 101.

viewer's remarks on historical evidence as justifier of performance practice, said: "It should be remembered about history . . . that what we know about history was only a small part of what was done, so that when we represent what we know about it, we are distorting it; and therefore to try and fill in a little of the creative energy — even if it's not exactly the same creative energy (because we'll never know what that is) — [helps us in] getting closer to a fuller picture." For Cooper, then, to realize Bach's intentions one needs not only knowledge but a vital impetus born of intuition to fill the gaps between the facts. This alone can convert knowledge into action.

To this Hogwood rejoined: "That's the wonderful thing, I think, about coming across new versions of pieces or new evidence. Suddenly that gives you this extra energy: 'Ah, a new set of instructions for embellishment . . . ah, wonderful!'" No *élan vital* here. What enables action on this view is a green light from the boss. The gaps between the facts can only be filled by new facts. Gaps will ever remain.

As I have suggested, the positivist viewpoint is ascendant today — obviously so among authenticists. One tends to patronize the idealistic viewpoint for naively confusing subject with object and for its mystical reliance on illusory nonknowledge. What a variety of sins such thinking may rationalize, we are apt to say today. Yet as essay 13 illustrates in detail, the positivistic viewpoint can lead to positions just as ludicrous and untenable, and just as potentially mischievous.

In any event, fidelity to something as malleably open to interpretation as the composer's intentions cannot be used as a yardstick by which the value of a performance may be measured, and it is not in professions of such fidelity that the unique essence of authentistic performance resides. Perhaps that essence can be located in the domain of hardware — in the "original instruments" we prize. But this can only be the case in so far as historical verisimilitude is the validator; and we have seen that that extent is not nearly as far as is often imagined. Besides, I sometimes wonder whether the craze for original instruments has anything much to do with historicism at all. One prominent advocate of "historical performance" (his term) for nineteenth-century music had this to say about an "original instruments" recording of the *Missa Solemnis*:

> I would be hard pressed to point up any significant difference between the vocal styles applied here and those in any of a half dozen representative modern recordings. There is something specious about arguing for instrumental authenticity while largely ignoring the vocal domain. It is certainly true that we know less about vocal techniques

and performance styles in the eighteenth and nineteenth centuries than we do about instrumental performance. But that is no reason to abandon the search.[31]

Many, I'm sure, would wish to debate the contention advanced here about the relative state of knowledge. But that is beside my point. What chiefly interests me is the idea that an indispensable earnest of authenticity is strangeness. Let us not abandon the search, the critic admonishes, simply because we have little idea of what we are searching for. He wants change, though he knows not what change he wants. Make it different, he seems to be saying, because difference is what counts. Make It New.

Who said that before? Why, Ezra Pound, of course, in the title to a testamentary book of essays, in its day a bible of modernism. And now we have come at last to the nub and essence of authentistic performance, as I see it. It is modern performance.

II

This may take a deal of explaining, since the vocabulary of conventional criticism opposes modern performance to what I propose calling by that name. Yet the ideal of authentistic performance grew up alongside modernism, shares its tenets, and will probably decline alongside it as well. Its values, its justification, and, yes, its authenticity, will only be revealed in conjunction with those of modernism. Historical verisimilitude, composers' intentions, original instruments, and all that, to the extent that they have a bearing on the question, have not been ends but means; and in most considerations of the issue they have been smoke screens. To put my thesis in a nutshell, I hold that "historical" performance today is not really historical; that a specious veneer of historicism clothes a performance style that is completely of our own time, and is in fact the most modern style around; and that the historical hardware has won its wide acceptance and above all its commercial viability precisely by virtue of its novelty, not its antiquity.

In essay 1 I raised the matter of modernism tangentially, chiefly in connection with the ideal of impersonality—"depersonalization" to use T. S. Eliot's word—that links modernist thinking to the values implicit in authentistic performance. Both regard the individual "as he is at the moment"—that is, as an ephemeral carbon-based, oxygen-breathing organism soon to expire, decay, and disappear, and who is

[31]Robert Winter, "The Emperor's New Clothes: Nineteenth-Century Instruments Revisited," *Nineteenth-Century Music* 7 (1984): 255.

prey to all the mundane subjective pleasures and pains that flesh is heir to—as a thing of no consequence. Eliot's envoi to what he called "the responsible person interested in poetry," reads as follows:

> To divert interest from the poet to the poetry is a laudable aim: for it would conduce to a juster estimation of actual poetry, good and bad. There are many people who appreciate the expression of sincere emotion in verse, and there is a smaller number of people who can appreciate technical excellence. But very few know when there is an expression of *significant* emotion, emotion which has its life in the poem and not in the history of the poet. The emotion of art is impersonal. And the poet cannot reach this impersonality without surrendering himself wholly to the work to be done. And he is not likely to know what is to be done unless he lives in what is not merely the present, but the present moment of the past, unless he is conscious, not of what is dead, but of what is already living.[32]

For a gloss on this beautifully gnomic text let us turn to Pound's *Make It New*, which, its title notwithstanding, consists mainly of studies of very old poetry, from the Troubadours to the Elizabethans. Under the heading of "A Few Dont's" for poets, we find this:

> Consider the way of the scientists rather than the way of an advertising agent for a new soap.
>
>   The scientist does not expect to be acclaimed as a great scientist until he has *discovered* something. He begins by learning what has been discovered already. He goes from that point onward. He does not bank on being a charming fellow personally. He does not expect his friends to applaud the results of his freshman class work. Freshmen in poetry are unfortunately not confined to a definite and recognizable class room. They are "all over the shop." Is it any wonder "the public is indifferent to poetry?"[33]

What is only personal is irrelevant. What is sought is a contribution of something valuable to the common wealth of art. And that means becoming well acquainted with that common wealth, which in turn means knowing history, or, in Eliot's terms, possessing "the historical sense," defined as "what makes a writer most acutely conscious of his place in time," and what impels him toward the "extinction of personality."[34]

It is no accident that both Eliot's maxims and Pound's were written during the First World War, the convulsion that truly ended

[32]"Tradition and the Individual Talent," in Frank Kermode (ed.), *Selected Prose of T.S. Eliot* (New York: Harcourt Brace Jovanovich, Farrar Straus and Giroux, 1975), 44.

[33]Ezra Pound, *Make It New* (London: Faber and Faber, 1934), 339.

[34]Eliot, "Tradition and the Individual Talent," 38, 40.

the nineteenth century and posed a hitherto inconceivable threat to all security and stability, whether of individual lives or of Culture and Civilization writ large. Refuge in order and precision, hostility to subjectivity, to the vagaries of personality, to whatever passes and decays—these were the inevitable reactions of all who were committed to the preservation of the high culture. The threat has only intensified since the days of Eliot and Pound, and high modernism has become even more intransigent, objectivist, elitist, and fearful of individual freedom of expression, which leads inexorably to the abyss. Examples can be found everywhere. A convenient one has appeared in the newspaper on the day I happen to be writing this. Lincoln Kirstein, comrade of Balanchine and sometime collaborator with Stravinsky, takes up the cudgels against "postmodernism," the code for whatever beleaguers the high culture today, with an attack on Isadora Duncan, dead these sixty years. She it is who, by personifying and glorifying the "exposure of a private personage's unique sensibility," led the way to the depravity of the present moment, when "exquisite care in craftsmanship, elegant spareness, historic obligation and humane responsibility are conveniently ignored by a generation of dance dilettantes." Isadora's legacy, writes Kirstein, "was reputation, not repertory." She was the antithesis of Nijinsky, whose "intense personifications used the broad language of a received academic vocabulary" and whose " 'self' remains mysterious." The peroration is borrowed from Saint Augustine: "I understand with complete certainty that what is subject to decay is inferior to that which is not, and without hesitation I placed that which cannot be harmed above that which can, and I saw that what remains constant is better than that which is changeable."[35]

We might already wish to draw an analogy with authentistic performance, which upholds a comparable goal—to arrest the decay of the music of the past by reversing the changeable vagaries of taste and restoring it to a timeless constancy. This would be a facile analogy, and one that accepted at face value what I hope I have shown to be a specious, or at least a debatable claim.

Let us instead press on. Shortly after I drew my first parallels between authentistic performance and modernist aesthetics, an extremely clever article by Daniel Leech-Wilkinson appeared in *Early Music*, as part of that journal's symposium on "The Limits of Authenticity." As a result of an experiment in which pairs of recordings (one authentistic, the other not) encompassing a wide range of repertory (from plainchant to Schubert) were compared, the author was able to report that

[35]Lincoln Kirstein, "The Curse of Isadora," *New York Times* (Sunday, 23 Nov. 1986), sec. 2, 1, 28.

in every case ... the stylistic contrast between the earlier and the "authentic" performance is essentially the same. The earlier performance—in accordance with the fashions of its time—shows greater variation of dynamics, speed and timbre, amounting to a performance which is more "emotional," more a personal "interpretation" of what the performers believe the composer to be "saying," while the more recent, "authentic" performance is characterized by relatively uniform tempo and dynamics, a "clean" sound and at least an attempt to avoid interpretive gestures beyond those notated or documented as part of period performance practice. In a nutshell, the difference is that between performer as "interpreter" and performer as "transmitter."

Leech-Wilkinson concluded that "the remarkable uniformity of approach which dominates early music performance . . . is nothing more than a reflection of current taste."[36]

I believe these observations may be considerably extended. For the most part, Leech-Wilkinson compared recordings of the 1950s and 1960s with recordings of the 1970s and 1980s. Had he compared recordings of the 1920s and 1930s with those in his earlier group, his conclusions would have been substantially the same, as they would have been were he to have compared early "electrics" with turn-of-the-century acoustic discs. Moreover, what he found to be true of performances involving repertory falling under the general—and ever-expanding—umbrella of "Early Music" would have been equally true of performances of virtually any repertory, including current repertory. Modern performance gets moderner and moderner, as Alice might say. Many who have made the comparison will tell you that Gary Graffman's Prokofiev, for example, sounds more like Prokofiev than Prokofiev's (ditto Sándor's Bartók or Tacchino's Poulenc). Changes in performing style in the twentieth century, no less than in past centuries, have been allied with changes in composing style, and with more general changes in aesthetic and philosophical outlook. Changes of this kind moreover, are never sudden, always gradual. To contemporaries, all periods are transitional and pluralistic. A multiplicity of styles is always available in any present, of which some are allied more with the past and others with the future. Only when the present becomes the past and the future becomes the present can we see which was which.

For a forcible reminder of this, we can listen today to Bach's Fifth Brandenburg Concerto, recorded at the Salzburg Festival in the Bach bicentennial year, 1950, by Willi Boskovsky on violin, Gustav Neidermayer on flute, and the string section of the Vienna Philharmonic under Wilhelm Furtwängler, who also plays the piano solo (Appendix,

---

[36]*Early Music*, 12 (1984): 14.

Recording No. 2a). It seems incredible that this performance happened so recently. It visits us now like the ghost of Jacob Marley, weighted down by generations of accrued tradition (some might wish to continue the Marley metaphor and call them accrued misdeeds), made crushingly palpable in Furtwängler's unforgettably ham-fisted continuo chords, banged out at full Bechstein blast with left hand *coll'ottava*. By comparison, *any* performance we may hear today will seem virtually weightless, reminding us of Karl Marx's definition of the modern experience as one in which "all that is solid melts into air."[37] This is Bach interpreted by a musician who still regarded Bach as Beethoven did — "not a brook but an ocean," and the fountainhead of contemporary music. The performance is a kind of sacramental act, a communion that renews contact with the source and strengthens the "perception, not only of the pastness of the past but of its presence . . . a sense of the timeless as well as the temporal and of the timeless and the temporal together," of which Eliot wrote in 1917. It embodies not an ahistorical vision of Bach, as we might be inclined to call it before reflecting, but the very opposite: a profoundly historical one in which the present actively participates. The pastness of the present is as much implied by it as the presence of the past. "Whoever has approved this idea of order will not find it preposterous," wrote Eliot, "that the past should be altered by the present as much as the present is directed by the past," and this because

> what happens when a new work of art is created is something that happens simultaneously to all the works of art which preceded it. The existing monuments form an ideal order among themselves, which is modified by the introduction of the new . . . work of art among them. The existing order is complete before the new work arrives; for order to persist after the supervention of novelty, the *whole* existing order must be, if ever so slightly, altered; and so the relations, proportions, values of each work of art toward the whole are readjusted; and this is conformity between the old and the new.[38]

So Furtwängler's Bach is no smug or mindless adaptation of Bach to the style of Wagner. It is a reaffirmation of the presence of Bach *in* Wagner and the simultaneous, reciprocal presence of Wagner in Bach. Without that perception, and its affirmation in the art of performance, Bach would fall out of the tradition, and so, deprived of their fount, would Beethoven, Brahms, and Wagner. All would become alien to all; the center would cease to hold.

[37]Karl Marx and Friedrich Engels, *Manifesto of the Communist Party* (1848), trans. Samuel F. Moore, in *Introduction to Contemporary Civilization in the West*, 2, 3rd edn. (New York: Columbia University Press, 1961), 683–84.
[38]Eliot, "Tradition and the Individual Talent," 38–39.

Artists who feel themselves heir to tradition in this way have a very exigent sense of canon. What is canonical is kin; what is not is alien. For German musicians of Furtwängler's generation, Bach was canonical but Handel was not. Schoenberg, who possessed these perceptions and was possessed by them to a rare degree—and who, according to his biographer, "was furious if one mentioned Handel in the same breath as Bach"[39]—made a "free transformation" of one of Handel's Concerti Grossi, Op. 6, that illustrates perfectly what Adorno (who hated the very idea of what we now call "authenticity") meant by calling the arrangements of Schoenberg and Webern "loyal . . . in being disloyal."[40] By violating every aspect of its sound and structure, Schoenberg sought to give Handel's music an "intensification of motival development," and especially a "solidity of form" that would prevent it from melting into air. By remedying an "insufficiency with respect to thematic invention and development [that] could satisfy no sincere contemporary of ours,"[41] Schoenberg sought to save at least this work of Handel's for the canon. The resulting "Concerto for String Quartet and Orchestra" was a rather extreme example of "the alteration of the past by the present." Webern's arrangement of the six-part Ricercar from the *Musical Offering*, of course, was another.

It would be a great mistake to call either Furtwängler's or Schoenberg's approaches naive. What can make them appear so is the fact that they rely on a sense of continuity—hence direct transmission—of tradition that many in the twentieth century believe to be lost. Eliot stated this sense of loss—or perhaps we should say, of rejection—quite explicitly, and in this rejection lies the challenge and the curse of modernism.

> If the only form of tradition, of handing down, consisted in following the ways of the immediate generation before us in a blind or timid adherence to its successes, "tradition" should positively be discouraged. We have seen many such simple currents soon lost in the sand; and novelty is better than repetition. Tradition is a matter of much wider significance. It cannot be inherited, and if you want it you must obtain it by great labour.[42]

Eliot was attempting an end run around the age of Romanticism and its catastrophic disorders. "It was romanticism that made the

---

[39]H. H. Stuckenschmidt, *Arnold Schoenberg: His Life, World and Work*, trans. Humphrey Searle (New York: Schirmer Books, 1978), 365.

[40]Theodor W. Adorno, "Bach Defended against His Devotees," in *Prisms*, trans. Samuel and Shierry Weber (Cambridge, Mass.: MIT Press, 1981), 146.

[41]Arnold Schoenberg, program note for Janssen Symphony Orchestra of Los Angeles, reprinted on sleeve of Columbia ML 4406 (1951).

[42]Eliot, "Tradition and the Individual Talent," 38.

revolution," wrote T. E. Hulme, who would die on the battlefields
of Flanders in 1917. "They [who] hate the revolution . . . hate romanticism."[43] His "they," of course, meant "we." In Hulme's view, Romanticism was the culminating phase of humanism, that fatal hubris
"which is the opposite of the doctrine of original sin: the belief
that man as a part of nature was after all something satisfactory." He
went on:

> The change which Copernicus is supposed to have brought about is the
> exact contrary of the fact. Before Copernicus, man was not the centre of
> the world; after Copernicus he was. You get a change from a certain
> profundity and intensity to that flat and insipid optimism which,
> passing through its first stage of decay in Rousseau, has finally culmi-
> nated in the state of slush in which we have the misfortune to live.[44]

That slush seeped into art through an excess of "vitality," Hulme's
term for a view of art that equates its beauty with its power to evoke a
pleasurable empathy:

> Any work of art [of this kind] we find beautiful is an objectification of
> our own pleasure in activity, and our own vitality. The worth of a line or
> form consists in the value of the life which it contains for us. Putting
> the matter more simply we may say that in this art there is always a
> feeling of liking for, and pleasure in, the forms and movements to be
> found in nature.[45]

And human nature above all.

Like Eliot, and like his mentor Wilhelm Worringer,[46] Hulme
chose all his examples from the visual arts or literature, where there
is no problem defining the natural forms and movements that serve as
models for art. But explicit statements of a vitalistic aesthetic of
music are far from uncommon. Hanslick, though an early and impla-
cable opponent of such a view, nevertheless summed it up well when
he admitted the analogy (to him a misleading analogy and irrelevant
to what is beautiful in music) between the dynamic properties of
music—"the ideas of intensity waxing and diminishing; of motion
hastening and lingering"—and the "forms" with which emotion pre-

[43]"Romanticism and Classicism," in T. E. Hulme, *Speculations: Essays on Humanism and the Philosophy of Art*, ed. Herbert Read (London: Routledge, 1924), 115.
[44]Hulme, "Modern Art and Its Philosophy," in *Speculations*, 80.
[45]Ibid., 85.
[46]See his *Abstraktion und Einfühlung* (Munich, 1908); a sizeable extract from the
introduction to this work, which furnished Hulme with his thesis, may be found (trans.
M. Bullock) in Francis Frascina and Charles Harrison (eds.), *Modern Art and Modernism: A Critical Anthology* (New York: Harper and Row, 1982), 150–64.

sents itself to our consciousness.[47] Later writers have formulated the idea in more general terms. Susanne Langer's way of putting it is that music reflects "the morphology of feeling,"[48] or, more loosely (after Carroll C. Pratt), that music may "sound the way moods feel." Even so recent a writer as Roger Sessions adhered to the notion, and expressed it more sweepingly than anyone else I have read: "What music conveys to us—and let it be emphasized, this is the *nature of the medium* itself, not the consciously formulated purpose of the composer—is the nature of our existence, as embodied in the movement that constitutes our innermost life: those inner gestures that lie behind not only our emotions, but our every impulse and action, which are in turn set in motion by these, and which in turn determine the ultimate character of life itself."[49]

None of the musical writers I have just quoted were professed vitalists, rather the contrary. They were all more or less opposed to the prevalent layman's notion of music as a "language of emotions," or a medium for concrete propositional expression. The vital quality they all point to is a potentiality that may or may not be harnessed (legitimately or otherwise) by a composer or performer. Any music that does seek to harness it will perforce emphasize the qualities to which Hanslick drew attention—the dynamic qualities of music, as expressed in fluctuations of tempo and intensity. That is why Romantic music—and Romantic performance practice—are more richly endowed than any other kind with crescendos and diminuendos, accelerandos and ritardandos, not to mention tempo rubato and a highly variegated timbral palette.

For a vitalist interpretation of Bach one could do no better than Furtwängler's rendition of the harpsichord "cadenza" in the first movement of the Fifth Brandenburg (Appendix, Recording No. 2a). It would be ridiculous to call it a "modern" performance. By 1950 it was already an anachronism, conclusive evidence that the performer had reached his artistic maturity before the First World War. That nobody plays Bach like Furtwängler any more goes without saying. But does anyone play Schumann like that any more? Chopin? Tchaikovsky?

Or consider Leopold Stokowski's interpretation of the opening of the Fifth Brandenburg (Appendix, Recording No. 2b). The presence of the harpsichord in this performance ought to show how far the use of "original instruments" will assure "authenticity." Stokowski had also reached his majority by the time of the First World War, and he was

[47]Eduard Hanslick, *The Beautiful in Music*, trans. Gustav Cohen (Indianapolis and New York: Bobbs-Merrill, 1957), 23.
[48]*Philosophy in a New Key* (New York: Mentor Books, 1948), 193.
[49]*Questions About Music* (New York: W. W. Norton, 1971), 45.

also brought up in an atmosphere where "vitalist" performance of all repertoires was the norm. And yet in this recording, made in 1961, an elephantine allargando at the end of the first ritornello has become less an expressive gesture than a purely formal one—or, to use a word that was being derided by some literary critics as "sanctified"[50] before I was born (so when will we musicologists wise up?), it has become a "structural" device of an offensively didactic kind, and the performance therefore is of a kind I believe we can all agree to call "mannered"—and doubly anachronistic, because it has lost its connection with the vitalistic aesthetic that had provided its justification.

To vitalist art (still following Worringer) Hulme opposed "geometrical" art, the kind which, he predicted, was going to gain ascendancy in the twentieth century. His superb description and account of it deserves to be quoted at some length:

> It most obviously exhibits no delight in nature and no striving after vitality. Its forms are always what can be described as stiff and lifeless. . . . [It embodies] the *tendency to abstraction*.
>
> What is the nature of this tendency? What is the condition of mind of the people whose art is governed by it?
>
> It can be described most generally as a feeling of separation in the face of outside nature.
>
> While a naturalistic art is the result of a happy pantheistic relation between man and the outside world, the tendency to abstraction, on the contrary, occurs in races whose attitude to the outside world is the exact contrary of this. . . .
>
> In art this state of mind results in a desire to create a certain abstract geometrical shape, which, being durable and permanent, shall be a refuge from the flux and impermanence of outside nature. The need which art satisfies here, is not the delight in the forms of nature, which is a characteristic of all vital arts, but the exact contrary. In the reproduction of natural objects there is an attempt to purify them of their characteristically living qualities in order to make them necessary and immovable. The changing is translated into something fixed and necessary. This leads to rigid lines and dead crystalline forms, for pure geometrical regularity gives a certain pleasure to men troubled by the obscurity of outside appearance. The geometrical line is something absolutely distinct from the messiness, the confusion, and the accidental details of existing things.[51]

Hulme's examples of "races" that inclined toward geometrical art included "primitive people," who "live in a world whose lack of order and seeming arbitrariness must inspire them with a certain fear"; but

---

[50]Cf. Robert Penn Warren, "Pure and Impure Poetry" (1942), in John Crowe Ransom (ed.), *The Kenyon Critics* (Cleveland and New York: World Publishing, 1951), 33.
[51]Hulme, *Speculations*, 85–87.

also the Egyptian, the Byzantine, and the postclassical pre-Renaissance Western civilization, all of them intent on an afterlife and hence full of religious contempt for the natural world. He did not mention— because, in an essay entitled "Modern Art" he did not need to—his own contemporaries, traumatized and dislocated first by the Industrial Revolution, then by war and political upheaval. As Yeats put it, "Nature, steel-bound or stone-built in the nineteenth century, became a flux where man drowned or swam."[52] Forster, less metaphorically, called it "this continual flux even in the hearts of men."[53] The feeling these images described was the great twentieth-century abjectness, the sense of "withdrawal, marginality, parasitism, and opposition— what we now call alienation."[54] Translate withdrawal into Latin roots and you get abstraction.

Escape from the flux led many early twentieth-century artists to primitive and archaic art, which shared the geometrical quality Hulme described: recall Picasso and his African ritual masks, or Pound and his Medieval poetry with its literally fixed forms. The great labor Eliot spoke of in connection with attaining to Tradition involved the deliberate seeking of points of contact with the Necessary and the Immovable, a determined quest to recover what in another essay Hulme called the "dry hardness which you get in the classics."[55] All of this resonates with some famous passages in Stravinsky's *Poetics of Music*, as where the great paradigmatic musical modernist avers that "the artist imposes a culture upon himself" and that "tradition results from a conscious and deliberate acceptance."[56] And you can be sure that it is to Stravinsky that we shall return.

But first let us return to Bach. A comparison of the beginnings of five different recordings of the Fifth Brandenburg Concerto, recorded over a fifty-year period from 1935 to 1985 (see Appendix, Recordings 2c–g), will show the changeover from the vital to the geometrical in twentieth-century performance practice. They display their individual uniquenesses and mutual differences, to be sure; but what they all have spectacularly in common is a fundamentally inelastic approach to those very dynamic properties that were so richly and purposely varied by Furtwängler. They all differ from Furtwängler's rendition infinitely more than they differ among themselves; the transition

[52]W. B. Yeats, "Introduction," *The Oxford Book of Modern Verse* (London, 1936), xxviii.

[53]E. M. Forster, *Howards End* (Harmondsworth: Penguin Books, 1941), 143.

[54]Roger Shattuck, "Catching Up with the Avant-Garde," *New York Review of Books* (18 December 1986): 66.

[55]Hulme, *Speculations*, 126–27.

[56]Igor Stravinsky, *Poetics of Music*, trans. Arthur Knoedel and Ingolf Dahl (Cambridge, Mass.: Harvard University Press, 1947), 56–57.

among them between what we are accustomed to call "modern" performances and authentistic ones on "original instruments" is in this context no thing of great moment. The earliest of them, by the Adolf Busch Chamber Orchestra—recorded in 1935 with Busch on violin, Marcel Moyse on flute, and the young Rudolf Serkin on piano—exhibits a bit more variation in loudness than the others (though even here the variations are more between the concertino and the tutti than within either group singly), and its tempo is noticeably slower than the others. The tempo is no less steady, though, which already forces attention away from the music's iconicity—that is, its capacity for analogizing human behaviour and feeling—and on to the reiterative rhythmic patterns, wherein resides music's closest analogy with geometry. The second and third in the sampling are virtually identical in tempo and in levelness of intensity, although the former was made in 1950 (the same year as Furtwängler's!) under Fritz Reiner and the latter was made about a decade and a half later by the Collegium Aureum—one of the earliest on "original instruments" and heavily touted as such in its day. The differing recording ambiences—very dry for Reiner, very live for the Collegium—almost make up for the radical difference in the size of the ensembles: in Reiner's recording there was a ripieno of two players to a part (for a total of ten) in addition to the soloists; in the Collegium Aureum version there were solo ripienists, and the violin soloist was also the first violin of the tutti, so that only seven players in all participated. The last pair of recordings are recent British contributions: the English Concert under Trevor Pinnock (1982) and the Academy of Ancient Music under Christopher Hogwood (1985). Their approach does not differ appreciably from the others, save perhaps in the lightness of tone, though as the performances grow progressively lighter as the sample progresses, lightness as such represents not a departure but rather the opposite. There is another way, however, in which the last pair of recordings do differ from their predecessors: the first three, in common with almost all recordings I have heard, whatever the vintage or the instrumentarium, relax very slightly (often imperceptibly to me without the use of a metronome) for the solo section, while Pinnock and Hogwood inflexibly maintain tempo. In Pinnock's case the players are obviously working at it against what appears to be a natural tendency, so that they actually seem subjectively to rush a bit.

In any case, there can be no disputing the fact that, in terms of Hulme's categories and compared with Furtwängler's performance, these are all of them geometrical renditions, not vitalistic ones, and they become more and more geometrical as they go along. What I do dispute, and emphatically, is that the concept of this style of performance had its origins in historical research or in aspirations toward historical verisimilitude, let alone respect for the composer's intentions. Wanda Landowska, decrying what she called the "objective" style of performing early music, wrote: "As for Bach, reducing to straightforwardness his involved, ornate and baroque lines would be like transforming a gothic cathedral into a skyscraper."[57] I don't know about the gothic cathedral, but when she said *skyscraper* she hit the nail on the head. What we have here is a case of what Virgil Thomson called "equalized tensions . . . the basis of streamlining and of all those other surface unifications that in art, as in engineering, make a work recognizable as belonging to our time and to no other."[58]

The historical research came later. Aspirations toward historical verisimilitude and (especially) appeals to the composer's intentions, were special pleading, rationalizations ex post facto. Virgil Thomson was under no illusions when he reviewed the performances of Landowska—who, he felt, "plays the harpsichord better than anybody else ever plays anything"[59]—in terms Landowska might have neither recognized nor approved. For him, it was the most modern playing around, precisely because it was the most geometrical. "Her especial and unique grandeur is her rhythm," he declared, after hearing her perform the *"Goldberg" Variations* in 1942:

> It is modern quantitative scansion at its purest. Benny Goodman himself can do no better. . . . Only in our day, through the dissemination of American and South American popular music, which differs from European in being more dependent on quantitative patterns than on strong pulsations, has a correct understanding of Bach's rhythm been possible and a technique invented for rendering it cleanly and forcibly. . . . The final achievement is a musical experience that clarifies the past by revealing it to us through the present.[60]

So by the time Schoenberg brought out his updated Handel Concerto Grosso, many if not most of his "sincere contemporaries" undoubtedly found it antiquated in concept.

By 1933 most modern musicians were well used to Hulme's categories—if not by his names, then by their own—and knew very well where they stood on the matter. Here is how Stravinsky summed it up in the *Poetics of Music*, relying on an article by his friend Pierre Souvtchinsky (who himself had relied upon Bergson, one of Hulme's mentors):

---

[57]*Landowska On Music*, 401.

[58]"Modernism Today" (1947), in Virgil Thomson, *Music Reviewed 1940–1954* (New York: Vintage Books, 1967), 233.

[59]Virgil Thomson, *The Musical Scene* (New York: Alfred A. Knopf, 1945), 203.

[60]Ibid., 202.

Mr. Souvtchinsky . . . presents us with two kinds of music: one which evolves parallel to the process of ontological time, embracing and penetrating it, inducing in the mind of the listener a feeling of euphoria and, so to speak, of "dynamic calm." The other kind runs ahead of, or counter to, this process. It is not self-contained in each momentary tonal unit. It dislocates the centers of attraction and gravity and sets itself up in the unstable; and this fact makes it particularly adaptable to the translation of the composer's emotive impulses. All music in which the will to expression is dominant belongs to the second type. . . .

Music that is based on ontological time is generally dominated by the principle of similarity. The music that adheres to psychological time likes to proceed by contrast. To these two principles which dominate the creative process correspond the fundamental concepts of variety and unity. . . . For myself, I have always [!] considered that in general it is more satisfactory to proceed by similarity rather than by contrast. Music thus gains strength in the measure that it does not succumb to the seductions of variety. What it loses in questionable riches it gains in true solidity.[61]

True solidity—again the rage against flux and impermanence, the same refuge in fixity and necessity, the same fear of melting into air. I would go so far as to suggest that all truly modern musical performance (and of course that includes the authentistic variety) treats the music performed as if it were composed—or at least performed—by Stravinsky.

III

If this seems an overly bold assertion, let us ask ourselves where a conductor such as Fritz Reiner, whose 1950 recording of the Fifth Brandenburg we have considered, would have got his very modern ideas about Baroque period style. You can be sure he never read his Dolmetsch. In the 1910s, when Dolmetsch's great guidebook came out, Reiner was in Dresden, hobnobbing with Nikisch, Muck, and Strauss, vitalists to a man, the last-named leaving us, in his compositions and arrangements, ample testimony to an utterly sentimentalized, fairyland vision of the eighteenth century. It must have been from the music of his own time that Reiner (as great musicians do in all periods) formed his ideas about the music of other times. Closely identified with Stravinsky's music in America (he conducted the Metropolitan première of *The Rake's Progress* shortly after recording the Brandenburgs), "*l'amico Fritz*" earned a grudging accolade from the Old Man—no lover of interpreters—in one of the

[61]Stravinsky, *Poetics of Music* (Bilingual edn., Cambridge, Mass.: Harvard University Press, 1970), 41, 43.

late books of conversation.[62] I believe it was Stravinsky who taught Reiner—and the rest of us—about Bach the geometrist, as it may have been Landowska—whom he heard as early as 1907—who taught Stravinsky.

The best theoretical formulation of the twentieth-century "geometrical" Bach style our recordings have documented can be found in Edward T. Cone's treatise on *Musical Form and Musical Performance*:

> Certainly the style of . . . the age of Bach and Handel is most memorably characterized by an important rhythmic feature: the uniformity of its metrical pulse. This is in turn but one facet of a regularity that pervades the texture of the music. As a result the typical movement of this period is indeed a *movement*, i.e., a piece composed in a single unvarying tempo. . . . Even when a movement juxtaposes two or more such units in clearly contrasted tempos, there is often an underlying arithmetical relation that, if observed in performance, unifies them. In this music, events of the same kind tend to happen either at the same rate of speed, or at precisely geared changes of rate. . . . In the best of this music, the contrapuntal texture, either actual or implied, sets up a hierarchy of events, each proceeding at its own rate, yet all under a strict metric control that extends from the entire phrase down to the smallest subdivision of the beat. . . . The beats seem to form a pre-existing framework that is independent of the musical events that it controls. One feels that before a note of the music was written, the beats were in place, regularly divided into appropriate sub-units, and regularly combined into measures; and that only after this abstract framework was in place, so to speak, was the music composed on it. . . . In performance, the result should be a relative equalization of the beats.[63]

The first point to observe about this fascinating document of twentieth-century taste is that it is profoundly antihistorical. What is presented as a self-evident feature of baroque music and an evaluation of its equally self-evident importance for determining the essential nature of baroque style is in fact a set of opinions uncorroborated by any contemporary witness. In fact, these are points no seventeenth- or eighteenth-century theorist or treatise writer ever made, to my knowledge. With respect to Bach, they can be traced back no further than Virgil Thomson and his "modern quantative scansion." In the second place we may note the close congruence between Cone's description of temporal and metrical regularity and Stravinsky's description of "a music based on ontological time." The critic pronounces the same positive value judgement on it as the composer:

---

[62]*Themes and Conclusions*, 225.
[63]Edward T. Cone, *Musical Form and Musical Performance* (New York: W. W. Norton, 1968), 59, 62, 70.

there is even the suggestion of the old "refuge from flux and impermanence" when Cone speaks of the abstract framework that preexists
(and, implicitly, outlasts) the individual composition. Where Cone
actually goes even further than Thomson or Stravinsky is where he
claims that the greater the pervasiveness of regularized metrical pulse
at multiple levels of texture, the better the music is—and this because
through the multileveled rhythmic structure a unifying hierarchy is
made manifest. Now if "structural" was the sanctified shibboleth of
the "new critical" 1930s and 1940s, surely "hierarchy" and "unifying"
were the sanctified words of the Schenkerian 1950s and 1960s, at least
in academic bastions of logical positivism, among which Cone's alma
mater occupied the premier position. This is Bach strictly as viewed
through Princetonian eyes.

And this ahistorical viewpoint led Cone into making a downright
erroneous prescription for performers: the equalized beat, reminiscent
once more of streamlining and skyscrapers. The author elaborates:

> We can best understand such metric play if we assume that in this style
> the primary metric unit is not the measure but the beat. This is not to
> say that the measure is unreal or purely conventional; but it is only one
> step in the hierarchical subdivision and combination of beats, which
> remain the unchanging elements. (Even the Late Baroque is, after all,
> not so far away from the Renaissance!) . . . Our orientation within the
> measure should be effected more by the actual musical profile than by
> applied accentuation (which, after all, was unavailable on two of Bach's
> favorite instruments).[64]

Harpsichordists and organists who have invested gallons of sweat
and tears in learning successfully to belie the concluding canard may
smirk or wince at pleasure. But the main point is that had the author
actually looked into any Baroque musical primer, from Quantz on
down, he would have found precious little about equalized beats, but
page upon page about meters and their allied dance rhythms, about
prosody, about good notes and bad—in short, about the measure as
primary metric unit and the concomitant necessity for applied accentuation. (And it is precisely in this that the late Baroque is in fact light
years from the Renaissance!) What Cone describes—and what all the
recordings in our batch, from Reiner to Hogwood, exemplify—is a
specifically twentieth-century style of Baroque performance that is
often linked with a certain invention of Mr. Elias Howe.

But if the sewing-machine style cannot be historically associated
with Bach, it can certainly be associated with the "neoclassic" Stra-

[64]Ibid., 66, 70.

vinsky. It is what Stravinsky and his spokesmen at one time called "monometric" rhythm.[65] Edward Cone's prime exhibit of the hierarchized metrical texture of Baroque music at its best comes from one of the episodes in the first movement of Bach's Concerto in D minor for harpsichord. Simultaneous patterning of steady sixteenths, steady eighths, quarter-note attacks, and syncopated half-note attacks (plus, later, syncopated quarters) does indeed make up an entrancing texture of time (ontological, that is) (Figure 4.1). There is no reason to assume that Bach or his contemporaries thought this fairly mechanistic passage noteworthy, let alone exemplary of the highest qualities of his style; but there can be no doubt that Stravinsky, on the lookout for models of geometrical solidity and equalized tensions, was struck by this very movement (and for the same reasons that Edward Cone was struck) — so struck, in fact, that he modeled the first movement of his Concerto for Piano and Winds on it. One clue of his dependency on this particular movement of Bach's is his adoption of the violinistic *bariolage* effects so uniquely endemic to these two keyboard concertos (the one by Bach obviously a transcription of a lost violin concerto that has been occasionally reconstructed) (Figures 4.2a and 4.2b).

Another is the peroration of Stravinsky's movement, the *Largo del principio*, where he sets up a rigid metrical matrix just like the one Cone admired in Bach, only more complex: sextolets in the piano right hand (beginning note-for-note identical to Bach's sixteenth-note figuration in Figure 4.1), large triplets in the left hand extracted hemiola-fashion from the sextolets by sampling every fourth note, quarter pulsations in the bass instruments, all against a theme in dotted rhythms (Figure 4.3).

Rigidly mechanical metrical structures like this one would characterize a number of influential Stravinsky compositions of the middle 1920s, including the *Sonate* (1924) and *Serenade* (1925) for piano, both of which he recorded—the former on a Duo-Art pianola roll in 1925, the latter on a set of ten-inch electrical discs issued by Columbia in 1934. Stravinsky's performance style gained an enormous prestige among progressive musicians in the 1920s and 1930s,

---

[65]See Nicolas Nabokov, "Stravinsky Now," *Partisan Review* 11 (1944): 332: "Look at any one of [Stravinsky's] bars and you will find that it is not the measure closed in by bar lines (as it would be in Mozart, for example), but the monometrical unit of the measure, the single beat which determines the life of his musical organism." The term goes back directly to the composer. A sketchbook dated 1919–22, which pertains to some of the earliest "neoclassic" pieces (*Octuor, Sonate*), also contains notations for a set of "Cinq Pièces monométriques." See the description of "Sketchbook G" in John Shepard, "The Stravinsky *Nachlass*: A Provisional List of Music Manuscripts," MLA *Notes* 40 (1984): 743.

Figure 4.1.   J. S. Bach, concerto in D minor for harpsicord, I, mm. 28–35

Figure 4.2a. J. S. Bach, concerto in D minor for harpsichord, I, mm. 148–56

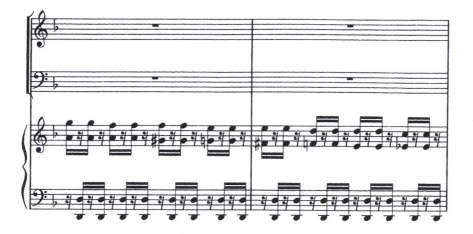

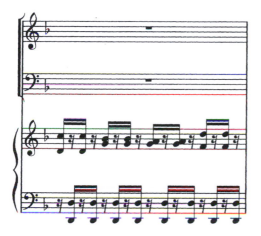

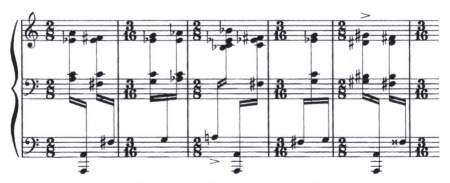

Figure 4.2b.   Stravinsky, Concerto for Piano and Winds, I, fig. 39

40 Più mosso ♩ = 166

tpt.

hn.

sf

tbn.

hn. 2,4 f

123

Figure 4.3. Stravinsky, Concerto for Piano and Winds, I, *Largo del principio*, fig. 45

Figure 4.3. (continued)

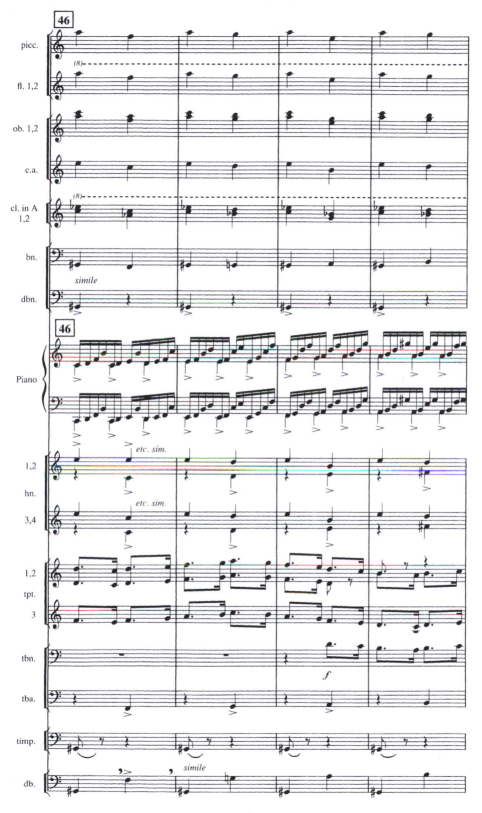

Figure 4.3. (continued)

when he was at the height of his career both as performer and as publicist, not only on behalf of his music, but on behalf of his philosophy of music, too. In newspaper *avertissements*, in pamphlets, in public orations on both sides of the Atlantic, and in his autobiography, Stravinsky propounded a philosophy of "pure music," and the properly "objective" manner of performance required to realize its purity. This he called "execution," and by defining it (in the *Poetics of Music*) as "the strict putting into effect of an explicit will that contains nothing beyond what it specifically commands," Stravinsky invoked the doctrine of quasi-religious fundamentalism alluded to before: what is not permitted is prohibited. "Execution" is contrasted, of course, with "interpretation," that old Stravinskian bugaboo. The whole "sixth lesson" of the *Poetics* is a sustained invective—perhaps exorcism would be an apter word—directed against the bugbear, for as Stravinsky puts it, "it is the conflict of these two principles—execution and interpretation—that is at the root of all the errors, all the sins, all the misunderstandings that interpose themselves between the musical work and the listener and prevent a faithful transmission of its message."[66] Stravinsky's ideal performer, then, is a "transmitter"—the very term Daniel Leech-Wilkinson used to distinguish authentistic performers from their "interpreter" forebears.

Stravinsky permits himself to couch the issue in sternly moralistic terms: "Between the executant . . . and the interpreter . . . there exists a difference in make-up that is of an ethical rather than of an esthetic order, a difference that presents a point of conscience." The point is that of scrupulous fidelity to the letter of the text, and an ascetic avoidance of unspecified nuance in the name of expression, or as Stravinsky stigmatizes it, in the name of "an immediate and facile success that flatters the vanity of the person who obtains it and perverts the taste of those who applaud it."[67] Worst of all are interpretations based on "extramusical" ideas; these are the real "criminal assaults" and "betrayals."[68] The highest quality in an executant, on the other hand, is "submission," defined in terms that seem as if borrowed from T. S. Eliot: "This submission demands a flexibility that itself requires, along with technical mastery, a sense of tradition, and, commanding the whole, an aristocratic culture that is not merely a question of acquired learning."[69] Ultimately Stravinsky boils it down to "good breeding" (*savoir-vivre*)—"a matter of common

[66]*Poetics of Music*, Bilingual edn., 163.
[67]Ibid., 165.
[68]Ibid., 167.
[69]Ibid., 171.

decency that a child may learn." The opposite of good breeding, of course, is vulgarity.

Stravinsky's illustrative example is uncannily pertinent to our present concern:

> *The Saint Matthew's Passion* by Johann Sebastian Bach is written for a chamber-music ensemble. Its first performance in Bach's lifetime was perfectly realized by a total force of thirty-four musicians, including soloists and chorus. That is known. And nevertheless in our day one does not hesitate to present the work, in complete disregard of the composer's wishes, with hundreds of performers, sometimes almost a thousand. This lack of understanding of the interpreter's obligations, this arrogant pride in numbers, this concupiscence of the many, betray a complete lack of musical education.[70]

We need not enter into a debate over the assumptions that inform this paragraph. We need not point to the epistemological difficulties Stravinsky skirts with the bland phrases "perfectly realized," and "the composer's wishes." Nor need we hire a psychologist to investigate what the phrase "concupiscence of the many" would have meant to a Russian aristocrat uprooted by the Bolsheviks. What interests us here is the early enunciation of principles that have become articles of faith in our age of authentistic performance: to wit, that the first performance of a work possesses a privileged authority, and that the composer's wishes are to be gauged in material rather than spiritual terms, to be measured, that is, in terms of sound, not "effect," precisely because sound, not effect, is measurable. Stravinsky goes on for the next five paragraphs to discuss the sound qualities of the St. Matthew Passion; he never stops to consider its effect, let alone its religious meaning.

It is of course not only noteworthy but inevitable that every instance of exaggeration, distortion, or malfeasance cited by Stravinsky in his lesson on performance ethics has to do with the same dynamic features, the nuances of tempo and intensity, discussed earlier when, using T. E. Hulme's terminology, we distinguished vitalist performance from geometrical. Stravinsky's categories are the same: what Hulme calls vital Stravinsky condemns as interpretation; what Hulme calls geometrical Stravinsky upholds as execution. For both of them the vital is vulgar, the geometrical elite. We may detect an echo of these categories, and also of Stravinsky's faith in the performance medium as guarantor of breeding, when Joseph Kerman tells us that "it is almost impossible to play Mozart emo-

---

[70]Ibid., 173.

tionally on a modern piano without sounding vulgar."[71] We may put these categories to the test by reference to a pair of recordings. An unabashedly vitalist (vulgar?) performance of the slow movement from Mozart's Sonata for two pianos in D major, K. 448, by Béla and Ditta Bartók (Appendix, Recording No. 4) features any number of tiny, unnotated, and hence (in Stravinskian terms) criminal and treacherous crescendi and diminuendi, accelerandi and ritardandi, and that most heinous of "sins" and "follies," according to Stravinsky's explicit designation in the *Poetics*: "a *crescendo* . . . is always accompanied by a speeding up of movement, while a slowing down never fails to accompany a *diminuendo*."[72] The recording was made in 1939, the year of Stravinsky's *Poetics*. Not all modern composers shared Stravinsky's ideas on performance, which only goes to show us yet again that all times and places, past and present, are ideologically heterogeneous. On the other hand, Stravinsky's own performance (with his son Soulima) of Mozart's Fugue in C minor, K. 426 (Appendix, Recording No. 4) is execution, pure and simple. You could not hope to find a drier, harder—in a word, more geometrical—performance of any music. You cannot say that the man did not practice what he preached.

It would be absurd to ask which of these two performances is the more authentic, or which is more faithful to Mozart's intentions. And the question would remain equally irrelevant and absurd had the renditions been played on fortepianos instead of modern grands. The difference between them is clearly an aesthetic and an ideological one, historical only to the extent that one exhibits a style of performance we take to be emblematic of nineteenth-century music making, while the other is obviously and wholly of the twentieth century. And we all know which of them lies closer to the norms of "authentistic" performance today.

Stravinsky's performance of Mozart's Fugue furnishes a perfect illustration of what Ortega y Gasset called a dehumanized art. The term was not meant to, nor should it, conjure up images of robots or of concentration camps. It meant an art purged of those "human, all too human" elements that to artists in the early twentieth century suggested ephemerality, inconstancy, mortality, in favor of abstract patterns and precisions suggesting transcendence of our muddy vesture of decay. Ortega's word "human," in this narrowly defined context, is once more a cognate to what Hulme had denoted by the word "vital." In his classic essay, "The Dehumanization of Art," first published in 1925, Ortega gave a startlingly complete and prescient

[71]*Contemplating Music*, 211.
[72]*Poetics*, 165.

description of the new twentieth-century aesthetic of what he felt the need pleonastically to dub "artistic art"—"an art for artists and not for the masses, for "quality" and not for hoi polloi."[73] It is a description that can be applied equally well to the performance style of new music seventy years ago and that of old music today. His description sounds many notes that have already been heard in our discussion so far: elitism, purism, insistence on scrupulous realization, and what Ortega calls "iconoclasm," that is, literally, the avoidance of iconicity and the kind of facile expressivity the latter often entails. He adds, and properly emphasizes, another dimension, though, one without which our discussion will never be complete. That is the element of demystification and irony. "The new style," he writes, "tends . . . to consider art as play and nothing else, . . . a thing of no transcending consequence."[74]

Beginning at least as far back as Hanslick, writers espousing a modern or anti-Romantic view of art have decried its abuse as an ersatz religion or narcosis. The fundamental mistake, on this view, was to confuse the idea of beauty—the legitimate domain of art, appealing, in Hanslick's words, to "the organ of pure contemplation, our *imagination*"[75]—with that of sublimity, formulated long ago by Longinus with respect to rhetoric, and associated by more recent writers with nature. The sublime consisted in "boldness and grandeur," and manifested itself in "the Pathetic, or power of raising the passions to a violent and even enthusiastic degree," in the words of William Smith, Longinus's eighteenth-century translator, for whom "enthusiasm" meant *intoxication*.[76] Eighteenth-century writers insisted on carefully distinguishing the sublime from the beautiful. For Edmund Burke they presented "a remarkable contrast," which he detailed as follows:

> Sublime objects are vast in their dimensions, beautiful ones comparatively small: beauty should be smooth and polished; the great is rugged and negligent . . . beauty should not be obscure; the great ought to be dark and gloomy: beauty should be light and delicate; the great ought to be solid and even massive. They are indeed ideas of a very different nature, one being founded on pain, the other on pleasure.[77]

---

[73]José Ortega y Gasset, *The Dehumanization of Art and Other Essays on Art, Culture and Literature*, trans. Helene Weyl (Princeton: Princeton University Press, 1968), 12.

[74]Ibid., 14.

[75]Hanslick, *The Beautiful in Music*, 11.

[76]Quoted in Peter le Huray and James Day, *Music and Aesthetics in the Eighteenth and Early-Nineteenth Centuries* (Cambridge: Cambridge University Press, 1981), 4.

[77]*A Philosophical Enquiry into the Origin of Our Ideas of the Sublime and the Beautiful* (1757), in Le Huray and Day, 70–71.

The history of music in the nineteenth century could be written in terms of the encroachment of the sublime upon the domain of the beautiful—of the "great" upon the pleasant—to the point where for some, with Wagner at their head, the former all but superseded the latter as the defining attribute of the art of tones. Not only that, but for Wagner, who more than any other musician invested his art with aspects of redemptive and ecstatic religion, the sublime was associated particularly with the fluctuant, dynamic aspects of his music—its waxing and waning, its harmonic fluidity, its oceanic, infinitely evolving *forma formans*—and its power and appeal, fundamentally wild and irrational, lay precisely in its "pathetic," intoxicant, and psychically contagious properties. All of this was profoundly repugnant to the early generation of modernists whose thought we have been dissecting. Ortega, speaking on their behalf, proclaimed that "art must not proceed by psychic contagion, for psychic contagion is an unconscious phenomenon, and art ought to be full clarity, high noon of the intellect." And, "aesthetic pleasure must be a seeing pleasure; for pleasures may be blind or seeing."[78] One thinks of Freud's famous dictum on the goal of psychoanalysis: "Where id was, there ego shall be."

It became a mission for twentieth-century artists to restore the distinction between bright, wide-awake beauty and blind, irrational sublimity, to reserve the former for art, and to give the latter back to life, nature, and religion. In this way neither art nor life would be degraded. Proponents of "die neue Sachlichkeit"—the "new actuality"—attacked the vaunted autonomy of the art work, along with the philosophy that put the creator and his personality at its centre. It is significant that theorists of the new actuality insist once again on the primacy of the ontological over the psychological, and emphasize (here we have perhaps a lingering echo of Futurism) quickness of tempo and mechanical uniformity of movement. Thus Boris Asafiev:

> Contemporary life, with its concentration of experience, its capricious rhythms, its cinematographic quality, its madly fast pace—the quality of this life has weaned us away from slow and leisurely contemplation. . . . [In] the field of music . . . responses can be seen in the striving for severity of construction, for clarity of writing, for concentration of the greatest tension within the shortest possible time, for the attainment of the greatest expression with the most economical expenditure of performing forces. As a result, there is a growing contrast in contemporary music between works built on the principle of maximum concentration, economy, and conciseness, and those which dispose their materials in breadth and employ the largest possible number of performers.

[78]Ortega, "*The Dehumanization of Art*," 27.

The former are notable for emotional and formal conciseness, for intensity of expression. . . . Emotional outpourings and formal breadth characterize the latter. . . . In the first case, the music asserts the dynamics of life; in the second it is ruled by an emotional hypnosis and a sterile hedonism. It is natural, therefore, that the new chamber music should have chosen the first style. . . . It has been unavoidably influenced by the impetuous current of our lives with its resilient rhythms, its flying tempi, and its subordination to the pulse of work. . . . The new chamber style is nearer to the street than to the salon, nearer to the life of public actuality than to that of philosophical seclusion. . . . Its style is essentially dynamic, for it is rooted in the sensations of contemporary life and culture and not merely in personal sentiments and emotions. Its style is energetic, active, and actual, and not reflectively romantic.[79]

This vivid description of an art debunked and off its pedestal was made in connection with Hindemith and Stravinsky.[80] How well it applies not only to twentieth-century composition, but to twentieth-century performance, will be evident if we return for a moment to the recordings of the Fifth Brandenburg Concerto we considered a while ago. The Furtwängler reading can be well described by invoking all the adjectives Burke associated with the sublime: vast, great, rugged, negligent, obscure, solid, massive. It exemplifies Asafiev's categories of slow and leisurely contemplation, emotional hypnosis, and formal breadth. The more recent the later performances, the more closely they conform to the attributes of Asafiev's "new chamber style": resilient rhythms, flying tempi, energy, activity, actuality, clarity, concision, the absence of subjective reflection. The metronome tells part of the story. Every performance described thus far has been as fast or faster than the last (figures give approximate metronome mark for a quarter note):

Furtwängler	c. 72
Stokowski	c. 84
Busch	c. 88
Reiner	c. 94
Collegium Aureum	c. 94
Pinnock	c. 96
Hogwood	c. 98

In addition, the performances grew progressively lighter and more buoyant: from a full symphonic string complement plus soloists (Furtwängler) to a mere half dozen players (Hogwood). Furtwängler

[79]Boris Asafiev, *A Book about Stravinsky* (1926), trans. Richard F. French (Ann Arbor: UMI Research Press, 1982), 97–99. Translation slightly adjusted in accordance with the original (Leningrad: Triton, 1929).

[80]The paragraph cited from *A Book about Stravinsky* had originally appeared in the Leningrad journal *Novaia muzyka*, in an article called "The New Chamber Style."

sought to invest the work with an imposing gravity—an importance, in short—of which modern performers have sought just as deliberately to divest it. After Hogwood's rendition, at once the lightest and the quickest, the piece seems ready virtually to blow away, or in Marx's phrase to melt into air.

And with this lightening, both material and spiritual, comes the element of irony, what Ortega called the "ban on all pathos" that inevitably arises as a "first consequence of the retreat of art upon itself." He even goes so far as to say "the modern inspiration . . . is invariably waggish." That may have been going too far, and Ortega immediately retreats a bit: "It is not that the content of the work is comical—that would mean a relapse into a mode or species of the "human" style—but that, whatever the content, the art itself is jesting. To look for fiction *as* fiction—which . . . modern art does—is a proposition that cannot be executed except with one's tongue in one's cheek."[81]

I believe this to be true both of modern creation and modern performance, but to avoid the potential misunderstanding to which Ortega calls attention, I would prefer to view modern irony not as a crisis of seriousness, but as a crisis of sincerity, of speaking truly and in one's own voice. So pervasive has this crisis become for music that a book has been devoted to it, which opens with a very provocative question:

> Music is a language. Such, at least, is the implicit assumption, if not the explicit assertion, of many who talk and write about it. . . . For we are told that music has meaning, although no two authorities seem able to agree on what that meaning is. There is consequently a great deal of discussion concerning just what music says and how, indeed, it can say anything. But in all this argument one question is seldom, if ever, asked: If music is a language, then who is speaking?[82]

This is a question, I submit, that could only have occurred to a musician in the twentieth century. Put to any premodern composer, it would have elicited an unhesitating, if unreflective (and philosophically perhaps untenable) reply: "Why, I am, of course!" And many performers would claim as much, too. The composer Schumann even allowed of the performer Liszt that his art was "not this or that style of pianoforte playing; it is rather the outward expression of a daring character."[83] Asked among the modernists, however, Cone's question

[81]Ortega, The Dehumanization of Art, 47.

[82]Edward T. Cone, *The Composer's Voice* (Berkeley and Los Angeles: University of California Press, 1974), 1.

[83]Quoted in Irving Kolodin (ed.), *The Composer as Listener* (New York: Collier Books, 1962), 262.

would produce a chorus akin to that elicited by the Little Red Hen: "'Not I,' said the composer; 'Not I,' said the performer." When art turns back on itself and its human content is denied, there is nothing left to express, as Stravinsky put it so bluntly in his autobiography. After the famous fighting words to the effect that "music, by its very nature, is essentially powerless to *express* anything at all," Stravinsky tried somewhat less successfully to formulate an alternative. Though a murky passage, its preoccupations are clear enough, and familiar: it takes us right back to the ontology of time, and to the idea that the content of art is its form.

> The phenomenon of music is given to us with the sole purpose of establishing an order in things, including, and particularly, the co-ordination between *man* and *time*. To be put into practice, its indispensable and single requirement is construction. Construction once completed, this order has been attained, and there is nothing more to be said.[84]

To ask "who is speaking," then, is to propound an irrelevancy, for it presupposes the existence of a speaker, a ghost in the machine. To the proponent of a dehumanized, geometricized art, literally no one is speaking. There is, I would suggest, no aspect of today's authentistic performance practice more pertinent to twentieth-century aesthetics, and none harder to justify on historical grounds, than its ambience of emotional detachment, its distancing of voice from utterance. This is easiest to observe, of course, when actual voices are present, singing words that possess an emotive import that has been embodied in the music. To a vitalist performer such as Otto Klemperer, for example, the Crucifixus of the B minor Mass is a statement about a matter of great human concern, emotionally intensified by Bach's rhetoric of chromaticism, dissonance, and melodic descent. Bach speaks of Christ's suffering and death, and the performers, identifying with Bach and Christ alike, speak directly to the listener out of their experience both lived and musical (Appendix, Recording No. 5a). To a modernist like Johannes Martini (Appendix, Recording No. 5b) the Crucifixus is a musical construction, some elements of which have generic semantic connotations—e.g., the tetrachordal ground bass[85]—and for that very reason may "speak for themselves," independent of the composer, who has not created but merely chosen them and set them in motion, and—needless to say—without any assistance from the executants.

---

[84]Stravinsky, *An Autobiography* (New York: W. W. Norton, 1962), 54.
[85]Cf. Ellen Rosand, "The Descending Tetrachord: An Emblem of Lament," *Musical Quarterly* 65 (1979): 346–59.

The exceedingly lightweight sonority and quick tempo of Martini's recording further serve the modernist aim of emotional distancing. I am quite convinced that this performance would have occasioned bewilderment on the part of any musician brought up with the doctrine of the affections. Such a musician would indeed have found it waggish. It comes, of course, from an album that advertises its fidelity to historical performance practice. That "performance practice" and expression can be divorced like this is a perfect symptom of modernist irony, and amply confirms Ortega's contention that to modern artists art is "a thing of no consequence."

If there is a historical resonance here, it is with something remoter than Bach and alien to him: we are transported back to the castle at Urbino, where Castiglione's courtiers sat discussing *sprezzatura*, that "certain noble negligence in singing," that marks the true aristocrat.[86] These sentiments found echo once again at the high tide of the Enlightenment, when Bach had been forgotten. Burney assures us that "music is an innocent luxury, unnecessary indeed, to our existence, but a great improvement and gratification of the sense of hearing";[87] while for Kant, it "merely plays with sensations."[88] Modernism has been a new Enlightenment, reacting to the Romantic as its predecessor had reacted to the Baroque. Virgil Thomson echoed Burney and Kant when, voicing what he made bold to call "the only twentieth-century musical aesthetic in the Western world," he asserted that "the only healthy thing music can do in our century is to stop trying to be impressive."[89] And in an introduction to one of Thomson's books, Nicolas Nabokov sounded off in a similar vein, at the top of his lungs:

> In order to become meaningful again music must rid itself of nineteenth-century habits, the clutches of historicism, and its immortality machine. Music should get itself defrocked like present-day priests and nuns who want to serve their community and enjoy life. It should forget

[86]Cf. Baldesar Castiglione, *The Book of the Courtier (Il Libro del cortegiano*, 1528), trans. Charles S. Singleton (Garden City, NY: Doubleday, 1959), 104. The phrase quoted in the text is from Giulio Caccini's *Nuove musiche* of 1601, trans. Piero Weiss, in Piero Weiss and Richard Taruskin (eds.), *Music in the Western World: A History in Documents* (New York: Schirmer Books, 1984), 170. Ultimately the Italian Renaissance insistence on aristocratic detachment derives from Aristotle, who in the *Politics* (Book 8) cautioned that too enthusiastic an involvement with musical performance compromises the status of a "free man."

[87]Charles Burney, *A General History of Music* (1776), ed. Frank Mercer (New York: Dover Books, 1957), vol. 1, 21.

[88]Immanuel Kant, *Critique of Judgment* (1790), trans, J. H. Bernard (New York: Hafner Press, 1951), 171.

[89]Virgil Thomson, "French Music Here" (1941), in *A Virgil Thomson Reader* (New York: Houghton Mifflin, 1981), 207.

about its nineteenth-century "beatification" (foretold by Goethe and accomplished by Wagner). The composer should stop being a public idol like a TV singer or a cinema actor. He should be again a juggler, a gamester, a trickster, and use all the newly developed techniques for his tricks and games. He should not compose for eternity, but for fleeting occasions and for the fun of it. He should then let his work disappear in Lethe, just as the thousands of seventeenth- and eighteenth-century operas, cantatas, and oratorios have fortunately disappeared. Only musicologists regret their absence.[90]

Surely many if not most of our recorded examples have already illustrated the applicability of these dicta to authentistic performance, and may begin to suggest a reason for the movement's burgeoning commercial success. The art works of the past, even as they are purportedly restored to their pristine sonic condition, are concomitantly devalued, decanonized, not quite taken seriously, reduced to sensuous play. And as the thousands of ephemerae at which Nabokov sneered have been resurrected, the classics of the repertory have been made to recede into their midst. Adorno decried this a generation ago, when he complained of the leveling tendency of what he called "objectivist" performances of Bach. "They say Bach, mean Telemann," he thundered at their perpetrators, accusing them of a blind refusal to recognize that "Bach's music is separated from the general level of his age by an astronomical distance."[91] Authentistic performers do seem determined to close this gap, which, if I may say it without necessarily embracing Adorno's moral indignation, testifies rather conclusively to their modernity.

Indeed, in pursuit of this goal they can go to lengths nowadays such as Adorno never dreamed of. Hogwood's text for the Fifth Brandenburg, for example, is not the standard, canonical one. His recording has sought to restore what is billed on the album as the *Urfassung*, the original version of the set, bringing with it a promise of hitherto unprecedented "authenticity." In practical terms this meant that the concerti were performed not from the text preserved in Bach's famous fair copy dedicated to the Margrave of Brandenburg, but from variant texts preserved in various manuscripts copied in Leipzig after Bach's death, which, to quote Mr. Hogwood's notes, "reveal the earlier forms of the Brandenburg Concertos." By subtle and (in my opinion) devious arguments, the authority of these miscellaneous secondary sources is elevated above that of the fair copy, "which carries a specious authority stemming more from its Dedication and calligraphy than from its value as source material." The two concertos that differ the most

[90]Nicolas Nabokov, "Twentieth-Century Makers of Music," Introduction to Virgil Thomson, *American Music Since 1910* (New York: Holt Rinehart Winston, 1971), xv.
[91]"Bach Defended against his Devotees," 145.

under this dispensation from their canonical forms are the First and the Fifth. Mr. Hogwood waxes positively indignant at the poor taste and opportunism that impelled Bach to revise them:

> His desire to impress the Margrave with variety above all is apparent, alarmingly in Concerto 1 where the revised version adds a new *concertante* third movement for the *violino piccolo* to a work that opens with a strongly *ripieno* movement; and in Concerto 5, where a harpsichord episode of nineteen bars is inflated out of all proportion to produce what is currently mistermed a "cadenza" of sixty-five bars.[92]

Let us recall Stravinsky's strictures, quoted above, about the "seductions of variety." In his recording, Mr. Hogwood has rectified Bach's lapse by reinstating the original nineteen-bar solo. Let me suggest that this conglomeration of shallow fireworks and harmonic barbarities, however "in proportion," and however it may conform to the performer's idea of the stylistic norms of its day, is poor music by any standard, and that by replacing it Bach judged it so. As a snapshot of Bach the improviser, it has its human interest to be sure, but it is unfinished composition at best. It is amusing to hear it as a once-only curio, but to offer it as a viable substitute for what Bach offered as representative of his best and most fully elaborated work is manifestly to devalue both that work and the critical sensibility that impelled its revision. Bach is indeed reduced here to the level of Nabokov's transitory gamester and trickster, as is Beethoven in Hogwood's "rhythmical, uncomplicated" renditions. And if I am not succeeding in keeping my indignation at bay, it is because I see here the ultimate perversion of the idea of authenticity: the elevation of what amounts to a rejected draft to the status of a viable alternative—and even a preferable one—because it is earlier, more in keeping with ex post facto historical generalizations, and less demanding on the listener. The utter spuriousness of the ploy is revealed in the fact that Hogwood's collection of early drafts is nonetheless being marketed as a rendition—and a particularly authentic one—of "The Brandenburg Concertos," a designation that has meaning only in conjunction with the canonical six in the calligraphic fair copy with dedication.

But even those less offended than I will have to agree that the immoderate reverence for the canon exemplified by Furtwängler and Schoenberg has been replaced by an equally immoderate irony. By being rendered so much less impressive than Furtwängler's, Hogwood's Bach is rendered correspondingly more modern.

[92]Notes to Oiseau-Lyre 414 187–1 (Bach: Brandenburg Concertos 1–6).

IV

To sum up the argument thus far, I hold that discussions of authentistic performance typically proceed from false premises. The split that is usually drawn between "modern performance" on the one hand and "historical performance" on the other is quite topsy-turvy. It is the latter that is truly modern performance—or rather, if you like, the avant-garde wing or cutting edge of modern performance—while the former represents the progressively weakening survival of an earlier style, inherited from the nineteenth century, one that is fast becoming historical. The difference between the two, as far as I can see, is best couched in terms borrowed from T. E. Hulme: nineteenth-century "vital" versus twentieth-century "geometrical." In light of this definition, modern performance, in the sense I use the term, can be seen as modernist performance, and its conceptual and aesthetic congruence with other manifestations of musical modernism stand revealed. What Carl Dahlhaus calls the "postulate of originality" and defines as "the dominant esthetic of [Wagner's] day" is still with us even if Wagner is not, and still decrees that music, both as to the style of its composition and the style of its performance "should be novel in order to rank as authentic."[93] When this is understood, it will appear no longer paradoxical but, on the contrary, very much in the nature of things that the same critics who can be counted upon predictably to tout the latterday representatives of High Modernism in music—Carter, Xenakis, Boulez—and who stand ready zealously to defend them against the vulgarian incursions of various so-called postmodernist trends, are the very ones most intransigently committed, as we have already observed, to the use of "original instruments" and all the rest of the "historical" paraphernalia. For we have become prevaricators and no longer call novelty by its right name.

But if the natural alliance between high modernism and authentistic performance can be thus readily discerned today, in the period of the senescence and decline of the former (and—who knows?—possibly the latter as well), it is just as conspicuous at the other end of their dual history, when both movements were in their fledgling years. Back in 1914 Ezra Pound wrote this:

> I have seen the god Pan and it was in this manner: I heard a bewildering and pervasive music moving from precision to precision within itself. Then I heard a different music, hollow and laughing. Then I looked up and saw two eyes like the eyes of a wood-creature peering at me over a brown piece of wood. Then someone said: Yes, once I was playing a fiddle in the forest and I walked into a wasps' nest.

[93]*The New Grove Wagner* (London: Macmillan, 1984), 104.

Comparing these things with what I can read of the Earliest and best authenticated appearances of Pan, I can but conclude that they relate to similar occurrences. It is true that I found myself later in a room covered with pictures of what we now call ancient instruments, and that when I picked up the brown tube of wood I found that it had ivory rings upon it. And no proper reed has ivory rings on it, by nature. Also, they told me it was a "recorder," whatever that is.[94]

It is the beginning of an essay entitled "Arnold Dolmetsch," which goes on to adumbrate very nearly every point I have been making about authentistic performance and the modern aesthetic. Here are a few more passages:

> This is the whole flaw of impressionist or "emotional" music as opposed to pattern music. It is like a drug: you must have more drug, and more noise each time, or this effect, this impression which works from the outside, in from the nerves and sensorium upon the self—is no use, its effect is constantly weaker and weaker. . . .

> The early music starts with the mystery of pattern; if you like, with the vortex of pattern; with something which is, first of all, music, and which is capable of being, after that, many things. What I call emotional, or impressionist music, starts with being emotion or impression and then becomes only approximately music. . . .

> As I believe that [Wyndham] Lewis and Picasso are capable of revitalizing the instinct of design so I believe that a return, an awakening to the possibilities, not necessarily of "Old" music, but of pattern music played on ancient instruments, is, perhaps, able to make music again a part of life, not merely a part of theatricals. The musician, the performing musician as distinct from the composer, might again be an interesting person, an artist, not merely a sort of manual saltimbanque or a stage hypnotist. It is, perhaps, a question of whether you want music, or whether you want to see an obsessed personality trying to "dominate" an audience. . . . It is music that exists for the sake of being music, not for the sake of, as they say, producing an impression.
>
> They tell me "everyone knows Dolmetsch who knows of old music, but not many people know of it." . . . Why is it that the fine things always seem to go on in a corner? Is it a judgment on democracy? Is it that what has once been the pleasure of the many, of the pre-Cromwellian many, has been permanently swept out of life? . . . Is it that the aristocracy, which ought to set the fashion, is too weakened and too unreal to perform the due functions of "aristocracy"? . . . Is it that real democracy can only exist under feudal conditions, when no man fears to recognize creative skill in his neighbor?[95]

---

[94]*Literary Essays of Ezra Pound*, ed. T. S. Eliot (New York: New Directions, 1968), 431.

[95]Ibid., 434–36.

It is all here: hatred of the revolution and the mob, the avoidance of living forms, the purity of art, art as scrupulous play of pattern, as wide-awake precision, as reflector of life as socially experienced. And over all, the twinkling ironic eye of Pan. Ortega, who knew not Dolmetsch, invoked the wood god, too: "The symbol of art is seen again in the magic flute of the Great God Pan which makes the young goats frisk at the edge of the grove. All modern art begins to appear comprehensible and in a way great when it is interpreted as an attempt to instill youthfulness into an ancient world."[96] And so, at its best, does authentistic performance.

An interest in "Early Music," meaning anything earlier than the Viennese classics, was taken as a sign of avant-gardism in Stravinsky's youth, something regarded with suspicion by more conservative artists, Stravinsky's teacher among them. Rimsky-Korsakov's diary for 9 March 1904 contains the following entry:

> This evening, together with Glazunov, I listened to the Johannes Passion [of Bach] at the Lutheran Church. Beautiful music, but it is music of an altogether different age and to sit through an entire oratorio at the present time is impossible. I am convinced that not only I, but everyone is bored, and if they say they enjoyed it then they're just lying through their teeth.[97]

Landowska was fond of quoting Eugen d'Albert's preface to his turn-of-the-century edition of the *Well-Tempered Clavier*: "I know there are people who can listen for hours to [Bach's] cantatas without showing any apparent boredom. These people are either hypocrites or pedants."[98] Those of us who know better than to be seduced by such quotations into a complacent sense of our own superiority to Rimsky-Korsakov and d'Albert will likely agree that Bach's lack of headway among such eminent musicians must have had something to do with the relationship between the kind of performances he was getting then and the expectations of his hearers. The fact that Bach's music has made such a fantastic, unprecedented headway in the ninety or so years since then obviously has to do with changes both in the performances and in the expectations. In light of such reflections, consider now the candid reaction of an ideally competent and sensitive listener to a recent performance of the St. Matthew Passion that was billed as a historical reconstruction of the work (as it happens, very much along the lines proposed by Stravinsky half a century ago):

[96]Ortega, "The Dehumanization of Art," 50.

[97]Mark Yankovsky *et al.* (eds.), *Rimskii-Korsakov: Issledovaniia, materialy, pis'ma* (Moscow: Izdatel'stvo Akademii nauk SSSR, 1954), vol. 2, 16–17.

[98]Quoted in *Landowska On Music*, 85.

> Since my early teens I have heard many renditions of Bach's *St Matthew Passion*, covering the full spectrum of twentieth-century performance practice, from traditional versions with enormous choirs and piano continuo through various realizations according to the ever-changing notions of "authenticity," and I have never failed to be intensely moved by this work. But, in every earlier performance I always found the piece long and heavy, and, in spite of the frequent cuts in the traditional performances, my reserves of concentration were sooner or later exhausted. In the uncut Bach Ensemble version I found myself for the first time totally involved to the very end, and I left the performance without the sense that the piece was overly long.[99]

The review goes on to emphasize many of the points we have dwelt upon in the present discussion: energetic tempi, clarity of texture, buoyant sonorities vouchsafed by small but variegated performing forces. These qualities would have been appreciated by Rimsky-Korsakov, too, who complained in his diary that it all sounded alike, that the choral writing was clumsy, that the tone color was uniform owing to "this incessant organ," and so on, all of which prevented the music from making an effect comparable to what he called "*our* music—a free music, music that plays with a succession of varied moods, music that employs all the most varied technical means, music that flows in varied and interesting forms."[100]

What can all this mean, except that in modern performances, including those modernistic ones I call authentistic, modern audiences have been discovering a Bach they *can* call their own—or, in other words, that Bach has at last been adapted with unprecedented success to modern taste. Our authentistic performers, whatever they may say or think they are doing, have begun to accomplish for the twentieth century what Mendelssohn *et al.* had accomplished for the nineteenth. They are reinterpreting Bach for their own time—that is, for our time—the way all deathless texts must be reinterpreted if they are in fact to remain deathless and exempt from what familiarity breeds.

That is why I wish to register my complete dissent from the usual gloomy diagnosis of the twentieth-century cultural impasse that the "authenticity movement" supposedly reveals. We have got our purposes, all right, and our stylistic preferences, and they are well and truly represented—authentically represented!—in our performances of music of all ages. This was quite dramatically illustrated at that

[99]Alexander Silbiger, "Conference Report: Johann Sebastian Bach: 300th Anniversary Celebration," *Journal of Musicology*, 4 (1985–86): 119.
[100]*Rimskii-Korsakov: Issledovaniia*, 17.

much-touted Battle of the Bands in September 1984, when the Chamber Music Society of Lincoln Center and the Academy of Ancient Music faced off on the stage of Alice Tully Hall. It was—despite the advance publicity and the differences in the ways Messrs. Cooper and Hogwood expressed themselves at intermission time—by no means the expected case of the Schleps vs. the Prigs. One heard dash and vigor from the British fiddles, and poise and clarity in the New Yorkers' playing. Both groups started their trills from above and neither eschewed string vibrato. Simon Standage played with the panache of the Galamian pupil he is, and Kenneth Cooper brought down the house with the unforgettable glitter and drive of his splendiferously embellished Fifth Brandenburg (replete with sixty-five bar "cadenza"). This was first-rate modern Bach from all hands. All of it was fleet, buoyant, and eminently geometrical. And it was not simply a matter of "convergence," nor one of the "mainstream" aping the "historians." The geometrical Bach, as we now know, was in place before the "historians" ever began to ply their wares.

So why all the bloodshed and recriminations? Why not simply recognize our modern Bach for what he is, and stop the nonsense about authenticity? As I see it, there are three reasons: (1) some enduring Dolmetsch-inspired mythology, (2) the belated intervention of positivist musicology, and (3) the ideology of our museum culture.

As Pound observed, Arnold Dolmetsch began his pioneering work "in a corner," and stayed there all his life. Though a muckraking critic like Shaw might, as we would now say, co-opt him as a stick with which to beat the Establishment,[101] the professional musicians of his day by and large wrote Dolmetsch off as a rustic crank. Unlike Landowska, who was only vaguely aware of him, Dolmetsch never toured the world. He was a local phenomenon, and once removed to Haslemere an isolated one. Nor was the level of his performance, or his family's, of a technical quality that could effectively challenge the musicians of the mainstream. Thus Dolmetsch and the musicians of his age stood as it were back to back; and as his life went on he adopted more and more the embattled and embittered tone of a voice crying in the wilderness—a tone that has remained characteristic of many of his heirs. In the Introduction to his magnum opus, *The Interpretation of the Music of the Seventeenth and Eighteenth Centuries,* published in 1915, Dolmetsch inveighed against the "prejudice and preconceived ideas" of "intolerant modernity." What he meant by modernity, however, was the musical world on which he had turned his back in the

---

[101]See Shaw's reviews of Dolmetsch's historical concerts in the early 1890s, collected in Bernard Shaw, *Music in London 1890–94* (New York: Vienna House, 1973), vols. 2 and 3, *passim.*

1880s, still preserved in aspic by Furtwängler in 1950. That world could indeed be characterized as a monolithic mainstream. Even by 1915, though, it had changed into a divided world, one faction of which (though probably unbeknown to Dolmetsch) was growing quite receptive to his message.

Or was it? From what we can gather from this very book, from Dolmetsch's attitudes toward "original instruments,"[102] and from the handful of recordings he made near the end of his life, it appears that Pound might have, as the saying lately goes, creatively misread the subject of his fascinating essay of 1914. Where Pound waxed enthusiastic over pattern and precision, Dolmetsch emphasized "what the Old Masters *felt* about their own music, what impressions they wished to convey, and, generally, what was the *Spirit of their Art*," and he purported to "show how erroneous is the idea, still entertained by some, that expression is a modern thing, and that the old music requires nothing beyond mechanical precision."[103] Dolmetsch's use of the word "modern" here is already a symptom of the confusion he has sown. But more to the point, it transpires that he was still a musician whom we might call an idealist and a vitalist, and he played little or no role in establishing the modernist style of performance that sustains early music playing today.

But be all that as it may, Dolmetsch bequeathed a mythology, to which many still unreflectingly subscribe, that cast a hated "present" that even by the time of its casting was receding into the past, against a "past" that was actually a constructed dogmatic fiction created in the present—for surely I need remind no one how many of the tenets of Dolmetsch's "historical style" (his overdotting, for one thing) have been seriously modified and in some cases overturned by subsequent research.

Meanwhile a seismic shift in musical sensibilities, brought on by the advent of modernism, was effecting a change in performance style for all music. It did not happen overnight, but after a couple of generations, say by the middle of the twentieth century, it was done. Anyone who still adheres to the division "modern" style versus "historical" style, then, is implicitly taking Furtwängler's Bach for the norm; which is to say, he is still living with Dolmetsch in the 1880s, a good century behind the times.

Now it was just around the time that the shift to what I call authentically modern performance was completed that academic

---

[102]See the account of Dolmetsch's harpsichord by Robert Donington, quoted by Laurence Dreyfus in "Early Music Defended against its Devotees: A Theory of Historical Performance in the Twentieth Century," *Musical Quarterly* 69 (1983): 305–6.

[103]Arnold Dolmetsch, *The Interpretation of the Music of the Seventeenth and Eighteenth Centuries* (London, 1915; 2nd edn. 1946; repr. 1969), xiii (italics original).

musicologists began turning their attention in a conspicuous way to performance practice. This can be viewed as part of a larger picture, the modernist takeover of the universities. In academic music studies, it was the heyday of logical positivism, symbolized, if you will, by the Princeton music department, which in the 1950s and 1960s was presided over by Milton Babbitt in composition and theory, and by Arthur Mendel in musicology.[104] Mendel (1905–79) had started his musical career in the 1920s as a composition pupil of Nadia Boulanger. In the 1930s he had been a prominent critic of new music (for the *Nation, Modern Music,* etc.). In the 1940s he was a choral conductor specializing in the music of Schütz and Bach. It is not surprising, given his background, that when he became an academic musicologist he should have made performance practice his speciality. He was among the earliest to do so; since his time, the number of such scholars has become legion.

Performance research as Mendel practiced it was a vastly different kind of enterprise from what it had been with Dolmetsch or Landowska. Positivist scholarship is interested in letter, not spirit. It sets up research experiments—"problems"—to be solved by applying rules of logic and evidence, the goal being avowedly to determine "What was done," not "What is to be done," let alone "How to do it." Direct application to actual performance is not the primary aim of such studies. They are not "utilitarian" but "pure research." Howard Mayer Brown has accurately characterized the nature of such scholarship when he insists upon the "dispassionate" suspension of "personal commitment" in the quest for a truth that ultimately represents—in the words of Leopold von Ranke, the father of *Historismus*—"the way it really was" (*wie es eigentlich gewesen*).[105] A perfect example of positivistic historicism in the realm of performance practice is Mendel's classic article, "Some Ambiguities of the Mensural System," which questions the prescriptive tempo relationships that have been established by modern editors in a wide range of fifteenth- and sixteenth-century music, demonstrates that contemporary theorists disagreed too often to be trusted uncritically, and ends with fully seven closely packed pages detailing dozens of individual unsolved problems in need of attack by future inductive research. The list is preceded by a more general prospectus that merits quoting at some length:

> What is needed, it seems to me, is not more articles advocating this or
> that interpretation of this or that theorist, or of a group of theorists

[104]For stimulating, partly autobiographical, reflections on this phase of academic music study and its consequences, see chap. 2 ("Musicology and Positivism: the Postwar Years") of Kerman, *Contemplating Music.*
[105]"Pedantry or Liberation," 39, 54.

arbitrarily selected, but rather an orderly method of gathering and sorting evidence from both the theorists and (particularly) the music itself. We do not know for most composers how consistent they were in their own mensural practice. We do not know what degree of consistency may have been imposed by publishers or copyists on different composers. We need to gather evidence of the mensural practice of each of the principal composers, each of the principal publishers, perhaps each of the principal anthologies.[106]

In one sense this agnosticism is quite salutary. It dismantles the historiographical dogmas of the Dolmetsches, and throws some cold light on their rejection of the unloved specious "present." But as Howard Mayer Brown has pointed out (tongue, one trusts, in cheek), a performer "seems to need the psychological protection of actually believing in what he is doing."[107] He cannot settle for a survey of the problem, he must, by performing, propose a solution. A performance simply cannot merely reflect the sketchy state of objective knowledge on a point of performance practice, it must proceed from the conviction that a full working knowledge is in the performers' (subjective) possession. While generations of scholars chew over Mendel's seven pages of problems, what is the poor performer who wants to sing some Josquin des Prez to do? Wait till all the evidence is in and all the articles are published? He will probably never open his mouth. Rejoice that the answers have not been found and he is free to do as he likes? That is certainly one possibility—but he who would do so risks rebuke from scholars whose implicit attitude seems to be, "Shut up until we can tell you what to do." This kind of destructive authoritarianism is rampant in reviews of performances of Medieval and Renaissance music, where just about any performance at all is open to the charge of "mixing . . . musicology and make-believe,"[108] if that is the kind of tack the reviewer wishes to take. Professor Mendel himself, sad to say, made a habit of giving performers, in Grout's words quoted earlier, a "bad conscience" about what they were doing, by challenging them to justify it on hard evidence. He presided over a terrifying workshop at the Josquin Festival Conference in 1971 on the performance of Josquin's Masses,[109] and used the positivistic inductive method as a veritable stick to beat modern performers. No matter

---

[106]Arthur Mendel, "Some Ambiguities of the Mensural System," in Harold Powers (ed.), *Studies in Music History: Essays for Oliver Strunk* (Princeton, NJ: Princeton University Press, 1968), 153.

[107]"Pedantry or Liberation," 55.

[108]David Hiley, record review in *Early Music*, 13 (1985): 597.

[109]A heavily edited transcript is available in Edward Lowinsky, in collaboration with Bonnie J. Blackburn (eds.), *Josquin des Prez* (London: Oxford University Press, 1976), 696–719.

what they did, Professor Mendel could find some theorist or source to say them nay. Nor can I ever forget the time Professor Mendel traveled up to New York to hear Nikolaus Harnoncourt lecture at Columbia about his ideas on Bach performance. The professor played the grand inquisitor: "But Mr. Harnoncourt, do you *know* that's true?" he intoned again and again. Mr. Harnoncourt could only splutter.

That is not the way. Joseph Kerman has chided me for "perpetuat[ing] old-fashioned stereotypes" of the musicologist *versus* the performer in essay 1.[110] I would like to think them outmoded, too, and as more scholars perform and more performers "schol," perhaps one day they will be. But the specter of Arthur Mendel continues to dance before me, and I feel we must still keep our guard up against holding the performer, as I put it there, "to the same strict standards of accountability we rightly demand of any scholar." For performers cannot realistically concern themselves with *wie es eigentlich gewesen*. Their job is to discover, if they are lucky, *wie es eigentlich uns gefällt*—how we really like it.

Really talented performers are always curious, and curious performers will always find what they need in the sources and theorists—what they need being ways of enriching and enlivening what they do. I have saved for discussion till now my favorite recording of the Fifth Brandenburg Concerto, the one directed by Gustav Leonhardt, recorded in Holland in 1976 (Appendix, Recording No. 2*h*). When discussing Edward Cone's model of Baroque performance practice, I observed that where he speaks of beat, musicians of the period invariably spoke of meter. Taking this aspect of historical evidence seriously has been the special distinction of the Dutch and Belgian Early Music performers of the last couple of decades. Their efforts have occasionally met with scorn, and in truth, when applied literalistically, their zealous downbeat-bashing can turn into self-parody. But applied with discretion and wit, what a lilt due attention to meter can impart! Leonhardt's performance is still squarely within the domain of the geometrical, as we have defined it, and in tempo it is on a par with Pinnock, who "placed" in our previous sampling at ♩ = 96. But the larger metrical units and the broader pulses lend a hint of iconicity to the performance—a sense of human gait. Hardnosed modernism here relaxes a bit, as well it might, its battle long since won. Leonhardt's recording also demonstrates the joyful results of thoroughly passionate and committed experiment with original instruments. His players have truly understood what, in essay 2, I described as the inestimable and indispensable heuristic value of the old instruments in freeing minds and hands to experience old music newly.

[110]*Contemplating Music*, 203.

What the result of such liberation will be, however, is unpredictable; and to presume that the use of historical instruments guarantees a historical result is simply preposterous.

Just how preposterous we can judge by comparing Leonhardt's recording with the recent one by the equally authentic Concentus Musicus under Harnoncourt (Appendix, Recording No. 2*i*). We will not have heard such a tempo since Stokowski's, nor nuances such as these since Furtwängler. It is vitalism redux. Nikolaus Harnoncourt shared with Leonhardt the Dutch government's Erasmus Prize in 1980 for their re-creations of Baroque music. Clearly, though, if one of them should happen to be re-creating the music of the Baroque, the other is baying at the moon. And if we think we know who is doing which, it is because we have accepted an authority, not because we are in possession of the truth. It is a fair guess that most Early Music connoisseurs today will side with Leonhardt in the matter of verisimilitude, and look upon Harnoncourt as a rebel. And in a way they would be right. Leonhardt's performance is well within the accepted canons of modernism, while Harnoncourt's is a challenge to them, not unlike the challenge lately issued by the so-called neoromantics to modernist canons of composition. We are in the midst of what may yet be another major shift in aesthetic and cultural values, and the fact that "Early Music" is reflecting it testifies to its vitality and its cultural authenticity.

As long as we speak of re-creations we can accept this kind of pluralism with equanimity and tolerance—which need not mean, of course, without a preference. It is when we talk about restoration that the trouble begins, and "authenticity" turns ugly.

Ever since we have had a concept of "classical" music we have implicitly regarded our musical institutions as museums and our performers as curators.[111] Curators do not own the artifacts in their charge. They are not free to dispose and use up at pleasure. They are caretakers, pledged to preserve them intact. Hence the negative value that lately attaches to the word "transcription." It has acquired a specious ring of vandalism, even forgery.

And hence the magical aura that has attached, in the minds of many, to "original instruments"; for they are artifacts as concretely,

[111]For illuminating reflections on this theme, see three articles by William Weber: "Mass Culture and the Reshaping of European Musical Taste," *International Review of the Aesthetics and Sociology of Music*, 8 (1977): 5–21; "The Contemporaneity of Eighteenth-Century Musical Taste," *Musical Quarterly*, 70 (1984): 175–94; "Wagner, Wagnerism, and Musical Idealism," in David C. Large and William Weber (eds.), *Wagnerism in European Culture and Politics* (Ithaca and London: Cornell University Press, 1984), 28–71; and two by J. Peter Burkholder: "Museum Pieces: The Historicist Mainstream in the Music of the Last Hundred Years," *Journal of Musicology*, 2 (1983): 115–34; "Brahms and Twentieth-Century Classical Music," *Nineteenth-Century Music*, 8 (1984): 75–83.

tangibly, and objectively authentic as an Old Master painting, and those who use them can claim ipso facto to be better curators than those who do not. But though the instruments are objects, the pieces they play are not. And hence the falseness, nay the evil, of the notion, so widespread at the moment, that the activity of our authentistic performer is tantamount to that of a restorer of paintings, who strips away the accumulated dust and grime of centuries to lay bare an original object in all its pristine splendor. In musical performance, neither what is removed nor what remains can be said to possess an objective ontological existence akin to that of dust or picture. Both what is "stripped" and what is "bared" are *acts* and both are interpretations—unless you can conceive of a performance, say, that has no tempo, or one that has no volume or tone color. For any tempo presupposes choice of tempo, any volume choice of volume, and choice is interpretation.

But that is not the worst of it. What is thought of as the "dirt" when musicians speak of restoring a piece of music is what people, acting out of an infinite variety of motives over the years, have done with it.[112] What is thought of as the "painting" by such musicians is an imaginary rendering in which "personal choices" have been "reduc[ed] to a minimum,"[113] and, ideally, eliminated. What this syllogism reduces to is: *people are dirt*.

And with that, of course, we return to our starting point, for this is another, less attractive way of stating the premise that underlies the whole modern movement. It is the dark side of dehumanization, the side that does evoke robots and concentration camps. We will not forget where Ezra Pound ended up, and why.

But we are not there yet, and Leonhardt's quirky Bach, to say nothing of Harnoncourt's, gives reassurance that the restoration ideal is far from universally shared. It is not the elimination of personal choice from performance that real artists desire, but its improvement and refreshment. And for this purpose original instruments, historical treatises, and all the rest have proven their value.

[112]Here, too, there is a bona fide modernist resonance. One of the last prose pieces to be published under Stravinsky's name contains this bit of heavy-handed ironizing about Leonard Bernstein: "Publicity often seems to be about all that is left of the arts. . . . Hence the spectacle, *also* almost the only one left, of the prisoners of publicity relentlessly driven to ever more desperate devices, as the condemned, in the Fifth Canto, are blown eternally by the unceasing winds. Recently one of music's superdamned (in this sense) was actually reduced to 'cleaning up' the score of . . . *Cavalleria Rusticana*, obvious as it must have been even to him that the accumulated dirt of bygone 'interpreters' was also the protective makeup that had kept the ghastly piece going this long." "Performing Arts," *Harper's* (June 1970): 38.

[113]Christopher Hogwood, quoted in Will Crutchfield, "A Report From the Battlefield" (see n. 4 above), 28.

The best indication of all that sterile restoration has not become the general ideal is that we have not acted upon our best means of achieving it, namely sound recordings. We have a much better idea of what music sounded like in Tchaikovsky's day than we will ever have of what it sounded like in Bach's day, and yet we do not hear performances of Tchaikovsky in our own day that sound like the Elman Quartet, for example, whose recorded interpretation of the famous "Andante cantabile" surely represents the kind of approach the composer expected (intended?) (Appendix, Recording No. 6).

Why not? Because it does not please us. Modern performance is an integrated thing. Our performances of Tchaikovsky are of a piece with our performances of Bach. That is what proves that they are of and for our time. And that is why, within the terms of the definition the foregoing statement implies, I do regard authentistic performances as authentic. As soon as a consensus develops that we must restore Tchaikovsky to his scoops and slides simply because that is what the evidence decrees,[114] I shall be the first to join in a chorus of lament for our Alexandrian age and the doom that it forebodes. It will mean we no longer care personally what we do or what we hear. Osip Mandelstam was revolted by nothing so much as what he called "omnivorous" or "haphazard" taste; to him it signified nihilism, an absence of values.[115] But as long as we know what we do want and what we do not want, and act upon that knowledge, we have values and are not dirt. We have authenticity.

POSTSCRIPT, 1994

Partly as a result of this very essay and the book of which it was a part, conditions have changed so as to lend this "ultimate" statement of the authenticity-as-modernism thesis something of a period flavor. Particularly dated, it seems to me, is the way it targets Christopher Hogwood as the authenticity ringleader. I would like to think that that is not only because so many new faces have emerged in the field since the middle of the eighties. I would like to think that popular perceptions about Early Music have matured.

[114]For a harbinger of such a viewpoint, see Jon Finson, "Performing Practice in the Late Nineteenth Century, with Special Reference to the Music of Brahms," *Musical Quarterly*, 70 (1984): 457–75. Sure enough, an attempt is made to rationalize (and sanctify) *portamenti* by calling them "structural."

[115]Nadezhda Mandelstam, *Hope Against Hope*, trans. Max Hayward (New York: Atheneum, 1970), 268.

When *Authenticity and Early Music* was finally published in 1988, the editor, Nicholas Kenyon, gave it a high-publicity launching on the BBC with a collage of interviews with the authors and their subjects. He got a lot of mileage, bless his heart, out of the concluding paragraphs of essay 4. I especially liked the little confession he managed to wring from Hogwood.

> **Q:** So how did this potent but misleading idea of cleaning the dirt from the painting, which is now under such strong attack, get established?
>
> **A:** Well, I think it's a simple metaphor for people who want an easy latchkey for this thing, and I quite agree that a lot of what one says to try and make the topic acceptable, explicable and attractive to the average consumer will not stand up to logical scrutiny, but it was never meant to.

I offer the foregoing in answer to the many who have accused me of flaying dead horses, or, as Andrew Porter puts it, of "driving a scholarly steamroller at Aunt Sallys that few serious musicians take seriously."[1] The frequency, and the intensity, with which this charge is made is ample testimony, in my view, to the life that remains in whatever horses I have been beating.[2] In fact, the horses are more alive than ever. In the wake of the Sistine Chapel debacle, even the art world has been alerted to the false claims to which restorers are given, and former defenders of such claims have begun to recant. The Warburg Institute's Charles Hope, for one, now allows that even in the case of painting it cannot be simply assumed that "we could remove centuries of accumulated dirt to reveal the pristine work of art beneath." This, as Hope now acknowledges, is because restoration is not solely restorative. It is "seldom undertaken solely to counter physical threats to works of art, such as cracking or flaking; rather it aims to improve their appearance." And, he finally admits, "just what constitutes an improvement is of course conditioned by current taste."[3] I think, moreover, that Andrew Porter puts his finger on what has alarmed my critics when he writes, with determined civility, that "Mr. Taruskin— possibly to his own dismay—gives comfort to people reluctant to hear, as he is not, the merits, as well as the musical failings, that have marked 'period' endeavor." I give no such comfort; the dismay is entirely Mr. Porter's, and it is a familiar sort of dismay, voiced most

[1]Andrew Porter, "Musical Events," *The New Yorker* (21 August 1989): 74.

[2]See also, for example, Charles Rosen ("The Shock of the Old," *New York Review of Books*, 19 July 1990, 46), who accuses me of reserving my "most crushing arguments . . . for opinions that no one really holds"; or Christopher Page ("A Revolt of the Ear," *Times Literary Supplement*, 24 February/2 March 1989, 20), who dismisses essay 4 as "using very substantial learning to obliterate some very insubstantial claims about authenticity made in publicity issued by record companies and in the occasional incautious sleeve-note."

[3]"Restoration or Ruination?," *New York Review of Books* (18 November 1993): 4.

consistently by apologists for the old Soviet Union or for the state of Israel: if there are faults, let them not be named aloud lest we comfort the enemy.

Such critics mistake my purpose. I do not think of the Early Music debates as the moral equivalent of war. I am well aware that many "Early Music" viewpoints are upheld not seriously at all, but altogether cynically. Yet I have always considered it important for musicologists to put their expertise at the service of "average consumers" and alert them to the possibility that they are being hoodwinked, not only by commercial interests but by complaisant academics, biased critics, and pretentious performers. Thanks to Nick Kenyon, I can cite Christopher Hogwood's words in confirmation.

I am grateful as well to Professor Andrew Roberts of the School of Oriental and African Studies, University of London, who advised me of the correct date for Ezra Pound's essay on Arnold Dolmetsch.

Recordings referred to in Essay 4

1. Bach, *Chromatic Fantasy* (Landowska) RCA LCT 1137
2. Bach, Fifth Brandenburg Concerto, First movement
    - (*a*) Vienna Philharmonic Orchestra
      Wilhelm Furtwängler, cond. and piano soloist
      Willi Boskovsky, violin
      Gustav Neidermayer, flute
      (Salzburg Festival, 1950)
      RECITAL RECORDS 515 (distributed by Discocorp, Berkeley)
    - (*b*) Philadelphia Orchestra, Leopold Stokowski, cond.
      Fernando Valenti, harpsichord
      Anshel Brusilow, violin
      William Kincaid, flute
      COLUMBIA MS 6313 (1961)
    - (*c*) Busch Chamber Orchestra
      Adolf Busch, violin and leader
      Marcel Moyse, flute
      Rudolf Serkin, piano
      ANGEL COLC 14 (originally recorded 1935)
    - (*d*) Fritz Reiner, cond. a pickup ensemble
      (ripieno: 2 on a part)
      Sylvia Marlowe, harpsichord
      Hugo Kolberg, violin
      Julius Baker, flute
      COLUMBIA ML 4283 (1950)

(e) Collegium Aureum (ripieni soli)
     Franzjosef Maier, violin and leader
     Hans-Martin Linde, flute
     Gustav Leonhardt, harpsichord
     RCA VICTROLA 6023 (originally Harmonia Mundi, c. 1965)

(f) The English Concert (ripieno: 1 [plus solo], 2, 2, 1, 1)
     Trevor Pinnock, harpsichord and leader
     Simon Standage, violin
     Lisa Beznosiuk, flute
     DG ARC 2742003 (1982)

(g) Academy of Ancient Music (ripieno:
     1 violin, 1 viola, violone [no cello])
     Christopher Hogwood, harpsichord and leader
     Catherine Mackintosh, violin
     Stephen Preston, flute
     OISEAU-LYRE 414 187-1 (1985)

(h) Gustav Leonhardt, harpsichord and leader
     (ripieni soli)
     Frans Brüggen, flute
     Sigiswald Kuijken, violin
     PRO-ARTE 2PAX-2001 (1976)

(i) Concentus Musicus Wien, Nikolaus Harnoncourt,
     dir. (ripieni soli)
     Leopold Stastny, flute
     Alice Harnoncourt, violin,
     Herbert Tachezi, harpsichord
     TELEFUNKEN 6.42840 AZ (1982)

3.   Mozart, Sonata in D, K. 448
     Béla and Ditta Bartók, pianos
     HUNGAROTON LPX 12334-38 (originally recorded Budapest,
     1939)

4.   Mozart, Fugue in C minor, K. 426
     Igor and Soulima Stravinsky, piano
     FRENCH COLUMBIA LFX-951/3 (recorded Paris, c. 1938)

5. (a) Bach, Crucifixus (B minor Mass)
     Otto Klemperer, cond.
     ANGEL S-3720 (c. 1963)

   (b) Bach, Crucifixus (B minor Mass)
     Johannes Martini, cond.
     MUSIKPRODUKTION DABRINGHAUS U. GRIMM 1146-47 (c. 1985)

6.   Tchaikovsky, Quartet No. 1, Op. 11 (Andante cantabile)
     Elman Quartet
     VICTOR RED SEAL 745575 (c. 1918)

5

What — or Where — Is the Original?

Kraków, Biblioteka Jagiellońska, Glogauer Liederbuch. Introduction by Jessie Ann Owens. (Renaissance Music in Facsimile, 6.) New York & London: Garland, 1986.

    Milan, Archivio della Veneranda Fabbrica del Duomo, Sezione Musicale. Introduction by Howard Mayer Brown. (Renaissance Music in Facsimile, 12.) New York & London: Garland, 1987.

    Vatican City, Biblioteca Apostolica Vaticana, Cappella Sistina MS 46. Introduction by Jeffrey J. Dean. (Renaissance Music in Facsimile, 21.) New York & London: Garland, 1986.

    Vatican City, Biblioteca Apostolica Vaticana, MS Chigi C VIII 234. Introduction by Herbert Kellman. (Renaissance Music in Facsimile, 22.) New York & London: Garland, 1987.

    Vatican City, Biblioteca Apostolica Vaticana, San Pietro B 80. Introduction by Christopher A. Reynolds. (Renaissance Music in Facsimile, 23.) New York & London: Garland, 1986.

    Trium vocum cantiones centum, à praestantissimis diversarum nationum ac linguarum musicis compositae. (Nuremberg: Johannes Petreius, 1541.) Introduction by Howard Mayer Brown. (Renaissance Music in Facsimile, 26.) New York & London: Garland, 1986.

Originally published as a review of six items from the Garland Publishing series Renaissance Music in Facsimile. Reprinted from *Notes: Quarterly Journal of the Music Library Association* 46 (1989–90): 792–97, by permission of the Music Library Association.

So what's to review? The music? That would be an impertinence. The scribes? Impertinent again, and gratuitous: they've been taking their lumps for centuries (besides, with every passing year they look smarter). There aren't even any editors to kick around. True, Howard Mayer Brown, Frank D'Accone, and Jessie Ann Owens are listed as editors in the publisher's brochure, but all they have done is choose the items to be photographed, write the introductions to some of them, and farm out the rest. Indeed, in their general introduction to the series they hint at the Death of the Editor. That will be something to return to, perhaps; but to cavil, in the presence of such bounty, either with the concept of this series or with the way it has been implemented would be most impertinent of all.

The six facsimile editions listed above are a sampling of some twenty-nine titles that have been issued thus far in a series comprising manuscripts and a few prints from seven European countries, covering genres from Mass to madrigal and a time span from the 1460s to the early seventeenth century. Choirbooks, partbooks, even scores are represented. The editors must be congratulated on their imaginative and comprehensive selection, a cross section of Renaissance mensural sources containing the widest possible range of musical and paleographical styles. The photography is of high quality (and the volume devoted to the exceptionally ornate and artistically significant Chigi Codex is bedizened with half a dozen breathtakingly beautiful color reproductions). Everything is as legible as possible (which does not always mean legible). The bindings are sturdy. The volumes open flat. The books have been printed on acid-free, 250-year-life paper (which somehow, given the contents, strikes me as funny). Introductions are concise, authoritative, and informative; that to the Chigi Codex, by the ever-questing, ever-generous Herbert Kellman, is a mine of new and fascinating iconographical lore. Jessie Ann Owens's table of contents to the Glogauer Liederbuch is the first such inventory to number the pieces correctly. Jeffrey Dean's meticulous breakdown of scribes in Cappella Sistina 46 will be invaluable to those on the lookout for "scribal concordances" (as Joshua Rifkin was first to call them) in other sources. Best of all, the publishers have announced their intention of following up on this initial issue with a yearly supplement of five or six volumes, "so that eventually a substantial corpus of facsimiles will allow students, performers and scholars easy access to some of the most important musical monuments of the period." All of us who love to root around in Renaissance sources, whether as performers, as historians, or (ahem) as editors, can only be grateful to the above-named trio and to Garland, their doughty publisher, for making us a fabulous gift. I ask only that in the future all the volumes be provided with concordances to modern editions (as only

Howard Mayer Brown has done among editors of the six titles under review) and that printed foliations be provided to supplement the erratic and ofttimes illegible ones in the manuscripts. But enough of quibbling. No research library can afford to be without these publications, and specialists in the period will want to have a few of the most relevant volumes in their personal collections. End of review.

But no, one cannot just let it go at that. For this series is not just a collection of old documents. It is itself a significant document of the state of the various disciplines whose activities intersect upon the repertory known as Early Music. As such it prompts reflection.

For quite some time the thrust of Renaissance musicology— following that of historical studies in general and possibly under pressure from the social sciences (and despite loud protests)—has been turning inexorably away from the Caesaristic mode of historiography that places the master or the individual masterpiece at the summit of the scholarly edifice. While important biographical research continues, while collected critical editions are still in progress (and still have major gaps to fill), and while analysis and criticism are still in their infancy, the most symptomatic studies of recent years have been those devoted to institutions, genres, and repertories. A glance at the contents of the major annuals—*Musica Disciplina, Early Music History*—will suffice to establish this much, as will a glance at the relevant pages in Cecil Adkins and Alis Dickinson's *Doctoral Dissertations in Musicology*. Nor is it a coincidence that the three most talked-about recent books on Renaissance music history (by Lewis Lockwood on Ferrara, Reinhard Strohm on Bruges, and Allan Atlas on Naples) have been primarily concerned with music in the context of court and civic institutions. In all three cases, moreover, the study of a music manuscript or a group of manuscripts (*Mod A-F, Las,* and *Bol Q16,* respectively, as they are known to their friends), in conjunction or alliance with archival research, provided the methodological focus. As Christopher Reynolds puts it in his introduction to San Pietro B 80, "paleographical details and archival data work hand in hand" reciprocally to illuminate a body of music and the social institutions within which it functioned (and Reynolds neatly illustrates the process by noting the chronological coincidence of the hiring of a bass singer at the Basilica San Pietro, as attested by the bursar's archives, with the layer of *SP B 80* that first contains four-part music).

A like concern motivates the present series. The editors' introduction speaks cogently about the value of source studies, not only (in their traditional application) as a means of illuminating "questions of chronology, attribution, and style," but also because musical sources are "artifacts that reflect the cultural milieu in which they were made." Indeed, every one of the individual introductions stresses the point. The Milanese *libroni* assembled by or for Gaffurius "ought to be studied for what they reveal about the conventional practices of cathedral choirs in western Europe about 1500, as well as for what they reveal about what was distinctively and idiosyncratically Milanese. . . . Reproducing [them] in facsimile may encourage such a broader view of their contents, in a way that the modern edition of most of their contents does not seem to have done." "Cappella Sistina 46 offers a microcosm of the Sistine scriptorium's activity in the first quarter of the sixteenth century." "San Pietro B 80 contributes significantly to our understanding of how an ecclesiastical institution—as opposed to a major court chapel—dealt with what was then a rapidly growing body of polyphony." The sumptuous Chigi Codex is "one of the most precious . . . of those invaluable sources of early music that not only offer us important repertories but also visibly, in other ways, bear witness to the social and artistic milieu of their origin and subsequent use." At the opposite socio-artistic extreme, the Glogauer Liederbuch "has been aptly described as containing *Gebrauchsmusik*, the ordinary music in common use that could be performed by local musicians. As such, it provides an interesting view of one aspect of musical life in fifteenth-century Europe." Even the lowly Petreius print has "importance . . . in revealing the tastes and levels of musical accomplishment in mid-sixteenth-century Germany."

Indeed, seeing the music, and particularly the more famous music (for I am an incorrigible Caesarist), in its natural habitat has a way of bringing it imaginatively to life that no other form of presentation can match. The motet manuscript Cappella Sistina 46, with its church-calendar organization—first the *temporale*, then the *sanctorale*, then the Marian antiphons, all pretty much in order—sets some great compositions by Josquin and Ockeghem (though one less by the latter than we used to think: as Jeffrey Dean points out on the basis of his own prior research, the setting of *Salve regina* in the manuscript is actually by Basiron) within a yearly round of evensong devotions that lend them a concreteness of purpose and hence a "reality" they do not have in the *Gesamtausgabe* or in the concert hall. It is good to be reminded that the works of the Renaissance masters were not "absolute" music but music that functioned in symbiosis with a social framework as yet undivorced from daily life.

Dean does his best to reinforce that impression by calling attention to such things as "the splash of wax from the great candle on the Sistine Chapel's music lectern on fol. 32" (in the photograph, I'm afraid, it's just a smudge); or (of more practical interest) the lines drawn through the staff by the papal singers the better to coordinate music and text. San Pietro B 80 sports such things as private notes

from scribe to chorister, which Christopher Reynolds ably interprets
in light of the archives (there is a *volue archangele*—"Turn, O Arch-
angel"—in the cantus part of a Kyrie on folio 71 that seems fairly
inscrutable if uplifting until Reynolds reveals that one of the sopra-
nists at the basilica was named Archangelo Blasio and that he was
being favored—or insulted—with a joshing reminder to turn the
page). The famous illuminations in the Chigi Codex shed a wealth of
light not only on matters of the manuscript's provenance and owner-
ship, but also on the music and its context. One item I cannot resist
citing, for its bearing on matters to which I have been a party, is
Herbert Kellman's identification of an emblem of the Order of the
Golden Fleece in the first initial of the first of the manuscript's four
consecutive *L'Homme armé* Masses (Busnoys's happily among them).[1]
Other illuminations make ironic or satirical commentary. "Two domestic scenes," Kellman reports, "seem to depict a man under attack
by mistress and maid, then reduced to observing through a window
the mistress and a youth at table, being served by the maid." For some
reason he neglects to mention that these scenes adorn the first opening of Ockeghem's *Missa Ma maistresse*!

So much for context and social commentary. The accessibility of
so many important Renaissance sources in facsimile will surely stim-
ulate research in these areas. Such must have been a primary purpose
of the series, and there could not have been a better one. As I hope I
have suggested, contextual studies need not necessarily entail the
disappearance of the masters or their masterworks (to cite the most
commonly voiced caveat). They can enhance critical understanding
of both.

Facsimile editions have their limitations, though, and these are
not always properly recognized by the editors in the general introduction, where some pretty dubious claims are made. For this reason,
some warnings to the unwary may be in order. First and foremost,
neither facsimile editions nor that singular oxymoronic artifact of
recent years, the "critical edition of a single source," offers the best or
most direct access to individual compositions.

Repertorial and codicological studies have always been part of the
methodology of Renaissance music study—and in particular, of the
editorial process—but they have loomed ever larger since the mid-
sixties, when Edward Lowinsky inaugurated his grandiose series
Monuments of Renaissance Music, the first and only one to be devoted exclusively to individual sources, not authors or compositions

---

[1] See R. Taruskin, "Antoine Busnoys and the *L'Homme Armé* Tradition," *Journal of
the American Musicological Society* 39 (1986): 255–93; also related correspondence in
JAMS 40 (1987): 149–53, 579–80, and 42 (1989): 443–52.

in the abstract or the ideal. Lowinsky's own contribution to the series—possibly its pretext—was his celebrated three-volume edition of the Medici Codex of 1518, in which one volume was devoted to a pioneering photographic facsimile of the source, one of the earliest such publications involving a sixteenth-century manuscript that presented no particular problem or oddity of paleography per se. It thus stands as a kind of godfather to the present series. Since then single-source editions have burgeoned (e.g., Allan Atlas's of the Cappella Giulia Chansonnier and Leeman Perkins and Howard Garey's of the Mellon Chansonnier), to the point where Philip Brett, in a recent essay, could speak of "codicocentricity" as one of the "ideological biases" of recent musical scholarship.[2]

Spurred by the advent of cheap photo-reproduction, numerous codicocentric facsimile editions appeared on the market prior to the inauguration of the present series, their evident success in appealing not only to scholars and libraries but to the ever-increasing ranks of mensurally-literate performers perhaps providing Garland with a preliminary earnest of commercial viability. Scanning my own shelf I spot the Trent Codices and the Mass volumes of Petrucci as reprinted by Vivarelli and Gullà, alongside various publications by the Boethius Press, Broude Bros., the Éditions Culture et Civilisation, and others. I have contributed to this flood tide myself, though not codicocentrically, with the anthologies of chanson *Bearbeitungen* (I wish we had an English word for it) issued by the now-defunct Ogni Sorte Editions. So long as the purpose of facsimile publication is viewed as didactic, and so long as the aim of codicocentric editing is conceived as documentary or historiographic, such projects are all to the good. Now that it has become such a well-implanted growth industry, in fact, I would like to see facsimile publication altogether supplant the "critical" editing of single sources, which has always struck me as a spurious activity (see essay 3).

It will not do, however, to claim that such a mode of presentation is inherently superior to that of traditional critical editing, or that by adopting it we have somehow transcended the whole issue of recension. And yet our trio of editors have subscribed to the assertion that "even the most splendid and critical of modern editions still offer us only a translation of the original rather than an exact reproduction." Just what, I should like to know, do they mean by "the original" in this context? If they mean the piece just as the composer wrote it (or "intended" it), then none of the publications in the present series remotely qualifies, as I am sure the editors are well aware. (The sole

[2]"Text, Context, and the Early Music Editor," in N. Kenyon, ed., *Authenticity and Early Music*, 101.

possible exception is the Chigi Codex, which—as Kellman points out—embodies "a kind of *editio princeps*" of Ockeghem's Masses and Regis's motets.) Yet they press on, superciliously, in a manner that has become lamentably familiar: "Translations are a good and sometimes essential aid to understanding the music, but they are inevitably and necessarily interpretations, always subject to the limited understanding of an editor, who might unwittingly obscure an essential element in attempting to prepare an accurate modern score, or who might fail to grasp some nuance conveyed in the original notation." Yet what are the redactions herewith presented in facsimile if not precisely what the editors affect to scorn? Are they anything but "inevitably and necessarily interpretations, . . . subject to the limited understanding of an editor [scribe]," who was just as liable as we are to misunderstand or misrepresent? Does mere age bestow authority tantamount to "originality"?

One cannot believe that the distinguished musicologists who wrote these sentences are so naive as to believe them. If proof is needed of the "limited understanding" the average manuscript redaction can evince, one need only investigate the several pieces that crop up in multiple versions within the very sampling under review. One such piece that I know well in all its variants, having recently prepared a critical edition of it, is an anonymous Magnificat (*octavi toni*), attributed on strong internal evidence to Busnoys, that appears both in San Pietro B 80 and in the first Milan *librone*. The San Pietro redaction has a great many small errors of pitch and duration, and in one case omits sesquialteral coloration. That of the Milan codex is much worse: in addition to just as many small errors (of the kind one expects to find in any manuscript redaction) it omits an entire voice part in the "Quia fecit." Neither source recognizes that the "Deposuit" is a fauxbourdon, and the Milan scribe compounds omission with commission in labeling the section a "Duo." The texting in both sources is haphazard; in the Milan source it is impossible. Although I would never claim that I have arrived at the "original," at least by conflating the two sources (and comparing the result with the explicitly attributed Magnificat of Busnoys) I managed to arrive at a redaction that is performable as it stands, which cannot be said of either fifteenth-century redaction.

Our series editors might answer this point with another claim from their general introduction, that by using the faulty facsimiles "performers are forced to come to grips with the music in the same way as the musicians who first performed it." ("In effect," they add, "they must imaginatively reconstruct the procedures followed by musicians in the fifteenth and sixteenth centuries, and gain thereby a kind of insight into the music (and quite possibly a freedom from dependence on the printed page) that cannot be achieved in any other way.") As a heuristic exercise such an undertaking is indeed valuable and praiseworthy. One learns to create the kind of ad hoc emergency redaction that was surely the fifteenth-century norm. But it is ridiculous, or at best disingenuous, to attempt to pass off such a redaction as "an exact reproduction" of a putative "original." Such thinking is of a piece with that other notorious "ideological bias" of our time, which automatically privileges the "authenticity" of the first performance. No one who attends new music concerts, or better yet who has had a piece played in one, will ever assent to such a notion.

Even for analytical or critical purposes, a facsimile edition is a poor substitute for a critical edition of any individual piece from the mensural period, when the standard performance formats were choirbooks and partbooks. The first and most essential task of an editor is to create a score, which was as necessary for study in the fifteenth or sixteenth century as it is now. In fact, two of the manuscript facsimiles issued by Garland testify to this: both the "Tregian Manuscript," an enormous miscellany prepared (that is, edited) by a musical recusant to while away his years in a London prison, and the "Tarasconi Codex," a large anthology of madrigals, consist of what we should now call study scores. They were not meant for performance but for perusal, just like our modern critical scores. Implicitly to denigrate the latter as an inherent distortion (because it is an "interpretation") is thus as historically baseless as it is misleading. It is however another accurate sign of our impersonal, nay antipersonal, times.

Finally, a word of caution to those attracted to these editions as recreational performance material. They will do best with those sources (invariably prints) that were actually prepared with amateur performers in mind, like the Petreius *Trium vocum cantiones centum* listed above, which the editors rightly call "an ideal introduction to the joys and difficulties of playing from original sources." Another such is the huge motet anthology *Novum et insigne opus musicum* (Nuremberg: Berg u. Neuber, 1558–59), whose three volumes make up items 27]ND29 in Garland's series. This will keep original-notation buffs contented for many months. In many if not most other cases, there will be far more difficulties than joys. The Cappella Sistina sources have been rendered only marginally legible by the ravages of time and "restoration." Scholars can (laboriously) dope them out but recreational performers should be warned off. The Milan *libroni*, as already intimated, are so error-ridden that one can only guess how Gaffurius's choir ever performed from them at all; and my experience suggests that a similar caveat, though perhaps a shade less strong, applies to the San Pietro manuscript as well. On the other hand, the Glogauer Liederbuch, though a mess, presents an attractive challenge to suitably patient and proficient mensuralists (and the music is wonderful). The Chigi Codex, of course, is gorgeous, and legible as only a "presentation" manuscript can be. *Kenner* and *Liebhaber* who know their Mass text cold and who are game to brave the *Missa Prolationum* or the *Missa Cuiusvis toni* will taste nirvana. For this volume alone, Garland Publishing has won a permanent place in my orisons.

6

The Modern Sound of Early Music

What does Early Music have to do with history? In theory, everything. In fact, very little. At the beginning, the movement was frankly antiquarian—a matter of reviving forgotten repertories and, with them, forgotten instruments and performing practices. Nobody objected to that, nor did most musicians even pay much attention to it. Now, it seems, Early Musickers are performing almost everything. They have laid claim to the standard repertory, and attention must be paid. More than that, sides are taken—the movement in its present phase has become controversial.

But on closer inspection, it becomes ever more apparent that "historical" performers who aim "to get to 'the truth' " (as the fortepianist Malcolm Bilson has put it) by using period instruments and reviving lost playing techniques actually pick and choose from history's wares. And they do so in a manner that says more about the values of the late twentieth century than about those of any earlier era.

Whatever the movement's aims or claims, absolutely no one performs pre-twentieth-century music as it would have been performed when new. This may be so easily verified that it is a wonder anyone still believes the contrary. Some examples:

• Frans Brüggen, appearing with his Orchestra of the 18th Century at Zellerbach Hall on the campus of the University of California at Berkeley, tells the audience during an intermission feature at the open dress rehearsal that the purpose of his enterprise is "to be obedient to the composer." He then conducts a performance of Beethoven's "Eroica" Symphony in which the composer's meticulously indicated tempos are all ignored.

Originally published as "The Spin Doctors of Early Music" in the Arts and Leisure section of the Sunday *New York Times*, 29 July 1990. Reprinted by permission of the *New York Times*.

- Roger Norrington launches a meteoric career as "historical" performer of the standard classical repertory with a cycle of Beethoven symphonies on CD in which the composer's metronome indications are not only (pretty much) followed, but also emblazoned on the containers in an act of pious bravado. Having set the tempos, however, the conductor adheres to them with dogged rigidity, contradicting every eyewitness report we have of Beethoven's own conducting, as well as the explicit instructions of eighteenth-century conducting manuals.

- Mr. Bilson and John Eliot Gardiner (the latter conducting the English Baroque Soloists) complete the first recorded cycle of Mozart piano concertos on "original instruments," representing the pieces in their true colors at last. But the notes they play, for the most part, are just the ones Mozart wrote. They do not add all the extra notes Mozart's audiences actually heard.

These performers and others like them can be counted on to flout historical evidence whenever it does not conform to their idea of "the truth." They do it knowingly. In fact, because they are so much more historically aware than conventionally trained musicians tend to be, they flout historical evidence more knowingly than do their "modern" counterparts. With the growing success of Early Music, we are increasingly surrounded by unhistorical sounds masquerading as historical—or "authentic," to use a word that more sophisticated performers now shun but that musical salesmen and spin doctors still spout to seduce the unwary consumer.

Some of these unhistorical sounds are really central to the concept of historical performance. Take the "countertenor" (male falsetto) voice. It is the very emblem of Early Music. No Baroque opera revival can get by without it. All the best historical vocal groups sport it, whether they sing Renaissance madrigals (the Consort of Musicke), the music of the pre-Reformation and Counter-Reformation Roman Catholic Church (the Hilliard Ensemble, the Tallis Scholars), or late medieval polyphony (the Gothic Voices).

There is no evidence that falsettists participated in any of these repertories when they were current. The voice was born in the English cathedral choir, and owes its modern currency to the success of Alfred Deller, an outstanding English cathedral alto, as pioneering protagonist of the modern Early Music revival in its antiquarian phase. It is no accident, then, that all of the vocal groups listed above are English, for they have founded their performing styles, as Deller did, on their own distinguished national traditions. Their excellence has bred emulation, establishing the English cathedral style as an international sonic norm for Early Music, and the model on which Early Music vocal production in all ranges is based.

The best one can do to justify the current vogue for countertenors on historical terms would be to say that, thanks to Deller's example, we now like to hear our Palestrina sung as it might have been sung by an Anglican choir in the sixteenth century. But in the sixteenth century no Anglican choir would have dreamed of singing Palestrina's music if they valued their lives.

There can be no historical justification at all for using an English cathedral voice in a Handel opera. Handel, who knew perfectly well what the falsettists of his adopted country sounded like, never wrote for them until he had abandoned opera for English-texted oratorios that drew upon indigenous talent and traditions. When (like us) he couldn't get a castrato for an opera performance, he happily dressed a woman in trousers and plumed helmet. Handel's women, we can be reasonably sure, sounded nothing like Alfred Deller. We can use women, too, of course, and sometimes do, but unless the woman is Marilyn Horne, we seem to prefer countertenors, demonstrably unhistorical though they be.

So is Early Music just a hoax? Are the Bruggens and Bilsons deceiving us, or themselves? Is "authentic" performance as inauthentic as all that?

Not at all. It is authentic indeed, far more authentic than its practitioners contend, perhaps more authentic than they know. Nothing said above about Messrs. Brüggen, Norrington, and Bilson or the rest should be taken in itself as criticism of the results they have obtained. They have been rightly acclaimed. Their commercial success is well deserved. Conventional performers are properly in awe and in fear of them. Why? Because, as we are all secretly aware, what we call historical performance is the sound of now, not then. It derives its authenticity not from its historical verisimilitude, but from its being for better or worse a true mirror of late-twentieth-century taste.

Being the true voice of one's time is (as Shaw might have said) roughly forty thousand times as vital and important as being the assumed voice of history. To be the expressive medium of one's own age is—obviously, no?—a far worthier aim than historical verisimilitude. What is verisimilitude, after all, but perceived correctness? And correctness is the paltriest of virtues. It is something to demand of students, not artists.

So why the confusion? Why do we make a pretense of historical performance when we're really creating something better? These questions are so bound up with the nature of late-twentieth-century taste that it would be better to postpone an answer till we've explored that taste a bit.

Without attempting an exhaustive inventory, one can suggest a few interrelated characteristics that exemplify current taste in the performance of classical music (and its composition, too, but that's a story for another day):

- It is text-centered, hence literalistic.
- It is impersonal, hence unfriendly to spontaneity.
- It is lightweight, hence leery of the profound or the sublime.

None of these traits began with Early Music, but Early Music has brought them all to a peak. Literalism is as old as Toscanini, who exhorted one and all to play what was set before them exactly as written ("com'è scritto"), regardless of "tradition." Impersonalism is as old as Stravinsky, who railed against "interpretation," and wanted his performers to be—just as Mr. Brüggen proclaimed himself—obedient "executants" of his will. Lightness is as old as Satie, inveterate debunker of artistic pretension in the name of mental health.

Taken together, the three positions are conventionally labeled antiromantic, though a closer look will reveal the ironic links binding at least the first two with the Romantic enthronement of the autocratic and infallible composer-creator, divorced from real-time music making. (There you have the real roots of "modern"—that is, Early—performance practice.)

What the three positions—enunciated by an Italian, a Russian, and a Frenchman in turn—also (and unquestionably) share is an anti-Teutonic bias. The style of performance they collectively describe has been a contender since the 1920s, dominant since the 1930s, virtually the only one since the 1950s and—as revamped and re-outfitted with a new instrumentarium—the one called "historical" (or "authentic") since the 1960s. Early Music is no earlier than that.

The text-centricity of Early Music is self-evident, and so is its literalism. That is what Early Musickers usually mean when they speak of fidelity to the composer's intentions. Pushed to a new level, it has brought us Mr. Bilson's Mozart, refreshingly rearticulated in conformity with a newly cleansed text; and it has brought us Mr. Norrington's Beethoven, radically reimagined so as to make those metronome settings work. (And they do!)

Less obvious (indeed, expediently denied) is the corollary, hostility to unwritten performance tradition, which accounts for not only Mr. Bilson's, but practically everyone's, reluctance to embellish the bare notes of the scores they execute. So even—nay, especially—in the most "obedient" Early Music performances of Mozart's piano concertos, the slow movements (and not only the slow movements) are fairly denuded of the raiment Mozart expected them to flaunt. The result is a kind of performance Mozart would have completely failed to understand—or to respect. So much for his intentions.

The impersonalism of Early Music has resulted in performances of unprecedented formal clarity and precision. It has also resulted in a newly militant reluctance to make the subtle, constant adjustments of tempo and dynamics on which expressivity depends, for these can have no sanction but personal feeling. That is why Mr. Norrington's tempos, though set in unprecedented conformity with Beethoven's prescriptions, are completely un-Beethovenian past the first measure, when Beethoven assumed that what he called the "tempo of feeling" would take over. It is an assumption the twentieth century (and only the twentieth century) has refused to make, and Beethoven would have listened to Mr. Norrington's renditions with utter discomfort and bewilderment.

The lightness of Early Music inheres in its very sounds—the period instruments, the countertenor voices, the small forces. For the high value placed on small forces there is no historical evidence, but there is a distinguished twentieth-century ("Neoclassical") literature for chamber orchestra, to which the Classical literature now conforms. The same ideal has recently been responsible for the resolute trivialization of some notable monuments of Germanic profundity, like the B minor Mass and the Choral Symphony.

We can't stand the sublime anymore, perhaps with good reason. (We know something the nineteenth century didn't know: namely, where Wagner led.) Do we need a fence around our good taste, not to say our moral purity? Then no German is above suspicion, not even Bach or Beethoven. If we are unwilling to give up their masterworks altogether, Early Music can render them handily innocuous. That may be a valid and necessary cultural critique, but it is not history.

Relics of the performance tradition to which all of this is a reaction are still available to today's ears in recordings by Willem Mengelberg, Artur Nikisch, Karl Muck, Wilhelm Furtwängler, and many others (including composers like Hans Pfitzner and Richard Strauss). They are instantly recognizable as premodern (and of course, echt-Teutonic). To hear them is to realize how far we've traveled from that phase of history. They show how fundamentally akin to standard modern performance practices are those that claim to be historical. The old recordings utterly debunk that pharisaical claim; for recordings are the hardest evidence of performance practice imaginable.

If we truly wanted to perform historically, we would begin by imitating early-twentieth-century recordings of late-nineteenth-century music and extrapolate back from there. Instead, as already implied, Early Music has been moving in the opposite direction. The pioneers extrapolated—from very soft evidence bolstered by very firm desiderata—a style of performing Renaissance and Baroque music, and from then on it has been a matter of speculative forward encroachment.

Even now, with the leading edge of the movement breaking into the mid–nineteenth century, these old recordings are not being utilized except on the antiquarian fringe. Why? Because to our modern taste they sound like caricatures. Nobody takes them seriously, least of all the Early Musickers. (Listen sometime to the single-sided acoustical 78 of Mischa Elman's quartet playing Tchaikovsky, circa 1914, and see if you can keep a straight face at their authentic scoops and slides, transmitted to Elman directly from his teacher Leopold Auer, for whom Tchaikovsky wrote his violin concerto.) We have our own tastes, our own ways and our own agenda. In case of conflict, they inevitably override the historical evidence. Which of course is how it should be—must be—if we have any sort of stake in our own culture. To take the opposite tack would be a profession of apathy.

So forget history. What Early Music has been doing is busily remaking the music of the past in the image of the present (necessary because we unfortunately have so little use for the actual music of the present), only calling the present by some other name.

Roger Norrington had just conducted a very jolly and spiffy performance of *Messiah* when we met in San Francisco a couple of Christmases ago. He was in an expansive mood. He began describing his latest forays into Romantic terrain and his plans for the future, which included Verdi.

"You'd be amazed how Classical Verdi really is," he said. "We're going to do him completely without this, you know"—here he screwed up his mouth into a caricature of an opera singer's, and emitted a tremulous *woo-woo*—"and it will be a revelation."

Hmm, I thought, Mr. Norrington is going to get all the way to the twentieth century without any woo-woo, and yet we know that somewhere along the line that old woo-woo certainly did exist. But more power to the man. If woo-woo is of no interest to him, he has every right to can it. And we have every right to love the result, as many of us do. Mozart's disdain and Beethoven's discomfort need not deter us. They are dead.

What *is* of interest, as I have suggested, is why we need the pretense—why Mr. Norrington needs to call his Verdi Classical instead of modern. It is because in the absence of a vital creative impulse classical music has become a chill museum. (The vitality, alas, is with other forms of music, in which performers behave very differently.) Our classical performers are the curators of their heritage, not its proprietors. They are sworn to preserve it and trained to be uncreative. So if you *are* creative, you have to hide the fact. You have to come on (to yourself as well as others) as a better curator, not a revamper.

Early Music has been the best curatorial credential of all, which is why it has never been as creative a movement as "historically" it ought to be. (Curators don't embellish or arrange, thank you, let alone improvise over a ground bass.) A violinist using a period bow can claim to be a better curator than one who does not, and one using a whole period violin is the best curator of all. A Roger Norrington remaking Verdi will seem a better curator if he calls his creation Classical rather than modern.

And here I must drop my dispassionate mask and deplore our afflicted cultural ecology, in which (as Randolph Coleman of Oberlin College has recently written) "the exorcising of *homo ludens* (man at play) forms the initial stage of our musical pedagogy." Mr. Coleman continues, "Repetition, standardization, virtuosity, accuracy, perfection, and professionalization (with its emphasis on patterns of conformity) are the terms of our teaching—not experimentation, idiosyncrasy, interaction, individuation, and especially not open-ended creative play." Mr. Coleman is talking about elite classical music training, of course, not the less lordly branches of our musical life, which have retained far more creativity.

Early Music, were it more truly "historical," might have formed a saving exception to this pattern; up to Mozart's time, at least, musical values were generally closer to those of what we now call pop than to those of our classical culture. But to ask that of Early Music may be asking the impossible. It is a product of the classical value system, after all, and its beneficiary. It cannot be expected to rebel. On the contrary, it has measurably advanced the perfectionist standards of its parent culture, pleasantly augmented its inventory of timbres and become perhaps the least moribund aspect of our classical musical life. That is accomplishment enough.

POSTSCRIPT, 1994

The droll publication history of this piece, and the most constructive correspondence it elicited, are reported in essay 7. Most of the correspondence was captiously antagonistic, doubtless owing to the headline the *Times* editors insisted on running over it. (An exception was a friendly correction from the critic Nicholas Deutsch, who wrote in to remind me that Handel did use countertenors in his oratorios; the text has been amended accordingly.) For a sample of the typical, bemusingly irrelevant response the piece elicited from musicians, I'll quote the portions of a really venomous letter from James Richman that the *Times* saw fit to print. (Mr. Richman was no stranger to me, incidentally. We performed together frequently in New York in olden days, and I was one of the founding members, along with him, of Concert Royal, a group he still directs.) This is what the *Times* printed, in the Arts and Leisure letters column for 26 August 1990:

> Anyone who remembers Richard Taruskin's arch-Romantic interpretations of Ockeghem and Couperin knows why he is so anxious to discredit the Early Music movement and the performance esthetic it has engendered. Mr. Taruskin's personal taste runs to 19th-century Russia (his specialty), and he would be quite happy if no one asked why a musicologist would prefer to play older music as if it were Tchaikovsky.
>
> Mr. Taruskin is at the heart of what is wrong with Early Music today. Instead of objective scholars, we have professors performing part-time; instead of impartial arbiters and keepers of the flame, we have involved personalities with axes to grind.
>
> Contrary to what Mr. Taruskin would have readers believe, there is a great deal of respect for the discoveries of modern research in the Early Music field. The vast majority of original-instrument performers take as much care as they can (short of bringing back the castrato voice) to follow the ways of the old masters. Honest mistakes are inevitable, but that is a different issue from the case of a musicologist deliberately picking and choosing from available data to justify his personal taste.
>
> A great deal of good work has been done, often by the very people Mr. Taruskin maligns, and it is a pity that his attitude casts such a negative pall over it. Great quantities of Western music are available today in informed performances as never before, thanks to dedicated performers who have broken the stranglehold of the 19th-century esthetic. As Early Music has for 25 years been a field driven primarily by the idealism of its proponents, that is an impressive achievement.

Not exactly the words of an "impartial arbiter," thank heaven. That is precisely the point: the last thing a performer ought to be is impartial. And, by and large, they are not. They care. Musicians like James Richman are committed artists, enthusiastically pursuing an ideal of beauty in which they fervently believe. As he says, they are idealists, and their idealism has no greater admirer than I. What I am waiting for is an end to the pretense that what Early Music performers are doing is (merely) historically correct. They are not ransacking history in pursuit of the truth. What they are looking for is permission.

Being human, when they find permission they are apt to believe that they have found the truth, and become "certain," to use Leo Treitler's word. Such certainty inevitably breeds intolerance. In the unedited version of his letter, Mr. Richman properly lauded the democratic leveling influence of positivistic research. Under positivism, "mere performers can be experts too":

> Most musicians accept new data when it comes their way, and a lot of them now know a great deal about the source materials which used to

be the exclusive territory of the "experts." This is a most wonderful development, completely in the spirit of the Enlightenment; each person is capable and free, by dint of careful examination of the evidence, to form his or her own reasoned conclusions.

Heaven help him or her, though, if those conclusions differ from Mr. Richman's.

Why has it been difficult or impossible for so many musicians to let go of the false perception that historical verisimilitude is in itself a measure of artistic worth? Why should another letter writer, David Pritchard, have assumed that I thought it was "ridiculous" to use countertenors in Handelian castrato roles, when all I said was that it is "demonstrably unhistorical"? But of course I gave the reason, as I see it, in the very article to which my correspondents responded; perhaps they never got to the end.

7

Tradition and Authority

Although I have written about Mozart and about Mozart performances, I am not a card-carrying Mozartean. Why, then, was I asked to address the Lincoln Center conference? It must have been because of my role in our ongoing War of the Buffoons, our dialogue of ancient and modern performance practitioners and theorists. In the spirit of buffoonery, then, let me change the subject. Let's take a break from Mozart and talk about Brahms. And then let's talk about Schubert, Prokofiev, and the Maori of New Zealand. And all the while we will be talking about Mozart just the same; because "Mozart," as we all know perfectly well, is not just Mozart. If Mozart were just Mozart, would we have spent a whole year having fits over him?

Modern? Historical?

My position in the War of the Buffoons can be simply stated. I have suggested that the ancients and moderns ought to exchange labels. What is usually called "modern performance" is in fact an ancient style, and what is usually called "historically authentic performance" is in fact a modern style. I have set this position out in a number of essays and reviews, and I can give their gist by briefly analyzing the latest salvo from the pamphlet wars: a piece by John Eliot Gardiner promoting his new recording of the Brahms Requiem.[1]

[1]J. E. Gardiner, "Brahms and the 'Human' Requiem," *Gramophone*, lxvii (1991): 1809–10.

Originally given as a talk at the Lincoln Cer. er conference, "Performing Mozart's Music," May 24, 1991, and published in *Early Music* 20 (May 1992): . 11–25. Reprinted by permission of Oxford University Press.

It observes all the usual conventions, beginning with the opening confession: "I used to find Brahms' Requiem a maudlin, rather depressing work." Tchaikovsky's dismal assessment of Brahms is thrown in as corroboration. The culprit, of course, is "misconception, anachronism and stylistic accretions, all conspiring towards dating [the work] and removing it from currency." But then comes revelation. With the right instruments, the right tempo and the right players ("whose daily fare [Brahms] isn't") the Requiem stands revealed as "radiant, full-blooded, and optimistic." Gardiner manages to praise his own lean cuisine recipe by identifying it as the composer's: "For all its harmonic richness there is not one gram of excess fat or indulgence in Brahms' [!] handling of his [!] orchestra, and with the chorus in full cry he [!] creates an awesome dynamic curve." Even the conductor's interpretive freedom is licensed by the composer's authority: tempo rubato in this performance, for instance, is founded not on the style of earlier performers—the baleful "crypto-Wagnerian approach" that had sapped the work's vitality—but on certain "wiggly lines pencilled into the conducting score" Brahms used at the first performance, representing "his sense of rubato," not yours or mine (or Gardiner's).

It is easier than usual to decode the message here. Far from a restoration, Gardiner and his players have accomplished a radical defamiliarization, achieved by means of a determined literalism, and governed by an ideal of fleet coolness and light that is wholly born of ironized twentieth-century taste. The involuntary giveaway is the calling of Brahms' contemporary, Tchaikovsky, as witness to the impoverishing effects of "misconception, anachronism and stylistic accretions." It is more obvious than ever that a performance so promoted is not a historically correct performance but a politically correct performance.

By now many readers will be feeling a familiar impatience with me. Why do I persist in debunking the hype rather than criticizing the performance itself? Why do I seem to dismiss (or as one of my exasperated critics has put it, "compulsively ridicule")[2] a movement that has so many beautiful achievements to its credit? Why am I so concerned with motives rather than with results?

But I have never derided the movement or the performances—or even the players. The most quoted line I have ever penned is the one in which I welcomed Roger Norrington as "the next great Beethoven conductor."[3] And though I have seemed at times thereafter to take

---

[2]L. Treitler, Letter to the Editor, *New York Times*, Arts & Leisure, 23 September 1990, 4.

[3]See essay 8. This time the protests came from the other side, e.g., Leo Black, ". . . 'More than Authenticity,' " *Musical Times* 132 (1991): 65.

Maestro Norrington rather severely to task,[4] he has not worn out his welcome with me. While never accepting their claims to historicity, I have had no less enthusiastic things to say about the work of Nicholas McGegan in Handel, Nikolaus Harnoncourt in Bach, and, in Mozart, Frans Brüggen, Malcolm Bilson, and John Eliot Gardiner, among many others.

Regarding the movement itself I have always held that, as a symptomatically modern phenomenon, it is not historical but *is* authentic. It is a message I have had great difficulty in getting across to musicians, because so many have invested so heavily in the false belief that authenticity can derive only from historical correctness. To deny the latter necessarily implies to them a denial of the former. They simply do not hear me when I say that what "historical" performers have actually accomplished is far more important and valuable than what they claim to have done. My reputation is now that of a hostile debunker, and it is as a debunker that I now find myself angrily debunked.

All I have ever debunked, however, has been the hype; and I persist in this disreputable waste of time, as many have called it, precisely because I want to rescue the notion of authenticity from that of historicity. I feel it is an urgent business for three reasons: first, because some of my musicologist colleagues have been throwing their weight — and that of our discipline generally — on the side of what amounts in my opinion to a dishonest claim of privilege; second, because the selective reading of historical evidence in support of an approved modern style has actually led to the repression of certain aspects of historical practice that might be very healthy to revive; third, because a more authentic understanding of what authenticity entails might make classical music more relevant to human needs and thus prolong its life in our culture.

I put my thesis most concisely, and most explicitly, in a short essay (No. 6 in the present collection), which I published in the summer of 1990 in the Arts and Leisure section of the Sunday *New York Times*. Intending the piece for the music page, I gave it a title that I hoped would make the main point inescapable: "It's Not Historical — It's Much Better Than That." When the Arts and Leisure staff decided to run it on the front page, the title had to be revised to include the word "music," so my editor substituted "The Modern Sound of Early Music." But when they decided to promote it from second to top lead, the task of putting a head to it passed out of the hands of Arts and Leisure to the higher editorial echelons. Scanning the essay, the Assistant Managing Editor of the paper found a phrase he couldn't

---

[4]See essay 9.

resist, and emblazoned it on top, even though it distorted the meaning of the piece in just the way I had hoped to avoid. The title that saw print—"The Spin Doctors of Early Music"—looked like a slander, and so I was not surprised to find intelligent musicians again misreading my message and accusing me, in the words of one irate letter-writer, of attempting "to discredit the Early Music movement and the performance esthetic it has engendered."[5]

Who Speaks for the Maori?

Along with the brickbats, however, came a communication from one who did not misunderstand: an anthropologist at the University of Kansas, who wrote with the welcome news that my article "resonates beautifully with some recent developments in anthropology and in history." His letter, accompanied by a reference to one of his own recent publications, went on:

> I was particularly pleased [that] you avoided the trap of debunking "historical" performances as inauthentic. Your analysis of how these represent contemporary values is convincing, and the point that a claim of reviving the past is actually a way of being original in today's world of music is a nice turn of the screw. One further turn is to recognize that essays like yours and mine are themselves reflections of our present orientations—specifically, the decenteredness and play of postmodern culture.[6]

Needless to say, I was elated to read this, and lost no time in looking up my correspondent's work, proceeding from there more deeply into anthropological and ethnomusicological terrain. It has been an education for me, and has led my considerations of the cultural meaning of musical performance practice to a new conceptual plane, and to a new evaluation of its sociopolitical significance. This article is offered as a preliminary account of the new direction I have been exploring, and the new questions it has raised for me.

My correspondent, Prof. Allan Hanson, is a specialist in Maori culture. His article, which has been a newsmaker in his field,[7] is called 'The Making of the Maori: Culture Invention and Its Logic.'[8] What he has discovered is that aspects of Maori cultural tradition,

---

[5]J. Richman, Letter to the Editor, *New York Times*, Arts & Leisure, 26 August 1990, 3. See the postscript to essay 6.

[6]A. Hanson, personal communication, 29 July 1990.

[7]See J. N. Wilford, "Anthropology Seen as Father of Maori Lore," *New York Times*, 20 Feb 1990.

[8]*American Anthropologist*. 91 (1989): 890–902.

including aspects as central as their mythology and their account of their origins as a people, were invented by the European anthropologists who studied them in the nineteenth and early twentieth centuries, and who—like the pioneers of "historical performance" as I have described them—supplemented isolated bits of observed or collected lore with connective tissue that was heavily colored by their own theories and prejudices.

This realization gave rise, on the one hand, not only to post-colonialist guilt,[9] but also to severe epistemological jitters among conservative anthropologists who felt—like some of my colleagues engaged in performance-practice research—that the legitimacy of their activity was under threat, and who tended therefore to resist or denounce a line of inquiry and reasoning that raised skeptical "questions about the nature of cultural reality and whether the information that anthropologists [or music historians] produce can possibly qualify as knowledge about that reality."[10] On the other hand, the new findings were resisted by the Maori themselves, who—like today's "historical" performers—had embraced the invented traditions as their authentic heritage, and drew from them their sense of cultural identity. So as to avoid offending Maori sensibilities, Hanson relates, New Zealand scholars of white European ("Pakeha") stock have had to moderate or repress their critique.[11] This parallels the way I have been accused of wishing to harm or kill the historical performance movement by denying its *raison d'être*.

Hanson argues that these findings should in themselves lead neither to rejection of the ethnographic enterprise nor to the delegitimation of Maori traditions, whatever their origins. "The fact that culture is an invention, and anthropology one of the inventing agents, should not engender suspicion or despair," he writes. In a like manner, I would contend, the fact that historical performance practice is an invention, and musicology one of the inventing agents, does not in itself call the authenticity of its products into question. Citing a wide variety of recent ethnographic studies involving peoples as diverse as the modern Greeks, the Quebecois, and the Hawaiian islanders, Hanson concludes that "when people invent their own tradition it is usually to legitimate or sanctify some current reality or aspiration." Among the newer generations of anthropologists, he writes, tradition

---

[9] For examples of how colonial officials, and anthropologists studying colonial Africa, have authored and imposed "traditions" on indigenous populations, see D. B. Coplan, "Ethnomusicology and the Meaning of Tradition," in *Ethnomusicology and Modern Music History*, ed. Stephen Blum *et al.* (Urbana and Chicago: University of Illinois Press, 1990), 35–48.

[10] Hanson, "The Making of the Maori," 890.

[11] Hanson, "The Making of the Maori," 895.

is now generally "understood quite literally to be an invention designed to serve contemporary purposes," and he quotes a colleague who defines tradition as "an attempt to read the present in terms of the past by writing the past in terms of the present."[12] That I believe this formulation to be wholly applicable to the current performance scene should be obvious. I have been saying it for years, almost in the same words. Not that I was by any means the first to do so: in his early essay, "On the Advantages and Disadvantages of History for Life," Nietzsche wrote, "we try to give ourselves a new past from which we should have liked to descend instead of the past from which we actually descended."[13]

But who needs Nietzsche? Each of us can confirm the truth of the observation introspectively. We all value our personal pasts and heritages selectively and create from them a personal mythology on which our sense of personal identity (read:authenticity) largely depends. Any historian or biographer who deals professionally with memoirs as source material has had to face the issue of constructed identity. (Having devoted long years to investigating Stravinsky I know this as well as anyone: I soon found, moreover, that it was not enough merely to catalog the composer's forgetfulnesses, mendacities, and (self-)deceptions; they turned out to be the very stuff of the Stravinsky character, as manifested not only in the memoirs but in the music.) Writ larger, the same point applies to whole cultures and civilizations; what Hanson says about the Maori is no different from what many cultural critics have been saying about us Pakehas. (Martin Bernal, for example, has devoted a major study to demonstrating that we trace Western civilization back to an "ancient Greece" that never existed until it was invented in the eighteenth century by the same theorists of classicism whose descendants invented the "Classical Period" to canonize the fine art of music in the West.)[14]

From all of this, Hanson suggests, "it follows that the analytical task is not to strip away the invented portions of culture as inauthen-

[12]Hanson, "The Making of the Maori," 890. The quotation is from L. Lindstrom, "Leftamap Kastom: The Political History of Tradition on Tanna, Vanuatu," *Mankind* 13 (1982): 316–29; compare the formulation of E. B. Thompson, quoted in Coplan, "Ethnomusicology," 40: "Tradition [is] dependent upon a symbolically constituted past whose horizons extend into the present."

[13]F. Nietzsche, "Vom Nutzen und Nachteil der Historie für das Leben," quoted in P. de Man, *Blindness and Insight* (2nd. ed., Minneapolis: University of Minnesota Press, 1983), pp. 49–50. Nietzsche continues: "But this is also dangerous, because it is so difficult to trace the limit of one's denial of the past, and because the newly invented nature is likely to be weaker than the previous one."

[14]M. Bernal, *Black Athena: The Afroasiatic Roots of Classical Civilization*, i: *The Fabrication of Ancient Greece, 1785–1985* (New Brunswick, NJ: Rutgers University Press, 1987).

tic, but to understand the process by which they acquire authenticity."[15] Just so. It is the process we want to investigate, so as to demystify it and perhaps free our imaginations to respond to a wider variety of stimuli, including stimuli from history, than our current historical performance orthodoxy allows. In previous studies I have concentrated on identifying that orthodoxy with modernism, our "tradition of the new," and on tracing its rise. Having said something about why it happened, I want to broach the question of how.

The Engine of Change

The assimilation of performance style to the tradition of the new was accompanied by a heavy assault on another kind of tradition, what from here on I shall call the "oral tradition." By "oral tradition" I do not mean necessarily a mouth-to-mouth tradition, but any tradition that is founded on listening and emulating. It is the ordinary handing-down from performer to performer that keeps musical repertories alive. Though we tend to think of the Western musical tradition as a literate one, permanently preserved in written artifacts, the written artifacts have always been mediated by oral traditions of the kind I am describing, as the more reflective historical musicologists—and particularly medievalists—are well aware.[16]

Ethnomusicologists go further: Charles Seeger asserted that "writing cannot be read—either in song or upon an instrument—without recourse to . . . oral tradition,"[17] though he recognized that, unless specially instructed,

> musicians can hardly be expected to regard the term seriously in speaking of a Beethoven symphony. They would recognize the role of oral transmission in the fine art of music if it were explained to them. But they would know it as plain "tradition"—the tradition of Joachim, Caruso, or De Reszke, or of Palestrina or Bach. In the former cases [Joachim, Caruso, De Reszke], they would be referring to very concrete musical realities ["performance practice"], transmitted largely by word of mouth. In the latter [Palestrina, Bach], they would be referring to

[15]Hanson, "The Making of the Maori," 898.

[16]See R. Crocker, "Is There Really a 'Written Tradition' in Music?," an unpublished paper quoted and discussed in J. Kerman, "A Few Canonic Variations," *Canons*, ed. Robert von Hallberg (Chicago: University of Chicago Press, 1984), 77–95. Kenneth Levy, David Hughes, Leo Treitler, and Hendrik van der Werf have also written extensively on the matter of "orality" and its implications, unquestionably the hottest issue in medieval musicology today. For a checklist of this literature, see the bibliography following Levy's article, "On Gregorian Orality" *JAMS*, 43 (1990): 185–227.

[17]C. Seeger, "Oral Tradition," *Funk and Wagnall's Dictionary of Folklore* (New York, 1950), 828.

substantial stylistic generalizations ["counterpoint"] conventionally
dealt with in written words.[18]

Until very recently these "concrete musical realities" were taken very
seriously indeed; conformity with oral tradition used to be what
conferred authenticity on interpretation. As recently as the 1960s
Josef Krips was proud to tell a San Francisco critic that he had his
Mozart direct from . . . Zemlinsky.[19] Some decades earlier Arthur
Friedheim, a pupil of Rubinstein and Liszt, found it altogether natural
to edit the works of Chopin to reflect his teachers' performances,
since their interpretations were integral to what he conceived as the
authentic Chopin tradition. Sergey Rachmaninoff, as record collectors may recall, also welcomed Rubinstein's mediation of the Chopin
tradition, taking the reprise of the funeral march in Chopin's Second
Sonata at Rubinstein's famous *fortissimo* instead of the composer's
piano. Whereas in the 1930s objection to such contamination was
generally written off as mere "purism" or pedantry, by the 1980s even a
musicologist known for her skepticism of scholarly orthodoxy declared
herself to be "astonished" that such things were once tolerated.[20]

Modern musicology has an altogether different concept of authenticity, and hence an altogether different concept of tradition. A
great deal of recent historical-performance theorizing has had for its
purpose the express denial or debunking of Seeger's "concrete musical
realities." There is by now a sizeable polemical literature devoted to
proving that what Seeger called "the oral tradition of writing" in
Western art music does not exist.

Robert Winter, writing in *the New Grove Dictionary of Musical
Instruments* in 1984, wrought some subtle and subversive changes
(as Nicholas Kenyon admiringly called them)[21] in a text Howard
Mayer Brown had written some ten years earlier for the article on
"Performing practice" in the original *New Grove Dictionary*. Accepting Seeger's "concrete musical realities" for styles and genres that had
never fallen out of active repertory, Brown had prefaced the discussion
with the subhead "Continuity of tradition," and stated that "the study
of performing practice in music since 1750 is fundamentally different
from the study of earlier performing practice," since "there is no 'lost
tradition' separating the modern performer from the music of Haydn,
Mozart, and their successors comparable with that which separates

[18]Seeger, "Oral Tradition," 825–26 (glosses in brackets mine).
[19]R. Commanday, "Alexander Zemlinsky's Chance for the Spotlight," *San Francisco Chronicle*, Datebook, 17 February 1991, 31.
[20]R. R. Subotnik, "On Grounding Chopin," in *Music and Society*, ed. R. Leppert and
S. McClary (Cambridge: Cambridge University Press, 1987), 111.
[21]N. Kenyon, "Introduction," *Early Music and Authenticity*, 11.

him from Machaut, or even from Monteverdi." Winter revised the subhead to read "Apparent continuity of tradition," and modified Brown's statement to read as follows:

> Superficially, there is a fundamental difference between the study of performing practice before 1750 and the study of it after that date. Unlike the music of Machaut or Monteverdi, the repertory from Haydn to Elliott Carter has been performed continuously since its creation. . . . But on closer examination neither the assumption of an unbroken performing history nor the corollary of an unbroken performance tradition stands up.[22]

Winter's "apparent continuity of tradition" chimes with Roger Norrington's dismissive phrase, "the perceived orchestral tradition," to denote what his performances have supplanted.[23] The reasons for calling such traditions illusory have to do in the first place, of course, with changes in hardware, but also (in Winter's case) with asserted disruptions in transmission: "Haydn," he writes, "left no accounts of Mozart's performing style," and "the degree of contact between Mozart and the young Beethoven in 1787 has never been reliably established." One can well imagine an ethnomusicologist like Seeger wondering that such considerations are deemed relevant to the transmission of performance style (or even composition style); he would doubtless have chalked it up to the historical musicologist's incurably bourgeois habit of fetishizing individuals and ignoring groups.

Both Winter and Neal Zaslaw, the latter writing in the recent *New Grove* handbook on *Performance Practice: Music after 1600,* heap scorn on the notion of precept and pedagogy as maintainers of continuous tradition. Krips's oral reception of Mozart from Zemlinsky or Friedheim's oral transmission of Chopin via Rubinstein and Liszt are for them only so much irresponsible complacency. Zaslaw, echoing a parallel statement by Winter, writes:

> Many 20th-century pianists could say that they had studied with someone who studied with Leschetizky who studied with Czerny who studied with Beethoven who studied with Haydn who knew Mozart. . . . But this patrimony, while it had indeed been continually handed down from generation to generation, had not remained unchanged. On the contrary, it is now clear beyond reasonable doubt that each generation modified what it received from its teachers' generation until the

[22]*New Grove Dictionary of Musical Instruments*, vol. 3, 53.

[23]D. Henahan, "St Luke's Orchestra with its New Director," *New York Times*, 7 December 1990.

manner of playing music of the Classical period had been altered almost beyond recognition.[24]

Who ever doubted it? The idea that "real" traditions are time capsules and only spurious ("apparent," "perceived") traditions modify what they transmit is seriously entertained by no one. By such a definition there have been no real traditions; to imply as much is fine strategy for undermining confidence in existing ones. But traditions, according to any informed definition, modify what they transmit virtually by definition, if not necessarily by design, working their transformations not only through the active intervention of the critical faculty, but also by what we might call interference. Oral traditions, especially in a musical culture as variegated as the Western fine art of music has become, are multiple, always contaminated, and highly suggestible, receptive to outside influence.[25]

"Mainstream" performers and performer-editors have always tacitly (if not, like Friedheim, openly) recognized that tradition did not merely preserve but adapted and potentially enriched what it sustained, modifying both the "objects" transmitted and the "subjects" who did the transmitting. While the "content" of the music—the part preserved in writing—could be thought of as fixed, its "style"—the manner in which it was presented—could be supplemented or updated practically without limit, without any sense that the object had been violated. Mozart or Schoenberg or Beecham vis-à-vis Handel, Berlioz or Wagner vis-à-vis Gluck, Mahler or Walton or Webern vis-à-vis Bach— all were perpetuators of oral tradition, paradoxical though it seems to say so, seeing their work as part of the legitimate life-support system that kept contemporary art in contact with yesterday's—and vice versa.

Cultural anthropologists and ethnomusicologists, perhaps needless to say, accept these conditions as given. Their literature emphasizes over and over again that traditions as they have existed in the real world have never been anything other than engines of change—perpetual, gradual, regenerative, unstoppable change. Few, if any, "persist . . . in opposing the notion 'traditional music,' like some ever-receding ethnographic horizon, to whatever it is that the folk are (alas!) actually performing, hearing, and dancing to now."[26] Seeger boldly defined tradition as "the handing on of acquired characteris-

---

[24]*Performance Practice: Music after 1600*, ed. H. M. Brown and S. Sadie (New York: W. W. Norton, 1989), 207.

[25]For a general discussion see B. Nettl, *The Study of Ethnomusicology* (Urbana: University of Illinois Press, 1983), chap. 13.

[26]Coplan, "Ethnomusicology," 47. For more trenchant criticism of ethnographic nostalgia, see J. Porter, "Muddying the Crystal Spring," in *Comparative Musicology and Anthropology of Music*, ed. B. Nettl and P. V. Bohlman (Chicago: University of Chicago Press, 1991), 113–30.

tics," observing that "whether or not acquired characteristics can be inherited biologically, there can be no doubt that they are inherited socially." Tradition, on this view, is the means by which "the younger members of a group can begin where the older leave off." And for all their guaranteed inconstancy, traditions are for Seeger "the principal survival mechanisms [of] human culture communities." As "a function of culture" music tradition is inescapably "a dynamic conception." If its products (and, I am tempted to add, its practices) appear to accumulate, *that* is the illusion ("entirely subjective and a direct result of our individual existences in general space-time"). On the contrary, "the repertoire as a whole and its relation to the culture . . . are in a constant state of flux."[27] These forty-year-old formulations of Seeger graphically anticipate the recent theories of cultural invention promulgated by Hanson and company, and apply to "the fine art of music" (as Seeger calls it) as well as they do to the folk musics that were his principal concern.

So the difference between a Krips and a Winter or between a Friedheim and a Zaslaw in their attitude toward the oral tradition has nothing to do with their respective consciousness of change. All have been fully conscious of change. The difference lies in the value placed on change. It is a matter of ideology. For the "ancients," nurtured on the ideal of progress plus faith in the individual genius of performers as well as composers, change was adaptation, survival, even improvement; for the "moderns," heirs to existential *Angst* plus a heavy dose of Germanic philology, change is loss, corruption, debasement, even vandalism.[28] (For us happy-go-lucky postmoderns, with our fluid, "decentered" view, change is interesting.) Tradition as such cannot honestly be denied, only deplored. In deploring it, Winter and Zaslaw have plenty of distinguished company, going back at least as far as Mahler ("Tradition ist Schlamperei") and Strauss ("the last bad performance").

Cheating at Telephone

But if socially sanctioned custom is to be dethroned as arbiter of style, what can replace the empowering sense of direct possession and

[27]All quotes from Seeger in this paragraph are from "Oral Tradition," 826.

[28]"Vandalism" was the preferred term at the Lincoln Center conference, applied especially to editors. As to corruption, compare D. K. Holoman, Introduction to "The 19th Century," *Performance Practice*, ed. Brown and Sadie, 323: "The proximity of the 19th century ensures that the central task in the study of its performance practice is to separate, among all the ore we have inherited, the practices that have survived unsullied from the past from those that have been corrupted by the vagaries of changing taste and fashion."

authoritative transmission such custom enables? Obviously one must draw one's energy from some other power source, some other authority. But which? Whose? The easy answer, of course, is the composer's, direct. Indeed, the idea of the composer as oracle, a vestigial residue of the Romantic cult of genius, has until quite recently been a foundation stone of modern performance ethics, invoked routinely by performers (especially conductors, and particularly when arguing with soloists), by musicologists, and by critics.

In the case of outstanding composer-conductors like Mahler, it is easy enough to see the antitraditional cult of the composer's authority for what it is, namely an assertion of personal authority. He debunked tradition in the heat of battle, in an effort to tame obstreperous performers. Among the *Schlampereien* he is said to have rooted out of his performances were the traditional appoggiaturas in Mozartean recitative, something the composer never imagined doing without. Mahler's alliance with the composer and his putative intentions was a way of pulling rank, and the composer was among those outranked. The same goes for Toscanini, who was known to claim alliance with an even higher authority. He once "apologized" to a musician he had insulted during one of his famous tantrums by protesting, "the trouble is, God tells me how He wants this music played, and you — you get in His way!"[29] Call it God or call it Mozart, the *force majeure* does not vary, and it always comes from within.

I would insist, in fact, that all who claim to speak directly for the composer are in fact asserting their own authority, even if they do not claim divine inspiration. I call it cheating at Telephone, the game in which A whispers a message to B, B to C, and so on, until the last player says it aloud to general hilarity. Not content to accept the whispered message from the one seated next to you, you get up from your seat and tiptoe round behind the other players to the first chair, which by now of course is empty; whereupon you sit yourself down in it and proclaim yourself the winner.

That obviously defeats the purpose of the game. The ploy, increasingly transparent, has been getting rare. (At the Lincoln Center conference it surfaced only once, when Jane Glover praised Sir Thomas Beecham's recording of Mozart's Symphony No. 39 for its "rapport with the composer," when all she could have meant was its rapport with her.) Its most recent prominent advocate was Edward T. Cone, in an essay published a decade ago under the title "The Authority of

[29]H. Taubman, *Music on my Beat* (New York: Simon and Schuster, 1943), 42. In this connection it is worth recalling the nickname Toscanini went by during his reign at La Scala; he was known as *il Dio* ("the God"): H. Sachs, *Toscanini* (Philadelphia: Lippincott, 1978), 138.

Music Criticism," where that authority was located precisely in its congruence with the composer's conception, "insofar as it can be ascertained" by research and analysis—even where it may turn out to have been "subconscious!"[30] One does not have to be a professed poststructuralist to see Cone's claim as circular and self-validating; but so is any claim to alliance with that vacant chair.

Le texte, c'est moi

It is more common today to invest final authority in the "text," the artifact that, under Seeger's definition of "the oral tradition of writing," represents the object negotiated by tradition. The text is rescued, as it were, from tradition (and, as we shall see, from the composer) and enshrined as autonomous, eternally fixed. There have been two distinct phases to this process.

The earlier one, which still has many adherents, was the "Urtext" movement, in which the score as the composer left it was regarded as a complete and self-sufficient directive, the incontestable final arbiter. There remained a site of contention, however, namely the unresolvable question as to which manifestation of the text (fair copy? first edition? corrected *Handexemplar*?) was entitled to the privileged status. The difficulty of hunting down that chimerical beast known as the *Fassung letzter Hand*, embodying the idealized final intentions of the author, finally led to Phase 2, epitomized by James Webster's much-repeated maxim that the score contains the truth and nothing but the truth, but not the whole truth.

On this view, the concept of text was enlarged to include not only the composer's actual notation but written evidence of all kinds (sketches, treatises, payment records, seating plans). As the notion of text expanded, the authority of the composer was correspondingly diminished. If we now expand the notion yet further to encompass all concrete physical objects inherited directly from the past (such as authentic period instruments), we shall come very close to the idea of textual authority that currently reigns among modernist musicians, including the historical kind.

Here, too, it is easy enough to show that ultimate authority rests not in the texts but in the interpreters (for texts do not speak for themselves); that texts, no less than composers, are routinely outranked, if only by other texts or types of text; that when choice among texts is exercised, the choice is irreducibly arbitrary, however

[30]*JAMS* 34 (1981): 1–18; esp. 12–14.

elaborately fiat be disguised as rule; hence (again) that all nontradi-
tional or antitraditional authority is discretionary authority; and,
finally, that "discretionary" is just a euphemism for personal and
subjective.

The surliest attack on oral tradition I have ever seen was made
by a committed textualist, Arthur Mendel (like Mahler and Toscanini
a conductor, but one recently turned scholar), in an essay published
under the title "The Services of Musicology to the Practical Musician." The diatribe, in which the word "tradition" never appears without impugning scare quotes, took the form of a huge gratuitous
footnote to a discussion of the musicologist's primary task, as Mendel
saw it — that of preparing editions of old music. It makes fascinating
reading not only for its rhetorical excess, but for the paradoxical
way it answers the inevitable question: If tradition is abolished,
what remains?

> Sometimes a significant part of the work of ascertaining the original
> meaning of notation consists in clearing away a mass of "tradition"
> attaching to the performance of a particular work or type of work.
>
> In the exercise of his interpretative imagination, a great performer,
> whose playing or singing carries particular conviction, introduces
> a hastening or slowing down of the tempo, a *sforzato* or a *piano subito*,
> a *Luftpause* or a *fermata*, that constitutes an integral part of his con-
> ception of the piece. Lesser men, then, in search of the secret of
> the compelling power of the greater artist's interpretation, grasp at the
> details in which it obviously differs from others — details which the
> great interpreter has not found explicit in the notation but which
> have been suggested to him by his own re-creative imagination. And
> the lesser men imagine that if they imitate these details they will
> achieve an effect similar to that of the performance in which the
> details occurred.
>
> Out of these imitations, and imitations of these imitations, are
> born performance "traditions," which by the time they have earned that
> impressive name have usually become meaningless distortions guarded
> with opinionated obstinacy and a sort of guild or secret-society ped-
> antry by those who have no conception of how they arose or what
> purpose they originally served. Probably few of them have any connec-
> tion with the composer. Whatever their origin, the musicologist must
> help the practical musician to free himself from any supposed obliga-
> tions imposed by them, and thus to make his own direct contact with
> the notation in which the composer has symbolized his intention and
> arrive at his own independent understanding of its meaning.[31]

Like so many others, Mendel represents "tradition" as a sort of
Nibelheim, populated exclusively by the stupid and the complacent,

[31]A. Mendel *et al., Some Aspects of Musicology* (Indianapolis: Bobbs-Merrill, 1957),
8–9.

measured against some Valhalla (here the abode of the intuitive elect).[32] The really glaring contradiction in his argument involves the relationship between the performer, whether "greater" or "lesser," the composer, and the notation. "Traditions" are rejected, "whatever their origin"(!), because they have no *demonstrable* connection with the composer. To the extent that they are not inherent in the notation, even the composer's intentions are thus thrown out of court. Anything unwritten is therefore unknowable and irrelevant to the performer's "obligation." (Also apparently unknowable is what distinguishes interpretive license born of a great artist's "integral conception" from "imitations of imitations"; the distinction is groundlessly invidious.) But who decides what is knowable from the writing and therefore binding?

Since it is presumably the "lesser" performer whom the musicologist addresses—the "greater" being exempted by virtue of his greatness—and since the lesser artist is so defined precisely by his incapacity for "independent understanding," it is not clear what sort of freedom such a musician enjoys by virtue of "direct contact with the notation in which the composer has symbolized his [unknowable] intention." In fact, by making the edition, the musicologist has undertaken to mediate between the "lesser" performer and the notation. Contact is not direct after all. What imposes an authentic "obligation," then, is the covertly paternalistic edition. Ultimate authority, on Mendel's view, rests not with the composer, not with the notation, but with Papa Doc, the musicologist.

The Price We Pay

Text-fetishism, the exaltation of scores over those who read or write them, has seriously distorted contemporary performance practice— notoriously so in the case of Mozart's concertos, where there has been an effort on the part of some musicologists to minimize the spontaneous aspects of their performance and, by forcing evidence, to place arbitrary quasi-Mendelian limits on the freedom of performers. Anachronistic notions of textual fidelity ("*Werktreue*"), of form (e.g., the

---

[32]Compare Philip Brett, who links traditional hostility toward tradition ("assimilating works *unthinkingly* to our mode of performing and perceiving" [italics added]) with more recent notions of enlightened discourse ("a sense of *difference*" [italics original]). See his "Text, Context, and the Early Music Editor," in *Authenticity and Early Music*, ed. N. Kenyon (Oxford: Oxford University Press, 1988), 114; or, for a more explicit statement, "Homosexuality and Music: A Conversation with Philip Brett," in L. D. Mass, *Homosexuality as Behavior and Identity* (Binghamton, N.Y.: Harrington Park Press, 1990), 53.

"double exposition," first described as such by Ebenezer Prout in 1895), and of "classical" concert decorum are projected back onto a repertory that actually embodied an aesthetic closer to that of today's pop culture.[33] It is evident that Mozart's actual performance practices are of far less interest to today's performers and those who instruct them than his texts. As a performer, Mozart is just part of the ignorable "tradition."[34]

But then so is Prokofiev, whom I cite not only because he too had an anniversary celebration in 1991, but because we have evidence of his performance practice such as we shall never have for Mozart. His own recordings of his piano music are available. But they have had virtually no impact on later performers, many of whom must surely have listened to them.

Consider the *Gavotta*, Op. 32, No. 3, composed in 1918 and recorded in 1932. The composer plays the opening pair of staccato quarter notes with a hesitation that leaves no doubt that they are an upbeat (meanwhile identifying the genre: eighteenth-century gavottes begin with an upbeat of a half-note's duration). The slurred eighth-note arpeggio that follows on the downbeat is rushed in compensation, seemingly in accordance with the old rule of tempo rubato, which Prokofiev may well have learned from his piano teacher, Anna Yesipova, not only the pupil but the former wife of Leschetizky ("who studied with Czerny who studied with Beethoven" etc.), or picked up from the performances of any number of virtuosos active in Russia in the first decade of this century. Later on it appears that slightly rushing the tempo was part and parcel of Prokofiev's way of executing fast slurs (and this is corroborated by other recordings of his, notably that of the Third Piano Concerto) (Figure 7.1.).

These features are completely absent in other recordings, for example, the recent one by Boris Berman, an established Prokofiev specialist who has recorded the composer's complete works for piano for Chandos. To hear it is to be finally convinced that, since texts

[33]For a detailed discussion of these points see essay 11.

[34] The one Mozart performer who actually tries to emulate Mozart the performer, Robert Levin, for that very reason remains an isolated and somewhat controversial figure in today's music world. As to the "pop" aesthetic of Mozart's day and the reluctance of today's musicologists to acknowledge it, compare Mozart's famous description of the behavior of the Paris audience at the première of his Symphony No. 31: "The audience, as I expected, said 'Shh!' at the soft beginning [of the finale], and then, as soon as they heard the forte that followed, immediately began to clap their hands" (letter to his father, 3 July 1778) with Neal Zaslaw's commentary: "The 1778 audience required new music and expressed its appreciation and understanding not only after each movement but—exceptionally—during a movement" (*Mozart's Symphonies* (Oxford: Oxford University Press, 1989), 311). The letter itself reveals that the audience's disconcertingly spontaneous behavior was not exceptional; Mozart had predicted it.

Figure 7.1.   Prokofiev, Gavotta, Op. 32, no. 3, mm. 1–8

outrank performers even when the performer is the composer, texts outrank composers, too. Of the oral traditions in which the composer participated so conspicuously, the younger pianist is oblivious. (One can even imagine him setting the composer straight on the matter of tempo: "It says here Allegro *non troppo,* Seryozha, *non troppo!*") For him dots and slurs are just dots and slurs, not tempo indications; he plays "just what's written," assuming the adequacy of what's written to the definition of the music as played even in the face of audible evidence to the contrary. He has accepted the notion, a veritable oral tradition in itself (though put in writing by Mendel), that to imitate the composer's rendition would be a "meaningless distortion." So my own piano teacher told me when I brought the piece in to my lesson. "But that's how Prokofiev plays it," I protested. "I don't care," he parried, "it's wrong."

Sometimes one hears it said that deviant authorial performances like Prokofiev's of Prokofiev or Debussy's of Debussy are valuable because they establish or clarify the limits of acceptability. But that is no help. I still wonder why we are so obsessed with setting those limits. What makes the whole matter doubly ironic is that study of Prokofiev's performance in conjunction with the score shows his apparent licenses to be perfectly consistent—that is, rule-bound—readings of the notation. There are even treatises that put such things in writing, though of course they do not mention Prokofiev. No, I do not mean that we are to accept Prokofiev's performance of his own piece because it is corroborated by Türk, only that blind modernist prejudice against the unwritten is also deaf.[35]

As a thought-experiment, let's imagine for a moment that Prokofiev's version was played by Berman, and Berman's by Prokofiev. Would not "Berman" now be dismissed out of hand as "mannered"? But more to the point—would not "Prokofiev's" literalistic rendition now assume *immense* authority, because it could now be used to bolster notions of *Werktreue*? It would now simplify rather than complicate our idea of what, exactly, defines or constitutes "the piece." A similar thought occurred to me at the Lincoln Center conference as I listened to Jacob Lateiner's loving description of the manuscript containing Mozart's Rondo in A minor, K. 511. I was fascinated by his account of a small alteration in the slurring at the end of the first phrase, and convinced when he characterized it as a stroke of genius. And yet, I had to wonder, would its sound, its effect, its meaning, or its genius be any different if, instead of occurring to Mozart in the act of writing the piece down, the change had occurred to Mr. Lateiner in the course of practicing or performing it? The answer must obviously be no, so far as the listener is concerned, and yet it is part and parcel of the *Werktreue* philosophy, as Mr. Lateiner himself outlined it, that any such spontaneous tampering is forbidden. It is plainly tautological (though, like all tautologies, irrefutable) to argue that a genuine stroke of genius can occur only to the composer; yet that tautology is the very root of the Urtext ideology (even in its expanded form), and it is among the factors that have so stifled the creativity of classical musicians since Mozart's time.

Sometimes I wish we could somehow abolish scores without abolishing pieces—that is, return music to a fully oral tradition, but with our cherished repertory intact. At the very least, I think, we would pay more attention, as listeners, to the kinds of things that make individual performances treasurable, and, as performers, we would be more inclined to emulate their charisma. Consider another case of "mannerism," one that resonates curiously with Prokofiev's way of doing his gavotte. Artur Schnabel's recorded performance of the little Schubert *Moment musical* in F minor[36] used to be controversial. The slurred pairs of sixteenths (often slurred onto the following eighth) are given a familiar little push by the venerable Viennese pianist, who studied, like Prokofiev's teacher, with Leschetizky. (I remember being exhorted as an adolescent by another of my own

---

[35]The literal truth of this statement is driven home by reviewers who have praised Berman's Prokofiev performances for realizing (to quote Peter G. Davis) "important defining qualities one hears in the composer's own recordings": *New York* 24/9 (13 May 1991): 98.

[36]Angel COLH-308, originally recorded in 1937

teachers, "If Schubert had wanted that, he would have written that"; to which I now would answer, "How?") Also unexpected and unnotated (and related) are the little *Luftpausen* that come before the cadences on A♭. On the other hand, Schnabel doesn't make much of the notated dynamics.

The notated dynamics are more faithfully observed (and lots of unnotated ones added) by another, younger Viennese, Paul Badura-Skoda, whose performance[37] otherwise resembles Schnabel's a great deal. He, too, indulges in that unwritten lilt on the paired sixteenths. Is he merely imitating the great man's invention? Was Schnabel imitating Leschetizky's? Does that mean, as Mendel would say, that they had "no conception of how [it] arose or what purpose [it] originally served"? Or are we dealing, in effect, with two artists who know how to say *Zwirnknäulerl*?[38] It's a Viennese thing; Sviatoslav Richter or Emil Gilels wouldn't understand, as we may hear in their recordings.[39]

But what, precisely, is its status? Does it go back to Schubert? Or does it represent the beginnings of "alteration almost beyond recognition"? Is it just a "perceived" or "apparent" tradition? Is it sanctioned by authority? Whose? Does it possess authority? For whom? Does it have validity? What validates it? Should editors take note of it? Should they undertake to free performers from "obligation" to it? Should critics endorse it? Should they condemn it? Should we draw the magic circle round "the piece" wide enough to include all rhythmic variants? If not, where will we place the limits? What will fall outside? When you start considering such questions, Robert Donington's "simple and categorical" retort to skeptics of performance-practice fundamentalism— "*Authenticity is congruity between music and performance*"—could hardly seem more complicated and indeterminate. " 'Do it now as it was originally done' is no bad start for getting round to that," he further specifies.[40] But since it transpires that "doing it as it was originally done" is exactly his definition of "congruity," and his only one, the clarification only compounds ambiguity with another impregnable tautology.

[37]Westminster XWN 18161, c. 1960

[38]See C. von Canon, "Zwirnknäulerl: A Note on the Performance of Johann Strauss *et al.*," *Nineteenth-Century Music* 2 (1978–79): 82–84. While breezily written, this is one of the few musicological discussions of performance practice to take "oral" traditions seriously, in this case quite literally oral; the article shows how characteristic Viennese dance rhythms reflect the rhythms of Viennese colloquial speech.

[39]Richter: Melodiya D-011755, released in the USA on Monitor MC 2057 (c. 1960); Gilels: Melodiya S-40082, released in the USA on Musical Heritage Society MHS 4025 (1979). Here, too, there is a nice irony: the piece was first published in the almanac *Album musical* (Vienna: Sauer & Leidesdorf, 1823) under the title "Air russe."

[40]R. Donington, "The Present Position of Authenticity," *Performance Practice Review* 2 (1989): 117.

Tradition Redux?

A humanist has been defined as one who rejects authority but respects tradition.[41] Our liberal educations were founded on that precept. The history of our century should have convinced us all by now that the aesthetically seductive simplicities of determinism and utopianism have got to be resisted wherever they may surface, and that the endlessly renegotiated social contract, dowdy patchwork though it be, is the only cause worth defending. That is why I find it so dispiriting, and ultimately sinister, that so much of the rhetoric in our ongoing War of the Buffoons has taken the opposite tack, respecting authority and rejecting tradition.

That is the authentic rhetoric of modernism, all right, as epitomized in the latest blast from Generalissimo Boulez, who "sing[s] the praises of amnesia" in a recent issue of *Early Music*.[42] Despite all the usual savagery of expression and violent imagery, his harangue is limp and quaint, for he naively mistook his audience. Far from the tribe of easily intimidated traditionalists he may have remembered from Early Music's age of antiquarian innocence, he was now addressing a readership of authoritarian amnesiacs every bit as intransigent as he. To shout "there is no such thing as tradition"[43] won't cow this crowd; they have been shouting it for years. Boulez never voiced any more militant hostility toward tradition than Clive Brown, who elsewhere in the same issue debunks a whole slew of Haydn recordings on period instruments because the players have not altogether expunged the memory of their training.[44]

It may be time for some countermilitancy—against authority, against utopia, against purity—on behalf of tradition as hermeneuts conceive it: cumulative, multiply authored, open, accommodating, above all *messy*, and therefore human. By all means let the stream of authentistic experimentation continue. At its best it is the best thing now going, and its commercial success is all the evidence we need of its authenticity. It is an authenticity born of its unquestionable relevance to our sense of ourselves at this moment, and to the culture we have invented. We like what is authentic because authentic is what we like. To seek any higher or more objective criterion is to confuse the goals of performance with those of research; that there is a difference I continue to insist. Authentistic performance, being the loyal

[41]E. Panofsky, *Meaning in the Visual Arts* (Chicago: University of Chicago Press, 1955), 3.

[42]P. Boulez, "The Vestal Virgin and the Fire-stealer: Memory, Creation and Authenticity," *Early Music* 18 (1990): 355.

[43]Ibid., 358.

[44]Record review, *Early Music* 18 (1990): 483–86.

child not of antiquity but of modernity, is in this sense quite traditional. It stands firmly in the receiving line of that grand game of
Telephone we call culture. Yet the hype continues to proclaim the
ugly opposite, and as long as the Emperor continues to parade I shall
be standing in the crowd with the other little boys.

I do see hopeful signs of counterinsurgency in some recent scholarly, critical, and even practical work. In a wide-ranging manual for
conductors currently in progress, David Epstein is attempting to
revive (or assert) the ideal of proportional tempo. His thesis is certainly not free of utopianism (nor am I much impressed by his frequent appeals to biological or historical necessity). But his empirical
surveys of tempo relationships in actual recorded performances have
revealed the way oral tradition has often imposed proportional tempo
relationships on works (such as the Schumann symphonies) whose
explicit metronome indications have not been coordinated proportionally. What I find so refreshing and liberating is that, instead of
turning this observation into a new stick for beating a tired old drum
on behalf of the infallible composer-creator, Epstein has the courage
to assert that in such cases the composer was wrong and tradition is
right.[45] The social mediation of the rhythmic structure, he implies,
has helped keep the music alive. That is what tradition is and does,
and why it is valuable. Though it contradicts the most hallowed
dogma of modernism to say so, the customer is not always wrong.

I think we are more open to this idea, even in the academy,
than we used to be. I'd like to think that an audience of academic
performance-practitioners might no longer react with quite so easy a
laugh as the one I observed only a few years ago when a crusading
scholar mocked a journalist for having called a traditional high note
in Verdi a gift from the Italian people to the composer. But then
reclaiming Verdi (and Donizetti, and Rossini) from the folk—which
meant zealously textualizing them—was one of the ways in which
Italian opera was redeemed for the canon in the 1960s and 1970s. It is a
measure of how far and how fast things have moved that a serious
musician like David Epstein can now acknowledge and even approve
the extent to which the German symphonic literature has become
folk music.

That is obviously a postmodern attitude, but it is not new. It is far
older, in fact, than the "historical" ideology it is in process of supplant-
ing. Not that historical performers will have no place in a decentered
musical polity. Their special opportunity—once they get past the
text-fetish and the bad conscience it breeds, and get truly historical—

---

[45]D. Epstein, *Shaping Time: Music, the Brain, and Performances* (New York:
Schirmer Books, 1995).

will be to point one possible way out of the desert of unspontaneous uncreativity in which classical music now languishes. They will only stand a chance of doing this, of course, if they aspire to say the next word, not have the last. They need to see themselves not as a substitute for the oral tradition, but as part of it.

And here, happily, I can end the sermon, because that is exactly what seems to be happening. Why has historical performance been improving so spectacularly over the last decade? Why do we hear so much less self-conscious downbeat bashing than we used to, so much less distracting *messa di voce*? It's not because the performers are reading better treatises (the treatises haven't changed), or because their hardware is improving (though of course it is). It's because they are not just chaining themselves to the documents. They are listening to and competing with one another, starting younger and with more experienced teachers, thinking of themselves increasingly as normal rather than as deviant or alienated members of musical society. In short, the movement has spawned a viable oral tradition. Around that authentic modern product I admire so much a hardy social practice has been growing up that obeys its own dictates, has its own momentum, is becoming more and more eclectic, contaminated, suggestible. Is this just wishful thinking? Perhaps not; Alfred Brendel has sensed the same phenomenon: "Principles, textbook rules and fixed ideas are [now] held in check by musicians for whom music is the sum of *all* its parts. Performances have become less dogmatic and more personal."[46]

So the engine of change is chugging away. Acquired characteristics are being inherited socially. The younger members of the group are beginning where the older leave off. Soon everyone will be improvising cadenzas, embellishing arias, extemporizing over grounds in a gratifying spirit of play—or they will if we'll let them. So let's forget utopia. Cut the authoritarian propaganda. No more special pleading! No more Eichmann defenses! Can we just stand back and let tradition have its way? I will if you will.

POSTSCRIPT, 1994

The rapprochement with ethnomusicology broached in this essay is by now a tangible decentering trend within the discipline of "unprefixed" musicology, evidence in its way of the emergence of a specifically musicological postmodernism. Scholars trained within ethno-

---

[46]A. Brendel, *Music Sounded Out* (New York: Farrar, Straus and Giroux, 1990), 223.

musicology (or its parent disciplines, anthropology and sociology) have begun to investigate Western art music and its institutions. The outstanding achievement of this type to date is Henry Kingsbury's *Music, Talent, and Performance*, to which reference is made in the Introduction. (A similar study of IRCAM, Pierre Boulez's technocratic empire, by the British scholar Georgina Born, will have been published by the time these words see the light.) Conversely, historical musicologists have been appropriating ethnomusicological attitudes and interrogative techniques, particularly as concerns the matters alluded to in footnote 16. Here the benchmark has been Peter Jeffery's *Re-Envisioning Past Musical Cultures: Ethnomusicology in the Study of Gregorian Chant* (Chicago: University of Chicago Press, 1992). Both Kingsbury's and Jeffery's work have much to teach the student of performance practice, whether the subject is approached from within (as an empirical research field) or from without (as a metamusicological case study).

With its radical opposition of tradition and pseudotraditionalism, the latter a legitimating front for modernist authoritarianism, the argument of essay 7 seems to resonate in various ways with those put forth in an influential book of essays coedited by the eminent British Marxist historian Eric Hobsbawm.[1] The editorial introduction contains a number of provocative statements that could easily slide undetected into various essays of mine, for example: "novelty is no less novel for being able to dress up easily as antiquity" (p. 5); or, "where [traditions] are invented, it is often not because old ways are no longer available or viable, but because they are deliberately not used or adapted" (p. 8). Elsewhere Hobsbawm speaks of a persistent pattern whereby movements in defense of tradition, or promoting the revival of traditions, coincide with, and appear in reaction to, socially disruptive historical events.

Hobsbawm sorts invented traditions into "three overlapping types":

a. those establishing or legitimizing or symbolizing social cohesion or the membership of groups, real or artificial communities
b. those establishing or legitimizing institutions, status, or relations of authority
c. those whose main purpose was socialization, the inculcation of beliefs, value systems, and conventions of behavior (p. 9).

Not surprisingly for a historian whose primary field of expertise is nationalism, Hobsbawm sees type a as prevalent, the other

---

[1]*The Invention of Tradition*, ed. Eric Hobsbawm and Terence Ranger (Cambridge: Cambridge University Press, 1983).

two (associated mainly with colonialism) "being regarded as implicit in or flowing from a sense of identification with a 'community' and/or the institutions representing, expressing or symbolizing it such as a 'nation.' "

Hobsbawm's "type b" does seem to jibe with certain aspects of performance-practice doctrine (cf. Neal Zaslaw's "documentary tradition," discussed in the Introduction). But until more research has been carried out on the institutional history of Early Music (something that, to my knowledge, has as yet been only investigated informally),[2] the extent to which Hobsbawm's model applies to the classical music scene cannot be assayed. Restraint in applying a model that contains so many notorious and volatile components is clearly indicated.

To leap incautiously to conclusions would smack of conspiracy theorizing, in which motives are irresponsibly inferred from perceived results. A fairly sweeping example of this kind of reasoning is the following assertion by Robert Walser, a scholar of popular music:

> Classical music is the sort of thing Eric Hobsbawm calls an "invented tradition," whereby present interests construct a cohesive past to establish or legitimise present-day institutions or social relations. The hodgepodge of the classical canon—aristocratic and bourgeois music; academic, sacred and secular; music for public concerts, private soirees and dancing—achieves its coherence through its function as the most prestigious musical culture of the twentieth century.[3]

The process of this "construction," often called "canonization," is well worth investigating, and a few musicologists and historians, some of whose work is cited in essay 4, have already undertaken the task.[4] It is by no means obvious, however, that this process of legitimation is an "invented" tradition by Hobsbawm's definition—that is, one with a single ascertainable origin and a single identifiable purpose—rather than simply a tradition as normally understood. (An example of a Hobsbawmian "invented tradition" would be the institution of Thanksgiving Day in the middle of the nineteenth century to legitimate a view of American history extending back to the seventeenth.) Nor is it obvious that top-down invented traditions differ from ordi-

---

[2]Both Harry Haskell's *The Early Music Revival: A History* (London: Thames and Hudson, 1988) and Howard Mayer Brown's "Pedantry or Liberation? A Sketch of the Historical Performance Movement," in the Kenyon collection, are anecdotal works, centered more on individuals and their careers than on institutions.

[3]Robert Walser, "Eruptions: Heavy Metal Appropriations of Classical Virtuosity," *Popular Music* 11 (1992): 265.

[4]An anthology of such studies, published since essay 4 came out, can be found in Katherine Bergeron and Philip V. Bohlman, ed., *Disciplining Music: Musicology and Its Canons* (Chicago: University of Chicago Press, 1992).

nary traditions in ways that would be relevant to Walser's thesis about classical music. According to Allan Hanson, whose work stimulated essay 7, they do not. (Recall the definition of "ordinary" tradition cited in Hanson's essay: "an attempt to read the present in terms of the past by writing the past in terms of the present.") Walser's attempt to expose the inauthenticity of the classical canon merely by noting its heterogeneity seems in any case to draw upon a discourse of purism he elsewhere, with the best of reasons, rejects, as do Hanson and most ethnomusicologists.

The question, as always, is how traditions, invented or otherwise, acquire their legitimacy, a question conspiracy theorists beg. Their skepticism is of course attractive, as Hobsbawm readily concedes, since the invention of tradition usually takes place for purposes of political (or, under capitalism, of commercial) manipulation. "To this extent," he writes, "conspiracy theorists opposed to such manipulation have not only plausibility but evidence on their side."[5] Where they fall short of critical standards is in their easy assumption that conspiratorial exploiters are omnipotent. As Hobsbawm puts it, "the most successful examples of manipulation are those which exploit practices which clearly meet a felt—not necessarily a clearly understood—need among particular bodies of people. . . . It is the historian's business to discover them retrospectively—but also to try to understand why, in terms of changing societies in changing historical situations, such needs came to be felt."[6] As I suggest in essay 4, what is needed, in short, is an account not only of the persuaders but of the persuaded; and what will emerge will be an understanding not only of "authenticity," but (as Allan Hanson assures us) of authenticity as well.

[5]*The Invention of Tradition*, 307.
[6]Ibid.

IN PRACTICE

BEETHOVEN

8

The New Antiquity

BEETHOVEN: Symphonies (3); Concertos for Piano and Orchestra (2); Overtures (2).

Mary Verney, fortepiano; Hanover Band, Monica Huggett and Caroline Brown, dir. NIMBUS (d) CD, NIM 5003, 5007, 5031.

BEETHOVEN: Symphony No. I, in C, Op. 21.

Orchestra of the Eighteenth Century, Frans Brüggen, cond. PHILIPS (d) CD, 416 329-2.

BEETHOVEN: Symphonies: No. 2, in D, Op. 36; No. 8, in F, Op. 93.

London Classical Players, Roger Norrington, cond. (David R. Murray, prod.) ANGEL REFLEXE (d) CD, CDC 47698.

BEETHOVEN: Symphony No. 3, in E-flat, Op. 55 ("Eroica").

Academy of Ancient Music, Christopher Hogwood, fortepiano and dir. (Peter Wadland, prod.) OISEAU-LYRE (d) CD, 417 235-2.

COMPARISON—Symphonies Nos. I, 2

Hogwood/Academy   OISEAU-LYRE CD. 414 338

I

"Early Music" has stretched its jaws again. It is engorging Beethoven, and has announced its designs on Schubert and Berlioz. In so doing, it has implicitly redefined itself, exacerbating all over again the

Originally published in *Opus* (October 1987): 31–41, 43, 63. Reprinted by permission.

tensions that have always attended its growth. It is time for another stocktaking and, possibly, some consciousness-raising both within the movement and without. What are its (cl)aims? What should they be? What has Early Music got to offer us?

For raising questions like these over the last several years, I seem to have acquired the reputation of a renegade among those in the movement for whom answers must be simple. Since I was among the first to question the No. 1 assumption on which the movement has based its claims—viz., that it is one of historical reconstruction and that therein lies its value—I am forever being chided for holding the simple-minded view that only complete and certain knowledge is knowledge at all, and that therefore research into performance prac-tice is futile. It is true that I have been eager to call attention to the inevitability of "gaps between the facts," and hence to the necessity for creative guesswork in any attempt at reconstruction, to the point where the word *reconstruction* is put into question. And I have always upheld the inspired guessers over their more pusillanimous col-leagues, who are content to let historical performance become a sort of lottery, according to the terms of which decisions and choices are dodged and the performer's approach dictated by the mere state of research over which, in his capacity as performer, he can exercise no control. "Because of this inescapable element of uncertainty," writes Standley Howell in a substantial and important review-essay in the *Journal of Musicological Research* (Vol. 7 [1986], No. 1) that covers some of the same recordings under review here, "some music historians have begun to wonder if the entire historical performance movement is misdirected. But our inability to achieve absolute authenticity should not prevent us from trying to understand as much as we can." The only obscurantist mentioned by name in the footnote accompanying these remarks is I.

Sorry, wrong number. All or nothing is not my hang-up. Research in an effort "to understand as much as we can" is never misdirected. That is the purpose of research. Howell goes on: "Historically-oriented performances can afford real insights into period musical style as long as we remember that all such efforts are experimental and subject to criticism and eventual revision." Of course. That, too, is in the very nature of historical research, of which experimental perfor-mance is a perfectly legitimate and honorable branch. If that were all that was claimed, no one would have heard a peep out of me.

But of course much more is claimed. The hornist Horace Fitz-patrick, writing on behalf of the Hanover Band, has let it be known that thanks to that group's efforts, "for the first time it is possi-ble to present the orchestral music of Ludwig van Beethoven to the listening public of today in a form which he would recognise." Clever ambiguity, that last word, laden to the brim with values of all kinds. Does it imply that Beethoven wouldn't know his own music in other renditions? Or that he would not admit their validity? Or, simply, that he would acknowledge, "Yes, that's how I did it." Any way you slice it, the Hanover Band is claiming privilege. It is claiming Beethoven's approval, and further, that his imprimatur makes its work in some way more edifying or nutritious for "the listening public of today." But how does that follow? When pressed on this score, authenticists who don the mantle of the composer's authority declare it to be a self-evident virtue. But the self-evidence is a product of a contemporary and very suspect ideology there is no reason to assume a nineteenth-century musician (even a very, very early nineteenth-century musician) would have shared (leaving aside, for the moment, whether the Hanover Band has earned the right to the claim at all). Does a text, in fact, embody a prescription for its interpretation? And if it does, is "original intention" immutable and binding, exempt forever from review or revision? I assume that those who accept the Hanover Band's claims at face value are prepared to go the distance with Mr. Meese on the matter of the constitution.

At once subtler and even more irresponsible are the claims Christopher Hogwood made, on launching his traversal of the Beethoven Nine, in a *Gramophone* puff piece (March 1986) that has become, I am happy to say, something of a *locus pudoris* among apologists for historical performance. He, too, claims to have reconsidered the repertoire "from the composer's point of view," and like most performers today (and all authenticists) he prefers to see "intentions" in terms of the letter of the text and empirical facts about the period (rather than in terms of the "spirit" of the text and the "effect" of the performance — for make no mistake about it: Authenticists are not the only ones to claim fidelity to Beethoven's intentions; everyone has claimed it, from Wagner and Bülow on down). So far Hogwood is merely echoing the divine Wanda, nobody's idea of an authenticist today, and her famous squelch (to whom? — the interlocutor differs with every telling): "All right, my dear, you go on playing Bach in your way, I'll go on playing him in his." But now hear this, for it's mind-boggling: Hogwood claims, by virtue of his historical approach, that "as in our appreciation of non-recreative art (painting, sculpture, literature), we can make our starting point what the work *is*, not what we would, with hindsight, design or expect it to be."

OK, I'll bite; what *is* a piece of music, anyway? If we could define this, we'd really know what "authenticity" was at last; for as Walter Benjamin put it over half a century ago in his famous essay, "The Work of Art in the Age of Mechanical Reproduction" (1936), "the presence of the original is the prerequisite to the concept of authenticity," and the "original" exerts its power over us by virtue of a fetishistic "aura," an atavism of art's origin in cult.

(The presence of a cultish or ritual element in our attitude toward art even today cannot be denied. It can be most easily seen, with respect to music, in the pleasure we continue to take in rehearing familiar works, something that, abetted by "music appreciation," "Great Performances," and the like [and here I can refer the reader to the chilling concluding chapters of Joseph Horowitz's *Understanding Toscanini*, without necessarily endorsing the author's diagnosis of the etiology of the disease he so effectively describes], has contributed to the universally deplored crisis of repertoire in our "classical music" establishment. Often it is claimed [e.g., by Leonard B. Meyer in his well-known essay of 1961, "On Rehearing Music"] that the pleasure of rehearing consists in perceiving new relationships and implications that had previously been missed or forgotten, and that tolerance for rehearing varies inversely with musical sophistication. The truth of these observations is probably consistent with the experience of each of us, to be sure. But just as surely we can all recall an experience like this: As children we are being read to sleep with a fairy tale we have heard fifty times and know by heart; mommy or daddy tries to expedite matters by skipping a page or a paragraph or a sentence; we immediately notice, are distressed, protest; the missing words are spoken for the fifty-first time, and, mollified and reassured, we fall happily asleep. Whatever novelty our fifty-first "Eroica" may contain for us, and however powerfully the experience of it may be renewed by a superlative or challenging rendition [another factor Meyer took into account, and to which we shall return], it is also the element of ritual intoning that pleases and entrances, and it is this element above all that lends an "aura" to the proceedings—one threatened, as we all know, by the easy availability of music in the age of recordings, something many composers [notably Stravinsky in his *Autobiography* and Britten in his Aspen Award speech] have decried.)

Now "aura," as Benjamin implied, increases directly with the perception of "authenticity," that is, originalhood. It keeps people, many of whom have reproductions of it tacked to their walls, crowding the Louvre to view the *Mona Lisa*, and it is that very aura that Hogwood, who makes explicit comparison with painting, seeks to arrogate for his "original" Beethoven. To return to the question, then, what is a musical "original"? To what extent can we say with Hogwood, "This *is* the piece" (say, the "Eroica"); or, "The piece *is* thus-and-so"?

There are three schools of thought on this matter: One holds that the musical work *is* the score, another that it *is* whatever the first performance was, and a third holds the question to be absurd.

II

Anyone who has really thought about the problem will be found in the third camp. Foremost among them is the Polish philosopher Roman Ingarden, who devoted a whole book to what Hogwood so blithely takes for granted, namely, *The Work of Music and the Problem of Its Identity*. Rejecting score because of its lack of specificity and performance because of its excessive contingency, he characterizes the musical work (in explicit contradistinction to those "nonrecreative" arts with which Hogwood presumptively associates it) as a "purely intentional object," using the word *intentional* in the highly specialized sense adopted by phenomenologists, for whom it denotes something that can exist only in thought (or in understanding). Such thinking about a piece of music does depend on the prior existence of score or performance or both, but the piece cannot be wholly identified with either. The score is a plan for the work and the performance an instance of it, but the work as such is a mental construct only.

Is this quibbling? If you think it is, try answering Ingarden's question, "Where is Chopin's B minor Sonata?" Is it there on your shelf, or here in the hall where Ashkenazy is playing? Or in the one where Horowitz is playing? And what about *my* shelf? Or maybe it is located in Chopin's manuscript (as the Hanover Band would probably maintain, since it makes such a selling point of the fact that it plays from facsimile materials)? That sounds like a reasonable way of settling the score, but what if the Chopin Institute in Warsaw and all its contents burned down? Would the sonata then cease to exist? (Unless, of course, you are one of those who think it hasn't existed—except in "transcriptions"—since Chopin himself last played it on his Erard piano. . . .)

Ingarden understood that there is more to a musical composition than its sounds. Musicians nowadays may find the title of his fifth chapter, "The Sounding and Nonsounding Elements and Moments of a Musical Work," unsatisfactory or paradoxical, but its contents are enlightening. His "nonsounding elements" include such things as rhythm, tempo, "movement," contour, and harmony (as well as what you'd expect, namely the "emotional" or "representational" qualities a piece may contain). We might at first blush insist on classifying rhythm, tempo, contour, and harmony among the sounding elements in a musical work, but upon reflection it becomes clear that all of these things are *relationships* among sounds as interpreted by a qualified listener.

The "tonic triad," for example, is not a sound, but a function assigned a sound within a syntactical and hierarchical system one must be trained to perceive. No mark made by pen or press on paper can be called inherently a tonic triad, nor can a group of tones depressed on a keyboard be called that without the mediation of theory. The tonic triad, then, inheres neither in the notation nor in the sounds, but it certainly inheres in the work as long as the work is performed among those who have learned the concept and have the ability to recognize it in context. For those who haven't, though they may attend a performance of the B minor Sonata, and though they may own a copy of the score, the B minor Sonata has no existence.

These ideas, though they may appear gratuitous or self-evident when enunciated so baldly, seem necessary to introduce into a discussion of the claims of historical performance, because so many of the movement's premises rest on an implicit denial of them. That is, they rest on an extremely, if tacitly, materialistic attitude toward the nature of music. In the course of a recent symposium at Oberlin College about "Historically-Informed Performance," for example, the question arose, as it so often does, why we advocate historical authenticity in the performance of early music, but not in performance of "early theater" (e.g., Shakespeare). Why don't we (yet) insist on historical pronunciation, or on boys in girls' roles, or on limiting theatrical resources to what may have been available in the sixteenth century? A very hot young critic who should have known better (no, who *does* know better) leaped in with the observation that in theater it's "the meaning of the sounds" that counts, while in music it's just "the sound of the sounds." He was gently reminded by a fellow panelist that music, too, communicates through "the meaning of the sounds," that is the relationships among them, even if the sounds have no easily defined external referents, such as words possess. But the absolutism to which the first speaker gave such hasty utterance does lie at the root of a lot of trendy nonsense about "authentic" performance.

Those who identify a musical work either with score or performance have to make the absolutist or materialist assumption—but that is the least of their difficulties. Take Nelson Goodman, the King of the Nominalists, who in *Languages of Art* comes up with a Theory of Notation that posits the score as absolute arbiter of a musical work's identity. This is anything but the ordinary, practical conception of a score. For Goodman the score does not prescribe the work but describes it. Immediately he has to assert two absurd corollaries. First, that only a note-perfect performance (i.e., one that, in Goodman's language, exhibits "full compliance" with the score) qualifies as an instance of the work in question. "The composer or musician is likely to protest indignantly at refusal to accept a performance with a few wrong notes [actually, with a single one] as an instance of a work; and he surely has ordinary usage on his side. But ordinary usage here points the way to disaster for theory." At which point we may well inquire, what price theory? Or more to the point, what is theory supposed to accomplish? "Common usage," for Goodman, in this case, "risks the consequence — in view of the transitivity of identity — that all performances whatsoever are of the same work. If we allow the least deviation, all assurance of work-preservation and score-preservation is lost; for by a series of one-note errors of omission, addition, and modification, we can go all the way from Beethoven's *Fifth Symphony* to *Three Blind Mice*." And never notice, right? Well, perhaps we would, even Professor Goodman, but since we can state no rule that would infallibly stipulate the point at which Beethoven's Fifth left off and "Three Blind Mice" began, not the slightest deviation from the text can be tolerated. (But which text? The autograph? The first printed editions? Parts or score? Peter Gülke's new critical edition? Your old yellow Eulenburg? My green Kalmus?)

Now what shall count as a deviation? Here is the second absurd corollary. Only notated signs whose meanings may be quantified in terms of relative frequency (pitch) or relative duration (rhythm) need be complied with; for only these *can* be complied with on Goodman's terms. Nonquantifiable specifications, including marks of expression, Italian words, and so forth, may be interpreted with unlimited latitude or ignored at pleasure, for they are "nonnotational." So, for example, "tempo specifications cannot be accounted integral parts of the defining score, but are rather auxiliary directions whose observance or nonobservance affects the quality of a performance but not the identity of the work." Unless, of course, they are metronomic indications, for these are quantitative, hence "notational," and therefore binding within the same rigid "compliance" rules for "work-preservation." We have an interesting situation here, indeed. As long as the first movement of Beethoven's Fifth Symphony carries the indication half note = 108, a performance at half note = 107 (or one containing so much as a single measure at half note = 107) does not qualify as an instance of the work; but if the words *Allegro con brio* had stood alone (as, from 1808 to 1817, they did), a performance of the piece lasting ten hours from beginning to end *would* qualify, so long as the relative durations indicated by the note values were meticulously observed. As will be all too apparent from the discussion that will follow, the requirement of metronomic compliance as posited by Goodman cannot be (humanly) realized. And what were the chances, given the realities of musical life in Vienna during Beethoven's lifetime, of a note-perfect performance between 1808 and 1817? Beethoven's Fifth, it transpires, has never been performed. (Wendy Carlos, quick, to the rescue!)

So we shall not wonder that Roman Ingarden dismissed as futile any attempt rigorously to define a musical work in terms of its score. The score is not meant to define the work, only to make its performance possible. Both phylogenetically and ontogenetically, music is anterior to its notation. (Though Goodman actually seems to think the opposite is true, when he distinguishes between a painting that is "autographic," i.e., wholly executed by the artist, and a musical work, which is "allographic" in that only the notation, not the sonic realization, is necessarily executed by the composer. There is considerable irony here, since this distinction leads Goodman to assert that "in music, unlike painting, there is no such thing as a forgery of a known work." Tell that to the Early Music hardware snobs I have written about, for instance in essay 13. But Goodman's dichotomy is fallacious on its face: Art forgeries are not generally of works but of artists. Van Megeeren did not copy "Vermeers" but Vermeer. And what is the difference between a Van Megeeren "Vermeer" and a Kreisler "Louis XIII," a "Mozart" by Marius Casadesus, a "Handel" by his brother Henri, or indeed the hundreds of musical manuscripts that have circulated over the last 250 years under the name "Pergolesi," some of them actually purporting to be autographs manufactured for sale to unsuspecting collectors—and here is the real equivalent to a forged painting, proving that music, too, can be "autographic".)

III

The remaining position—that a musical work *"is"* whatever took place at the first performance—though it is the least tenable of all, is nonetheless the one explicitly espoused by Hogwood and the Hanover Band. Hogwood led up to his point about what a Beethoven symphony *is* with the following argument:

> The urge towards grandiose sonorities with which we traditionally credit Beethoven is in fact only applicable in certain cases. The Eighth Symphony, for instance, first played in the large Redoutensaal in 1814, is described by Beethoven himself: "At my last concert . . . there were 18 violins, 18 seconds, 14 violas, 12 violoncelli, 7 contra-basses, 2 contra-bassoons." This last remark suggests that, as often happened in the large nineteenth-century festive orchestra, the wind parts were doubled. Two weeks before the performance of the Ninth Symphony, a letter to the Director of the Kärnthnerthor Theater asks that room be found on stage for 24 violins, 10 violas, 12 basses and cellos and double the usual number of woodwinds. In one of the conversation books used by Beethoven to combat his deafness we note that "20 to 24 for each part in the chorus are already at hand."
>
> The re-establishment of such historical figures in performances of the symphonies reinforces the *continuing* revolutionary nature of Beethoven's writing, and helps the modern listener discover the *differences* of scale, as well as thought and intention, between all nine works.

Implicit here is the notion that Beethoven wrote and scored his symphonies with the venue and occasion of the premiere in mind. And that is a great deal to imply. The reader may already have been wondering, in fact, what the quoted list of instruments from the Redoutensaal concert in 1814 had to do with what the Eighth Symphony *"is,"* since the symphony as written contains no part at all for contrabassoon. Like the Seventh (composed the previous year) it is a lightly scored composition compared with the Fifth and Sixth Symphonies, or even the Third: There are no trombones, and all winds and brass are in pairs.

That Redoutensaal concert also included a revival of *Wellington's Victory*, however. All efforts were bent on this occasion to surpass the effect produced by the *Wellington* premiere the year before (in a program that had included the first performance of the Seventh Symphony as well) at a monster concert organized by Maelzel to promote his mechanical orchestra machine, the Panharmonicon (he had not yet come up with the metronome). The reason for hiring the Redoutensaal had been its shape, or rather that of its backstage area: "With the help of the long corridors and the rooms opposite to each other," wrote Anton Schindler, Beethoven's amanuensis, "the opposing forces (i.e., the bands and cannonades representing the English and the French) were enabled to approach each other and the desired illusion was strikingly achieved." The English and French forces, in this ideal realization, each consisted of large wind bands, and when they were combined for the Battle, the orchestra required contained two piccolos, two flutes, two oboes, four clarinets, four bassoons, four horns, four trumpets, three trombones, and sundry percussion—to which the contrabassoons (one for the English and one for the French) were surely added to reinforce the string bass as the foundation of this extraordinary *Harmonie*, the way they customarily functioned in Austrian military bands (and the way the contrabassoon would go on functioning even in Brahms's First Symphony, six decades later). The sixty-nine strings Beethoven listed in his diary were necessary to counterbalance the unheard-of twenty-seven winds, plus percussionists.

Did these ninety-six-plus musicians all participate in the Eighth? Of course not. Though it is the piece that matters to us now, it was clearly just along for the ride on 27 February 1814 (for a benefit concert had to include a premiere). How many musicians were dismissed when it was played? This we simply cannot say—although they must have included the two contrabassoonists, as well as the trombonists and percussionists (or does Hogwood plan to treat us to an Eighth replete with triangles and cog rattles?). If we do assume that all the rest of the *Wellington* band played in the Eighth, moreover, we'll have to assume that two extra oboists were hired just for it. Does that make sense? Even if we decide it does, we are left with the conclusion that the big band sound of the premiere had less to do with what the Eighth *"is"* than with the fortuities of the occasion, and particularly with its noisy bedfellow. A lesson we may draw from this is that Beethoven's approach to scoring (or more precisely, to the medium of performance) in his symphonies was pragmatic rather than idealistic, and that hence no actual realization, then or now, may be said to embody the composer's "thought and intention." The only conclusion the evidence permits us to draw is that where orchestral performance was concerned, the more seems definitely to have been the merrier. We are free to adopt a more fastidious standard if we wish; we may indeed decide on an ideal sound for this music. But if we do, it will represent not "the composer's point of view" but our own.

Not even the assumption that Beethoven's forces tended to increase in a steady progression, and that this was his "continuing revolution," can be taken seriously. It is a preconception inherited from precisely the Romantic stereotype authenticists purport to deconstruct. As A. Peter Brown of Indiana University has shown, performances of Haydn's oratorios had routinely employed forces as large as those at Beethoven's disposal in 1813 and 1814 (and the gigantic complement Beethoven demanded for the Ninth—a complement reflected in the Wellingtonish scoring of the work, the last movement of which includes parts for piccolo, four horns, three trombones, contrabassoon, and three percussionists—is obviously related to the fact that his last symphony is half oratorio). As already intimated, no steady progression in orchestra size may be deduced from Beethoven's scoring as such. The nonstring (i.e., one-on-a-part) contingent for the First, Second, Seventh, and Eighth Symphonies, composed over the fourteen years 1799–1813, is uniform. (The "Eroica" departs from the norm only by the addition of a single horn; the Fifth and Sixth add trombones and piccolo; and the Fifth, uniquely before the Ninth, has a contrabassoon. The Fourth, with its single flute, is Beethoven's most lightly scored symphony.)

As to actual complement, Howell (in the essay cited above) deduced from a collation of data in various recent secondary sources (most notably the work of the Viennese scholar Otto Biba) that orchestra size varied according to venue (in ascending order of size: noble house, theater, concert series in rented hall or restaurant, choral "festival") and that all of these possibilities were theoretically open to Beethoven throughout his career in Vienna, subject to limitations chiefly of purse. To decide that one represents the ideal (or the "normal," as the Hanover Band would have it) is arbitrary or self-serving. I choose the latter adjective advisedly, given Fitzpatrick's tortured attempt, in his notes to the Hanover Band's recording of the First

Symphony, to establish (on the basis of a payment receipt in the Austrian State Archive) the exact size of the "normal" orchestra that played the first performance of that work at twenty-nine musicians, which number just happens to coincide with the number of musicians participating in the recording (if one doesn't count the inaudible, pseudohistorical "continuo" fortepianist).

The number of musicians paid is no guide to the number who played, since virtually all public concerts mixed amateur and professional players. Howell convincingly argues that the number of musicians participating in the premiere of the First was "at least 35 and probably 40 or more," and, on Biba's data, that if one had to choose a number to represent "normal" (if not normative) practice for a symphony performance in Beethoven's Vienna, that number would most likely be in the neighborhood of fifty or fifty-five—larger than the complement employed on *any* of the recordings presently under review. (Brüggen, with forty-four, comes closest, and probably does represent the strength of sound heard at the First's premiere, if not the chimerical "ideal" for the piece.) It is understandable that Early Music ensembles today cannot muster the numbers needed to represent the early nineteenth-century norm. One day they will no doubt be able to do so. What will Fitzpatrick say then?

There are larger issues at stake here. Positivistic *Musikwissenschaft* instills a misplaced sense of strict accountability in performers aspiring to "authenticity." They feel they must back up what they do with quantitative data rather than qualitative judgment, even if the data must be fudged. "Imitating the orchestra that played a specific concert is a convenient way of avoiding a decision about how large the orchestra should be," Howell shrewdly notes, "and early music groups resort to it all too often." Indeed I would go further. To rely only on fragmentary available (or less fragmentary manipulated) evidence amounts to a sort of musicological Eichmann defense. And when the "orders" such musicians pledge themselves to follow come *only* from fortuitously preserved and arbitrarily selected performance data, not even from the composer, the result becomes a wholly circular enterprise that leads, far from the promised liberation and renewal, to reductivism and stereotype. When Hogwood speaks of "what the work *is*, not what we would . . . design or expect it to be," his *we* inevitably, if paradoxically, includes Beethoven. And this goes equally, if not more so, for the Hanover Band. Many aspects of its performances, from small details to all-encompassing principles, might be cited as illustration of this curious "unintentional fallacy," as we might call it. I will cite two.

In its performance of the Fifth Symphony, the Hanover Band does the scherzo in the expanded fivefold form (scherzo-trio-scherzo-trio-scherzo, plus coda) Beethoven later employed in the Seventh Symphony. This follows the autograph, "and, one assumes, would therefore have been played at the first performance," according to the sleeve note. That is enough to confer final authority on the procedure, even though the first edition (parts only: Breitkopf and Härtel, 1809), as well as the professionally copied score (proofread and corrected by Beethoven) from which the edition was prepared, already gives the standard ABA scherzo and trio format. Evidently Beethoven changed his mind within a year of the premiere, and never changed it again (the 1826 first edition of the score agrees with the 1809 parts). Nothing he could do, however, can take away the authority of the first performance for those who have committed themselves to it a priori as the arbiter of the work's identity, and who prefer submission to any authority to the burdensome exercise of judgment.

The Hanover Band's sleeve annotator, at any rate, does not defend the group's decision on the basis of judgment, preferring to explain the discrepancy between autograph and first edition in a manner downright insulting to the composer: "That [the five-part format] was abandoned some [!] years later could be due to nothing more than an error in printing not picked up by Beethoven, or perhaps a feeling that such a 'Minuet & Trio' da capo was old-fashioned and unsuited to such an extended composition." The latter suggestion was manufactured out of whole cloth (there was no such "old-fashioned" convention to which Beethoven was at first putatively adhering), and the suggestion that it was nothing more than a typo is preposterous, since the "expanded" version requires a separate ending. It all comes down to a preference for "facts" over anyone's designs (along with an arbitrary decision as to what will constitute a "fact"); or, put another way, an ostensible preference for value-free "what" questions over value-laden "why" questions.

The matter of the scherzo's form in the Fifth is minuscule, however, compared with the general approach to tempo in all the symphonies; and disregard (pronounced in Hogwood's case, total in that of the Hanover Band) for Beethoven's metronome markings is the biggest surprise these performances have to offer, in view of their claims to Beethoven's "recognition," let alone ultimate "is-ness."

IV

Here, too, it seems to have been the factitious conferral of authority on the first performances, irrespective of any later Beethovenian "hindsight" or "design," that provided the performers with their excuse. Maelzel's metronome having been introduced only in 1815, the settings now associated with the Beethoven symphonies through the Eighth were part of neither the original texts nor the original published performance materials, which contained only the impressionistic "nonnotational" verbal indicators that either vouchsafed performers a Goodmanian bliss of unlimited discretion, or conversely, locked them into a rigid adherence to convention, depending on how you prefer to look at things.

The metronome settings for the first eight symphonies were supplied in one fell swoop by Beethoven's publisher S. A. Steiner, at first in the pages of the *Allgemeine musikalische Zeitung*, the leading German music periodical of the day (issue of 17 December 1817—see Figure 1). Because of the delay, because no autograph document survives to corroborate the claim that the settings were "determined by the Author himself (*vom Verf[asser] selbst . . . bestimmt*)," because Schindler claimed Beethoven later repudiated the metronome, because of the composer's physical handicaps, and for any number of other reasons, conventional-minded performers, for whom Beethoven's markings have always been a nuisance and a threat, have always been able to find ways of impugning their authority, in favor of . . . what?

In the nineteenth century the question seems simple enough: It was in favor of the inspirational *elastischer Takt*, the Wagnerian "pure Adagio" that "cannot be taken too slow," and all the rest of what "enlightened" musicians today like to regard as the interpretive baggage of the Bad Old Days. But why does the Hanover Band, which regards and advertises itself as the cutting edge of authentic performance for this repertoire, which insists Beethoven would have "recognized" its work, and which accepts a certain Viennese payment receipt as holy writ, nevertheless flatly state that "these tempi are not at all suitable"? Suitable, again I ask, to what?

Before attempting to answer this question, let me interpolate, lest this line of argument be misunderstood, that in my view metronome fundamentalism is no more deserving of intellectual respect than any other kind of fundamentalism. I am familiar with all the objections, including Beethoven's own (on the autograph of his song "Nord oder Süd" of 1817, the year of his symphony settings): "100 according to Mälzel, but this applies only to the first measures, as feeling has its own tempo." Debussy echoed this a century later in a letter to his publisher Durand: "You want my opinion about the metronomic indications? They are true for just one measure." In between, Weber had this to say: "We have no correct measurements in music. They only exist in the feeling heart and if they cannot be found there, the metronome will not help." And Brahms: "The numbers found in my compositions have been talked into me by my friends, for

Metronome settings for Beethoven's Symphonies 1–8, as published in the Vienna music journal *Allgemeine musikalische Zeitung* (17 December 1817).

I myself never believed that my blood and a mechanical instrument can agree so well." (Also, I am fully aware that human psychology is such that an imagined tempo is apt to be very different from the tempo the imaginer himself will produce in actual performance. A comparison between Stravinsky's markings and his many recorded performances is sufficient to establish this much.) Nonetheless, even if metronomic rigidity is rejected, *initial* choice of tempo must be based on something given, as all our writers agree (and for proof of this, see Hector Berlioz's funny story about Mendelssohn in his *Memoirs*).

Now musicians like Hogwood and the leaders of the Hanover Band are not the type to be justifying their ways by appeals to the feeling heart or to their blood. How do they justify their tempos, then? Hogwood, for all his aggressive volubility on other matters, keeps mum on this subject. The Hanover Band has published its reasoning, which runs as follows: First, "Beethoven inherited the conventions of tempo which were in use during the latter part of the eighteenth century." Second, "the evidence of these conventions and the technical demands of the instruments of the time combine to suggest that fast movements were played slower than we are accustomed today, and slow movements faster." Third, "applying this principle restores the metric proportion between the opening Adagio of the [First] Symphony and the ensuing Allegro," a principle of coordination that holds good elsewhere, too.

This is a salad of unexamined assumptions, tortured reasoning, and special pleading. The first point would seem calculated to suggest that Beethoven was as uncritical of "eighteenth-century conventions" as his "authentic" interpreters, while we know him—not only on the basis of Romantic legends, but on solid documentary evidence—to have been highly skeptical of them. Hence his welcoming the metronome in the first place, of course, which makes possible a *specific*, not generic, approach to tempo. In a letter to Ignaz von Mosel, who had published an encomium to the metronome in the *AMZ* shortly before Beethoven's list of tempos appeared there, he wrote:

> I heartily rejoice in the same opinion . . . in regard to terms indicating time-measure which have been handed down to us from the barbarous period in music. For, only to name one thing, what can be more senseless than *Allegro* which, once for all, means *merry*, and how far off are we frequently from such a conception of this time-measure, in that the music itself expresses something quite contrary to the term. . . . As for me, I have often thought of giving up these senseless terms, Allegro, Andante, Adagio, Presto, and for this Mälzel's Metronome offers the best opportunity.

That Fitzpatrick actually quotes this letter to show Beethoven's "uncertainty" with regard to proper tempo is an indication of how tortuous his reasoning can become in his determination to dismiss the composer's testimony.

In the last full year of his life, 1826, Beethoven's letters are full of *"Metronomisierungen"* (so much for Schindler). That of 13 October, to Schott, gives the full breakdown of tempos for the Ninth Symphony, in the same format as the 1817 list, and obviously meant to supplement the latter (the composer even asks his publisher to "have them specially printed"). A somewhat later letter promises metronome markings for the Quartet, Op. 135, earnestly demanding that Schott wait for them before printing the piece, and going on to make the following very pointed remarks, which refute the implications of the Hanover Band's first and third points equally:

> In our age such things [as metronome marks] are certainly necessary; also I hear from Berlin that the first performance of the [Ninth] Symphony went off with enthusiasm, which I ascribe in great part to the metronome marking. We can scarcely have any more *tempi ordinari*, for one must follow the ideas of unfettered genius.

What are "*tempi ordinari*" but the generic, conventionalized ones the Hanover Band purports to reinstate—most particularly, the proportionally calibrated relationships between tempos to which our friend Fitzpatrick refers in the extract quoted. It is a willful throwback to what Beethoven regarded as "the barbarous period of music."

Proportional tempos were inherent in the notation of music until about 1600. Thereafter, their use is not demonstrable, only inferrable from the histories of various genres. The last genre for which there is widespread scholarly agreement as to its "proportionality" is the French overture of the Lullian opera and the German orchestral suite. But even here there is room for dissent, and it is precisely the increasing use of Italian verbal indications that testifies to the weakening hold of the *tempi ordinari* through the seventeenth and eighteenth centuries. The assumption Fitzpatrick makes with respect to Beethoven's First Symphony cannot even be responsibly maintained for Haydn's First.

As to the doctrine that faster-was-slower-and-slower-was-faster, it is something we all learn from our childhood piano teachers, but it is unsupported by any reliable contemporary evidence. In my opinion, it rests on a tacitly patronizing attitude toward the attainments of performers before the nineteenth-century Age of the Virtuoso. This much may be inferred from Fitzpatrick's reference to the "technical demands of the instruments." Say, rather, the technical attainments of our present-day players of those instruments, who are complacently assumed to be at least as proficient as their forebears. It is in any case a piece of special pleading, which becomes particularly poignant in the case of the 1817 metronome markings, for (even assuming they are not Beethoven's) they provide hard contemporary evidence that contradicts the received wisdom of tempo then and now. The fast tempos—indeed, practically all the tempos—are faster than what is considered normal today, and in some cases faster than what is even now considered practicable. So ingrained is the old wives' tale, though, that it is actually taken as evidence to weigh against that of the 1817 tempos—to outweigh it, in fact.

Not that the scholarly Hanover Band is without an authority for its highhanded rejection of the evidence. The sleeve annotator even cites one at some length: "Some of Beethoven's tempo indications will be found not completely appropriate to the character of a given piece. Thus some Symphonic movements seem to us marked too fast. . . ." And who is this speaking? Why, it's Gustav Nottebohm, writing in 1872, three years after Wagner's *Über das Dirigieren*, which set the standard for the late-nineteenth-century tradition of Beethoven interpretation. In other words, the Hanover Band has mounted an elaborate pseudohistorical justification of its Victorian preconceptions about the "character" of Beethoven's music. When we add to this its too-candid admission that adopting what it is pleased to call "a late 18th-century concept of tempo," in preference to the markings of 1817, "solves certain problems of both technique and ensemble," the spuriousness of its pretensions to "authenticity" is fully revealed.

V

From all the points of view thus far discussed, neither the Hanover Band's performances nor those of the Academy of Ancient Music can be fairly described as "accurately old," to quote the last words of Hogwood's *Gramophone* puff. But that is only because no one's performances can claim to be that. There is no unmediated access to the past. All "pasts" are constructed in a present, as Faulkner understood so well when he said, "The past is not dead; it isn't even past." The Beethoven constructed by the Band and the Academy is just as much a figment as that constructed by Wagner and Bülow; only the angle of the distorting lens has been altered. In some ways, moreover, I feel sure the new view is if anything less faithful to Beethoven than that which it claims to have supplanted.

By readopting the old-fashioned method of dual leadership from the concertmaster's chair and the keyboard, for example, both the Band and the Academy have sought to abandon what Hogwood has called "the 'maestro' concept of direction," through which Beethoven's music has been traduced over the last century-and-a-half. They heap implicit scorn on the conductor who "indicates[s] expression to the orchestra by all manner of singular bodily movements," who tears his arms "with great vehemence asunder" to indicate a sforzando, who at *piano* crouches down "lower and lower as he desire[s] the degree of softness," and who "if a crescendo then enter[s] . . . gradually [rises] up again and at the entrance of the *forte* jump[s] into the air" with a shout. Leonard Bernstein? Michael Tilson Thomas? No, it's Beethoven, the first Maestro if you please, conducting in 1813 (described by Louis Spohr). The " 'maestro' concept" started somewhere, after all, and that starting point, so far as we can tell, was precisely the figure from whom it is now being stripped in an effort to dismantle a legend. In its place we are offered a new legend: Beethoven, Preserver of the Eighteenth-Century Tradition.

That's perfectly all right. It's really no loss to us that the Hanover Band's or the Academy's performances cannot be "accurately old." The pretension to accuracy appeals not to "the aesthetic response"—or whatever it was Gertrude Stein invoked when, asked to comment on modern art, she stated simply, "I like to look at it"—but to what Joseph Alsop has recently dubbed "the historical response," an inevitable, if secondary, component of art appreciation in cultures that have turned works of art into pedigreed commodities. Far more important, aesthetically, is the other virtue Hogwood claims for "his" "original" Beethoven: that of being "terrifyingly new." In Hogwood's view, and that of the Hanover Band, this goes hand in hand with the dethroning of the maestro, the theory being that the very fact of conductorlessness, together with the use of period instruments, strips away generations of accrued spuriosity, baring the "brand old" work to be gazed on plain. The favored metaphor, as we all know by now, is that of the museum restorer's workshop, and it is tiresomely rehearsed in Clive Brown's notes to the Academy's recording of the first two symphonies. With specific reference to the maestroless mode of orchestral leadership, however, Brown makes some claims that are worth examining. "One very important consequence of the prevalent method of directing an orchestra from the violin or keyboard," he writes,

> was that the performances must almost entirely have lacked the wider variety of nuance and tempo modification which were later to be considered the hall-marks of a conductor's interpretation: the old system inevitably necessitated a constant pulse in the music. . . . The net results of reviving the instruments and performance practices of Beethoven's period are a brighter, clearer sound, sharper contrasts, and uncomplicated, rhythmical performances.

All of which is presumed to come with the force of revelation.

It doesn't, though, because the kind of high-profile, interventionist "maestro" interpretations here called into question are not those of today, or even of yesterday. To find Beethoven performances that are significantly more elastic in tempo and "nuance" than the ones Hogwood directs from the fortepiano bench or Monica Huggett from the Hanover Band's concertmaster seat, you have to go back to the interpretations of old German Idealists like Wilhelm Furtwängler (d. 1954) at the very latest. Furtwängler was actually already rather tame and "modern" compared with the likes of Richard Strauss, Hans

Pfitzner, and Willem Mengelberg, all of whom have left us recordings of Beethoven's symphonies. Pfitzner's Third and Sixth, and Strauss's Fifth, all recorded in Berlin in the late '20s, have been reissued on InSync cassettes (4146, 4128). Mengelberg's First, recorded shortly before the Second World War, near the end of his tenure with the Concertgebouw Orchestra, can be heard, along with the Second, on a Philips CD (416200–2). In its way it is the most revealing exemplar I know of Beethoven performance in the Bad Old Days, since the work on which the operation is performed is one whose "Classical" proportions and proprieties throw the "Romantic" and (by today's standards) alien conducting style into sharpest relief. Mengelberg's approach to the First Symphony is worth a brief description as foil to those under review.

To begin at the beginning, there is no way of calculating Mengelberg's tempo for the Adagio molto until the fifth measure is reached. All the half-note chords in bars 1–3 carry unwritten fermatas (as do the rests at the ends of bars 1 and 2). The crescendo to the cadence in bar 3 is accompanied by an unwritten *molto allargando*; the cadential chord at the fourth downbeat is again held out of time; and finally motion gets under way in the five-note pickup that follows, which proceeds through an accelerando to the fifth downbeat, where at last a steady tempo is established. That tempo is eighth note = 73 (cf. Beethoven's 88), and it holds, more or less, till the last bar of the Adagio (allowing for a very broad interpretation of Beethoven's own *tenuto* markings on the quarter-note chords in bars 8 and 10). The ascending scale in the last bar is taken *molto ritenuto* to an unwritten fermata on the top note, and the concluding group of four thirty-seconds is taken, in a fashion that has become standard practice, as sixteenths in the tempo of the main part of the first movement, the Allegro con brio (in keeping with Beethoven's evident intention: cf. the four sixteenths that precede the recapitulation).

That tempo is a surprise: the fastest one I have encountered on records (half note = 115; cf. Beethoven's 112). Contrast—far "sharper contrasts," indeed, than anything Clive Brown had in mind—was for Mengelberg its own reward. The major deviations thereafter include two sudden leaps (to a whopping 123 at the beginning of the development section, and to 118 from a previous ritard at the recap), and two notable holdbacks, one relatively subtle, the other fairly gross. The subtle one involves the sustained wind chords between the string phrases in the main theme. They are played *molto tenuto* to magnify the effect of the crescendo. The gross one involves the cello-bass pianissimo passage that acts as a bridge between the second theme and the codetta. Both in the exposition and in the recapitulation, Mengelberg brusquely reins in the four staccato fortissimo chords preceding the passage so that it starts way under tempo (in the low 90s by the metronome) and gradually regains both the original tempo and the loud volume over its whole eleven-measure expanse, played as a steadily mounting accelerando-cum-crescendo. (Beethoven marks the crescendo from *pp* to *f* over the last two-and-a-half bars only.)

In Mengelberg's performance we can see the same coordination of tempo variation with variation in other musical parameters that Will Crutchfield discussed with insight in an article on early Brahms interpreters in the August 1986 *Opus*. The case emphasized there, "the equation of crescendo with acceleration and diminuendo with ritard," is often taken as paradigmatic for "Romantic" (or, in Virgil Thomson's well-known opinion, for "European") interpretation generally; and it clearly is what prompted Mengelberg's treatment of the cello-bass passage. It is not the whole story, though. The coordination can be inverse as well as direct (as in Mengelberg's treatment of the beginning of the slow introduction), which seems more a hortatory device than an "expressive" one. And there is a whole other dimension to the matter as well, particularly significant, it would appear, for Beethoven interpretation: the direct coordination of tempo with levels of rhythmic activity. Rhythmic contrasts and progressions alike are consistently underscored by the *elastischer Takt*. Mengelberg's tenuto on the whole-note wind chords in the first theme has the effect of dramatically heightening the contrast between the fast rhythmic motion of the strings and the stasis that interrupts and paces it. (It's a nice effect, and I don't blame the maestroless Hanover Band one bit for copying it, even though according to Brown's theory it can't.)

In the second movement (Andante cantabile con moto), Mengelberg (like practically everyone else) sacrifices the *con moto* to the *cantabile* at the outset, with a tempo of eighth note = 85 (cf. Beethoven's 120). But that's just the outset. Throughout the movement the tempo varies with the level of rhythmic activity, and at the latter's peak—the D-flat major passage shortly after the first double bar, where the strings have ten bars of chugging dotted rhythms in sixteenths and thirty-seconds—Mengelberg is winging away at eighth note = 101. (He also is most careful to distinguish these rhythms from the sixteenth-note triplets with which they occasionally coexist.)

Other reasons for modifying tempo with Mengelberg include chromatic harmony (as in the second strain of the Menuetto, which on the da capo is treated to a really jarring *molto ritenuto*), and what we might call the *Kehraus* (i.e., "clearing out the dance hall") accelerating coda (something Beethoven actually notated into the finale of the Fifth Symphony). Once past the introduction, the conductor's basic tempo for the last movement (Allegro molto e vivace) is half note = 80, again the fastest I've heard on records and closer to Beethoven's marking (88) than any other, including the latest batch of "authentic" renditions. The last thirty-eight bars are taken through an exciting stretto, so that the symphony actually ends, in Mengelberg's rendition, just where Beethoven marked it.

Before proceeding to any comparisons, it might be well to note two things. First, the idea that older performances, especially those of the Germanic school, were slower than more recent ones is nothing but a myth, as Beethoven's metronome marks already imply, but as Mengelberg's recording palpably proves. His Beethoven tends to confirm Harold Schonberg's theory of the Glacial Shift, according to which performances of the standard repertoire have been getting steadily slower (or, to put it another way, the works have been getting longer) since Schonberg started keeping track about half a century ago. Second, and more important, the "liberties" and "licenses" the old-time maestros allowed themselves were not as arbitrary, inspirational, or *ad hoc* as they are usually made out to be, but followed rules derived from basic principles of rhetoric that could be defined and, if one wished, even codified. They were fully rational, though it was "feeling' they served, and though they were surely so thoroughly internalized as to appear instinctive. *And they are with us still*, all disclaimers notwithstanding. As we shall see, Beethoven's "tempo of feeling" claims its due even from those who profess to have renounced it, and think their methods have precluded it. The difference between a Hogwood and a Mengelberg, when all is said and done, is a matter of degree.

It's a mighty big degree, of course, and past a certain point quantity does determine quality. But it was not our latter-day "authenticists" who made the decisive step across that line. It was Toscanini, the prophet of the "uncomplicated, rhythmical performance," and Maestro of Maestros. The "authenticists," or their spokesmen, are claiming credit for yesterday's revolution.

Much has been written of late about the phenomenon of Toscanini and all its consequences. I don't want to stir that polemical pot. But I would like briefly to consider what Toscanini has meant to twentieth-century performance practice from what may be a useful perspective. One of the essential Toscanini paradoxes, articulated by Thomson and others, was that this musician, notorious for his reactionary taste, nonetheless did more than anyone else toward modernizing musical performance and musical perception alike. He was the great simplifier and depersonalizer of music. This was something that could easily be compared with streamlining, with abstraction, with all kinds of twentieth-century artistic manifestations and creeds. And Toscanini's approach, in particular his insistence on playing *"com'è scritto"* (whether or not he actually did so), was likewise easy to reconcile with the widespread objectivism and "anti-interpretationism" of the "middle half" of the twentieth century, given strongest expression in the writings of Stravinsky.

But these are facile parallels that may obscure profounder cultural issues. The latter may be briefly (and, of course, oversimply) described in terms of a dichotomy given early formulation by a German scholar named August Halm, and lately revived by Carl Dahlhaus in his very influential recent history of nineteenth-century music. This view sees the nineteenth-century musical scene in terms of two opposing cultures. Stanford University musicologist Karol Berger has recently put it all quite brilliantly into a nutshell, characterizing the dichotomy as one between

> the Italo-French culture of opera and the Austro-German instrumental tradition: the former relying on self-sufficient expressive vocal melody and, increasingly, on large-scale rhythmic and metric organization, texture, and timbre; the latter on the logic of harmonic and thematic relationships. While the dramatic tradition preserved the aesthetic premises of the Enlightenment, according to which music served a function and invited enjoyment, the instrumental tradition encouraged a new Romantic aesthetics of autonomous music, whose meaning resided solely within itself and which, consequently, invited understanding rather than mere enjoyment.

Toscanini was the great crossover artist of the twentieth century. Reared in the "first" culture and trained in the opera pit, he applied its values to the symphonic masterworks of the "second," producing radically unfussy, synoptically architectonic renditions that were electrifying in their "large-scale rhythmic and metric organization," and "invited [nay, compelled] enjoyment," not reflection. While it would be grossly reductive (and dismissive) merely to say he conducted Wagner (another supreme cross-over artist, but in the other direction) as if he were Verdi, or that every Toscanini trait can be subsumed under the adjective "Italianate," a large part of the Maestro's irresistible fascination (and let's not forget how successful he was in his heyday with German and Austrian audiences, who found his performances revelatory) may surely be attributed to his alien perspective. He defamiliarized the repertoire and made it new again, in performances of staggering technical mastery and irresistible visceral appeal. And it was not modernism he embodied, but the very opposite. As the Halm/Dahlhaus paradigm suggests, Toscanini was as un-Romantic as Stravinsky, perhaps, but not out of commitment to *Neue Sachlichkeit* or anything of the kind. He was an avatar of a pre-Romantic aesthetic.

That is not to say, of course, that he was "Classical." That term was coined, in the heat of battle, in the nineteenth century. It is anachronistic when applied to Haydn, Mozart, and Beethoven, who were universally regarded as the first musical Romantics by the generation (that of E.T.A. Hoffmann) who defined the Romantic aesthetic, the very same generation that first had the notion of "absolute" music. Our modern-day, confused and confusing style periodization notwithstanding, Mozart and Beethoven, at least, *were*, in any historically meaningful sense of the word, Romantics, and Beethoven was the very fountainhead of the tradition that is now being challenged in his name (for proof of this, see Hoffmann's own widely anthologized writings, or Rose Rosengard Subotnik's analysis of Mozart in light of Kant, published in *Music and Civilization*, W.W. Norton's 1984 festschrift for Paul Henry Lang).

It was Toscanini, then, who pioneered the un-Romantic deconstruction of Romantic music, and the force of his example was such that it has become an absolute standard in our time. It defines "modern performance" of the German classics. *Every* prominent conductor today, whatever the tradition to which he professes allegiance, is in reality the follower of Toscanini. Which is to say: Although conductors in the German tradition may still adopt tempos slower than Toscanini's (and as we have already seen, they may be more likely to do so now in defiance of him than were earlier generations), their performances are far more "rhythmical, uncomplicated," and architectonic than those of their spontaneous (or pseudospontaneous), "poetic" forebears who stemmed truly from the Romantic tradition founded by Beethoven (the *elastischer Takt*, according to Brahms, was "no recent invention"). A Karajan performance, or a Solti (or, to go back a bit, a Reiner or a Szell) is far more like a Toscanini than anyone's is like a Mengelberg. The latter's tradition is dead (and undoubtedly due for an "authentistic" revival).

A few facts and figures to back this up:

Toscanini recorded the Beethoven First several times. I have listened carefully to two of his versions: that of 1937 with the BBC Symphony, and the NBC Symphony rendition issued a dozen or so years later as part of a complete Nine. They are quite different. The much-admired BBC recording (for someone reared, as I was, on the NBC version) is quite relaxed and even a little "Romantic" (and very sloppy, the record's reputation and that of the orchestra notwithstanding). Toscanini even molds the "cello theme" in the first movement a little, à la Mengelberg, though far, far less conspicuously. With him it's just a dip from a basic rate of half note = c. 104 to c. 99, followed by an almost instant regaining of the tempo, long before the crescendo (scrupulously executed where Beethoven notated it) takes place. As David Hall put it, way back in the 1948 edition of *The Record Book*, "there is just enough elasticity here to keep the performance from becoming metronomic." If that is so, then the NBC rendition *is* metronomic. The first movement hugs its basic tempo of half note = 107 (close enough to count as *com'è scritto* for anyone but Nelson Goodman) with remarkable steadiness (or rigidity, in case you don't like it). Noticeable deviations in the exposition are only these: half note = 111 at the beginning of the bridge (the first kinetic tutti); 103 at the second theme; 98 at the "cello theme." The double bar is reached right on target, followed by a little lurch (to half note = 111 again) at the beginning of the development section.

Now what is remarkable is that virtually every subsequent recording I've tested adheres astonishingly closely to these basic parameters of variability, whatever its actual tempo. Shown in Table 8.1 is a sampling chosen for diversity: the Germanic mainstream represented by Karajan's first stereo recording (1961, with the Berlin Philharmonic); the avowedly "modernist" viewpoint by René Leibowitz (Schoenberg's pupil and Boulez's teacher), conducting the Royal Philharmonic (the recording may have had other incarnations, but I know it only from an integral set issued—I blush—by Reader's Digest, c. 1962); and the recent "authentistic" position by Hogwood and Hanover (Beethoven's single marking, recall, is half note = 112).

With the exception of the "traditionally" slower second theme, where the authenticists were obviously on special guard not to relax (and where, not realizing they had speeded up for the bridge, they unwittingly set the second theme *faster* than the first), the pattern is uniformity itself. Within the exposition, the first tutti is *everybody's* high point, the "cello theme" everybody's low point. In every case the beginning of the development is faster than the beginning of the exposition. That is apparently the "tempo of feeling" for this music, and it had been Mengelberg's, too. But how compressed (or actually repressed?) the range of variability has become since his time. Where Mengelberg's variations had covered a range of thirty points or more on the metronome, Toscanini's cover thirteen (both times, the earlier one contemporaneous with Mengelberg's recording); "maestroless" Hogwood's a healthy eighteen (though I have an idea his jump to 114 at the development was the product of a splice);

Table 8.1	Toscanini/BBC	Toscanini/NBC	Karajan	Leibowitz	Hanover Hogwood	
Allegro	104	107	96	112	86	104
Bridge	112	111	99	114	90	107
Second theme	104	103	95	106	90	107
"Cello theme"	99	98	92	105	85	96
Development	109	111	97	113	90	114

Leibowitz's nine; Karajan's seven; and Hanover's five. I'm sure you didn't expect Karajan's range to be so much more compressed than Hogwood's, even discounting the anomalous 114; it shows that if the other "maestroless" performance, that of the Hanover Band, is the steadiest/rigidest, that is the product of a contemporary ideology, not the inevitable result of a historical performance practice. As to tempo, what does it tell us that the authentistic Hanover Band is farthest of all from Beethoven's marking, or that modernistic Leibowitz starts right on the money, with variation, according to the "tempo of feeling," both above and below? (And while I'm on the subject I'd like to put in a word for Leibowitz's set, which I find enormously stimulating and at times illuminating. In the First, his sforzandos put everyone else's quite in the shade, including those who claim "sharper contrasts" to be their unique achievement, while some of the brass attacks, e.g., the trumpet-horn octaves that initiate the retransition, startle no matter how well one knows the piece, and not just because of the fast tempo. This is a recording that cries out for reissue and wide dissemination!)

VI

In sum, I must declare fraudulent both the claim of accuracy and that of novelty for the recordings of the Hanover Band and the Academy of Ancient Music. They have no right to the privilege they assert. Their endeavors must stand or fall by the same standards as everyone else's. And as sure as pride goeth before them, they fall.

Hogwood's do so for the usual reasons: His performances are dull run-throughs, devoid of detail, with nothing at all to impart to anyone who is really listening. One cannot hear his "Eroica," in particular, without mounting irritation. That such a job is foisted on the public, accompanied moreover by such a clamor of hype, must set a new standard for chutzpah.

Don't look for any sign of chutzpah in the playing, though; Hogwood seems to have rededicated the symphony "To Celebrate the Memory of a Great Nebbish." The first movement (dotted-half = 60 by Beethoven's prescription) is set at a flabby, self-satisfied 49 (47 at the exposition repeat), midway between those performances that characterize Beethoven's heroics "broadly," with a tempo in the low-to-mid-40s (Furtwängler, Walter, Solti, etc.) and those that do so "athletically," in the low 50s (Toscanini, Kleiber, Karajan). Not that these alternatives exhaust the possibilities by any means. Pfitzner—like other Germans of his generation, no doubt—is a case apart. His tempo fluctuates between 44 and 53 even within the first theme. Like it or not, you are definitely engaged.

And then there are the modernist wild men, Leibowitz (in the Reader's Digest set), Hermann Scherchen (in his second recording with the Vienna State Opera Orchestra for Westminster, 1958), and most recently Michael Gielen with the Cincinnati Symphony (Vox), who have actually tried to take Beethoven's tempo marking seriously. William Malloch ("Toward a 'New' [Old] Minuet," August 1985 *Opus*) sees Gielen's finely played recording as superseding its predecessors, but I am not altogether sure. It is true that Scherchen's and Leibowitz's recordings were scrappy studio rush jobs, in which the conductors' efforts were often dissipated against the players' tendency to revert to the tempos they were used to. Ensemble is to laugh, perhaps, but the struggle is terribly involving. There is an air of authentic excitement about them (and you may interpret the adjective any way you wish). Leibowitz never got his men past 56 to the dotted-half, but Scherchen breaks through to 60 about fifty bars into the development section, and one feels, listening, the way Roger Bannister's fans must have felt watching their man complete his 3'59" mile. At the height of the coda Scherchen hits 62, and it's hats in the air! (At this point, though under the mark, Leibowitz pulls off another magnificent coup with his brass, bringing to the fore the martial trumpet-timpani tattoos that all too often get buried beneath the ripping wind scales.)

Cheap thrills? Maybe, but anything is preferable to the utter lack of characterization Hogwood offers, all cloaked up in the mantle of authenticity. Authenticists pride themselves on having taken a cold hard look at the details and markings that slaves to tradition take for granted or miss. Where then are Hogwood's sforzandos and piano subitos (including the absolutely crucial one nineteen bars before the end of the first movement)? And what is the "Eroica" without them? The playing falls for long stretches into that unmodulated sight-reading dynamic studio hacks call "mezzo-fortissimo," even (incredibly) when the second theme is reached in the recapitulation.

Felix Weingartner's dowdy old *Ratschläge für Aufführungen klassischer Symphonien* (1906, translated by Jessie Crosland under the title *On the Performance of Beethoven's Symphonies*), justly regarded as a period piece (even by Weingartner himself at the end of his life, according to an anecdote retailed by Adrian Boult) for its copious recommended rescorings, nonetheless points out many fine distinctions among Beethoven's markings that are worth the attention not only of conductors, but of all critical listeners. Hogwood, clearly, never thought to look into it (indeed, he seems at times only superficially acquainted with the music itself), for if he had, he would have paid some attention to the difference between the *sfp* markings that grace the articulation of the "new theme" in the development the first time it is enunciated (in E minor) and the *sf*s that appear in its second statement (A minor). As Weingartner points out, "we can conclude that the second passage has to be played with a somewhat more intensified expression than the first, so that it is not simply a transposed repetition, but is destined also to form a transition to the energetic period" that follows. (I recommend the observation of this distinction to the reader as a touchstone for telling the men from the boys among performers of this symphony.) Needless to say, there is no trace of this or any other strategy in Hogwood's reading. Nor has any thought been given to balance (the maestro's first task, after all); we just get what comes out of each instrument, independently interpreting its own dynamic markings. No doubt this is part of Hogwood's conception of authenticity, but it's just a dodge to avoid yet another issue. Ensemble, however, is excellent. Like most Early Music groups, the Academy of Ancient Music evidently considers its job of preparation done as soon as everybody is together.

In the less intensely individual First and Second Symphonies, the Academy's performances are a bit less offensive, but still maddeningly bland and complacent (I can't say innocuous, because the hype *has* been harmful). If a choice had to be made between them, I'd much prefer the Hanover Band here, because the playing of its individual members is often committed and beautiful. The unaccompanied second-violin theme at the beginning of the Andante in the First is quite exquisitely shaped, even if the tempo does plod. Second beats are turned into lovely "feminine endings" (the influence of the players' extensive Baroque experience, no doubt), and there is a winning swelling (through the four slurred eighths) and a lovely dwelling on the melodic high point in the sixth measure. The ascending woodwind scales in thirds in the coda to the finale are a treat (though the same winds are painfully out of tune in the descending dotted scales in thirds near the beginning of the Second Symphony). Though it may be the result of the undersize ensemble, I was much taken with the translucence of the textures, as in measures 310ff. in the first movement of the Second, an unusually knotted contrapuntal passage, where the lower strings in thirds come through much more clearly than in other performances I've heard. The woodwind sforzandos in the third-movement trio are also beguiling; and the finale, in which the Band finally gets off its bottom and plays at a tempo within shooting distance of Beethoven's, is just the sort of colorful Haydnesque romp the composer must have set out to create, as a counterweight to his despair over the onset of his deafness (that very movement, of all things, was most closely contemporaneous with the heart-rending Heiligenstadt Testament).

Not even the Hanover Band's scrawny, inadequate Fifth is without individual instrumental felicities that can be savored. You've probably never actually heard the clarinets playing along with the string unisons at the very beginning, for example. Now you can (at the very end of the second fermata, as the strings fade away). Nor, in all likelihood, have you ever really heard the piccolo as a separate color in the final unison. It's fierce. For some reason the Band found Beethoven's tempos more "suitable" in the Fifth than in the other symphonies it has recorded. In the finale, it actually exceeds the marking by a good bit; and while Howell, for one, chides the group for making the movement sound "superficial and lightweight," I welcome the demonstration that Beethoven's markings are well within the bounds of feasibility. An ensemble of more appropriate size, playing at the Hanover Band's tempo, would surely have the whole audience shouting, "*Vive l'Empereur!*"

Which is why I look forward to hearing the Fifth one day in a performance by Frans Brüggen and the Orchestra of the Eighteenth Century. For sheer coloristic and instrumental values, their recording of the First Symphony is tops. Not only are the players thoroughly steeped in that peculiarly "analytical" idiom of Early Music performance endemic to the Low Countries, which places such a premium on highly profiled etching of short phrase units, and not only are the "original" instruments played with unparalleled suppleness and mastery (kudos especially to the clarinetists!), but Brüggen understands the potential of a period band to magnify, not diminish, the "size" of the music it performs. Forty musicians striving at fullest tilt to project the very top of their repertoire, the "newest" and most demanding music composed for their instruments, make a much grander impression than sixty or more laying back so as not to transgress the bounds of "style" or "taste." Their performance is viscerally involving from first to last. The tenutos in the slow introduction have real suspense. The tremolos in the first movement, thanks to the dry, crisp articulation of the strings, crackle like no others I've heard. Brüggen's tempo in the last movement is actually a shade slower than Hogwood's (half note = 78 vs. 79; cf. Beethoven's 88), yet the performance sounds much faster because the band is a little bigger and the playing much, much more committed. (There is actually a bit of overlap in personnel between Brüggen's band and Hogwood's; I'm sure those players have an interesting story to tell.) Brüggen's string players (particularly the cellos) are the clearest I've heard in the fast scales at the beginning of the finale's development section. Their legato/staccato contrasts are delightfully lithe and effortless, with no loss of momentum. And his wind players realize the "laughing" Mozartean retransition (replete with a knockout of a *piano subito*) to memorable perfection. The finale, in short, is as good as I'd ever want to hear it.

The rest of the performance, despite all its undoubted virtues, is not. Brüggen's infatuation with size allows much of the work to go bloated and sentimental, and the Menuetto is conceived quite inappositely (except from a virtuoso wind player's perspective, that is) as a sort of Mendelssohnian scherzo, at a tempo far beyond Beethoven's indication, which types the piece as a late-eighteenth-century *Deutscher Tanz*, not a harbinger of jet propulsion. The slow introduction of the first movement is promisingly brisk (eighth note = 83 to Hogwood's 77 and the Hanover Band's 73, the same as Mengelberg's), but then, when passing into the Allegro con brio, Brüggen actually puts into effect the anachronistic gear-shift of *tempi ordinari* preached (but not actually practiced) by the Hanover Band. The eighth note becomes the half note, producing the logiest tempo on records. (Like everyone else, Brüggen speeds up to the tutti at the bridge, and finds his true pace at half note = 91, but this is still the slowest in my sample.) By the time he has reached the recap, Brüggen has at least passed Karajan and the Hanover Band, but he's still ponderous, and, the discrepancy with the opening tempo being keenly felt, trivial (an unusual combination that adds up, for me, to sentimental). But the playing qua playing is often matchless; and I warn you that after hearing Brüggen's gorgeous winds, you'll find the sound of a "modern" wind complement in the "Classical" repertoire insufferably pinched, tight, and wobbly.

VII

And now hats off, gentlemen. I had feared I would have to end this piece on a note of skepticism and rejection, in the face of which it would be harder than ever to continue protesting my belief in the movement to whose aims I subscribe but whose actual achievements I seem forever to be disparaging. But in Roger Norrington and the London Classical Players I can point at last to musicians whose work exemplifies every principle I hold dear, and who are keeping the promise of authenticity in ways their colleagues and competitors, most of them, have not begun to imagine.

What is that promise, and why is it rarely kept? The answer to the second question is that the nature of the promise is usually unrecognized, even within the movement, and even by its best practitioners. I was once brought up quite short, reading an interview with Nikolaus Harnoncourt, one of the "early musicians" I admire most. Asked by his interlocutor to contrast his kind of playing with "modern performance," he exploded in sarcasm: "Modern performance? Modern performance? I'd like to hear a really modern performance. The kind of performance you have in mind is not modern. It's a compound of nineteenth-century training, unreflective geniality, and ignorance. There is no modern performance." Beg to differ, Mr. Harnoncourt. There *is* a modern performance, and you are one of its chief exponents. What you and your colleagues are doing, whatever it is you say or think you are doing, is reinventing music in the image of the twentieth century (and none too soon—we're practically into the next one). What Dahlhaus has called the "postulate of originality" and defined as "the dominant aesthetic belief" since Beethoven's own day, is with us still, and it still decrees that music "should be novel in order to rank as authentic." That is the chief appeal, whether you measure by aesthetic standards or commercial ones, of the "authenticity" movement. It appeals by virtue of its novelty, not its antiquity. And that is just as it should be. What I so often find myself decrying is that, owing perhaps chiefly but far from exclusively to the influence of academic musicology, we have become prevaricators, and no longer call novelty by its right name.

Not Norrington. He has seen through the cultish cant. "The point about playing Beethoven on old instruments, of course, is to make him sound new," he writes in the refreshingly forthright "Performance Note" accompanying his recording of the Second and Eighth Symphonies. Sew that into a sampler and hang it on the wall. And also this: Discussing the role of historical evidence in the renewal of style, he writes, "Our aim is to rediscover these great masterpieces, not by ignoring all this evidence, but by placing as much reliance on it as on our own musicianship and interpretative powers." Many think they are doing this, but, as we have seen in the case of Hogwood and the Hanover Band, few actually do. Norrington knows that in order to rediscover anything one must first remake oneself, and one must do this by challenging and bringing to consciousness all the prejudices and knee-jerk habits one never knew one had.

How? By taking evidence on faith and absolutely seriously, and then painstakingly building up one's "own musicianship and interpretative powers" around it. It is a kind of inspired literalism he advocates and practices, which must begin with submission (for one cannot strip oneself down from within) but proceeds by means of a highly critical process of experimentation in which anything and everything is rejected that does not accord with the *donnée*. What I read between the lines of Norrington's "Performance Note" reminds me of one of my favorite Stravinsky remarks, made to a young composer toying with the idea of adopting the serial method, who asked him what to do if you find a note is theoretically right but musically wrong. "You must learn to hear it as musically right," said Igor

Fyodorovich. Do not change your givens. Change yourself. That is the only way one learns.

But choose your givens with care! Again Norrington cuts through the cant so zealously propagated by Hogwood and the Hanover Band:

> Orchestra size was not a crucial factor. Orchestras played equally in very small and very large formations. . . . Pitch [given an absurd emphasis by Fitzpatrick in his notes to the Hanover Band recordings] was not crucial either: it varied all over Europe, and even within one town. . . . What *were* absolutely crucial were speeds, note-lengths, bowing and phrasing.

Speeds! Norrington publishes Beethoven's tempo markings right on the back of his CD, where the movements are listed. It is not only an act of bravado, it is a *profession de foi*. It is from the tempos that his approach derives, the very tempos all the others flee. And it must be so, for no other givens are nearly so specific. He does not begin, then, by asking whether Beethoven's tempos are "suitable"; he *assumes* they are, for you have to start your strip-down somewhere. Everything else can go, but they must stay! Everything else must be made to fit them. Though treatises do survive with information about articulations, phrasings, and all the rest, instrumental techniques cannot be assimilated in the abstract, but only as applied in real musical contexts to real musical problems, with nothing taken for granted.

So it comes down to the tempos, with articulations, phrasings, and balances imagined afresh so as to make them work. And work they do! From the very beginning of the slow introduction to the first movement of the Second Symphony, this is a performance to rank with the great ones, and one to make all other authenticists who have assayed this repertoire hang their heads. Norrington fearlessly takes Beethoven's eighth note = 84 at its face value, heedless of Weingartner's warning that "the metronome mark does not agree with the direction *adagio molto*." Wrong! The task, rather, is to make the *adagio molto* agree with the metronome mark; and by dint of flawlessly executed legatos, perfectly calibrated accents, and marvelously controlled string articulations, Norrington and his Players succeed. *It does not sound rushed.* It has the poise and certainty of movement that always characterize a *tempo giusto*; and it has the spaciousness and relaxation of a true adagio. (By comparison, Toscanini at eighth note = 77 sounds frenetic, while Hogwood and Hanover, at 65 and 66, are merely dull, even logier than Karajan.)

The London Classical Players, under their inspired leader, achieve the kind of memorable "modern" characterization of the music Scherchen and Leibowitz went after, but at a level of ensemble execution circumstances barred their predecessors from approaching. And what a wealth of detail the performances contain! An *fp* is one thing, an *sfp* another, an *sf* yet another (and when you hear the two horns play their dissonant major second, *sf*, in the twenty-second measure of the introduction, you'll know you're hearing Modern Music, vintage 1802). A note marked staccato is one thing; a note unmarked is another, *equally specific*, thing; and neither is anything like what you've heard in other performances.

Problems of balance are met head-on and conquered. At measures 158–65 in the first Allegro of the Second Symphony, where Weingartner flatly states that winds and strings cannot be balanced at fortissimo and prescribes a reorchestration (throwing in a homily for good measure: "A radical change cannot be held to be impious; on the contrary, in my opinion it is urgently demanded by a pious veneration for the great work of the great master"), the threatened winds fairly shriek defiance in Norrington's rendition (as they do in Toscanini's— need I add that they are inaudible in the Hanover Band recording and nearly so in Hogwood's?). And you have never heard a Beethovenian *piano subito* till you've heard the one introducing the retransition (m. 212) as performed here. It's like hitting a speed bump.

To go on describing this performance would mean merely offering a travelogue of favorite sounds and shapes. Listen for yourself and find your own. I want only to add that, like all first-class Beethovenists, Norrington has the gift of molding a whole movement into a coherent shape with a single overriding contour. The moment of glory in the first movement of the Second comes at that blazing chain of suspensions in the coda (mm. 336–40) where the trumpets in D suddenly rise to their top register to join the horns, fortissimo. It tells, both architectonically and dramaturgically, like nothing any other performance has to offer; and listening to it, mouth agape, I felt I understood for the first time how listeners in the '20s and '30s must have reacted to that other inspired literalist and defamiliarizer, Toscanini. Like his in legend, this rendition is something truly new and transcendent. While listening to it, I was so totally drawn in that I repeatedly forgot to check this or that passage with my "tap-mode" metronome, or even follow the score. Having heard it, I find myself changed in my own perceptions and appetites, so that all familiar performances of the symphony, at least for now, sound faded and jaded. Beethoven has been radically "made strange" again, and (just as, long ago, it must have been with Toscanini), one is made to feel that the strange face into which one gazes is truer than the face one thought one knew so well. At the very least, I have a new appreciation of the greatness of the Second Symphony. It has never seemed so imposing. The period band makes a ferocious sound; and, all repeats in place, it lasts well over half an hour even at Norrington's (that is, Beethoven's) torrid tempos. It seems a veritable "Eroica."

(The performance of the Eighth Symphony, while boldly characterized and in every way satisfying, was for me not quite the transforming experience the Second had been. Could this have had something
to do with the fact that Norrington compromised a bit with the
tempos in the outer movements? In the finale I have to concede that
Beethoven's whole note = 84 may have been unrealistic. At Norrington's 74 the eighth-note triplets already sound like a buzz saw; any
faster they'd turn into a tremolo. I can't tell from the performance
itself, though, why Norrington reduced Beethoven's dotted-half = 69
in the first movement to 57. Wouldn't a more irrepressible momentum have made the movement even more [as Stravinsky called it] "a
miracle of growth"? Or perhaps my reaction has been influenced by
Malloch's shrewd observation that "unless the first movement is
played at [Beethoven's] fast one-to-a-bar waltzlike tempo . . . , the
whole point of contrast will be lost between it and the later three-to-
a-bar old-fashioned Tempo di minuetto third movement." Still, there
are wonders here. I refer students to the last page of the Allegretto,
where Norrington makes such a telling contrast between notes with
staccato dots and those without.)

So I have no hesitation in saying that this recording represents a
breakthrough, not just in "Early Music" performance, but in Beethoven
performance *tout court*; nor have I any doubt that Roger Norrington is
to be the next great Beethoven conductor. It gratifies me beyond measure that a Beethoven interpreter of stature should have emerged from
the ranks of Early Music (and given the present achievement, what a
parochial misnomer "Early Music" seems). But it doesn't surprise me in
the least. That was always the movement's promise, indeed its raison
d'être. Up to now, though, its dominant figures have often been confused as to aims, and hence as to means. Brown, in his notes for
Hogwood, writes complacently that "in the 185 years since the premiere of the First Symphony, each generation has claimed Beethoven
for its own and has performed his works according to its own tastes,"
the implication being that from now on, by golly, things are gonna be
different. Norrington has understood, and shown us all, that this
generation will not differ from the others, that Early Music is in fact to
be this generation's way of claiming Beethoven for its (our) own, and
that that is what authenticity means. I don't know whether his work
will prove as marketable as Hogwood's. Probably not: You have to pay
attention to it. But Norrington's cycle is the one that will make a real
difference, if it shocks us out of our comfortable genetic fallacies and
persuades us at last that our "authenticity movement," far from a sterile
restoration of a static, authoritarian *is* that never was, can play a major
role in the endless process of renewal that keeps our cherished repertoire alive. *That* is tradition; the other is just another *Schlamperei*.

9

Resisting the Ninth

BEETHOVEN, **Symphony No. 9, in D Minor, Op. 125.**
Yvonne Kenny, soprano; Sarah Walker, mezzo; Patrick Power, tenor; Petteri Salomaa, bass; Schütz Choir of London; London Classical Players; Roger Norrington, cond. EMI CDC 7 49221 2.

Something that used to puzzle fans who listened to the souvenir recordings of the old Hoffnung Music Festivals without having attended them was the extra roar of laughter that would swell up during the applause at the conclusion of each travesty. It was the response to a favorite sight gag: the conductor would customarily leap off the podium and bound over to shake the kettledrummer's hand instead of the concertmaster's. And that is just what I felt like doing after hearing this extraordinary recording of Beethoven's Ninth Symphony. Always something of a timpani concerto among symphonies—besides the famous solos in the Scherzo there is the horripilating tattoo that all but drowns out the first movement recapitulation, the confiding exchanges with the cellos and basses in the third movement coda, the shimmering roll that supports the most visionary moment in the finale, and much besides—the Ninth is enhanced immeasurably on this occasion by the stupendous playing of Robert Howes and the superbly responsive instrument on which he deploys his sticks.

Nor is Howes the only London Classical Player one wants to single out for special thanks. There is the fourth hornist whose perfectly pitched, beautifully phrased solo in the Adagio makes one almost regret the invention of the valve-horn, whose even tone robs the famous C-flat major scale of so much of its other-worldly quality, a quality that — as Berlioz always claimed, and as one is now persuaded — Beethoven cannily planned the stopped tones to produce. (I cannot name the player because the roster lists five hornists; there must have been some subbing at the sessions.) There are the cellos and basses (in equal numbers!), led respectively by Susan Sheppard and Barry Guy, who make such an unforgettable assertion—"mais *in Tempo*," as Beethoven wanted it—out of the recitatives at the beginning of the finale, and then settle down into the most happily poised, least hortatory or sentimental enunciation of the Joy theme you'll ever want to hear. The second time around they are joined by the warm and brotherly bassoon of Felix Warnock and well seconded in the vocal exposition by a young Finnish baritone named Petteri Salomaa. Nor would it do to pass over concertmaster John Holloway and his first fiddles, who execute with such breathtaking precision the figurations in the Adagio, made more challenging than ever by the unheard of tempo.

But then, all the members of this extraordinary band of sixty-five deserve to have their hands clasped and their backs slapped for their contributions to this outstanding enterprise, as do the remaining vocal soloists and, certainly not least, the fifty singers in the Schütz Choir of London. Among their names one recognizes many a familiar English Early Music chorister, but the sound here is as far as may be imagined from the cathedral-tot timbre normally associated with the various groups of Clerkes and Scholars from which they hail. (I have actually been hearing a bit of grumbling about this, which astonishes me; but never fear, those who would prefer countertenors and ephebe-impersonators in the chorus and coryphées from Count Dracula's Hofkapelle have probably only to wait until the other Early Music Beethoven traversals currently in progress get around to the Ninth.) The singing and playing are so ardently committed, so imbued with mission and with risk, and yet withal so deucedly *accomplished*, as to put this recording in a class by itself, and not only among period instrument endeavors.

Finally, there is the mastermind behind it all, Roger Norrington, about whom I have already written admiringly and at length. His outstanding virtues are in evidence again, particularly what I have called his inspired literalism—meaning his conviction that Beethoven's tempi and expression markings are not something applied to the notes and rests as a mere suggestion for interpretation, but an essential aspect of the musical thought—and his gift for finding sounds to fit the signs and then molding the performance into a vividly imagined and projected *Gestalt* that takes shape in the ear's mind and lives thereafter in the ear's memory as a compelling representation of a masterpiece's unique sonic profile: its "true content," as Heinrich Schenker would have called it.

I will give one example of this from the Ninth to stand for many. After the first great unison statement of the theme as it finally coalesces at the beginning of the first movement, there is a rising scalewise continuation from the tonic D to B♭, the pitch that will function, unconventionally, as alternate tone center for this movement (and later, as primary center for the Adagio). The notes of this ascent, all marked *sforzando,* are notated very strangely: as dotted eighths separated by sixteenth rests. Most performers of the piece will notice the *sf* marking here, and articulate the passage with strong detached accents, separated by those effective rhetorical pauses known as *Luftpausen.* Norrington has realized that the strange rhythmic articulation, which recurs elsewhere in the movement in other dynamic contexts, is in fact thematic, and must be given a very distinctive sound in performance. So he has the players sustain the intensity of the *sf* through the full written value of the notes, and then very precisely measure off the exact length of the rest. The effect is very halting and ungainly—the musical equivalent, perhaps, of a wheeze. However we choose to interpret it, though, we certainly recognize it (as in other performances we do not) on each of its returns, no matter what the local dynamic level or melodic contour, and through it we recognize that all passages so marked are related in some important way, whether we wish to call the relationship structural or affective (if, indeed, a distinction is called for). The most striking instances of this thematic recurrence are at m. 196 and again at mm. 214–17 in the development section, where they are preceded by the most exquisitely calibrated transitions in the winds from staccatos, through slurred staccatos (the latter coinciding with a rarity in Beethoven's instrumental music—an expressly marked ritard), to the "wheeze" itself. While other conductors may fairly claim to have been attentive to the subtle differences in Beethoven's markings, only Norrington so consistently comes up with such distinctive and easily recognizable sound-analogs to each notational idiosyncrasy or nuance. It is his special genius.

All of which is so much more vital and important than mere historical verisimilitude—as (I would have thought) would be as obvious to Norrington as it is to me—that I find it quite confounding and disappointing to read sentences redolent of the usual earlie musicke cant over Norrington's signature in the notes:

> In this series we aim to recreate these past masterpieces, not according to recent interpretative tradition, but by the traditions of the early

nineteenth century. In this way, paradoxically, we are sure that they will speak to us more vividly today. In particular we want to restore the Ninth Symphony to the humane, quicksilver thought-world of the Classical Period, whose greatest progeny it is.

Alas, this is Judge Bork stuff. And I will only stage a confirmation hearing to the extent of pointing out that the Classical Period was something Beethoven never heard of (it being a fictive term and concept produced by Romantic historiography); that the "humane, quicksilver thought world" Norrington very successfully evokes in this performance is something he has created according to his own interpretive lights—by far the most "recent interpretative tradition" around today—and is in no demonstrable sense a restoration; and that therefore there is no paradox. Norrington is doing what important interpreters have always done (quite often, as here, with a palliating smokescreen of restoration), namely, recasting tradition in contemporary terms and according to contemporary taste. The ostensibly restorative element in his performances is really what I have called his literalism; and scrupulous literalism in matters of art and interpretation, as well as the "wit and humor" that Norrington goes on to describe as "classical traits," are really quintessential components of the modernist viewpoint. They serve the cause of aesthetic distancing, and as such actually run counter, I believe, to the impulse that produced the Ninth. But that need bother us only if we accept Norrington's contention that his work embodies "the known intentions of the composer." It does not, for it cannot, beyond matters that may be expressed as quantities.

II

These matters, and Norrington's well-advertised compliance with them, are the most obviously newsworthy features of this performance, and they have already been much discussed—and rather misleadingly—in print. Because Norrington has built his interpretive approach around fidelity to Beethoven's notorious metronome markings, he has acquired a reputation as the fastest Beethoven conductor in the West. One reviewer has elaborately contrasted Norrington's rendition with the monumental performance conducted by Wilhelm Furtwängler on the occasion of the postwar reopening of the Bayreuth Festival in 1951—an occasion that, fraught with countless cultural, political, and plain emotional overtones, must have told mightily on the rendition. Here is his report, quoted from the music page of the Sunday *New York Times* for 7 February 1988:

> Furtwängler['s] is much, much slower. It can't help being slower. Its
> instruments have greater weight. Today's strings need more time to
> accelerate past this downward pull of gravity; modern brass sound has
> more brilliance, more resonating power, requiring a certain space be-
> tween it and our ears.
>
> Mr. Norrington's tempos dance lightly because they can—they
> bear less burden. Lessened gravity frees them. Because ancient instru-
> ments retain sound with relative difficulty, our ears must hurry before
> the sound goes away. . . .
>
> Furtwängler, for all his outmoded modernity—his progressive
> incorrectness—advises us that the past exists only as we think of it
> right now. . . . Mr. Norrington's wonderful musicians and their ardent
> explorations of history argue eloquently in a different direction.

It is a feat to get so much so wrong in so little space. Furtwängler,
to begin with, was as dubious a representative of "modernity" in 1951
as he is today. On the contrary, his performances preserved in aspic a
century-old tradition of Beethoven interpretation that went back precisely to the great figure the Bayreuth Festival worships. This was no
secret in 1951; indeed that anachronistic link with Wagner was precisely what made Furtwängler indispensable to the occasion his
performance celebrated, and he surely did all he could, in the event, to
emphasize it. His, not Norrington's, is the voice of history.

But beyond that, a careful hearing of his rendition alongside
Norrington's will show just the opposite of what the *Times* reviewer
attempted to prove. The Wagnerian gravity of Furtwängler's performance had nothing to do with the instruments being used, except
insofar as the tone color, particularly of the brasses, revealed the
Ninth's Wagnerian affinities: the first movement recap is pure *Dutch-
man*, and there is an unforgettable glimpse of *Götterdämmerung* in
the finale (mm. 193–98), due not only to tone color but to a massive
accelerando. His tempi are eternally in flux, accelerating and de-
celerating in great waves that often pass Norrington's steady paces in
both directions, though the point of departure is usually—and necessarily, given the propensity to fluctuate—much slower. The essential
difference between the two is not a matter of speed as such, but one of
Norrington's Apollonian regularity (an artifact of the twentieth century and only of it) versus Furtwängler's variability, amounting at
times to climaxes of truly Bacchic frenzy. Just listen to him lead his
elephantine "modern" band through the last Prestissimo of the finale
(mm. 920*ff*), where Norrington—who has calibrated his tempo (half
note = 146) to build on the previous Prestissimo (m. 851), marked by
Beethoven at half note = 132—is actually the slowest on record (cf.
Klemperer, the previous record-holder, at 150). Furtwängler is by far
the fastest, and keeps getting faster. By the end of the movement he
has broken 200, and left my metronome behind in the dust.

So please, let there be no more uninformed, deterministic talk about period instruments and their magical power to make a performance all by themselves. Such talk is evasive and simplistic at best, destructive of all judgment and values at worst. Nor, as we have already seen, are Norrington's (that is, Beethoven's) tempi uniformly faster than the norm.

The only tempo, in fact, that will surprise the knowledgeable listener with its quickness is that of the third movement, the Adagio molto e cantabile, where the Wagnerian tradition, to which even Toscanini bowed in this instance, established itself somewhere between one-half and two-thirds of the rate Beethoven indicated. (A breakdown based on the recordings listed at the end of this chapter: Beethoven marked the initial value of the quarter note at 60 — i.e., one a second; Furtwängler begins at 30 and actually decelerates from there; Walter's basic pulse is 35; Karajan's is 38; Klemperer's is unexpectedly the fastest among traditionalists — he moves around between 39 and 46; while Toscanini, no iconoclast this time, hovers around 40 with many leaps and dips.) Norrington is just shy of Beethoven's mark around 58 (René Leibowitz had set the previous modernist benchmark at 52), though he is forced to slacken the heavily embellished second variation to around 50 to accommodate the first violins' triplet sixteenths and thirty-seconds. Which puts him not so far ahead of his faster predecessors.

Norrington's basic tempo for the first movement, held pretty steady throughout at quarter note = 80–82, is a good notch slower than the 88 Beethoven marked, and also slower than Leibowitz (ca. 90) and even Walter (ca. 84). Furtwängler begins this movement as if it were *Das Rheingold*, with a tempo under 50; but one of his Dionysiac lunges in the recapitulation (the dozen bars before letter P) actually brings him up into the 80s, past Norrington, though by letter Q (the famous horn solo) he has subsided to 67, and by the coda (the equally famous chromatic dead march ostinato) he is back in the 50s, where he remains. His notion of proper tempo, obviously, is a function of his affective reading of the music — something that was de rigueur in the late nineteenth century, verboten in the late twentieth. As to the early nineteenth century, the period of the symphony, vide infra.

In the Scherzo, Norrington and Furtwängler begin, mirabile dictu, at the same tempo (full measure = 117–20), which is just a mite faster than the one indicated by Beethoven (116) and quite a bit slower than Toscanini at 124, Leibowitz at 130, and Karajan at 131 (Klemperer lumbers egregiously at 102). Norrington holds fast to his initial pace, while Furtwängler is all over the map (the steadier the rhythmic writing, the faster his tempo; he hits a peak of 123 around letter A). That Norrington, for all his touted dependence on the markings, is not slavish or pedantic about them is evident in the second half of the Scherzo, where he (again like Furtwängler) sets the *Ritmo de tre battute* slower than the opening and accelerates from there, regaining his original tempo at the return of the *Ritmo di quattro*.

The Trio is another newsmaker—but for its slowness. Alone in the field, Norrington accepts Beethoven's marking (half note = 116 in cut time) as valid. Everyone else, following tradition, rejects it as an error: for how could Beethoven have intended a Presto following a stringendo to revert to the tempo of his initial Molto vivace—indeed, to sound slower, since there is now twice as much time between downbeats as before? Even Klemperer is faster than Norrington here, as is Furtwängler, and—by a wide margin—Toscanini (150–60), Karajan (152), and Walter (156). As for Leibowitz, he evidently believed that the intended mark was whole note (i.e., full measure) = 116—against the plain physical evidence of Beethoven's manuscript, available in published facsimile since 1924. Trying valiantly for what was clearly impossible, he ended up at half note = 180. That the result sounded ridiculous in its flat contradiction of Beethoven's pastoral imagery did not deter him in his quest for literal authenticity. (I should add that by the time the horns get their turn at the trio tune, Klemperer, having slackened to 96, manages to snatch the slowness trophy from Norrington.)

All of Norrington's departures from the range of the familiar in the finale are in the direction of moderation where others take things to extremes. Some are radical. The Alla Marcia variation (m. 331) and the entire double fugue that follows are taken at tempi chosen to accord with Beethoven's setting for the Allegro assai vivace (dotted-quarter = 84). Norrington is not really that close to Beethoven, in fact, but at 94 for the Alla Marcia and 100–02 for the fugue, he is far slower than anyone else on record, especially Furtwängler, who is again the fastest (130; 140), and gets faster as he approaches the choral outburst at letter M, although not without a radical dip (to 90) to reflect the brief harmonic shift toward the minor mode that sets off the climax. At letter M Norrington is slower than his slowest rival (who else but Klemperer?) by a good twenty-five points on the metronome (101 vs. 126). Furtwängler, at 137, is bested at the other extreme only by Toscanini's furious 191. There has been no mark to indicate any tempo change from Beethoven, incidentally, since the 84 at the Alla Marcia.

At the Andante maestoso ("Seid umschlungen, Millionen"), all those who had been careering in the 120s and 130s come to a virtual standstill, with those commonly perceived antipodes, Toscanini and Furtwängler again tied at the lower extreme (ca. 56 to the half note). Norrington is exactly at Beethoven's indicated tempo (72), which puts him alone on the opposite end. Thus Toscanini's tempo contrast covers 135 points on the metronome, Norrington's a mere 29. At the ensuing Adagio ("Ihr stürzt nieder, Millionen?"), where everyone else's tempo congeals into the forties, Norrington (at half note = 56) is again alone out front at a tempo close to Beethoven's indication (60).

With the second double fugue (Allegro energico, dotted half note = 84), it's a whole new horse race. Now Norrington is at the rear, at 90, and Furtwängler is in a frenzy at 115. When Beethoven jacks the tempo up to half note = 120 for the coda, Norrington again tracks him closely, which puts him briefly ahead of the pack (only Toscanini is faster, at 123); Furtwängler and Walter start slowly—Walter all the way back to 94—but accelerate madly so that they can slam into the Poco adagio at m. 810 like two tons of bricks. Norrington barely breaks stride and resumes the same tempo as before when Beethoven marks Tempo I at m. 814. Furtwängler continues to apply the whip here, passing Norrington and Toscanini by the time the next Poco adagio is reached (the one for the soloists at m. 832; Norrington's quartet must have blessed him for relaxing so little). From then on it's Prestissimo al fine, with Furtwängler achieving lift-off as noted, except for the Maestoso at m. 916, where Norrington keeps close to Beethoven's marking (quarter = 60), and Furtwängler skates clear off the metronome at the other end, with a tempo below 30.

The surprising upshot of this comparison is that Norrington's finale is the safest and sanest (humanest and quicksilverest?), while Furtwängler's apparently lives by the precept that anything is all right if it is enough so. That was Wagner's philosophy, too, where conducting Beethoven was concerned. And, though we will never know what Beethoven would have made of Norrington's performance, we can be sure that Wagner would have detested it. It is in light of the Wagnerian tradition, and nothing more recent than that, that Norrington's performance is "revisionist."

But that is not where its virtue lies. I have given all the foregoing figures just to set the factual record straight and clear the air of misconceptions, not because the tempi, any more than the instruments, will automatically make the performance great or authentic. Having chosen our tempi we still have to make the performance. And though it is easy enough to say that we are rejecting the nineteenth century in favor of the eighteenth (Stravinsky said it, after all, some six or seven decades ago), "eighteenth" here is only a stand-in for "twentieth," since the twentieth century is the one that has always loved to wear masks, and still does.

So what shall we make of the twentieth-century viewpoint on the Ninth, insofar as Norrington's performance represents it? Full of admiration as I am for the execution per se, grateful as I am for a rendition so novel and provocative that it has forced me to think harder about the piece than ever before, still I find I cannot simply give myself up to it, as I was so happy to do with some of Norrington's previous recordings. And I think I know why.

III

For a century and a half and more now, Beethoven's "Symphonie mit Schluss-chor über Schiller's Ode: 'An die Freude' " has surely been the most strenuously resisted masterpiece in the canon of symphonic music. Immediately notorious, it was received with skepticism wherever it was performed in the early years of its existence, as Robin Wallace has shown in his documentary study, *Beethoven's Critics*, which traces the reception of Beethoven's music during the composer's lifetime and for a short time thereafter. Throughout the nineteenth century, hostile voices continued to be raised against it. For Louis Spohr, who had known Beethoven in Vienna in his youth, and played under his baton, the Ninth was a monstrosity that could only be explained in terms of its creator's deafness:

> His constant endeavor to be original and to open new paths, could no longer as formerly, be preserved from error by the guidance of the ear. Was it then to be wondered at that his works became more and more eccentric, unconnected, and incomprehensible? . . . Yes! I must even reckon the much admired Ninth Symphony among them, the three first movements of which, in spite of some solitary flashes of genius, are to me worse than all of the eight previous Symphonies, the fourth movement of which is in my opinion so monstrous and tasteless, and in its grasp of Schiller's Ode so trivial, that I cannot even now understand how a genius like Beethoven's could have written it. I find in it another proof of what I already remarked in Vienna, that Beethoven was wanting in aesthetical feeling and in a sense of the beautiful.

For Fanny Mendelssohn, who heard it under her brother's direction on its Düsseldorf premiere in 1836, the symphony was "so grand and in parts so abominable, as only the work of the greatest composer could be, . . . a gigantic tragedy with a conclusion meant to be dithyrambic, but falling from its height into the opposite extreme— into burlesque." It was the Ninth that gave maximum credence to the complaint confided by the nineteen-year-old Schubert to his diary against "that eccentricity [of Beethoven's] which joins and confuses the tragic with the comic, the agreeable with the repulsive, heroism with howlings and the holiest with harlequinades."

The only nineteenth-century musicians who embraced the Ninth without reservation were those whose own aesthetic program it could seem to validate. This brings us back to Wagner, of course, for whom the Ninth sounded the death knell of "pure music" and finished off the symphony as a viable independent genre. "The last symphony of Beethoven," Wagner wrote, outlining his vision of *The Art Work of the Future*, "is the redemption of Music from out her own peculiar element into the realm of *universal art*—and this, of course, by the incorporation of The Word in the guise of its *Schluss-chor*. "It is the human evangel of the art of the future"—that is, of Wagner's art. "Beyond it no forward step is possible," within the realm of instrumental music, "for upon it the perfect artwork of the future alone can follow, the *universal drama* to which Beethoven had forged the key." A classic co-optation, this.

The contention that the Ninth represented the summit of Beethoven's art or that it embodied the inexorable will of History only intensified the backlash against it, even—or above all—among those who acknowledged its greatness. "Do not search for the abnormal in him," Schumann had preached to Beethoven's devotees. "Do not illustrate his genius with the Ninth Symphony alone, no matter how great its audacity and scope." It was Brahms, of course, who made the most pointed critique of the Ninth along these lines with his famous near-quotation of its choral theme in the finale of his own First Symphony in 1876. This was no simple homage or oath of fealty such as one finds in so many late-nineteenth-century symphonies (e.g., by Franck, Bruckner, Mahler), which chiefly resonate with involuntary echoes of Beethoven's first movement. By bringing the choral theme back within an instrumental context, Brahms, as it were, corrected the wrong turn Beethoven had taken, with what dire results for the Master's corybantic followers.

Not even in the twentieth century, when the canon has become the ossified object of a wholly distracted, automatic genuflection, and when Beethoven's technical and stylistic audacities have long since been absorbed into the language and vastly exceeded, has the Ninth entirely succeeded in going down. Resistance remains and has become increasingly generalized. Thomas Mann had Adrian Leverkühn, the composer-protagonist of *Doctor Faustus*, cry "I want to revoke the Ninth Symphony!" On a somewhat less exalted plane, Ned Rorem refers to it in one of his diaries as "the first piece of junk in the grand style," which I single out for quotation since I heard Mr. Rorem repeat the assertion only a few years ago (this time he called it "utter trash") at a colloquium with student composers at Columbia University, and I could observe the smiles of mischievous complicity on the faces of many members of that audience of serious young musicians that went out reflexively to meet the one on Rorem's own. That made me think about the Ninth's special status, all right. It seemed perfectly clear to me that mentioning another piece could never have elicited such a surefire response (as Mr. Rorem, a frequent public speaker, must know very well). To cast aspersions at a symphony by Tchaikovsky or a tone poem by Liszt would have seemed merely superfluous, while insulting any other Beethoven piece (even the "Eroica" or the Fifth) would have called forth confusion and consternation, I'm sure. The Ninth, it seems, is among connoisseurs preeminently the Piece You Love To Hate, no less now than a century and a half ago. Why? Because it is at once incomprehensible and irresistible, and because it is at once awesome and naive.

IV

There has been a lot of interesting critical writing about the Ninth lately, betokening a restlessness within the musical-intellectual community that may reflect large issues. We seem to be experiencing a general revolt against the formalist viewpoints—whether intellectualist or epicurean—that have been part and parcel of modernist thinking on the arts, and a return to hermeneutics (that is, "reading" a work of art for its "meanings") as a proper mode of critical inquiry. It is natural that the Ninth has become a focal point of this ferment because, as Leo Treitler puts it,

> more than any other work of the Tradition, it *demands* interpretation. It does so in and of itself because it blatantly confounds efforts to account for its events on strictly formalist terms, but also by virtue of the interpretational, or hermeneutic, field in which it has been transmitted to us.

The last clause is a warning, to those inclined to pursue Original Intent, that the meaning of the Ninth—or any other text or artwork—depends "both on the tradition in which it was composed and the tradition that it has generated," the latter tradition having arisen precisely out of the inadequacy of the former to account fully for the work. Why *does* the kettledrum practically drown out the first movement's recapitulation? Why *does* the submediant (B♭) replace the more usual mediant (F) as the symphony's antipodal tonal region? Why do the horns have their strange solos in the first and third movements, and why are there four of them (to mention only events that have figured in our discussion thus far)?

The Ninth poses more questions like these than any other Beethoven symphony—perhaps more than any symphony by anyone else up to the time when composers began purposely loading their symphonies with symbols and sphinxes (this being the tradition that the Ninth "generated"). And they are questions neither textbooks of harmony nor textbooks of form nor histories of music will ever answer, questions next to which the most obvious novelty—the choral finale and the introduction of The Word—seems quite unproblematical. Treitler's point, which seems indubitable, shows how wrong Wagner was to declare that the introduction of a text rendered the symphony "articulate" and its meaning explicit. Despite the text, maybe to some extent even because of it, the meanings of this symphony remain mysterious.

Other analysts and critics have attempted hermeneutic interpretations of the formal and tonal structures of the symphony (e.g., Ernest Sanders, as long ago as 1964) and, along more specialized lines, of its specific imagery for representing the Deity all through the work, but especially in the finale (William Kinderman). Kinderman's study takes into account both concurrent compositions, as they evolved in Beethoven's sketchbooks alongside the Ninth (the *Missa solemnis,* the String Quartet in E-flat, op. 127), and also what is known of Beethoven's response to the philosophy of Kant. Maynard Solomon, in an especially rich and pregnant essay, has analyzed the meanings of the Ninth in terms of recurrent musical imagery of all kinds— martial, pastoral, ecclesiastical—and in terms of a complicated network of thematic reminiscences and forecasts. (Here, incidentally, Solomon revives a long-debated and seemingly long-since-rejected exegesis of the work by the Russian critic Alexander Serov, who claimed to transmit an insight of Wagner; its resurrection followed Robert Winter's demonstration, on the basis of a sketch study, that the theme of the Ode to Joy was in fact fully evolved before the first three movements were composed.) These thematic forecasts prefigure the Elysium named in the finale and turn the symphony into an embodiment of the primordial mythic structure of a quest. As Solomon summarizes this aspect of his inquiry:

> A multiplicity of drives converges in the Ninth Symphony's finale—for a visionary D major to overcome the power of D minor [and casting the tonality of D major as "visionary" resonates beautifully with its use in the third movement, where it inhabits the interludes of unearthly stillness that mysteriously intrude between the variations in B-♭]; for a theme adequate to represent "Joy, divine spark of the Gods"; for Elysium, with its promise of brotherhood, reconciliation, and eternal life; for a recovery of the classical ideal of humanity united with Nature. And more: for a Deity who transcends any particularizations of religious creed; for a fusion of Christian and Pagan beliefs, a marriage of Faust and Helen.

Yet Solomon is careful to affirm that "the precise nature of Beethoven's programmatic intentions will always remain open: . . . the Ninth

Symphony is a symbol the totality of whose referents cannot be known and whose full effects will never be experienced." And further, most pertinently, that "in refusing to accept the mythic design as the ultimate or sole meaning of the symphony we remain true to the nature of music, whose meanings are beyond translation — and beyond intentionality."

The message is clear. We may interpret Beethoven's meanings in endless ways, depending on our perspicacity and our interests (Solomon himself proceeds to biographical and psychological speculations that will not interest everyone or shed what all might agree to regard as relevant light on the symphony). What we may not do, on this view, is on the one hand to claim to have arrived at a definitive interpretation, or on the other to deny the reality of this semiotic dimension or its relevance to the meanings of the work.

V

Meanings like these had not figured in eighteenth-century musical discourse. That century had its semiotic codes, all right — its *Affektenlehre,* its *sinfonia caracteristica* (the genre to which the "Pastoral" Symphony belongs, as do also, perhaps, the "Eroica" and the Fifth), and so forth. But such embodied meanings, whether emotive or descriptive, were always *public* meanings. No one needs to interpret the "Pastoral" Symphony. If we do need to have certain eighteenth-century genres interpreted for us by historians — the expressive conventions of Baroque opera, for example — that is only because we have lost the code through desuetude, not because it was esoteric. Some Baroque genres (sacred ones) did, it is true, occasionally embody esoteric meanings of a theological sort, to which hermeneutic techniques need to be applied, but these were survivals of a pre-Enlightenment aesthetic and were rejected between Bach's time and Beethoven's. During that time, moreover, musical illustrations and emotive gestures were delimited by what was universally taken to be the nature of beauty and the purpose of art. As Mozart himself insisted, "music, even in the most terrible situations, must never offend the ear, but must please the listener, or in other words must never cease to be music."

The meanings embodied in the Ninth Symphony, as in the late quartets, are no longer public in this way. Though they are clearly crucial components of the works, they cannot be fully comprehended according to some socially sanctioned code. They have become subjective, hermetic, gnomic. They are not so private as to render the musical discourse altogether unintelligible, but they do render its message ineffable and to that extent, oracular. In the Ninth, at least up to the finale, inspiration thus calls out to inspiration. Intuitive grasp, aided of course by whatever can be gleaned by code or study or experience, is the only mode of understanding available. And that must be what Beethoven meant by insisting, in his late years, that he was not merely a composer (*Tonsetzer*) but a tone-poet (*Tondichter*).

Nor can the meanings in his works be simply bracketed off as "extramusical," since as we have seen, inscrutable *musical* events and relationships are what hint to us of their existence (the drumroll, the key contrasts, the horn music). Bracket the meanings and no self-explanatory musical utterance remains. Most obviously, too, many of the musical events most closely bound up with these meanings do offend the ear (besides that shattering drumroll, think of the *Schreckensfanfare* at the outset of the finale, in the second of which the D minor triad and the diminished-seventh chord on its leading tone are sounded together as a seven-tone harmony whose level of dissonance would not be matched until the days of Strauss and Mahler). However much they may move or thrill, they cannot be said to please the listener. By Mozartean standards they aren't music; and by composing them, Beethoven tells us that he doesn't care what we think of them (or of him), that they are in fact bigger than we are.

Which is another way of saying that they are sublime. We tend nowadays to interchange the words "beautiful" and "sublime" in our everyday language, perhaps even in our critical vocabulary; but eighteenth-century writers were careful to distinguish them as virtual opposites. Recall Edmund Burke, quoted in essay 4, who contrasted the smallness, the lightness, and the pleasurableness of the Beautiful with the vastness, the obscurity, the painfulness of the Sublime. Nineteenth-century *Tonkunst* displayed a determined progress from the one pole to the other, from the pleasant to the "great."

Quite obviously the Ninth was a milestone—perhaps even the point of departure—along this path. All the adjectives Burke applies to the "great"—vast, rugged, negligent, dark, gloomy, solid, massive—suit its first three movements to perfection, even as the adjectives applied to "beauty"—small, smooth, polished, light, delicate—seem altogether alien to it. Spohr was right after all. Beethoven did lack a sense of beauty. Or rather, he rejected the assumption on which Spohr based his judgement, that to be beautiful—i.e., pleasing—was the only proper aim of art.

Even the Eighth Symphony is, by and large, a conventionally "beautiful" piece by comparison with its successor. And here let us take note that as much time separates the dates of completion of the Eighth and the Ninth—twelve years (1812–24)—as those of the Eighth and the First (1800–12). There is just no comparing the Ninth with its fellows, or with any contemporary composition, for that matter. Nicholas Temperley rightly observes, in the *New Grove Dictionary* (s.v. "Symphony"), that

> the Choral Symphony . . . can only be treated as a solitary masterpiece, with no immediate predecessor or successor; in this it resembles the symphonies of the radical Romantics . . . and the immense influence it had was on the late-nineteenth-century composers, not on those of its own time.

Solitary, vast, awe-inspiring, the Ninth reminds everyone of a mountain. It makes us uncomfortable. "We live in the valley of the Ninth Symphony—that we cannot help," says Joseph Kerman. Why the resignation? Why should we wish it otherwise? Because of the finale, of course, and the impossible problem of tone it has created, especially for us in the fallen twentieth century. That it is a catastrophic descent cannot be denied. Beethoven even tags it so for us, when he has his baritone ask for something *angenehmere*—something more pleasing—after the horror fanfares in which sublimity reaches far past the threshold of pain. And the pleasure, as the nature of the Joy theme at once announces, is to be an eminently public pleasure, annulling the private pain Beethoven had previously disclosed to us. Kerman calls the theme "half folklike, blinding in its demagogic innocence." Is *this* the Elysium to which our noble quest has delivered us, the realm glimpsed mistily through visionary modulations amid the crags and ravines of earlier movements? And who are all this riffraff, with their beery *Männerchöre* and sauerkraut bands? Our brothers? And the juxtaposition of all this with the disclosure of God's presence "above the stars?" No, it is all too much!

So much we may already read in nineteenth-century reactions to the finale, which register—through the fastidious charge of bathos—a characteristic dismay that Beethoven apparently took his democracy straight. In the twentieth century, the problem has been compounded. Not only have artists of our time once again rejected intimations of the sublime as the proper role of art—for a Ned Rorem, the "grand style" already implies a "piece of junk"; his expression is a pleonasm—but we have our problems with demagogues who preach to us about the brotherhood of man. We have been too badly burned by those who have promised Elysium and given us Gulags and gas chambers. Our suspicions may not extend to Beethoven himself, as they do to Wagner, whom so many find personally repellent; rightly or wrongly, we seem to respect his naiveté. But we can hardly share it, or live happily with it.

For that reason his work, no less than Wagner's, needs neutering. And the way in which the twentieth century has until recently been

neutering the Ninth has been to say to it, paraphrasing Alice's triumphant rejoinder to the Queen of Hearts, "Why, you're nothing but a
pack of notes!" Formalist analysis, beginning with Schenker's huge
tome of 1912, has been our dodge—and our scalpel. For those who
cannot reject it outright, deflecting attention from "meaning" to
"structure" has been the primary means of resisting the Ninth.

VI

And it is to that tradition of what we might call sublimated resistance
that Roger Norrington's brilliant recorded performance seems to be-
long. By turning its attention wholly on the notes and realizing these
with unprecedented lucidity, it has managed to avoid confrontation
with the troubling meanings. Never has the Ninth seemed so effable.
And when all is said and done, and though as an admirer of Norrington's work I say it with reluctance and regret, the result has been a
trivialization.

The best illustration of all comes right at the beginning, the
famous beginning that was so unprecedented in the symphonic literature, and so influential on its later development. No symphony had
ever started, as the Ninth does, so amorphously, at the very threshold
of audibility, with a tremolo on an open fifth that discloses neither
tempo nor mode. Such vagueness became a Romantic cliché, but its
beginnings with Beethoven do not really denote "an enjoyment of
sensuousness as opposed to structure and articulation," as Edward
Lippman has succinctly defined "The Tonal Ideal of Romanticism."
Beethoven's gesture marks a transcendence of the Enlightened viewpoint on art, which saw art as imitation of nature—nature, for music,
being speech and simple song—and its replacement by a metaphysical idea according to which music, as Lippman puts it, "possesses a
mysterious and self-contained character that stands in opposition to
the world of every day experience," so that the beginning of a composition is like "the unveiling of a secret domain."

Norrington, with his passion for clarity and his genius for vivid
articulation, plays this gambit utterly false and frustrates its magical
effect. The tremolo in second violin and cello, notated as a sextolet, is
articulated like a nervous little tarantella with six eminently count-
able sixteenths to the bar and an accent on every down beat: DIG-a-da-
dig-a-da DIG-a-da-dig-a-da. The quality of time is kinetic, not hover-
ing. With the beats and measures so highly organized, and the tempo
so regular, the gradual coalescing of the theme proceeds like a clock-
work, or like an advancing army. The metrical displacement of the
entries as the passage moves to its culmination—surely intended to

maintain vagueness and prevent kinetic regularity from ever setting in—emerges as precise syncopations. No secret domain gets unveiled. Great success in realizing the letter of the score here has led to a falsification of its spirit.[1] No one would glean from the opening of this performance the intimations of the cosmic and the infinite to which Nietzsche gave expression in a passage from *Human, All Too Human*—"The thinker feels himself floating above the earth in an astral dome, with the dream of immortality in his heart: all the stars seem to glimmer about him, and the earth seems to sink ever further downward"—an impression that links up presciently with that other tremolando-ridden passage in the finale when God's dwelling place "beyond the stars" is invoked. Here again, vagueness is assured by the vertical superimposition of quarter-note triplets in the winds against sixteenths in the strings. And this passage, in turn, is the very one that resonates with Beethoven's reading of Kant, whom he perceived as equating "the moral law within us, and the starry heavens above us."

A reading of the Ninth as a pack of notes, even an inspired reading of the notes like Norrington's, leaves us very far from the truth of the work, for all that our knowledge of the latter is doomed to incompleteness. Illuminating readings of the score—and here I must place Furtwängler's in a class of its own—are those that make the kind of connections discussed in the last paragraph. It is that kind of performance, which may be achieved with any instruments using any tempos, that truly counts as an interpretation in the hermeneutic sense.

Though full of surface distortions, Furtwängler's performance makes disclosure after spinetingling disclosure of the spiritual content of the music by means of inspirational, unnotated emphases, pointing to unsuspected musical parallels that link widely dispersed passages. It was not until I heard Furtwängler's unnotated tenutos in m. 24 of the first movement, and his unnotated molto ritardandos two bars later, that I realized the significance of the enigmatic E-flat-major chord (a "Neapolitan," but in root position, not the conventional "sixth"), which moves to a diminished-seventh chord on Eﾮ in m. 27. These are the precise harmonies that, in the last movement, introduce

---

[1]It could be argued, of course, that Beethoven's notation is exact, and the claim of vagueness is based on a preconception. The sort of "spirit" I am looking for, one could contend, demands a different sort of notation, i.e., an "unmeasured" tremolo. The latter, though, seems not to have been a part of Beethoven's notational vocabulary. The earliest symphonic score in which I have spotted it is Berlioz's *Symphonie fantastique* of 1830, though Adam Carse, in his *History of Orchestration*, cites operatic precedents going back to the eighteenth century. Beethoven's use of the sextolet, contradicting the subdivisions at the melodic surface, would seem to be evidence that Beethoven's intended effect was the very blur that Norrington has triumphantly clarified.

Beethoven's depiction of the "starry dome" beyond which God makes his abode, the "denouement of the entire symphony," to quote Treitler. It is the chord progression that, with the addition of A in the bass, leads finally and securely to the never-again-to-be-questioned D major of Elysium, the very progression the first movement never gets to consummate. It is the progression the timpani tries so hard to insist upon at the first movement recapitulation, but can never browbeat the bass instruments into vouchsafing: their unstable F♯ falls inexorably to F♮, and Elysium is lost. (At mm. 326–27, timpani still raging, the "beyond the stars" progression is assayed once more, but again to no avail; D♭ major again fails to materialize.)

Again, it was thanks to Furtwängler—who with courageous initiative decided that the *fortissimo* for the brass's F at m. 132 in the Adagio should also apply to the low strings' D♭ a bar later—that I was able, to my astonishment, to perceive another foreshadowing of the deity in the last movement: the chord progression here is the same heaven-storming submediant that no one can miss where the chorus proclaims, "Und der Cherub steht vor Gott!" Next to revelations such as these, textual and metronomic matters recede to a somewhat secondary importance, and preoccupation with them seems evasive.

As long as we are on the subject of the third movement, let me add that Norrington fails to realize what seems to me the most eminent potential advantage of adhering to Beethoven's metronomic indication. With the music going fast enough to place the rhythmic pulse on the half note (or the dotted-half in the last variation)—which is how Norrington correctly justifies the marking "Adagio molto" in conjunction with what seems such a quick metronomic setting—it ought finally to be possible to hear the winds sing the original theme ("e cantabile") at its original speed behind the violin filigree in the two variations. At conventional "modern" tempi the wind line loses its melodic coherence, and the lyrical impulse devolves inappropriately upon the violins, turning the embroidery into the essential design, as happens when one gets up too close to a painting or a building. The faster tempo might have enabled our ears to step back and observe the sonic texture as one can see from the score Beethoven intended it to be observed. Yet either because he had not shaken the customarily skewed perspective, or because he was too eager to show off the accomplishments of his magnificent first fiddles, Norrington allowed their athletic filigree to go on occupying the sonic foreground, robbing the music of its visionary calm. Indeed, it takes on more flagrantly than ever that sentimentally contorted Biedermeier aspect so many have unjustly decried in the piece as a lapse of style or taste. Said Vaughan Williams: "I cannot get out of my head the picture of Beethoven playing the pianoforte in a fashionable Viennese salon."

VII

The curiously restrained finale is another example of what I would call sublimated resistance to Beethoven's message, for all that it is played in unprecedented accord with Beethoven's metronome marks. It is the prime example, in fact, in keeping with the difficulty the movement presents to twentieth-century sensibilities. This paradoxical situation arises out of what seems a basic misapprehension about the meaning of metronome marks, and our tendency to confuse a twentieth-century approach to tempo with a fictive notion of "classical" performance practice. It is worth some close discussion.

Reviewing Karajan's first stereophonic traversal of the complete Beethoven symphonies back in 1964, Paul Henry Lang asserted that "a steady and relentless tempo . . . is a *sine qua non* of classic symphonic thought," in urgent need of reinstatement to counter "the excessive tempo alterations and wayward phrasing that the mistaken identification of Beethoven with Romanticism called forth." This has been the conventional wisdom now for at least half a century, but it is not a historically tenable viewpoint—quite the opposite, in fact. In essay 8 I suggested that this notion of "Classical" style emerged when the aesthetics of the Italian opera house were applied to the performance of "absolute" music, a phenomenon of which Toscanini was the chief protagonist, and that it had never existed before the First World War. I have also suggested that the identification of Beethoven with Romanticism was not at all mistaken, and the Ninth offers the best corroboration. By setting Schiller, the preeminent German theorist of the Sublime and of individual creative freedom, after all, Beethoven made the identification himself. Romanticism, in any case, was something that existed in Beethoven's time. "Classicism," as we use the term today (mainly as a stick with which to beat the Romantics), was not.

Goaded now by my dissatisfaction with Norrington's finale, I want to pursue this general point into narrower and more specific matters of evidence. Where is the authority for the ideal of a "steady and relentless tempo" in Beethoven? What eighteenth- or early-nineteenth-century writer upheld it? The matter is so taken for granted these days that chapter and verse are rarely adduced, or even called for. In fact, the only citations I have been able to find are the two that Lang happened to quote in his old Karajan review; and as I discovered in the process of verifying them, Lang's citations were tendentiously distorted.

The first is attributed to Gluck: "If the tempo is changed in 'Che farò senza Euridice,' it becomes fit for a Punch and Judy show." This seems pretty definite, as well as colorful. But what Gluck actually

wrote, in his letter of dedication of his opera *Paride ed Elena* to
the Duke of Braganza in 1770, was this: "By changing very little in
the expression of my aria for Orfeo, 'Che farò senza Euridice,' it
might be turned into a little puppet dance. A note more or less
sustained, a *rinforzo* distorted either in time or in volume, an appoggiatura out of place, a trill, a cadenza, a run can easily ruin a whole
scene in such an opera. . . ."[2] He isn't talking about tempo at all,
but about the tendency of singers to be careless with their embellishments and dynamics. To the extent that the remark might be extrapolated to tempo, it could only refer to a poorly chosen one (in this
case, obviously, one that is too fast), rather than failure to maintain a
steady pace.

More seriously doctored is the second authority, the German
pastor and dilettante composer Carl Ludwig Junker (1748–97; Lang
elevated him to the rank of a "classic authority on eighteenth-century
practices"), who in 1782 published a little handbook entitled *Some of
the Chief Duties of a Musical Director* ("Einige der vornehmsten
Pflichten eines Capellmeisters oder Musikdirektors"), from which
Lang extracted the following sentence (the interpolation in brackets is
his): "Modifications of tempo can be better expressed by the composer
himself, by his setting and coloring [i.e., by the note values employed
and by the nature of the orchestration] than by the tempo changes
caused by the conductor." Even before checking it is clear that this is
garbled; it makes no sense. One cannot tell whether the conductor is
being exhorted to forbear or the composer is being encouraged to be
more specific. Does the writer want more modification or does he
want less?

It turns out that the remark has been quoted out of context, and
that Junker was really saying virtually the opposite of what Lang
purported to prove by quoting him. Here is the original statement:

> It is true that the composer, through his writing itself, through the
> various types of nuances [available to him], could better and more com-
> pletely express these modifications than the conductor [could] by varying
> the musical time-sequence; but it is just as true that the two of them,
> composer and performer, must work hand in hand, and that variation in
> the time-sequence, as an auxiliary art, remains indispensable.

Junker actually introduces the matter of tempo-modification by
invoking Lang's "steady and relentless tempo" (*eine völlig gleich-*

[2]The original Italian: "Non ci vuol nulla, per che la mia Aria nell'Orfeo: 'Che farò
senza Euridice,' mutando solamente qualche cosa nella maniera dell'espressione, di-
venti un saltarello da Burattini. Una nota più o meno tenuta, un rinforzo trascurato di
tempo, o di voce, un appoggiatura fuor di luogo, un trillo, un passagio, una volata, puo
rovinare tutta una scena in un Opera simile."

förmige Bewegung), but only as a straw-man (p. 36). He then continues with this rhetorical question:

> Must every piece be performed at the given tempo straight through to the end, without ever inclining toward a greater speed or slowness? Or ought this tempo, even right in the middle of the piece, be somewhat adjusted, ought it be accelerated, ought it be held back?

The first alternative is not even given consideration. The only choice, it turns out, is between accelerating and holding back. Stated in most general terms, the reason for constant tempo adjustments goes right to the heart of matters aesthetic. The sentence that immediately precedes the one quoted by Lang reads as follows: "There is no passion whose movement, itself wholly uniform, might be so circumscribed; it ranges, throughout, through various modifications of movement." And elsewhere, with regard to contrasting moods, Junker observes that

> Nothing is sudden in nature; no change takes place through instantaneous transformation of opposing moods, no expression changes at a bound into its opposite. There are intermediate shades, which an expression must go through if it wishes to change into its opposite.[3]

Thus musical movement (*Bewegung*) is a function of the "movements" of the spirit. Only as long as the unitary Cartesian view of the latter remained in force could a conception of "a steady, relentless tempo" hold sway. Such a tempo might have been appropriate to music conceived in terms of the Doctrine of the Affections (though I

---

[3]The original passages in Junker, all from the section entitled "On Tempo" (*Von der Bewegung*), are as follows:

Dass diese Modifikationen, der Komponist, durch seinen Satz selbst, durch die verschiedenen Arten der Kolorierung, besser und vollständiger ausdrücken könne, als der Direktor, durch die Veränderung der musikalischen Zeitfolge, bleibt richtig; aber eben so richtig bleibt es, dass beyde, Se[t]zer und Ausführer, einander in die Hände arbeiten müssen, und dass die Veränderung der Zeitfolge, als unterordnete Kunst, nothwendig bleibe (p. 37).

Muss jedes Stück, ganz bis zu Ende, in der nemlichen Bewegung, die sich niemahls, weder einer grössern Geschwindigkeit noch Langsamkeit nähert, vorgetragen werden? Oder darf diese Bewegung, selbst in der Mitte des Tonstücks, etwas abgeändert; darf sie beschleunigt, darf sie zurück gehalten werden (p. 36)?

Es gibt keine Leydenschaft, deren Bewegung, sich selbst immer gleichartig, abgezirkelt seyn sollte; Sie wälzt sich durch verschiedene Modifikationen der Bewegung hindurch (pp. 35–36).

Nichts ist Sprung in der Natur; keine Veränderung geschiehet durch die augenblickliche Verwechslung, entgegengesetzer Bestimmungen, keine Empfindung geht durch einen Sprung in ihre entgegengesetzte über. Es giebt Mitteltöne, die eine Empfindung durchgehen muss, wenn sie zu ihrer entgegengesetzen über gehen will (pp. 27–28n).

know of no contemporary writer who says so explicitly), but it was effectively banished by the advent of "Sentiment." Or, to put it in terms of conventional style-periodization, Lang might conceivably have been describing the tempo conceptions of the Baroque, but surely not those of the Classical period. Junker's Capellmeister, it transpires, was a Furtwängler, not a Norrington.

And so, I continue to maintain, was Beethoven, for whom metronome markings were good "only for the first measures, as feeling has its own tempo." No one, to my knowledge, ever maintained a position to the contrary before the twentieth century, when for reasons completely unrelated to the matters at hand, composers began demanding an "objective," depersonalized performance style for their own music, and performers allowed this rigid "neoclassical" mode of execution to rub off on what by then had solidified into the "classical" repertory, minus the neo.

But even supposing Gluck and Junker had meant just what Lang said they meant, by what lights do pronouncements of the 1770s and '80s apply to the music Beethoven wrote in the 1820s, or the way in which it should be performed? Over the half-century in question momentous changes had taken place in orchestral practice: baton conducting, for one thing, had decisively replaced the "presiding" fiddler or keyboard strummer. And while eyewitness commentators on Beethoven's style of playing the piano — Schindler, Ries, Czerny — tend to contradict one another (though please note Czerny: "His playing, like his compositions, was far ahead of his time"), descriptions of his conducting are unanimous. To the familiar ones by Czerny and Spohr, let me add this one by Ignaz von Seyfried, the music director of the Theater-an-den-Wien: "He was very particular about expression, the delicate nuances, the equable distribution of light and shade as well as an effective *tempo rubato*. . . ." —a *tempo rubato* that Beethoven pioneered in orchestral performance, and that was the primary impetus for the switch in orchestra leadership from the keyboard to the baton in the first place.

Anton Schindler actually tried to transcribe Beethoven's *tempo rubato* for aspiring conductors. His *Life of Beethoven* (1840) contains a sizable extract from the Larghetto of the Second Symphony, marked by Schindler to reflect what he heard — or so he says — when Beethoven conducted the piece himself (Figure 9.1, pp. 258–59). Now as we all know, Schindler was, or could be, a great fibber. Should we believe him this time? Ignaz Moscheles, who edited Schindler's book in its English translation (1841), and who knew Beethoven for a while as well as Schindler did (he prepared the piano reduction of *Fidelio* under Beethoven's supervision), was among those who believed. He added a footnote to Schindler's discussion: "I agree with M. Schindler in these remarks. The slight deviations of time recommended must give life and expression, not only to this movement, but also to the imaginative compositions of all the great masters."

VIII

Roger Norrington, who knows more about conducting and about Beethoven than I'll ever know, surely knows all this. How, then, can we understand his very streamlined and steady performance of the choral finale to the Ninth except as a knowing anachronism, an effort to purge the piece of the traits which continue to embarrass many twentieth-century musicians? He knows better than I do that he is following no historical mandate when he allows the remarkably slow tempo at which he begins the Alla Marcia variation to govern all the 264 measures that ensue before Beethoven's next metronomic indication—a span that takes in the whole fugal development and the radiant choral recapitulation in D major. True enough, the "tempo of feeling" ineluctably pulls him along a little as the music progresses, but his effort to restrain it is quite annoyingly audible. I'll wager he would agree with me that Beethoven's tempo for the Alla Marcia—a good ten points, actually, below the tempo Norrington actually adopts—was meant to apply only to the pokey start in the bassoons and big drum, if it applies to anything at all;[4] that by the time the tenor enters, the tempo should have revved up considerably; and that the clear intention of the whole 264-bar stretch is to portray a mounting wave—or better, a spreading infection—of Elysian delirium. But, child of the twentieth century that he is, Norrington is suspicious of what Ortega y Gasset called an art that "proceed[s] by psychic contagion, for psychic contagion is an unconscious phenomenon, and art ought to be full clarity, high noon of the intellect." In its effort to bridle what Beethoven sought to unleash, moreover, Norrington's performance of the Ninth finale remains true to that Anglo-Saxon

---

[4]This tempo has been questioned by many—even Norrington, by implication, when he told a *Gramophone* interviewer that "the only really suspect [metronome] marks occur in the Ninth. Beethoven made his metronome markings for all the symphonies soon after writing the Ninth [actually in 1817, the year in which he made his first sketches for his last symphony], and he obviously knew the first eight rather better than he knew the Ninth" ("The Symphony as Opera?" *The Gramophone* 44 [1987]: 1222). Even though inaccurate in its historical details, this statement seems very sensible to me, and it applies above all to the tempo of the Alla Marcia variation. It has even been suggested (by Hermann Beck) that the metronome setting was meant to refer to the dotted half note, not the dotted-quarter, which would exactly double the tempo to which Norrington adheres with such determination. Toscanini, on the evidence of his NBC Symphony recording, seems to have shared Beck's opinion.

Beethoven, Symphony No. 2, II, mm. 55–75, purportedly edited by Schindler to reflect the composer's performance practice (Anton F. Schindler, *The Life of Beethoven*, trans. and ed. Ignace Moscheles [London, 1841], pp. 143–44).

pudeur which prompted Sir George Grove, at the height of the Victorian era, to censure the "restless, boisterous spirit [that] occasionally manifests itself, not in keeping with the English feeling of the solemnity, even the sanctity of the subject."

This, then, is the ultimate resister's Ninth, a Ninth to mollify and reassure those many of us who have come to hate the piece—or rather, who hate what the piece has come to stand for. The question is whether what the piece has come to stand for—that sublimity, that naiveté, that ecstasy of natural religion, that bathos—is something inherent in the Ninth, or something that has accreted to it. To take the latter view is, I firmly believe, to take the easy way out, and that is what Roger Norrington and his forces, with magnificent dedication, conviction, and technical panache, have accomplished. In so doing, Norrington has again shown himself, as he did with the Second and Eighth, to be a truly authentic voice of the late twentieth century.

To resist the resistance, to make peace with this score on its own terms, may not be possible in our time. It would signal recovery of an optimism that our century's wars, upheavals, atrocities, and holocausts—and the despairing attendant cynicism that has from the beginning undergirded the modern movement—may have precluded once and for all. Yet the fact that we continue to insult and distort Beethoven's gigantic affirmation shows that it is still under our skins, that it still troubles the conscience of trivial artists like Ned Rorem, that it still awakens in us longings for what we can no longer believe in, but wish we could. We are still in the valley of the Ninth.
And so there's hope.

THE NINTH: A READER

Kerman, Joseph. Chapter 7 ("Voice"), in *The Beethoven Quartets* (New York: Norton, 1979).

Kinderman, William. "Beethoven's Symbol for the Deity in the *Missa solemnis* and the Ninth Symphony," *Nineteenth-Century Music* 9 (1985): 102–18.

Lang, Paul Henry. "Editorial" [on Beethoven symphony recordings], *Musical Quarterly* 50 (1964): 77–90.

Lippman, Edward. "The Tonal Ideal of Romanticism," in *Festschrift Walter Wiora*, ed. Ludwig Finscher and Christoph-Hellmut Mahling (Kassel & New York: Bärenreiter, 1967), 419–26.

Sanders, Ernest H. "Form and Content in the Finale of Beethoven's Ninth Symphony," *Musical Quarterly* 50 (1964): 59–76.

Solomon, Maynard. "Beethoven's Ninth Symphony: A Search for Order," *Nineteenth-Century Music* 10 (1986): 3–23.

Treitler, Leo. "History, Criticism, and Beethoven's Ninth Symphony," *Nineteenth-Century Music* 3 (1980): 193–210.

———. " 'To Worship That Celestial Sound': Motives for Analysis," *Journal of Musicology* 1 (1982): 153–70.

Vaughan Williams, Ralph. *Some Thoughts on Beethoven's Choral Symphony, etc.* (London: Oxford University Press, 1953).

Wallace, Robin. *Beethoven's Critics* (Cambridge: Cambridge University Press, 1986).

Winter, Robert. "The Sketches for the 'Ode to Joy'," in *Beethoven, Performers, and Critics,* ed. Robert Winter and Bruce Carr (Detroit: Wayne State University Press, 1980), 176–214.

RECORDINGS CITED FOR COMPARISON

Furtwängler 1951. Elizabeth Schwarzkopf, soprano; Elisabeth Höngen, mezzo; Hans Hopf, tenor; Otto Edelmann, baritone; Bayreuth Festival Chorus and Orchestra. ANGEL CDC-47081

Karajan 1962. Gundula Janowitz, soprano; Hilde Rössl-Majdan, contralto; Waldemar Kmentt, tenor; Walter Berry, baritone; Vienna Singverein (dir. R. Schmid); Berlin Philharmonic Orchestra. DEUTSCHE GRAMMOPHON 2534349

Klemperer c. 1960. Aase Nordmo Lövberg, soprano; Christa Ludwig, mezzo; Waldemar Kmentt, tenor; Hans Hotter, baritone; Philharmonia Chorus (dir. W. Pitz); Philharmonia Orchestra. ANGEL AE-34428

Leibowitz 1961. Inge Borkh, soprano; Ruth Siewert, contralto; Richard Lewis, tenor; Ludwig Weber, bass; Beecham Choral Society; Royal Philharmonic Orchestra. READERS DIGEST RDS-34

Toscanini 1952. Eileen Farrell, soprano; Nan Merriman, mezzo; Jan Peerce, tenor; Norman Scott, baritone; Robert Shaw Chorale (dir. R. Shaw); NBC Symphony Orchestra. RCA VICTROLA 1607

Walter 1957. Frances Yeend, soprano; Martha Lipton, mezzo; David Lloyd, tenor; Mack Harrell, baritone; Westminster Choir (dir. J. F. Williamson). COLUMBIA ODYSSEY 32160322E

MOZART

10

An Icon for Our Time

The walls, so they say, have ears; and during the coming pair of seasons, encompassing the bicentennial year of Mozart's death, the walls of Lincoln Center are slated to absorb every one of the composer's works, from the little Andante "pour le clavecin" in sister Nannerl's notebook, composed just after his fifth birthday (if Papa Leopold, who inscribed the little harpsichord piece, is to be believed), to the Requiem, on which he was working when he died, just 30 years, 10 months and 1 week later.

In that short span Mozart managed to compose such a quantity of music that it takes a book of a thousand pages just to list it adequately (the "Chronological-Thematic Catalogue" by Ludwig Köchel, now in its sixth revised edition). And that quantity is of such a quality that the best of it is still our standard of perfection in music, never to be surpassed (since perfection, as a standard, has long since gone out of style).

Mozart is the very earliest composer by whom works in practically every genre he cultivated have been maintained in an unbroken public performing tradition to our own time; except for Handel's oratorios, nothing earlier has lasted in this way. Haydn, Mozart's great contemporary, has survived only in part; his operas, for example, have perished irrevocably, as periodic attempts to revive them unfailingly prove. Bach returned only after a time underground.

Mozart is so familiar that some performers have been going out of their way to defamiliarize him, whether by updating him or by embalming him in "historical" timbres. Those supremely provocative opera productions of Peter Sellars try to have it both ways. The works

Originally published as "Why Mozart Has Become an Icon for Today" in the Arts and Leisure supplement ("Season Preview") of the Sunday *New York Times*, 9 September 1990. Reprinted by permission of the *New York Times*.

are updated on the stage, embalmed in the pit—a perfect paradigm of post-modernism, perhaps, and yet another unmasking of the pseudohistoricism of "Early Music."

But that sort of approach will probably not be much in evidence in the orgy of veneration at Lincoln Center. Sentimental adoration has been the order of the day for Mozart since time immemorial. Dissenting voices have now and then been raised. "There are ways to hate Mozart," John Cage amiably announced one day (though, disappointingly, he failed to list them). Frederick Delius grumbled, "If a man tells me he likes Mozart, I know in advance he's a bad musician." But such talk is probably just talk, revealing a greater distaste for the cult than for its object.

For Mozart is our foundation stone, our icon and our pedigree. Celebrating him means celebrating ourselves. In him we see our species transcendent, effortlessly bringing forth what Bernard Shaw called "the only music yet written that would not sound out of place in the mouth of God." From there to actual deification is just a step. "I love Mozart as the musical Christ," wrote Tchaikovsky. "I do not think this comparison is blasphemous. Mozart was as pure as an angel, and his music is full of divine beauty . . . the culminating point of all beauty in the sphere of music."

The sheer harmonious perfection of Mozart has given us our notion of musical Eden, sometimes called the "Classical" period, an eighteenth-century fairyland invented by the tortured and driven artists of the nineteenth century, who looked upon Mozart's mythically prodigal powers of spontaneous invention (a myth that has been somewhat debunked by recent scholarship) with a reverence bordering on terror. They invented "Salieri" to punish the careless god-child for shaming them but aspired, withal, to his exalted station. The dying Mahler's last word, according to his widow—uttered when he was past hearing surrounding voices, and possibly enjoying the heavenly reception many accounts of borderline death-experience relate—was "Mozart!"

Until recently, when interest in Mozart suddenly exploded as a result of commercial theatrical and cinematic exploitation, a taste for Mozart was a connoisseur's taste—"a mark of caste," to quote Shaw again. For many, Mozart was and is problematic. Within his lifetime, Mozart's music was thought brash, overspiced, and too complicated for the average listener. ("Too many notes, my dear Mozart," said the Emperor.) In the nineteenth century, a cult of Mozart sprang up among the literary—not, for the most part, among musicians—that emphasized his violence, his sensuality, and his power to subvert.

In his celebrated book *The Classical Style*, Charles Rosen has revived this strain of Romantic Mozart worship, insisting eloquently that Mozart's music "cannot be fully appreciated . . . without re-creating in our own minds the conditions in which it could still seem dangerous." Some readers may also recall Virgil Thomson's once famous piece "Mozart's Leftism," in which Mozart's true liberalism (understated, between-the-lines, to be discerned by the discerning) was contrasted with the overtly proclaimed populism of Beethoven, "an old fraud who just talked about human rights and dignity but who was really an irascible, intolerant, and scheming careerist."

More recently, radical critics like Rose Rosengard Subotnik and Susan McClary have suggested that some of Mozart's later music carries the seeds of disintegration—stylistic, psychological, even social. This shocking message can be found, they argue, not just in the operas that inspired Romantic thinkers like E.T.A. Hoffmann or Søren Kierkegaard with their idea of Mozart's "demon," but in instrumental works as well. And what shocked Mozart's more sensitive contemporaries may shock us, too, if we're still sensitive.

In the last three symphonies, Ms. Subotnik discerns (for the first time in music) evidence of a "critical world view," meaning a sense of reality that is no longer fully supported by social norms, but must be personally constructed and defended. The high level of unsettling chromaticism in these works (traditionally symbolic of the irrational), their tendency to unify movements by means of shared forms or melodic motives (deliberately shoring up coherence in a way that implies a threat to it), and the calculated disruptions in the musical continuity, she argues, add up to an unprecedented portrayal of a mind under stress. Mozart, for her, is the first composer who suffers as we do from the malaise of modernity.

Ms. McClary, concentrating on the concertos, finds evidence of social alienation in the relationship between the soloist and the accompanying group. In a close technical reading of the slow movement of the G major Piano Concerto (K. 453), she finds the orchestra to be no simple accompanist but an antagonist that dominates and ultimately crushes the individual (soloist), whose personal needs are "blatantly sacrificed to the overpowering requirements of social convention." She finds a special bitterness in the movement's "harmonious closure," for the harmony masks repression.

To continue to uphold Mozart as the embodiment of "pure order," Ms. McClary concludes, is really to uphold "an icon of the old cultural order for purposes of warding off—or at least institutionally marginalizing—the increasingly successful encroachments of new, previously disenfranchised producers (ethnic minorities, members of the working class, women) and forms of culture." Ms. McClary invites us to identify with Mozart as their representative.

There can be no denying the relevance of such a view to the sorry life Mozart ended up leading in the real world. (The life he was privileged to lead in his creative imagination is of course a closed book to us, though we sometimes like to pretend his manuscripts and sketches give us access to it.) Ms. McClary's characterization of her pianist-protagonist—self-dramatizing, exhibitionistic, maladjusted—chimes with, and may well be influenced by, the unvarnished (or devarnished) Mozart portrait that has emerged of late from revisionist biographies like that of Wolfgang Hildesheimer, now a dozen years old. (Since Hildesheimer, demystification has progressed apace; medical historians now confidently pronounce the idyllic god-child to have been an obsessional, anal-fixated, paranoiac personality—in a word, infantile, meaning anything but childlike.)

It is always a question how far we are justified in reading an artist's work in terms of his life; and Ms. McClary's work carries the further burden, insofar as the musical and academic establishments are concerned, of an explicit political agenda. Still, her voice, and Ms. Subotnik's, have been heard.

Neal Zaslaw, adviser and scholar-in-residence to Lincoln Center's bicentennial festivities, and nobody's idea of a scholarly maverick, ends his just-published, grandly conceived and executed survey, *Mozart's Symphonies: Context, Performance Practice, Reception* (Oxford University Press), with a searching consideration along similar lines of the "Jupiter" Symphony finale, concluding that it "perhaps gives us a glimpse of Mozart's dreaming of escaping his oppressive past and giving utterance to his fondest hopes and highest aspirations of the future"—by which we are to understand everyone's past and everyone's future. There seems to be an increasing awareness—though it is definitely a minority awareness—that at its highest and best, Mozart's music embodies not only beautiful sounds but profound and sometimes terrible meanings.

So maybe it was not just out of laziness or incomprehension that audiences used to have a very selective relationship with Mozart's vast output. Maybe they had a notion of what was highest and best in it, and what kind of messages they wished to derive from it. Three operas, a half-dozen symphonies, a few concertos, and a handful of chamber and keyboard works—with greatly disproportionate emphasis on the works in minor keys, of which Mozart actually wrote very few: these used to constitute the active Mozart repertory, with the rest relegated to secondary categories of "historical interest," if not oblivion.

As early as 1799, a reviewer, after acknowledging Mozart's supreme genius, remarked of a quartet of early Mozart symphonies, just published for the first time, "it does not follow that everything of the sort that Mozart wrote is worth preserving, nor does it follow that after his death people should without exception collect and publish everything he wrote, especially in his younger years."

Wrong, says Mr. Zaslaw, who in his recent book is quick to turn around (inconsistently, it could seem, in light of his remarks on the "Jupiter" finale) and warn that such strictures are founded on a fundamental error. The reviewer, he alleges, was guilty of "confusing the general change in symphonic style between c. 1774 and 1799 with Mozart's personal development as a composer." It's not Mozart's fault, in other words, if his earlier works seem superficial to listeners who know his later ones—and it's not fair of us to entertain a preference.

Moreover, Mr. Zaslaw argues, modern notions of what art is all about are anachronistic to most of Mozart's work, and irrelevant to its evaluation. The "fundamental thesis" of his book is that "Mozart's symphonies, far from being 'art for art's sake,' were *Gebrauchsmusik*—music for use, functional music—which, when divorced from its original setting, loses some of its meaning." His mission, carried out with zeal and erudition, has been to restore a sense of the original context to Mozart's work, thereby to recover the lost meaning—and thereby, too, willy-nilly to inhibit contemporary judgment.

Laudable as it is from the standpoint of "disinterested" scholarship, the enterprise is open to question as criticism. It rests on the implicit assumption, still regnant in the musical academy, that the meaning of an artwork is complete at the time of creation, and that the passage of time entails nothing but loss of meaning. Tradition, in this view, is only noise and distortion, a cosmic game of "telephone."

Another view is possible. Contexts, it may be argued, are not simply lost but changed. The venues and social milieus in which Mozart symphonies are now "used"—the concert hall, the stereo-equipped home or automobile—are inescapably different from those the works inhabited when new (theaters, churches, aristocratic soirees). Change of context adds as much meaning as it may take away.

This applies to apprehension as well as to consumption. For us today, *Don Giovanni*, say, is not just the opera Mozart and da Ponte knew, bearing only the meanings it had for them and for the audience that greeted it in Prague two centuries ago. *Don Giovanni* is also something E.T.A. Hoffmann has known and construed, and Kierkegaard, and Charles Rosen, and Peter Sellars. Its meaning for us is mediated by all that has been thought and said about it since opening night, and is therefore incomparably richer than it was in 1787. Reconstruction of the original meaning, assuming it could be recaptured pure, should add its valuable mite to the pile, but cannot replace it. For that, were it possible, would be an impoverishment.

Such a position, alas, is not fashionable in our age of Authenticity. Judge Bork, rejected by the United States Senate, seems to have found a haven in the musical-intellectual community. Approach things for what they are (that is, were), we are enjoined, and judge them not. Enjoy. Uncritical acceptance of the past (coupled—it could scarcely be by coincidence—with an ultracritical reception of the present) is now the rule.

We tend to despise those who have been picky in the face of Mozart's cornucopia. It is with no little self-congratulation that some critics have celebrated the indiscriminateness of what is now considered enlightened taste, and in particular the abandonment of any ethical dimension to artistic judgment. (See what happens now if you voice any principled objection to the cruel and cynical *Così Fan Tutte*.) Yet respect it or not, the Romantics, who—mindlessly, we are told—valued in Mozart only their own reflection, definitely had a criterion. Do we?

Intransigence, which (when coupled with passion) is what lends all authority to criticism, is on the wane. The recent revised edition of Joseph Kerman's classically crusty *Opera as Drama* now makes room for Mozart's *Idomeneo*. Not that there is anything wrong with *Idomeneo* (that is, with its inspired music), but including it considerably softens the book's curmudgeonly old thesis (advanced pointedly against a "flabby relativism" that holds everything to be "all right on its own terms") that opera lost its dramatic way after Purcell and did not recover it till Mozart met up with da Ponte. Now we read, "most of us would rather have notes by Mozart than drama by anyone else," and "what gives *Idomeneo* a certain haunting power as drama," despite its problems, "is its basic subject matter."

So, flabby or firm, relativism is on the rise, and musicology, always a great omnivore, has been its accomplice.

But there is something else, too, behind our plan to put the Köchel catalog on parade, something '80s-ish and ugly. The demystification of Mozart, which began in earnest, and in honest if somewhat reckless fashion with Hildesheimer's biography, turned dishonest and trivializing and vastly remystifying with "Amadoose" (which is how you must pronounce it at the video store). The careless god-child of Romantic legend has become the braying ass of ours, glorified in the popular imagination as a boorish bumpkin who was "good at what he does," a cynical Gladstone Gander, gifted and successful far beyond his moral deserts—and to be loved for it. That, it gives pain to acknowledge, is our current Mozartean self-reflection. Our musical Christ has turned yuppie.

Accordingly, it is as the object—the symbol, even—of conspicuous musical consumption that he has at last become popular in the decade now ending. There is something dismally authentic about this, to be sure. The ideal (if that is the word) of conspicuous consumption was what motivated eighteenth-century aristocratic patronage of the arts. Some economic historians, for whom it symbolizes decadence, call it "quantitative luxury," and it is to be thanked or blamed for all the reams of faceless *Gebrauchsmusik* that have come down to us from Mozart's time.

Mozart consumption today, far more than at any time past including his own, is undeniably a matter of quantitative luxury, and his masterworks have indeed begun to recede into the faceless mass (or haven't you tuned in lately to FM?). More records of Mozart are now issued and bought than of any other composer, as a glance at the bimonthly listings in *Fanfare* magazine will quickly confirm. Philips Records, like Lincoln Center, has announced a complete Mozart for sale. Record clubs now offer him as their primary (if still relatively infinitesimal) "classical" inducement. As little as ten years ago, it was not so.

This last bit of intelligence comes from an editorial in the latest issue of *19th-Century Music*, the toniest of all academic music journals. The editors go on to ruminate that Mozart is "the 1980s' not-so-secret code word—as in 'Mostly Mozart'—for user-friendly classical music, their paradigm of Old-Age-New-Age music if not their very metonymy for nonthreatening sound *tout court*." Take that, Mr. Rosen, Ms. Subotnik.

But it's hard to disagree with the diagnosis. And in that light, it's hard not to see in Lincoln Center's bicentennial gourmandizing a musical Trump Tower, less a Mozart-fest than a K. Mart (as in Köchel, the numbers man). Somehow it doesn't seem much of a celebration anymore.

On the brighter side, there have lately been some solid strides in Mozartean performance practice. Admirable research continues, the latest notable contributions being those of Mr. Zaslaw on matters of orchestral execution, William Malloch on minuets (play them faster!), Jean-Pierre Marty on tempos (standardize them!), Hugh Macdonald on repeats (observe them!), Will Crutchfield on appoggiaturas (add them!), David Grayson on instrumental embellishment (go to town!).

Predictably, "historical" performers have been quickest to adopt the recommendations that entail the least creativity (Mr. Crutchfield and Mr. Grayson in particular have been getting a lot of backtalk), though the pianist Robert Levin's astonishing yeoman work in the concertos (yes, he improvises his cadenzas) will no doubt inspire rivalry ere long, much to everyone's benefit.

On the more ordinary level of scrupulous text rendition, Mozart performance on period instruments becomes more mellifluent and convincing year by year. The viability of the fortepiano is no longer at issue, thanks to the work of Malcolm Bilson, Melvyn Tan, Steven Lubin, Penelope Crawford, and others. Mr. Lubin's chamber group, the Mozartean Players, is setting a high standard in the very difficult medium of keyboard plus strings.

And then there are the period orchestras, permanently established by now in Boston, New York, Washington, San Francisco, Ann Arbor, Toronto, and other North American cities (if we may parochially ignore England and the European continent for the moment). Because of all this specialist activity, everyone, it seems, is playing Mozart with a new fluency these days, whatever the make or model of their instruments.

But (to end this jeremiad with a proper caveat) if we no longer care what we play, does it matter how we play it? Is the coolness that is so essential a part of our enlightened "historical" performance style a true reflection of history, or is it, like the wholesale consumption of the Köchel catalog, a mark of lessened commitment?

Laurence Dreyfus, a Bach scholar and viola da gambist who is at the forefront of historical performance today, is troubled by the latter possibility. Why, he asked aloud at the recent Berkeley Festival and Exhibition "Music in History," must one "continue to turn to the remastered recordings from 60 years ago in order to experience the passionate rapture that accompanies a musician engaged wholly with the artwork?" What is missing, he contends, "is the insight that the giants of our pantheon are great to the extent that they learn to represent the depths of melancholy, and melancholy, as Kant recognized, was a kind of secret key to the sublime."

This comes very close to the Subotnik-McClary position on what made Mozart Kant's greatest musical contemporary. It's not something we are likely to recapture by turning him back into a purveyor of "functional music."

POSTSCRIPT, 1994

If you are introduced to your audience as a comedian, all you have to do is say "Good evening," and some impressionable soul will laugh. If, rightly or wrongly, you have acquired the reputation of an enemy of "historical performance," then no matter what you write, somebody will read it as another bash. That, at any rate, is the only way I can explain the reaction to this piece. The unfriendliest riposte came from Leo Treitler (whose writings on Mozart I could easily seem to be endorsing), who read my passing reference to Peter Sellars as a "sneer at the inconsistency of . . . setting . . . *Figaro* in Trump Tower and modern dress while the recitatives are accompanied by an 18th-century fortepiano. Perhaps he prefers 18th-century costumes and accompaniment by a Romantic pianoforte or Baroque harpsichord? Did he dislike something about the Sellars production beyond the idea of it?"

But I did not say I disliked it. (I don't dislike it.) I merely reported it—or rather them, since I did not single out *Figaro* from the other Sellars productions—as an example of defamiliarization, which they obviously are. Indeed, what I pointed out about the Sellars productions was their consistency, not their inconsistency, seeing the updating on the stage and the authenticity in the pit as working in harness to defamiliarize the thrice-familiar sounds and stage images of a trio of beloved operas.

But once you have been identified as a polemicist, you can no longer be a reporter. Many were those who read Rose Subotnik's or Susan McClary's positions as mine. Kenneth LaFave, who writes for the *Phoenix Gazette* and seems to be the Rush Limbaugh of music criticism, protested my "clenched-fist diatribe," my "tired neo-Marxist attempt to make music the slave of history," and my "insipidly narrow attitude" that "the possible ways of viewing Mozart reduce to two: either Mozart was a mere 'functionary,' providing agreeable tunes, or his music was the voice of revolutionary ethos." In short, the response to this piece, while gratifying in its sheer extent (it was quoted in *Time* magazine and the *Wall Street Journal*, and reprinted in Paris, Singapore, and Tel Aviv), gave ample support to those cynics who contend that readers don't read books, and listeners don't listen to music: all we read and hear are reputations.

A refreshing contrast was the response of Wye J. Allanbrook, an outstanding Mozart scholar, who took equally sharp issue with me, but with a recognizable me. At a bicentennial symposium in Washington organized by the Woodrow Wilson International Center for Scholars, Prof. Allanbrook read a stimulating paper entitled "Mozart's Tunes and the Comedy of Closure," in which she decried the "naive and uncritical" exaltation of what she called "the Gloomy Mozart." It is unnecessary, she claimed, to counter the tendency toward sentimental adoration with so selective and extreme an alternative ("tragic") reading of Mozart's work. From there she went on to show how one can view him properly within the conventions of his time (conventions that demanded reconciliation of conflicts, i.e., comic closure) and still see him freshly and in a way that is relevant to contemporary intellectual concerns. In any case, she wrote, "it is a curious quirk of the psychology of our fallen nature that when we hear that a reading of a text or art work enshrines that same fallen nature we feel better."

I could still quibble if I wished: I did recognize the rarity of the tragic mood in Mozart (as indicated by the rarity of the minor mode in his works), and, again, sooner reported than espoused the Romantic viewpoint that glorified dark readings. Nor do I regard such an outlook as "indiscriminate" (Prof. Allanbrook's word) or conformist; on the contrary, I upheld it as a discriminating viewpoint, one (and only one) possible antidote to the indiscriminateness with which Mozart was being consumed, under cover of veneration, in 1991. I am glad though, to have irritated Prof. Allanbrook into producing an equally, if oppositely, discriminating reading of Mozart, and I hope that her very rich essay will soon be published.

II

A Mozart Wholly Ours

The collaboration of fortepianist Malcolm Bilson and John Eliot Gardiner on a complete Mozart piano concerto cycle was inaugurated amid loud publicity in 1983, and the first releases appeared on Archiv the next year. Commenting in the February 1987 issue of *Opus* on the K. 414 and K. 450 recordings (in connection with a "competing" release by Steven Lubin), I cautioned that it was perhaps "too early yet for hosannas and fanfares." That was then. Now the series is complete, and it is time to throw caution to the English Baroque Soloists' winds! Get out the trumpets and the drums! Calooh, calay! Great performing is great performing; it renders questions of performance practice, historical verisimilitude, authenticity, call it what you will, utterly moot. And in their later recordings (mostly of the later concertos, but also—even especially!—of K. 238), Bilson, Gardiner, and the English Baroque Soloists have realized a level of performance that has to be termed great, whether we are speaking of matters technical or aesthetic. At such a level, the two are one.

This achievement not only casts a treasured body of repertory in a new and blazing light, and not only settles once and for all the question of the fortepiano's viability as a concert instrument for today. Far more than that, it holds up a mirror in which we may see ourselves, the musicians and music lovers of the late twentieth century, and all our values, reflected with blinding clarity. (If that is what Joseph Kerman meant when, concluding a searching review-essay in the *New York Review of Books* [May 18, 1989], he called Bilson's Mozart performances "exemplary"—that is, exemplifying—then the word could not have been better chosen. But that is the fourth definition of the word in my dictionary. Anyone reading Kerman might well think he had the first meaning in mind, which has to do with norms and models for

Originally published in *Musical America* (May 1990): 32–41.

imitation. That would be unfortunate; the very last thing we want to be doing at this auspicious moment is setting limits.)

Exemplifying what? Our values, our selves. It is perfectly evident that these performances, despite the period hardware they employ, reflect neither the practices nor the values of Mozart's time. And that, of course, is quite all right. There is no reason in the world why they should, barring reasons of purely didactic (or possibly sci-fi) curiosity. And there is no way that they could, for reasons that go far beyond the state of available evidence or the performers' intentions. The virtues of these performances are much more important than that: they are the virtues of contemporaneity, of nowness. Since "nows" inevitably become "thens," they are ephemeral virtues. But while the moment lasts, they are the Mozart performances that are most wholly ours; and that is why we shall cherish them.

Yet historical claims have been made about these performances nevertheless, and they go on being made. They must be disposed of, since they come not only from the commercial sector but from the writer of the encyclopedic program notes to the series, Bilson's Cornell colleague Neal Zaslaw, a respected expert on late-eighteenth-century performance practice. Professor Zaslaw singles out four practices as especially "relevant" to the reconstruction of a period style for Mozart's piano concertos. In the first place, there is due emphasis on the role of the wind instruments ("their characteristic colors, the weight they lend to the tuttis, their clarification of the harmony and voice-leading") as an integral part of Mozart's palette, even in the concertos where the composer himself declared them dispensable. Second, Zaslaw mentions the use of reduced strings to accompany the solo sections ("to enhance dynamic and timbral contrasts, to overcome the problem of insufficient rehearsal time, to minimize potential difficulties of balance between fortepiano and orchestra, and perhaps also to create more flexible accompaniments"). The third practice cited is the use of the fortepiano to accompany the tuttis, continuo-fashion ("not only of benefit to an orchestra's ensemble; it also adds an almost subliminal ictus generally characteristic of orchestral sound of the period"); the fourth is the matter of cadenzas and *Eingänge* (" 'lead-ins'—brief cadenzas 'leading in' to one or more of the returns of the rondo refrains" in finales).

There is no disputing the importance of these points, or the success with which at least three of them have been realized in these recordings. The playing of the winds here is the very stuff of legends. Their timbres are so vivid, their intonation so impeccable, their presence so much a part (as we now see) of what makes Mozart Mozart as to put a whole new slant on our concept of color for this music. No one who has heard these recordings will ever be content again with a standard orchestral blend in the Classical repertory. The discovery, or rediscovery, of a new color scheme has unquestionably been the major revelation of the "Early Music" incursion into that eminent domain. In the later concertos (that is, from K. 450 on), the wind solos are among the major attractions of these discs. There is an especially long episode of *Harmonie*-heaven in the slow movement of K. 482 (the largest and most varied of the concertos and, as of this writing, my personal favorite); and a little later on, the (alas unidentified) flutist and bassoonist sing the operatic duet of your dreams.

Not that one would wish to slight the contribution of the string players to these extraordinary performances: the most exquisite single moment for me was the very beginning of the Andante from K. 467—yes, the very one that has been so polluted by sentimental cinematic exploitation. The texture—legato over staccato over pizzicato—is fabulously unblended, the first fiddles' phrasing is a miracle of nuance, and the very audible addition of just the right amount of vibrato to their dissonant appoggiatura brings ecstasy. Yet of calculation one hears no hint. The whole thing "flows like oil," as Mozart used to say when particularly pleased, thanks in part to the artful near-accommodation of the double-dotted notation in the tune to the triplet rhythms running beneath.

Another major revelation, and one that has already been much acclaimed, is the new perspective on the relationship between the solo instrument and the orchestra that is vouchsafed by the second and third points summarized above. The soloist and band are more deeply and productively involved with one another than later became the concerto rule. Which is not to say that the fortepiano cannot rear up and dominate the mass when that is the composer's wish, as in the finale of K. 466. It can be an obstreperous little cur: just listen to it growl and bark in the first movement of K. 537, the orchestra trying hard to maintain decorum. As many have noted, the use of the fortepiano and the period band, engaging the very top of their repertoire for all they're worth, seems to magnify this music far beyond the capabilities of their stronger "modern" (that is, nineteenth-century) counterparts, who have to scale back for fear of mud and bombast. The larger the piece, the truer this is. The opening of K. 503 has never sounded so majestic (and Gardiner's initiative helps: he extends the silence between the opening chords with unwritten fermatas); in most performances, Mozart's grand gestures seem fairly empty, and the piece had never been one of my favorites. Nor had the rondo ever seemed so well proportioned to the massive opening movement as in Bilson and Gardiner's generous rendition.

Yes, indeed, in the right hands the period instruments can make all the difference! (But, in "the right hands"—that is, hands rightly schooled, controlled by minds rightly stimulated—so could any instruments, and I must continue to protest the overemphasis of what is at root a false issue, one that Zaslaw, unfortunately, fudges badly when he discusses in the liner notes, under the heading "Classical instruments," matters of playing technique that could be applied to standard conservatory instruments if only conservatories taught such things.)

Still, the four issues raised by Zaslaw do not by any means exhaust the "relevant" questions of historical performance practice for this music—that is, if relevance may be gauged by controversy engendered. His selectivity is in fact quite suspect. And his discussion of the fourth point—cadenzas and "lead-ins"—is marred by a downright prevarication. He is at pains to minimize the extent to which these interpolations were actually improvised: if they were, he argues, "why would written-out cadenzas for most of Mozart's piano concertos (and sometimes two or three for a single movement) have come down to us?" While allowing that they were "undoubtedly sometimes written for [Mozart's] sister or his pupils rather than himself," he nevertheless wishes us to believe that Mozart's own cadenzas (that is, the ones he played), "although conceived and performed in an improvisatory style, were usually carefully prepared beforehand."

Now we *know* that is not true. Not only Mozart but all virtuosos of his day improvised in public all the time. No concert was complete without improvisations, and to give the impression that Mozart couldn't really do it but had to resort to subterfuge (Zaslaw also cites "C. P. E. Bach's instructions for 'improvising' fantasias," as if Bach wrote his treatise to instruct the likes of Mozart)—well, that's quite an insult! Not only did Mozart improvise fantasias and cadenzas, he (like Beethoven) was known to "improvise" the whole piano part in a newly written concerto from blank staves or from a bass line. (For an idea of what Mozart could do, see the autograph pages from the **"Coronation"** Concerto, K. 537, reproduced in Emanuel Winternitz's *Musical Autographs from Monteverdi to Hindemith* [Dover]; the published piano part, first issued three years after Mozart's death, is the work of an unidentified arranger.)

Zaslaw's equivocation with regard to the cadenzas (which Bilson, of course, does not improvise, instead using Mozart's or other didactic ones when available and writing his own very serviceable ones as a last resort) is of a piece with his arbitrarily restricted view of the fortepiano's continuo role, which he couches in terms of an unwarrantably confident historical assertion: "Mozart usually accompanied the orchestra during tutti passages, playing the bass-line with the left hand, and with the right sometimes playing chords, sometimes doubling the bass-line at the octave, sometimes doubling the treble instruments." Couldn't that right hand have contributed something beyond what the treble instruments were already playing? This oversight, in turn, is of a piece with Zaslaw's unaccountable silence on what is surely the most controversial of all Mozartean subjects, that of ornamentation and, ultimately, florid embellishment.

That it was common practice in Mozart's day, and that he was its preeminent master, no one can doubt. But with few exceptions, modern performers and those who instruct them maintain a negative—or, at best, an embarrassed—attitude toward the custom. Scholarly performers (Bilson among them) who otherwise proclaim themselves in favor of historical practices and authentic instruments as avenues "to get to 'the truth,' whatever that is" (as Bilson put it to an interviewer in the summer 1989 *Piano Quarterly*) suddenly raise fastidious objections to all but the most modest embellishment—so modest that I'm sure Mozart would not have recognized it as such. Frederick Neumann, author of the most thorough scholarly investigation of the subject (*Ornamentation and Improvisation in Mozart* [Princeton, 1986]), rails and fulminates against the kind of "desecration" we know Mozart to have practiced and expected, and exhorts performers to refrain from what is not absolutely "necessary" (which is to say from *any* embellishment, for embellishment, by its very definition, is never "necessary").

What is the reason for this double standard, this blind spot? To answer this question, we have to go to the very root of our present-day cultural attitudes. What we will discover will also unravel the paradox with which this essay began: how it is that performances seemingly in search of the past should actually be so revealing of the present.

"We have good reason to assume," writes Professor Neumann in the introduction to his book, "that no fundamental change has occurred in the aesthetics of performance" since Mozart's time, and that "we are therefore on fairly firm ground in assuming the basic identity of an informed, cultivated taste of today with the one Mozart expected to encounter in his audiences." Nothing could be easier to disprove.

Performance aesthetics in the realm of (small-c) classical music today, especially among those (like Neumann) interested in the question of performance practice, are dominated by the search for "authenticity"—a word whose notoriously elusive meaning can best be captured (as it is normally intended by musicians) by translating it into German, in which it is usually called not *Authentizität* (though the word exists) but *Werktreue*, "fidelity to the work." Central to this concept is an idealized notion of what a musical work is: something wholly realized by its creator, fixed in writing, and thus capable of being preserved. Fidelity is that which enables preservation: scrupulous execution according to the creator's intentions, divined either directly from explicit notation or indirectly through study of contemporary conventions and circumstances. At the center, then, stands the text, and the *werktreu* performer (and scholar, and editor, and critic) is there to serve it. That is our modern idea of "the truth." Literacy breeds literalism.

Literalism is not necessarily a failing. Pursued with commitment and passion, it can inspire. An inspired literalism can work wonders in making old music sound new. By now we have seen this happen often enough (besides Bilson and Gardiner, think of Roger Norrington and Christopher Page — but also think of Charles Rosen or Alfred Brendel). Still, the process is worth a close look.

The first thing a committed literalist wants to ascertain is the authenticity of his text. So, the Early Music performer today has either trained himself to be a textual critic or hires one. In the present case, the texts of the New Mozart Edition, in progress since the time of Mozart's *first* bicentennial, have been checked by Prof. Zaslaw against the sources, some of which only fairly recently resurfaced (in Poland) from their protective storage during World War 2. Since I followed these performances with my Kalmus reprints of the old Breitkopf & Härtel edition, I can report that this textual work has borne some notable fruit. In two cases, missing music has been recovered: two bars in the first-movement recapitulation of K. 482, and a whole seven-bar structural phrase in the opening tutti of K. 595. (But doesn't Zaslaw owe us an explanation of this one? Was it based on a new source or more accurate source reading, or was it a conjecture based on analogous passages elsewhere in the movement?) Even more telling — and delightful! — is a case of removal. A fierce tutti entrance in the first-movement recapitulation of K. 449, which in the old edition followed a deceptive cadence in the solo part, now breaks in on the soloist's preparatory trill a measure earlier, it apparently having been found that the old editors had counted a superfluous bar of rests in the orchestral parts. The effect is wonderfully jarring.

But if these are the biggest fish in the editorial net, they are not the most important ones. The really significant result of all the recent checking and cross-checking of sources has been the restoration of Mozart's original dynamic indications and, most of all, his articulation and expression marks: the slurs, the accents, the wedges, and the dots. These newly restored marks have been the basis for a total conceptual overhaul, on the part of the newest breed of literalists, of our whole manner of articulating — that is, "speaking" — Mozart's music, and one to which the use of original instruments is said to be indispensable. Whether or not the last point is true — I have my doubts — there can be no denying either the beauty or the communicative power of the new rhetorical approach, which is based not on the long legato lines of romantic music but on short, pointed phrases in exact alliance with the metrical scheme and in continual dialogue with one another.

For me, perhaps only because I am familiar enough with Bilson's playing to take its extraordinary articulateness for granted, the most compelling textual and textural revelations on this level came from Gardiner's band, lending the orchestral playing an unprecedented presence and authority. The first such revelation to strike me (only because I listened to the concertos in order) was the scrupulous differentiation in the second first-movement theme of K. 238 between the slurred and unslurred resolutions of the syncopated eighths. Most performers today would probably routinely standardize them, thinking the disparity a product of oversight. For all I (or Gardiner) know, it may be just that, but to assume that the composer intended what he presented (since you cannot know the opposite to be the case) is a matter of new-literalist faith. And what a spectacular result! The very end of the movement is the feminine ending to end all feminine endings. It is obviously polemical and therefore perhaps overdone (but that's true of "authentic" playing in general: eighteenth-century musicians never had nineteenth-century musicians to react against); yet, hearing it, one can only agree that extremism in the pursuit of *Werktreue* is no vice.

More familiar examples would include the pronounced pairing of the half notes (and their separation from the ensuing quarter) in the woodwinds' theme in the first movement of K. 466. The standard rendition, which slurs all three notes, makes for a far less distinctive and memorable shape — and this is a shape that really needs to be memorable, for it returns "cyclically" (and uniquely in all of Mozart's concertos) in the finale. To cite another case, only a fanatical rage for meticulous execution can have produced the precision weighting of the string chords that accompany the piano theme at measures 71–84 in the finale of K. 482 (recurring just before the end of the movement) according to their metrical position and their notation as eighths or quarters. Nothing short of excruciating attention to detail could possibly beget such breezy vivacity. For a final example of *werktreu* zealotry, consider the main theme from the Larghetto of the "*Coronation*" Concerto (K. 537), as articulated first by Bilson, then by the band. It starts with four notes that are identical in pitch and rhythm (four quarters on E in *alla breve* time). They are first paired in accordance with the half-note pulse (and doing this on the keyboard is no mean feat), and then the pairs are paired, precisely weighted in accordance with the prevailing beat structure. Precious? Yes indeed — in all senses of the word.

These achievements are unquestionable advances, and Bilson is well entitled to his pride in them. Twice in his *Piano Quarterly* interview, he compares himself with Rudolf Serkin, no doubt chosen for having been a prime exponent of *Werktreue* in the days before the concept had become ineluctably bound up with period hardware. It is a gauntlet I simply had to pick up, so I compared one of Bilson's performances with a representative one by Serkin, that of K. 459 with the Cleveland Orchestra under another doughty old *Werktreuer*, George Szell (Columbia MS 6534, recorded in 1963). There was no contest at all. After Bilson and Gardiner, the older recording was simply unlistenable. The orchestra (The Cleveland Orchestra! Under George Szell!!) was painfully out of tune, the tempos clunky, the timbres dull. Phrases lacked lilt (every eighth note in the $\frac{6}{8}$ Allegretto seemed to have an accent; the Allegretto sounded like an Andantino molto pesante). Serkin's legato occluded the sculptured shapes of his melodic lines. His cadenzas lacked drama and fantasy. In short, hearing this performance after Bilson and Gardiner's felt like going to sleep. And while the recorded sound quality undoubtedly played a part in this impression, I think it was the smallest part. Never was I better convinced that the new approach to Mozart, for all that the instruments are "smaller," makes him much, much bigger.

Yet the virtues of that approach, its zealous preciosity on all levels from text to articulation to expression to execution are precisely what make it so completely representative of our time and so foreign to Mozart's. I do not just mean that the performances we hear today are better prepared than Mozart could have expected. Zaslaw quotes from Leopold Mozart's famous letters home to Salzburg in which he reported about his son's concert activities in Vienna. Orchestral sight-reading was the rule and rehearsal a rare luxury, and there was no such thing as a conductor. While Zaslaw is quite right to point out that the existence of a common practice made up to a certain extent for these deficiencies, it is implausible that our present-day standards of ensemble performance—standards Bilson and Gardiner have measurably advanced—could possibly have existed in Mozart's day.

That is obviously no reason to renounce them, nor is it sensible to assume Mozart wouldn't have appreciated them if he'd had the chance. But it is nevertheless striking that he never complained about these aspects of the conditions in which he worked. I do not believe it ever occurred to him to wish for a change. And that is because present-day standards of textual fidelity and precision execution are not self-evident virtues. They are products of our value system, products of *Werktreue*, and (*pace* Neumann) of very secondary relevance to the value system that reigned in Mozart's time.

What was that value system? Zaslaw, in his liner notes, gives us an excellent clue. Discussing the strange lack of contemporary critical writing on Mozart's concertos, he quotes from a recent socioeconomic study of musical reception. The "eighteenth century's point of view" on works of music turns out to have been far from idealized in the sense to which we now subscribe. Works were not considered constituents of a repertory or a canon, they were the commodities necessary for the "carrying on of musical 'daily business,'" in which the central figure was not the creator but the performer, whether domestic amateur consuming new works at home or charismatic professional plying his trade in salons and theaters at a transcendent level of execution.

In either case, the performer was not there to serve the work; the work was there to serve the performer. Preservation was of no account at all. Neumann's reference to the "informed, cultivated taste of today"—namely, the taste of what we now call the classical audience—had absolutely no place in this sphere of activity. The modern, scrupulous performer who caters to this taste was almost unknown (I say "almost" because the latter period of Mozart's activity was the very time when our modern preservationist values were being born, for example in the antiquarian circle of Baron von Swieten, but certainly not in the context of the concerto). We are on the horns of what is by now a familiar dilemma: a performer in the spirit of Mozart's age could never satisfy today's standards of "authenticity," and the very fact that we seek authenticity (that is, *Werktreue*) precludes our achieving fidelity to the spirit of Mozart's age. If you want to know how we are supposed to feel about charismatic performers in our age of authenticity, you have only to read the chary inanities about Vladimir Horowitz in the *New Grove Dictionary of Music and Musicians.*

Now what was this "spirit of Mozart's age"? To ascertain it we have only to look to our own musical "daily business," which is the business of pop. How the various paths diverged is a story for another time, but that we now have a divided musical culture is perhaps the most salient fact of our musical life, and our chief difference from our counterparts in the past.

Pop (or jazz) culture, in starkest contrast to classical, has a concept of work-identity so fluid as to be practically indefinable. (It is a famous unsolved problem of musicology, in fact.) Classical performers are constantly exhorted to make themselves into transparent vessels: Zaslaw rails at one point against ignorant performers who are "reduced [!] to . . . seeking a personal 'interpretation' based on such necessary intangibles as musicality, taste, instinct or inspiration." These, of course, are qualities pop or jazz musicians, and their audiences, prize without irony or apology. Indeed, they are an absolute requirement. To perform a standard without attempting to give it an inimitable personal imprint would be unthinkable to a "stylist" in those domains. And audiences reward and reinforce that attempt in ways that are far more direct and natural than are possible within the decorous and ritualized etiquette observed by (or forced upon) classical audiences. Pop or jazz listeners applaud spontaneously on recognizing both standard and imprint, and offer similar rewards to any noteworthy or pleasantly surprising feature of the performance as it happens, whether a difficult lick, or a high note, or (most flattering to all concerned) some sort of allusion or in-joke. Needless to say, the pop performer is always on the lookout for ways of eliciting this kind of on-the-spot recognition. We've all seen them angle for it, heads cocked, eyes a-twinkle (yes, Horowitz, too . . . and that is what "the last of the Romantics" really means).

So did Mozart. His letters and his concert reviews give ample testimony to the brisk interaction he enjoyed with his audiences. Here are parts of his description of the premiere performance of his *"Paris"* Symphony:

> Just in the middle of the first Allegro there was a Passage I was sure would please. All the listeners went into raptures over it—applauded heartily. But as, when I wrote it, I was quite aware of its Effect, I introduced it once more towards the end—and it was applauded all over again. . . . I had heard that final Allegros, here, must begin in the same way as the first ones, all the instruments playing together, mostly in unison. I began mine with nothing but the 1st and 2nd violins playing softly for 8 bars—then there is a sudden *forte*. Consequently, the listeners (just as I had anticipated) all went "Sh!" in the soft passage—then came the sudden *forte*—and no sooner did they hear the *forte* than they all clapped their hands.

And here is a report, furnished by Zaslaw, of a Mozart recital in Prague:

> Indeed, we did not know what to admire the more—the extraordinary composition, or the extraordinary playing; both together made a total impression on our souls that could only be compared to sweet enchantment! But at the end of the concert, when Mozart extemporized alone for more than half an hour at the fortepiano, raising our delight to the highest degree, our enchantment dissolved into loud, overwhelming applause.

So to imagine that Mozart could have let an unvaried reiteration pass in public (let alone a whole binary repeat, as Bilson does in the finale of K. 453 and elsewhere); or that he meant his shorthand notations in block chords or in figuration for left hand alone as anything but blueprints for flights of fancy (both can be found on a single page in the first movement of K. 451, which Bilson obediently executes *com'è scritto*); or that (to cite a well-known crux from the slow movement of K. 595) when he doubled the violins and flutes at the octave he intended the piano to follow passively along with the upper line, its accompanying chords creating all kinds of forbidden parallels with the lower (that's what Bilson does, like everyone else, and it sounds just awful) — to imagine these vain things is patently to misconstrue the nature of the works and their motivating aesthetic.

And yet it is a necessary misconstruction, for to admit a performance practice that exalts spontaneous creativity over work-preservation, and that when exercised at the highest level can actually threaten work-identity, would violate the most fundamental tenet of our classical music culture, that of *Werktreue*. To perform Mozart as Mozart expected to be performed implicitly denies his status as a classic, thus threatening our most cherished concepts of repertory and canon. Our way of rendering him today is a case (a "classic" case indeed) of what cultural critics call "appropriation." (Still, anachronistic though modern concepts of repertory and canon may be to Mozart's concertos, they are not so far off that their application may not easily be rationalized; and so Zaslaw can write, "Nonetheless, by the 1780s western Europe already had its connoisseurs and collectors of 'art for art's sake' who must have recognized the extraordinary qualities of Mozart's music. . . . ")

Malcolm Bilson for one (and, I'll bet, John Eliot Gardiner for another) is perfectly aware of all of this. In the *Piano Quarterly* interview alluded to above, Bilson chose to answer one critic who had voiced the hope that fortepianists of the future would supply "thickets of slow-movement embellishment that will make every performance unique" with the bland assurance that "we already know pretty much all there is to be found out about ornamentation in the eighteenth century; unless somebody finds a compact disk of Mozart playing the fortepiano, I don't think we're going to find anything else." I believe him. I'm sure he knows all there is to know about embellishment. The question is, why doesn't he do it? And by now we know the answer.

In fairness, though (and with pleasure), I should add that, whether goaded by critics or by his own musical quests, Bilson has loosened up to the point where I wish he would remake all the concertos he recorded before 1986. The latest releases in the series — especially those containing K. 466, K. 482, K. 491, K. 537 (where even Neumann would have to concede the necessity for ornamentation), K. 595, and the Concert Rondo, K. 386 — do contain fleeting passages of often lovely florid embellishment, as well as a much more varied approach to tempo and timbre. An artist whom (on the analogy to Rachmaninoff's reference to Schnabel as "the great Adagio player") I had always thought of as "the great finale player" has developed a new poise and depth. (On the other hand, the recordings of K. 242, for three pianos, and K. 365, for two, are duds. What should have been marvelously unbuttoned and competitive renditions displaying the joys of trade-off and fake-out are polite and decorous to a colossal fault. Ego problems, no doubt, considering what hams pianists II and III [Robert Levin and Melvyn Tan] are known to be.) In his latest recordings — and especially that of K. 238, my nominee for the most nearly perfect performance of the set — Bilson explores "worlds of fortepiano color as yet undreamt of" such as the critic to whom he responded in the *Piano Quarterly* had hoped one day to hear. (In the interview, Bilson wrongly but very tellingly assumed the critic had been talking about improved instruments.) Bilson's rubatos, once virtually nonexistent, are becoming a trademark. In short, he is becoming Rubinstein. (I mean this literally: on a hunch, I compared Bilson's superbly relaxed and nuanced recording of K. 488 with my old favorite by Arthur Rubinstein and Alfred Wallenstein on RCA [LSC 2634, recorded in 1962], and, far from the outcome of the Serkin experiment, found the tempos to be *identical* and the phrasing of the opening solo in the slow movement nearly so, allowing for the fact that by Bilsonian standards even Rubinstein's playing is more or less everywhere underarticulated.)

Yet I would less like to see comfortable compromise with the "mainstream" at this point than continued experimentation and progress, particularly in the vexed domain of creative spontaneity. (And that is why I have to object when Bilson, excellent artist though he is, is held up as an example.) It is an important enterprise, because it could entail a contribution to the "postmodern" project, that breaking down of walls between high and pop culture that could save them both for "an informed, cultivated taste of today," as Neumann puts it, a taste that is not being very well served at present from either camp. There have not been too many successful experiments of this kind yet, God knows; but it's too soon to give up hope.

My hopes right now are pinned on Robert Levin, Bilson's uncharacteristically reticent partner in K. 365. Until very recently, I knew his work as a Mozart concerto soloist only by hearsay — in particular, ecstatic reports of his triumphant performance of K. 491 at a 1989 Mozartfest in Ann Arbor. Now I've heard him in action, a friend having lent me a tape of Levin's Sarasota Festival rendition of K. 467 (on a modern grand, and it doesn't matter a bit). I can see why people have been amazed. From the first, you know something is up. The soloist not only accompanies the opening tutti, his right hand keeps up a running commentary ("graffiti!" Neumann would no doubt sniff). Opportunities for flashy embellishment are seized not only in the slow movement but in all of them, with some really extraordinary impromptu "extra" variations in the finale. His rubatos in the Andante, far more distending than anything Bilson has dared (yet fully in keeping with Mozart's own description of the practice) really tug at the heart. And Levin actually commands the intellectual and digital means to improvise his cadenzas. (How can you tell, you say? You can tell because, if written down, the improvisations would have faults of composition by Mozartean standards.) It's all quite electrifying, even if, as I think, it must inevitably stop short of what the composer would have done. (Mozart, after all, had no inhibiting sense of himself as a "classic.")

The question is, could it work on records? Perhaps not. Recording is never kind to spontaneity. Recorded performances have their own permanence; they are also "texts" of a sort. The existence of sound recording as a factor in our musical life has obviously been a tremendous spur on the evolution of *Werktreue* toward our recent "authentistic" extremism. A performance like Levin's (or, to be sure, like Mozart's) on a CD would be a virtual contradiction in terms, and it might grate. But we don't know that till we've tried it, and it's just the sort of thing some enterprising, well-subsidized European label will be surely game to try. Levin, resident in Germany, must be negotiating with some such firm even as we speak. Stay tuned.

MOZART: Concertos for Piano(s) and Orchestra (23); Rondos for Piano and Orchestra (2).

Malcolm Bilson, fortepiano; Robert Levin and Melvyn Tan, fortepianos; English Baroque Soloists, John Eliot Gardiner, cond. Andreas Holschneider, prod. ARCHIV CD. All recordings are DDD.

Concertos for Piano and Orchestra: No. 5, in D, K. 175; No. 8, in C, K. 246; Rondos for Piano and Orchestra: in D, K. 382; in A, K. 386.

ARCHIV CD: 415 990-2. Playing time: 60:16. (Recorded April 1985 [K. 175, K. 246], April 1986 [K. 382], and October 1986 [K. 386].)

Concerto for Piano and Orchestra, No. 6, in B-flat, K. 238; Concerto for Three Pianos and Orchestra, No. 7, in F, K. 242; Concerto for Two Pianos and Orchestra, No. 10, in E-flat, K. 365.

ARCHIV CD: 427 317-2. Playing time: 67:32. (Recorded October 1987.)

Concertos for Piano and Orchestra: No. 9, in E-flat, K. 271; No. 11, in F, K. 413.

ARCHIV CD: 410 905-2. Playing time: 52:28. (Recorded in 1983.)

Concertos for Piano and Orchestra: No. 12, in A, K. 414; No. 14, in E-flat, K. 449.

ARCHIV CD: 413 463-2. Playing time: 45:26. (Recorded in 1983.)

Concertos for Piano and Orchestra: No. 13, in C, K. 415; No. 15, in B-flat, K. 450.

ARCHIV CD: 413 464-2. Playing time: 49:11. (Recorded in 1983.)

Concertos for Piano and Orchestra: No. 16, in D, K. 451; No. 17, in G, K. 453.

ARCHIV CD: 415 525-2. Playing time: 53:05. (Recorded April 1985.)

Concertos for Piano and Orchestra: No. 18, in B-flat, K. 456; No. 19, in F, K. 459.

ARCHIV CD: 415 111-2. Playing time: 55:19. (Recorded April 1984.)

Concertos for Piano and Orchestra: No. 20, in D minor, K. 466; No. 21, in C, K. 467.

ARCHIV CD: 419 609-2. Playing time: 57:38. (Recorded April 1986.)

Concertos for Piano and Orchestra: No. 22, in E-flat, K. 482; No. 23, in A, K. 488.

ARCHIV CD: 423 595-2. Playing time: 59:47. (Recorded March 1987.)

Concertos for Piano and Orchestra: No. 24, in C minor, K. 491; No. 27, in B-flat, K. 595.

ARCHIV CD: 427 652-2. Also CS. Playing time: 62:41. (Recorded May 1988.)

Concertos for Piano and Orchestra: No. 25, in C, K. 503; No. 26, in D, K. 537 ("Coronation").

ARCHIV CD: 423 119-2. Playing time: 60:37. (Recorded October 1986.)

POSTSCRIPT, 1994

In the years since this essay first appeared, the scholarly project of freezing Mozart in writing and denying the variable aspects of his performance practice has continued apace, even as the dazzling pianistic work of Robert Levin (alas, still untapped for a major recording project as of this writing) has gone on threatening it. Uncreative correctness continues to be the scholarly ideal, and the historical Mozart is tamed to conform to it.

In connection with the 1991 bicentennial, the Cambridge University Press inaugurated a scholarly series, Cambridge Studies in Performance Practice, with a volume of Mozart essays (*Perspectives on Mozart Performance*, ed. R. Larry Todd and Peter Williams). One of them, "Mozart the Fortepianist" by Katalin Komlós, assembles a great deal of evidence to give the lie to those scholars, such as the ones quoted in essay 11, who want to minimize the role of improvisation in eighteenth-century performance practice or, more generally, to downgrade the importance of ephemeral performance occasions or of the value of spontaneity to the whole idea Mozart inherited of what "music" was. One of Komlós's quotations, from the 1833 autobiography of the Abbé Stadler, Mozart's long-surviving contemporary, reflects with special irony on current musicological cant:

> In the art of free improvisation Mozart had no equal. His improvisations were as well-ordered as if he had had them lying written out before him. This led several to think that, when he performed an improvisation in public, he must have thought everything out, and practised it, beforehand. Albrechtsberger thought so too. But one evening they met at a musical soiree; Mozart was in a good mood and demanded a theme of Albrechtsberger. The latter played him an old German popular song. Mozart sat down and improvised in this theme for an hour in such a way as to excite general admiration and show by means of variations and fugues (in which he never departed from the theme) that he was master of every aspect of the musician's art.

Yet even Komlós respects the ideological fence that has been erected around the last eight concertos, declaring their cadenzas to be no longer products of spontaneous virtuosity but rather "an integral, organic part of the composition" (three buzzwords in one phrase!). Against the clear physical evidence of the sources the author holds these concertos to be preternaturally immune from historical or stylistic investigation, or from enhancement in performance: "their individuality and completeness," Komlós writes, "is beyond technical detail."

One of the staunchest upholders of the organicist mystique, and hence one of the scholars most hostile today to the idea of extemporization and variability in the performance of masterworks, is Christoph Wolff, who contributed another article, "Cadenzas and Styles of Improvisation in Mozart's Piano Concertos," to the Cambridge symposium. He still wants to believe, or wants us to believe, that Mozart wrote out cadenzas for himself, and that he did so because the idea of "cadenzas as improvisatory elements" failed to "correspond and harmonise" with his development as a composer (p. 228). The mere existence of a few scattered cadenza manuscripts—only "a relatively small portion" (p. 238) of what Mozart is tautologically assumed to have committed to paper—is taken as evidence in support of what thereby becomes a wholly circular argument. ("By habit," we are told, "he jealously guarded his personal performance materials" [p. 230]; "The cadenza manuscripts demonstrate [!] that it was apparently important for Mozart to write the cadenzas down rather than to play them completely *ex tempore*. He may have altered minor details or even major portions in the act of performance. The sources suggest, however, that he generally followed his elaborate and carefully planned improvisatory [?] designs" [p. 231].)

More evidence of this kind is drawn from a letter to his father in which Mozart wrote, "I composed it for myself and no one else but my dear sister must play it [p. 230]." But "it" was not a cadenza; it was the Concert Rondo, K. 382, for which no autograph cadenza survives. Another letter to Leopold forces Wolff into a tour de force of equivocation. Mozart writes:

> I shall send the cadenzas and *Eingänge* to my dear sister at the first opportunity. I have not yet altered the introductions in the rondo, for whenever I play this concerto [K. 271], I always play whatever occurs to me at the moment.

Wolff glosses as follows (p. 232):

> This concluding remark clearly refers to spontaneous improvisation, but there are two aspects worth considering: (1) Mozart specifically mentions the fact that he had not yet "altered the *Eingänge*" in the K. 271 finale, i.e. that he had not made the apparently necessary stylistic adjustments in the cadenzas of this Salzburg concerto from the 1770s; (2) improvisations on the spur of the moment may indeed be an essential element of the earlier Salzburg cadenza style, but less so in regard to the new Viennese style.

Stylistic "evolution"—evolution toward the "organic"—is the magic bullet. Wolff elaborates:

> The chronology of Mozart's cadenza style reflects a move from the motivically free-wheeling fantasia manner to motivically and metrically tightly controlled improvisational gestures which are gradually more and more removed from genuine improvisation and, instead, come much closer to compositional elaboration. Developmental aspects also play an increasingly significant role in that the principal

thematic material undergoes further transformations in the cadenza. In many instances he also revises the cadenzas by further refining certain key passages. The fact that [in revising] he more often than not preserves the principal ideas of his cadenzas manifests his increasingly "anti-improvisatory" approach. The cadenzas furnished Mozart, the composer/performer, with an important vehicle permitting him to make adjustments to a work that received its basically fixed *Gestalt* after the completion of the score and the copying of the performing parts.

We are privileged here to witness the birth of a mythological being: Mozart the anti-improviser, a figment of the zealously "anti-improvisatory approach" of modern Mozart scholarship. The cadenza, in this view, has become a means of editorial commentary, of additional composerly control over a wholly finished, idealized work-object. The complexity and abstract "control" of Mozart's late cadenzas preclude improvisation, Wolff thinks, just as Albrechtsberger had thought two centuries before him. The irrelevance of such an idealized notion of cadenza-function to the "musical daily business" of Mozart's day is obvious. It receives its support from the familiar ahistorical historian's notion of a Mozart cut loose from the life of his times.

The interesting task is not merely to debunk the notion but to understand the zeal with which it is defended. There is an element of desperation in it, the same finger-in-the-dike anxiety that motivated Peter Williams's attack on essay 1. If performers are given their heads, if performance values are restored to their historical position vis-à-vis composerly ones for this repertoire, just think of all the dreadful performances we will hear! But think of all the dreadful performances we hear now. The only difference is in the nature of the dreadfulness: dreadfully unstylish versus dreadfully boring. It were more healthy, I think, to concentrate on the best potential result rather than the worst. When this shift of perspective is made, anti-improvisatory argument and mythmaking fall instantly away.

Not that it is necessary to restore improvisation to Mozart's concertos in order to have great performances. The recordings of Artur Schnabel, rather eagerly sacrificed by Joseph Kerman in his *New York Review* encomium to those of Malcolm Bilson, are in their way every bit as "exemplary." Schnabel grew up under a wholly different ideological regimen from Mozart, was sustained by a wholly different musical ecology. Where the artist of Mozart's day valued spontaneity, wit, and nonchalance, Schnabel's day placed the premium on perfection and profundity. Where Mozart's sister Nannerl (quoted by Komlós) could recall of him that he never practiced past the age of seven, "for he always had to improvise, to play at sight, and to play concerts in front of people, and that was his whole *exercicium*," Schnabel was brought up under the post-Czerny regime of daily practice, scales, etudes, and all the rest, with an eye toward a consummateness of technique that nobody cared to acquire until the performer had become a museum caretaker, pledged to preserve intact the accumulated wealth of the ages. The mystique of performance passed from that of creating ephemeral excitement to that of producing a flawless reproduction. The skills most prized were those of producing a perfectly even tone, of connecting such tones in seamless legatos, of excreting stylistic or technical "impurities."

Both sets of tasks and skills are equally difficult, both equally rare in their fullest development. As Leschetizky, Schnabel's teacher, once observed, "it is harder to play six bars well on the piano than to conduct the whole of Beethoven's Ninth Symphony." With standards of tone production and legato so high, instruments had to "evolve" to further their achievement.

Schnabel's performance of the Larghetto from K. 595, recorded in 1934 with the London Symphony under Sir John Barbirolli, is a miracle of a kind it would never have occurred to Mozart or any of his contemporaries to attempt. The tempo is at an extreme of slowness that could never have been so much as conceived of until pianos existed that could provide a tonal envelope to sustain it. The legato is of a smoothness that no pianist could have thought of producing until a whole century of emulating famous pianistic "touches" had gone by. Every note is sculpted and considered in a way that completely denies and rejects the spontaneous values of the eighteenth century, as well as those of the contemporary "*U-Musik*" (*Unterhaltungsmusik*, "entertainment music") in which eighteenth-century values lived on, and against which the "serious" artists of the nineteenth and twentieth centuries defined their esthetic goals. Schnabel's performance is as authentic a representative of that esthetic and those goals as the depersonalized but still anti-improvisatory Mozart constructed by Professors Zaslaw and Wolff is a representative of late-twentieth-century modernism.

And Schnabel's sculptural, un-Mozartean legato allows him to finesse that awful "crux" of parallel octaves in the Larghetto of K. 595 in a way that enchants the ear and haunts the memory. Indeed the whole piece is characterized — made memorable — in a way that, for all its excellences, the Bilson approach cannot match. It may be argued, of course, that characterizing "whole pieces" is only a relevant task once the idea of pieces as wholes had been reified and objectified by the nineteenth-century work-ideal, and is just as anachronistic to Mozart as the Schnabel tempo and the Schnabel legato. But if that is to be the authentistic defense, then the whole idea of *Werktreue* has lost its grounding, and the project of "authenticity" is reenmeshed in paradox. Until we rid our thinking of its horror of anachronism, we will never achieve, or reachieve, an integrated, which is to say authentic, Mozartean performance practice such as Schnabel, to say nothing of Mozart, possessed.

12

Old (New) Instruments, New (Old) Tempos

MOZART: **Symphonies: No. 31, in D, K. 297 ("Paris");
No. 35, in D, K. 385 ("Haffner"); No. 40, in G minor,
K. 550.**

Orchestra of the Eighteenth Century, Frans Brüggen,
cond. PHILIPS CD, 416 329-2, 490-2 (recorded in performance,
May 1985).

These are wonderful performances of their kind. But if you buy them, you should be aware of what their kind is: namely, nineteenth-century renditions on eighteenth-century instruments.

They make a marvelous sound, and feature an endless array of instrumental felicities. The "Paris" Symphony, in particular, comes off brilliantly, for it is a virtual study in marvelous sounds and instrumental felicities—a send-up, in fact, of the empty orchestral pyrotechnics then fashionable in the French capital, as Mozart confided in a couple of funny letters to his father. The period band really digs into the showy fanfares and rockets of the first movement. I admired, too, the gorgeous string curtsy at the beginning of the Andantino, where the oft-deplored "Amsterdam swell" and the nonvibrato production are exquisitely apropos. And in the finale I was struck by the superb articulation of the whole notes at the head of the second theme, which, carried over into the contrapuntal development, floods the texture with light.

Originally published in *Opus* (December 1987): 45–46. Reprinted by permission.

The instruments really do make a difference here. And so does the fact that the texts performed are those of the Neue Mozart Ausgabe. In the "Paris" and "Haffner" Symphonies, this affects not only the details of rhythm and articulation, but also ornamentation and even (in the "Paris" slow movement) harmony. (Of course, these are not the first recorded performances to use the new edition; not only has there been the Academy of Ancient Music *intégrale*, the Harnoncourt/ Concertgebouw, etc., but also an alumni band of the National Orchestral Association under Leon Barzin, who, way back in the Mozart bicentennial year of 1956, stole a march on the NMA and the whole authenticity crowd by making a spirited recording of the "Haffner" directly from the autograph full score, which was then in the Association's possession.)

And yet, Brüggen's tempos are everywhere in line with what we're used to, not with what a sizable, not-to-be-sneezed-at body of evidence tells us about eighteenth-century norms. This evidence — much of which, as it concerned minuets, was provocatively summarized by William Malloch a couple of years ago ("Toward a 'New' [Old] Minuet," *Opus*, August 1985) — has been accumulating since the very earliest days of authenticity revivalism and even before, but such has been that movement's obsession with hardware that no period band has as yet made any significant use of it.

Some of this evidence is encoded in mechanical cylinders; some of it consists of metronome indications by early-nineteenth-century musicians like Carl Czerny and Johann Nepomuk Hummel who had studied early in life with the eighteenth-century greats. All of it, by the way, emphatically supports Beethoven's controversial "*Metronomisierungen*" (see essays 8 and 9); which may be one reason why today's artists are leery of it. Admit Hummel's tempos for Mozart, and you'll have to admit Beethoven's tempos for Beethoven. Now that Roger Norrington is vindicating Beethoven's tempos so compellingly, maybe his example will inspire those who purport to give us eighteenth-century-style Mozart and Haydn to scrutinize their assumptions.

But maybe I'm being as optimistic as Malloch, who so confidently predicted imminent change in line with the evidence he presented in 1985. Since then the Academy of Ancient Music has begun issuing its dispiriting Beethoven cycle at stodgy Victorian tempos. And while Brüggen's beautifully played Mozart is anything but dispiriting, still, a chance has been missed. For if our finest "Classical" period band is not going to broach the matter of period tempo, who will?

A comparison between Brüggen's tempos in the "Haffner" Symphony and those found in Hummel's piano arrangement, made in the early 1820s, will show how far modern ideas about eighteenth-century tempo have strayed from the evident historical reality (so far, in fact, that Virgil Thomson could decry Toscanini's minuet tempos, the closest in their day to the Hummelian norm, for what Thomson took to be their manifest inauthenticity). In the first movement, where Hummel indicated half note = 88, Brüggen (evidently following the conventional view of the movement as a sweeping rhetorical statement — those opening octaves! — rather than an Allegro con spirito, as Mozart described it) sets the half note at 71. According to the comparative tables assembled by Robert Münster a quarter-century ago in the *Mozart Jahrbuch ("Authentische Tempi zu den Sechs Letzten Sinfonien W. A. Mozarts?,"* the article that first drew attention to Hummel's arrangements as a source of information), this is slower not only than Toscanini but even Klemperer, and faster only (within Münster's sample) than Bruno Walter. Hummel marked the Andante at eighth note = 100. Brüggen's tempo (82) accords with Beecham's, the fastest in prestereo days. (For the record, Barzin clocked in at 83, and Hogwood/Schröder at 84, also Beechamesque rather than Hummelian, though faster than the Kappelmeisterly norm, which, to go by Münster's table, hovers around 76.)

In the Menuetto, as Malloch has already noted, nobody on records comes within leagues of an eighteenth-century pace. Where Hummel set his metronome at dotted-half = 66 (and by the way, it's of the utmost importance to note that Hummel counts the minuet "in one," not, like all conductors today, however authentistic, "in three"), Brüggen's is more than a third slower at 42. His tempo, in fact, exactly matches those of Jochum, Klemperer, Krips, and Henry Swoboda in Münster's sample; it is, one can't help noting, the twentieth-century *tempo ordinario* for this music — and for that very reason should have been suspect in the eyes of a Brüggen or a Schröder (the Academy tempo is hardly less ordinary at dotted-half = 44, exactly two-thirds Hummel).

Hummel did not set a metronomic tempo for the finale, but Czerny's four-hands arrangement puts the quarter note at 152, only slightly faster than Brüggen's 144. The sudden congruence still reflects our contemporary common practice, though, since Münster's tables demonstrate that modern recordings deviate least of all from the Hummelian or Czernian standard in duple-metered finales.

The lesson all these comparisons teach is an eye-opening one, and also a little painful. "What does it matter," said Stravinsky in 1957, when Early Music was on its wobbly first legs, "if the trills, the ornamentation, and the instruments themselves are all correct in the performance of a Bach concerto if the tempo is absurd?" For Mozart, no less than for Bach (or for Stravinsky), tempo is "the principal performance problem." True, Brüggen's performances don't sound absurd; they sound beautiful. And, as any number of fine pianists will tell you, attempts at performing Beethoven's music at Beethoven's tempos often *do* sound absurd. But all this just goes to show that, as the saying goes, we have all grown up absurd with respect to this repertoire. Hey, that's OK. We have every right to prefer what we prefer. The question is, can we go on unreflectively preferring what we're used to and still talk about "authenticity"? These marvelous Brüggen performances point up all too well, in their very marvelousness, what has always seemed to me a fatal flaw in the authenticity movement—viz., its preoccupation with the sound-surface ("the trills, the ornamentation, and the instruments themselves," to which we might add, for these performances, the *premiers coups d'archet* and the "Mannheim rockets") coupled with neglect, even denial, at times, of what lies behind it. ("What?", comes back the new-critical chorus, vintage 1940, "Something more? Music should not mean but be!" Authenticity is a child of its time.)

So keep all these caveats in mind when I tell you that the G minor Symphony receives a truly great performance from the Orchestra of the Eighteenth Century and its charismatic maestro. The tempos are a shade less absurd than in the "Haffner," it is true, although the minuet still hobbles along at two-thirds Hummel (dotted-half = 55 vs. 76; even Richard Strauss, in the 1920s, went faster). The finale, at half note = 134, is close enough to Hummel's 152 for jazz, though slower than Jochum's or (would you believe?) Karajan's. The Andante is by far the most "going" (i.e., *andante*) yet recorded (eighth note = 106 to Hummel's 116), and the effect of the tempo on the music is utterly transforming! It's really "in two" for once, with a delightful lilt on the eighth notes such as only "early musicians" seem to know how to impart; the dissonant harmonies (e.g., at letter B) can be heard linearly, in terms of their resolutions; and the inspired harmonic detours through which the sectional cadences are delayed emerge with warmth and tenderness (the players carefully distinguishing the legatos and the forte from the unslurred fortes and sforzandos elsewhere), minus the pompous bathos more usually encountered.

The first movement, however, where modern performances are often quite in accord with Hummel's marking (half note = 108), is pushed to about 116. That is not what is good about it. I hope I have not created the simplistic impression that faster is better for this music. What is not merely good but revelatory is the phrasing, in which the suprametrical grouping of bars (what is often called the "larger rhythm" of the piece) emerges with a matchless dynamic cohesion, at once lending the music a poignant but not overly pathetic songfulness (what Schumann must have meant when he wrote of this movement's "Hellenic grace") and ensuring that the famous departures from symmetry at this higher rhythmical level (something analysts have been chewing over for many decades) continually tease what Milton Babbitt likes to call "the ear's mind." These musicians have really written the book, once and for all, on "feminine endings" (listen not only to their unforgettable enunciation of the main theme, so often sentimentalized, but also to the cadence at letter E, right before the second theme in the recapitulation). Add to that such miracles of translucent balance (evidently untampered with by the engineers, for this is—incredibly—a live, real-time performance) as the bassoon counterpoint to the main theme at the recap, or the addition of the horns at the "rounding" of the second half of the minuet's trio, and you see why this is a recording to be treasured until an equally accomplished band finally does something about the minuet tempo.

The only thing I guarantee you won't like about it is Philips' fault, not Brüggen's or his band's. How long are we going to have to put up with the outdated ego-trippery of canned applause at the end of a live-performance recording? That should have gone out with pretape 78s, where it was sometimes unavoidable (though even then it could be abused: A Soviet friend once showed me, in Moscow, a set of five ten-inch 78-rpm records that preserved Joseph Stalin's victory address at the end of the "Great Patriotic War"; Sides 1–9 contained the speech, Side 10 was the applause [did the NKVD make sure you played it?]). After an experience like this G minor, the spell-shattering noise is an abomination.

BACH

13

Backslide or Harbinger?

BACH: **Sonatas for Viola da gamba and Harpsichord:
No. I, in G, S. 1027; No. 2, in D, S. 1028; No. 3, in G
minor, S. 1029.**

Mischa Maisky, cello: Martha Argerich, piano. (Hanno
Rinke, prod.) DEUTSCHE GRAMMOPHON (d) CD, 415 471–2.

COMPARISONS:

Casals, Baumgartner (1950) CBS LP. 32768 (5)
Rose, Gould (1974) CBS LP. 32934

The Early Music boom has made things pretty easy for reviewers. It is
now possible to pass judgment on a performance one has not yet
heard. One very prominent reviewer announced an impending series
of recitals, at which two prominent New York musicians would
perform the Beethoven sonatas for piano and cello, by sniffing, "They
are fine artists, but [!] they play modern instruments. . . . I look forward to [their] recitals but will know them . . . for what they are:
transcriptions, in effect, in which Beethoven's tone colors, textures,
attacks, and sonic durations are inevitably altered." Pity the poor fine
artists, thus consigned, as Dante consigned the Greek philosophers,
to the upper reaches of Hell. Elsewhere our critic contrasted their
"transcriptions" with the real McCoy, a performance on "original
instruments," in which "Beethoven's music rang out more bravely,
more beautifully, and in better balance" than modern instruments
could achieve, and (it follows) with Beethoven's tone colors, textures,
attacks, and sonic durations unaltered.

Originally published in *Opus* (April 1987): 22–25. Reprinted by permission.

But a moment's reflection will unmask this ploy. In neither case did the critic hear Beethoven's tone colors or sonic durations. He heard the tone colors and sonic durations of a cello and a piano. (What, by the way, is a sonic duration?) Nor did he hear Beethoven's attacks. He heard the attacks of a cellist and a pianist. We have here a spectacular instance of what has become a widespread and obnoxious fallacy: taking the instrument for the player and (in this case) even for the composer. Facile intransigence like this smacks of the kind of snobbery one is more used to encountering in those drama critics who will assure you that any old troupe of British actors will turn in a performance of any play superior to that of any troupe of Americans. In either case the critic has absolved himself from the exercise of his proper function, which is to evaluate specifics, not legislate class distinctions. Performances, even when they are not evaluated, as here, in advance, are too often evaluated for their class connections, rather than for their accomplishment. It is not, however, what you'd call a class act on the part of the critic. It's bigotry.

Which is not to deny that "original instruments" may possess some practical advantages over their modern counterparts in the performance of certain repertoires. In the case of Beethoven's cello sonatas, it is quite true that a proper balance is more easily achieved when a "fortepiano" vies with a cello of similar vintage than when a grand pianoforte contends with its modern string counterpart, for modern keyboard instruments have gained more power vis-à-vis their ancestors than have modern strings. It is quite true, to return to our critic's account, that "a pianist can play his heart out, whack out sforzandos, rumble through bass figuration on an early instrument without drowning his partner," and with both instruments functioning at top power the music is (subjectively) magnified. It makes little sense, however, to say that "on a big Steinway he must throttle back and render the written score at half power." What is the power of the written score? Now it's tones and notes that are being confused.

But if a better balance is easier to achieve in one medium than in another, then those working in the harder medium deserve greater credit for their balances, no? They are the ones who must consider, weigh, adopt strategies, not just open the throttle and zoom. No matter the instrument, it's in the strategies and considerations that the artistry of performance resides—not in the hardware, in short, but in the software of brain and muscle (and, dare one add nowadays, heart?).

Still, why make things hard for oneself? Why go on playing the music of the past on the instruments of the present? Why not cut up our heritage into a multiplicity of specialist domains? Precisely because then it stops being our heritage, if by heritage we mean our common patrimony, that part of the past that is still present and available to us all. The Early Music movement denies the presentness of the past, whether that past be the era of the Carolingians or that of Carter, whose works, however new, are in the past by the time we hear them. Appreciation, in this view, is always an act of historical imagination; no work of art may be comprehended, or even apprehended, except in terms of its historicity. At least since the nineteenth century, this has been an assumption on which Western cultural consciousness has rested. Our musical culture has been, ever since the very concept of "classical" music was born (again, in the nineteenth century), a museum culture, and it was inevitable that musicians would eventually become imbued with the mentality of curators and restorers. Hence the negative value that attaches nowadays to the word "transcription." It has acquired a specious ring of vandalism, even of forgery. (Since a forgery, being condemned by definition, needs no special evaluation, it follows that the more a critic can dismiss a priori as "transcription," the less actual judgment he'll have to pass, and the less risk he runs of error. Like all snobberies, this one is born of fear and lassitude.)

It was not always so, and it has been the encroachment of "early music" on the standard rep that has brought painfully to the consciousness of many what had been its tacit, hence unacknowledged if not actually repressed, threat to our sense of heritage, thus inspiring a backlash. To a greater extent than ever, we now have two cultures in classical music: the openly historicizing one nowadays identified with Early Music, but just as characteristic of that senescent movement known as modernism, and the so-called "mainstream," formerly smugly oblivious of any competition, now embattled and defensive, allied willy-nilly with a seismic cultural shift that in its early stage we call "postmodernism," but which will surely have another name by the time it joins modernism in history.

The postmodernist stance, like the newly self-conscious mainstream one, is a reassertion of consumer values as against the caretaker culture of the museum. It seeks to annul the claims of linear history, whether by attempting to stanch the flow of time itself (hence the attractions of motionless "minimalism") or by collaging disparate historical styles, as it were neutralizing their historicity (think of Rochberg's *Concord* Quartets). It revels in cross-temporal and cross-cultural "transpositions" of all kinds, exemplified, on the one hand, by Peter Sellars's Handel productions and, on the other, by Bach on the Moog and Vivaldi on the koto. In reaction to the shrinkage of historicist performance (and composition) into little pools of elite specialization, the unacademic mainstream is expanding into a vast pluralistic ocean, in which the past is once again regarded as available and unfragmented, to be disposed of in the present as we will, without snobbery and without bigotry. Transcriptions are coming back—real transcriptions, not the kind of thing snobs call by that word. Liszt's operatic and symphonic arrangements are developing a cult following in the concert hall, perhaps due in the first instance to the 1986 centenary, but destined, I believe, to outlast it. And you can find young artists nowadays programming and even creating Bach-Busoni, Bach-Siloti, and (despite the academic outcry: See Paul Henry Lang in the June 1986 *Opus*) Bach-Sitkovetsky.

It is in this ocean of possibilities that performance of past music on present instruments will find its redemption—so long as the manner of its performance is truly postmodern, that is, deconstructive, intertextual, transgressive.

And that is why I prefer to view this recording of the Bach gamba sonatas on modern cello and piano, played in fiery fearless fashion by a pair of youngish virtuosos, not as an anachronistic throwback to a complacent mainstream that preceded modernist/historicist performance, but as a harbinger of what might one day replace it. Bigoted critics who dismiss in advance performances of Beethoven on these instruments will not wait to hear this "transcription" before condemning it, and hardware snobbery is surely the ascendant position today among taste-makers. Cellists and pianists, evidently intimidated, have lately shied away from this repertoire—which, however, has by no means led to its neglect, thanks to the rise of a new generation of talented and skillful gambists and harpsichordists who can negotiate Bach's none-too-grateful writing for the instruments quite convincingly (though I would as yet call no recording on these instruments— and I've probably heard them all—inspired). There are at present only three cello-piano versions in the catalog, and the other two are by artists of much older generations. Comparison is interesting.

Miraculously, the 1950 Prades performance by Pablo Casals and Paul Baumgartner still survives. Though the seventy-three-year-old Casals's fingers had slowed a bit, this recording preserves a startling memento of what Bach performance was like in prefragmentation, premodernist days. NOT ONE NOTE COLD, as Casals can be heard exhorting the musicians on the *Brandenburg* Concerto rehearsal disc from Marlboro that Columbia circulated as a bonus years ago. The cellist's melodic line throbs and churns restlessly, incessantly (the pianist one forgets almost immediately, only partly because of the skewed balance).

The shape of the unfolding line takes complete precedence, in fact, over anything a good modernist critic would call "structural." Bach's fugues, ritornello plans, binary designs, all fade far into the perceptual background, crowded out by that urgently emotive melodic outpouring. From what nowadays we would claim for an historically informed point of view the performance is an absurdity, and yet it's riveting, enthralling. This is an artist who communes not with his art and its history, but with his fellows. He speaks with his cello, and it is impossible not to listen. I'm not at all sure, moreover, that in an age when fugues, ritornello plans, and binary designs were the standard and predictable patterns into which practically all musical thought was channeled, performers and listeners didn't take them for granted and concentrate on the music's narrativity rather than its "structures." Who wants to concentrate on the same stereotypes over and over again? (We do, that's who, when we listen to our Hogwood records.)

Casals, lucky genius, did not have to face the "modern problem," so memorably defined by Auden, in his great essay on Yeats, as that of being "no longer supported by tradition without being aware of it." Casals did not have to choose a style, only excel in one: nor did he have to place himself in history. It's easy now to dismiss him (in the words of Stravinsky, chief architect of the modern problem for musicians) for "playing Bach in the style of Brahms." But that misses the whole point, which is that Casals, till the year he reached his majority, was Brahms's contemporary, and that he (like Brahms) grew up regarding Bach as the fountainhead of contemporary music, not as the speaker of a dead language in need of philological revival.

Casals's musical world was at one with itself, and it is that wholeness of experience and identification his playing still conveys. For him not only did Brahms contain Bach (we can see this, too), but Bach contained Brahms as well; Casals possessed the sense, described by Eliot (in terms, of course, of letters, but just as true for music) "that the whole of the literature of Europe from Homer . . . has a simultaneous existence and composes a simultaneous order," and resides within each Individual Talent that accepts the Tradition. "Whoever has approved this idea of order," wrote Eliot, "will not find it preposterous that the past should be altered by the present as much as the present is directed by the past." Casals's Bach, then, had been altered by Brahms, we can even say "influenced" by Brahms, before Casals had ever touched him. Casals's playing therefore bespeaks terms of intimacy with Bach that modern historical performances, though they may make sounds that more closely resemble those of performances in Bach's time, can never aspire to. Casals really owned his Bach, for he felt really owned by Bach. These bonds have been put asunder by modernism, and they can never be retied.

We can only envy Casals now, not emulate him. The immediacy of his ties to Bach arose partly out of the fact that he belonged to an historical epoch that in most important ways resembled Bach's more than it did ours. No artist who has come to his maturity since the First World War can feel the presentness of the past the way Casals could, and no mere conservatory course can ever hope to compensate for this loss. The corollary to the "modern problem," to return to Auden, is that "every individual who wishes to bring order and coherence into the stream of sensations, emotions, and ideas entering his consciousness, from without and within, is forced to do deliberately for himself what in previous ages had been done for him by family, custom, church, and state, namely the choice of the principles and presuppositions in terms of which he can make sense of his experience." This is the old existentialist dilemma: the greatest of all twentieth-century clichés, perhaps, but still frightening, since its proper solution is alone what lends authenticity to action and to life. As Auden suggests, the reason authenticity has become such a cursed *issue* in our day is precisely this: that be it in ethics or in musical performance practice (and maybe this is why they are so often and so crudely confused), authenticity is a condition to which, in the fallen twentieth century, one must aspire, while Casals, in his prelapsarian day, could simply inherit it.

Auden once more, and for the last time: "There are, of course, always authorities in each field, but which expert he is to consult and which he is to believe are matters on which [the modern artist] is obliged to exercise his own free choice. This is very annoying for the artist as it takes up much time which he would greatly prefer to spend on his proper work, where he is a professional and not an amateur." Hence the tendency to escape from freedom into certainties too easily adopted and worn. Blind submission to authority—whether it takes the form of unreflecting obedience to one's conservatory teacher (whose authority stems from *his* teacher, and so on) or reliance on "original instruments," and other historical hardware—is the usual method nowadays for evading the responsibility of choice and decision. Today's truly authentic interpreters of music of the past (whatever the vintage of the instruments they play) are the ones whose styles owe the least to generalized precept and the most to acute, personal, and highly specific observation. The great name here, of course, is Glenn Gould.

Gould's recording of the Bach gamba sonatas (with Leonard Rose along for the ride, as Baumgartner was along for the ride with Casals) is one of the great beacon fires of postmodernist performance *avant le mot*. There is literally nothing in these readings either of Bach-the-Baroque-composer or of Bach-the-contemporary-of-Brahms. And, by the way, the recording completely gives the lie to those who complain that the grand piano cannot achieve a proper balance with a cello. On the contrary: This is the only recording of these sonatas ever made in which the balance among the contrapuntal lines is absolutely perfect (which means, of course, highly flexible and variable). It is achieved by exploiting pianistic resources of selective accentuation unavailable to the harpsichord, and by Rose's unhistorically, even unnaturally (but in the context of these performances brilliantly appropriate) *détaché* bowing, which matches Gould's famously ahistorical, idiosyncratic keyboard touch, and was obviously inspired by it. Above all, the balance was achieved by working toward it on the basis of the text alone, without any interference from preconceptions as to what the instruments can or ought to be able to do, either "now" or "then."

Where Casals had placed emphasis on "singing" (read: speaking, and hence expressive) line, Gould places it on texture—not "Bach's textures," as our unreflecting modernists would call them (when working in an anachronistic medium, one is at least protected from committing naive "intentional fallacies" like that), but the texture of the three-part counterpoint embodied in the writing. It is realized in a crystalline and eerily idealized way so that it remains a frozen "text," not a spontaneous "act"—a play of pure sound-pattern as unrelated as possible to the characteristic of any historically fixed, hence ephemeral, medium of performance (if he could, I'm sure Gould would have preferred to work, like Stockhausen, in sine tones). In order to distill this essence, the pianist actually makes supremely (some would no doubt say, criminally) free with the letter of the text. Not only does he distend the rhythm so as to achieve a maximum independence between the lines played by his two hands, but he adds chords ad lib, doubles parts at the octave and the third (!), improvises melismata to the point where they become virtual graffiti (e.g., in the first movement of the Second Sonata), interpolates extra voices, usually in the middle of the texture as harmonic fill, but in at least one memorable instance (the third movement of the Second Sonata) in imitation against the main tune. And that uncanny, extraordinary, disembodied touch! I have no idea how he produced the rolled chords in the right hand in the third movement of the First Sonata, for example; I only know that they have been haunting me now for a dozen years, and that Gould's is the only recording of these too familiar works that continues to give me refreshment.

What does all this have to do with Baroque performance practice? Exactly nothing, except insofar as we know that Baroque performers made free with texts. Did they make as free with them as Gould? Hard to say. What he does sounds more like the kind of thing Liszt is reputed to have done when performing familiar scores (but wait: Doesn't Bach's pupil Lorenz Mizler tell us that Bach "accompanies every thoroughbass to a solo so that one thinks it is a piece of concerted music and as if the melody he plays in the right hand were written beforehand"?). And if Alfred Brendel warns us that we should not emulate Liszt's playing even of Liszt ("he would be better served by ardent, if critical, devotion than by performers pretending to be another Liszt"), that must be put down to lingering modernist *pudeur*. Gould was very arrogant and pretentious, no doubt. But I'm sure he never thought himself another Bach. He knew he was the first Gould—and the last. George Szell was right. That nut *was* a genius.

Having invoked Casals and Gould, what shall we make of Argerich and Maisky? They're neither nuts nor geniuses. They're a hell of a team, though, far more so than Casals/Baumgartner or Gould/Rose. They cannot match Casals in premodernist conviction or Gould in postmodernist originality—who could?—but they are unmatched for uninhibited virtuosity. What appeals to me in these performances is the unabashed exploitation of the modern instrumental medium to make points ("structural" points at that) about the music in a way historical instruments cannot do. For example, Argerich emphasizes proto-sonata-ish "double returns" (main theme in original key) by increased tonal weight and minutely lengthened articulation. Harpsichordists make such points by means of agogics. When pianists imitate this, their playing loses its pianistic integrity (as does Argerich's at times, when she copies the harpsichordish *style brisé* at cadences). Maisky is not afraid to underscore his melodic points with portamentos, though sometimes he elides phrase endings into beginnings in a way that suggests not so much a considered expressive distortion as an unexamined Piatigorskian residue.

Argerich now and then takes off on the text in a somewhat Gouldish fashion, but tentatively. That is why I call this recording a harbinger, not a fully fledged mainstream counterattack. It has lots of personality and joie de vivre, though, and better represents the good humor and informality of Bach's chamber music than any of the rather dour and straitlaced gamba-harpsichord versions currently available (and not just in this country—I make no exception for the overrated Leonhardt/Kuijken import, cult following though it has acquired). I look forward to its being surpassed both from within the mainstream and from the modernist/historicist camp, and have reviewed it and its predecessors at such length mainly in an effort to combat invidious prejudice. At bottom I guess I'm just an old-fashioned liberal pleading for tolerance and peaceful coexistence, and convinced (to paraphrase the National Rifle Association, normally no friend to us bleeding hearts) that instruments do not play music, people do.

POSTSCRIPT, 1994

It was inevitable that the reviewing fraternity would rise up in defense of its own. My protest against Andrew Porter's hardware snobbery (for his were the incredible words quoted at the outset: see his *New Yorker* column for 3 November 1986) provoked a rejoinder from Will Crutchfield, then a staff reviewer for the *New York Times*. In a "Critic's Notebook" column (16 April 1987), he chided me for "seeming to confer the status of a high cause" on the use of "modern" (or rather, as he pointed out, nineteenth-century) instruments for old music. But no, the only cause I cherish is that of playing with understanding and personal commitment, qualities I welcome from all quarters. What I detest is giving the instrument—any instrument, old or new—credit for what the performer has accomplished.

A month or so after his Critic's Notebook, Crutchfield praised the Boston Early Music Festival Orchestra in a *Times* review by noting that "the more one hears Handel on period instruments, the more one realizes how individual and particular are the orchestral pieces that have sometimes seemed cut in a generic pattern." A splendid point is vitiated by again putting the instruments first. By dint of study and application, including application to the task of learning to play a new—er, old—instrument, the best specialist performers get much closer to their chosen repertory than their "mainstream" counterparts manage to do. Like mother seals, they can distinguish the individual features of what look to outsiders like undifferentiated, interchangeable beings; and they can impart their awareness of individual difference to their audiences. That is why their renditions can seem revelatory. Difference is what they reveal. How insulting it is to imply that all it takes is the right instrument to achieve this, or that using the right instrument is what gave the players their vision. It is just the other way around: those who have the vision will want to use the old—er, new—instruments.

14

Facing Up, Finally, to Bach's Dark Vision

The Teldec Bach Cantatas

Teldec's series of Bach church cantatas, begun in 1971, when the German label was still called Telefunken, is now complete on eighty-three CDs, assembled in forty-five packages. Almost incredibly, enough Bach church cantatas are lost to fill another forty-nine CDs.

The Teldec series includes one hundred ninety of the two hundred surviving works, with one recorded in two versions. Of the other ten items, five have been found to be spurious, including the much-recorded Nos. 53 and 189, and five are fragmentary works or reworkings—"parodies"—of other compositions.

Teldec's performances use a variety of European boy choirs and two period-instrument ensembles. The cellist and conductor Nikolaus Harnoncourt leads the Vienna Concentus Musicus, perhaps the oldest period-instrument ensemble still in business, and the harpsichordist and organist Gustav Leonhardt leads the Amsterdam-based Leonhardt Consort.

The series has prominently featured soloists who were or went on to become international stars, including the flutist Frans Bruggen, the countertenor Paul Esswood and the baritones Max von Egmond and, lately, Thomas Hampson. The one singer associated with the project from first release to last was the tenor Kurt Equiluz.

Originally published in the Arts and Leisure section of the Sunday *New York Times*, 27 January 1991. Reprinted by permission of the *New York Times*.

And now for something altogether unreviewable: eighty-three compact disks containing almost two hundred church cantatas by Johann Sebastian Bach as recorded by Teldec over an eighteen-year period (thirteen years longer than it took to write them) by a who's who of Early Music virtuosos under the joint direction of Gustav Leonhardt and Nikolaus Harnoncourt.

Eerie is the only word for the virtual silence that has greeted the end of this project, inaugurated in 1971 amid considerable fanfare and controversy. Completion was announced for 1985, the Bach tricentennial year. Had that deadline been achieved, no doubt, we would have heard more about it. Meanwhile, a competing series, inaugurated in 1975 under the leadership of the German choral specialist Helmuth Rilling, did make it to the finish line in time.

Although the Rilling traversal relied on standard instruments and a traditional (alas, rather drab if dependable) performance style, it possessed a certain musicological cachet. It was issued in the revolutionary new chronological order of cantatas that was established in the 1950's by a heroic team of German scholars, while the Teldec project followed the aimless order of the nineteenth-century Bach Gesellschaft edition. The Rilling version is also marginally more complete, since it includes the fragmentary works and parodies.

Most injurious of all to the newsworthiness of the Teldec series, perhaps, is the fact that along the way it stopped reflecting the absolute cutting edge of fashion in Bachian performance practice. In 1971, even sympathetic scholars could find the Leonhardt-Harnoncourt approach disconcerting, what with its clipped nonlegato articulations, its rhythmic alterations and dislocations, its easily satirized dynamic bulges, its brusquely punctuated recitatives, its flippant tempos, not to mention the tiny forces, the green and sickly sounding boy soprano soloists, above all the recalcitrant, sometimes ill-tuned "original instruments." Some were downright indignant at the loss of traditional scale and weight. The venerable musicologist Paul Henry Lang blasted the "frail performances with inadequate ensembles," and what he saw as the craven sacrifice of spiritual values to safe and shallow scholarly "objectivity."

Yet by the early 1980s, the ground had shifted to the point where Mr. Leonhardt and Mr. Harnoncourt had become middle-of-the-roaders. The authenticity spotlight was stolen by proponents of ever more radical theories of historical Bach performance, the most notorious being the elimination of the chorus altogether in favor of single voices. For today's authenticity mavens the Teldec performances are not nearly frail enough.

The British quarterly *Early Music* has been ignoring the series since the 1986 releases, when Mr. Harnoncourt's work in parti-

cular was primly dismissed as having "no advantages over traditional 'Romantic' interpretations," because it did not sufficiently respect what the reviewer was pleased to call "the implications of the
music itself."

The music itself—what might that be? Though blandly invoked as
if it were a self-evident ideal, it is really a problematical and anachronistic notion. Bach would not have understood it. Its fount was
the late-eighteenth-century Enlightenment, the antimetaphysical
Age of Reason. It was an Enlightened music historian named Charles
Burney who in the 1770s penned the definition of music that is still
paraphrased in most dictionaries: "the art of pleasing by the succession and combination of agreeable sounds." If Burney's words ring
true, it is because modern musicians—composers, scholars and performers of every stripe—are essentially formalists at heart. And so are
modern listeners.

We all tend to exalt what Stravinsky called the *matière sonore*—
the material sound of music—over immaterial meaning (the "extramusical content," if you will). Listeners value performances to the
extent that they are beautiful-sounding. Performers strive hardest for
clean execution and beautiful tone. Composers and scholars define
and explain musical meaning primarily in terms of an abstract
("purely musical") sound-syntax. When pressed to a logical extreme,
some have even attempted to deny the reality of musical expressivity.

Because of his unparalleled technical mastery and his habit of
pinning down in precise notation so much more than his contemporaries cared to do, Bach is often looked upon as music's formalist
supreme. The disproportionate visibility of his highly patterned instrumental music nowadays abets this perception, as do Bach's late
quasi-scholastic testaments, *The Art of Fugue*, and particularly *The
Musical Offering*, which after all arose out of contact with his son's
employer, Frederick the Great of Prussia, ardent Enlightener of the
German lands.

The Enlightened, secularized view of Bach is the one advanced by
most modern scholarship. The six columns devoted to the cantatas in
the *New Grove Dictionary of Music and Musicians* contain nothing
but a taxonomy, a sterile formal classification. Lip service is paid to
the composer's "unfailing expressive profundity," but the whole question of expression is assimilated to innocuous notions of beautiful
form, as if to lure attention away from rhetoric and imagery and onto
"the music itself."

According to such a taste, whether the genuine eighteenth-
century article or its modern simulacrum, all music stands or falls as
distinguished entertainment. "I don't mind so much if a performance

is unhistorical," Roger Norrington told a reporter last summer, attempting an end run around the vexed notion of authenticity, "but I do mind if it isn't fun."

How utterly irrelevant this whole esthetic is to the Bach of the cantatas! How irrelevant, therefore, the cantatas are to our modern concert life. Small wonder that scarcely half a dozen out of two hundred are or ever will be known to concertgoers.

And a thoroughly unrepresentative lot it is, too, even if we exclude the fun items like the "Coffee" and "Peasant" Cantatas from the list. The favored handful includes gaudy display pieces like No. 51, *Jauchzet Gott in allen Landen*, the one church cantata Bach ever composed for a woman's voice. It includes officiously celebratory ones on familiar hymns like No. 80, *Ein' feste Burg*, usually performed—not here!—in a big band arrangement by the composer's son Wilhelm Friedemann. And it includes uncharacteristic imitations of what Bach called "the pretty little Dresden tunes" (that is, opera) like No. 140, *Wachet auf*, with its love duets between Christ and the Christian soul.

Anyone exposed to Bach's full range (as now, thanks to these records, one can be) knows that the hearty, genial, lyrical Bach of the concert hall is not the essential Bach. The essential Bach was an avatar of a pre-Enlightened—and when push came to shove, a violently anti-Enlightened—temper. His music was a medium of truth, not beauty. And the truth he served was bitter. His works persuade us—no, *reveal* to us—that the world is filth and horror, that humans are helpless, that life is pain, that reason is a snare.

The sounds Bach combined in church were often anything but agreeable, to recall Dr. Burney's prescription, for Bach's purpose there was never just to please. If he pleased, it was only to cajole. When his sounds were agreeable, it was only to point out an escape from worldly woe in heavenly submission. Just as often he aimed to torture the ear: when the world was his subject, he wrote music that for sheer deliberate ugliness has perhaps been approached—by Mahler, possibly, at times—but never equaled. (Did Mahler ever write anything as noisomely discordant as Bach's portrayal, in the opening chorus of Cantata No. 101, of strife, plague, want and care?)

Such music cannot be prettified in performance without essential loss. For with Bach—the essential Bach—there is no "music itself." His concept of music derived from and inevitably contained The Word, and the word was Luther's.

It is a predicament Bach's Enlightened rediscoverers recognized from the very first. Carl Friedrich Zelter, the conductor of the Berlin Singakademie, wrote of it to Goethe in 1827, two years before his pupil Mendelssohn revived the St. Matthew Passion. Communion with Bach's music, Zelter felt, was a means "toward apperception and awe of the Truth," but there was an obstacle: "the altogether contemptible German church texts, which suffer from the earnest polemic of the Reformation."

This was something the Enlightened mind could only resist. "The thick fog of belief stirs up nothing but disbelief," Zelter complained, with the result that Bach's sacred output "will doubtless long remain a secret, since it cannot be compared with the music we know at present."

The effort to save "the music itself" (which could be adapted to contemporary taste) from its motivating esthetic (which could not) set a vast sanitizing project in motion. It has been going on from Mendelssohn's day to our own, and has for nearly two centuries been keeping the essential Bach at bay, absent equally from the pages of *Grove* and from the latest pretty one-on-a-part renditions.

It is because they have refused to participate in the cover-up that the work of Mr. Leonhardt and (especially) Mr. Harnoncourt has been difficult of acceptance. The two divided the cantatas up, it would appear, according to temperament. Mr. Leonhardt, the Early Music movement's patrician guru, took most of the pastoral pieces, leaving the really tough sermons to the suitably fearless and contentious Mr. Harnoncourt. (Occasionally, as in Volume 40, they cast themselves whimsically against type, with the result that the phlegmatic Mr. Leonhardt unfortunately ended up playing the most neurotic piece of all—the organ solo in Cantata No. 170 that Bach himself called "an infernal bawling and drawling.")

Like any true guru, Mr. Leonhardt does not justify his ways. It is one of the stranger features of the Teldec series that the regular section in the program books devoted to "Notes on the Performance" contains only remarks by Mr. Harnoncourt on "his" cantatas. By putting his cards on the table, Mr. Harnoncourt invites backtalk; Mr. Leonhardt's seraphic silence silences.

Yet since Mr. Harnoncourt's approach is the more challenging and the riskier, his success is all the more estimable. There is a danger of intentional fallacy in trying to account for that success, but what may well have started out as mere literalism seems to have been subverted by the essential Bach into a new, authentic musical evangelism.

Mr. Harnoncourt's style has taken on attributes that "performance practice" alone could never have vouchsafed. They can only have come from those "contemptible" Lutheran texts and their unaccommodating polemic. His increasingly hortatory and unbeautiful way of performing Bach reached a peak about halfway through the series, and the intervening decade has done nothing to lessen its power to shock—or disgust. If you seek contact with the essential Bach at full hideous strength, Mr. Harnoncourt's performances remain the only place to go.

It feels not only invidious but ridiculous to be singling out one recording from a yard-high stack. But in Volume 41, released in 1988, the essential Bach speaks through Mr. Harnoncourt with a special vehemence. Cantata No. 178, *Wo Gott der Herr nicht bei uns hält*, begins with a French overture straight from hell, a portrait of a world without God in which (as Dostoyevsky later noted) all things are possible and there is no hope. Mr. Harnoncourt applies to the dotted rhythms the awful Gnashville sound he has gradually developed for such occasions, the strings of the Concentus Musicus hurling their bows at their instruments from a great height, producing as much scratch as tone.

The "chorale-recitative" that follows illustrates the futility of human effort with a bass that is continually and arbitrarily disrupted. It is played with greatly exaggerated dynamics to underscore—needlessly, most proper authenticists would insist—the bare message of the notes. After an aria depicting a Satan-engineered shipwreck with nauseous melismas and a chorale verse evoking persecution with a crowd of claustrophobically close and syncopated imitations, we reach the heart of the cantata.

A glossed chorale verse about raging beasts finally dispenses with word-painting, which depends on mechanisms of wit and can be taken as humor. It harks back instead to the wellsprings of the Baroque in grossly exaggerated speech contours, something akin to wild gesticulation.

Now Bach the anti-Enlightener comes into his own, with a frantic tenor aria, "Shut up, stumbling Reason!" ("Schweig nur, taumelnde Vernunft!"). Past the first line the message of the text is one of comfort: "To them who trust in Jesus ever, the Door of Mercy closes never," to quote the doggerel translation in the program booklet. But Bach is fixated on that fierce and derisive opening line—indeed, on just the opening word. Out of it he builds practically the whole first section of his da capo aria, crowding all the rest into a cursory and soon superseded middle. Over and over the tenor shrieks, "Schweig nur, schweig!," leaping now a sixth, now a seventh, now an octave. Meanwhile, the accompanying orchestra, reason's surrogate, reels and lurches violently.

This one is not for you, Dr. Burney. Hands off, Maestro Norrington. There is no way this music can ever be fun. In fact, it is terrifying—perhaps more now than in Bach's own time, since we have greater reason than Bach's contemporaries ever had to wince at the sound of a high-pitched German voice stridently shouting reason down.

The cantata that follows on the same disk—No. 179, *Siehe du, dass deine Gottesfurcht nicht Heuchelei sei*—is harsh and minatory: "See to it that your fear of God is no sham!" The performance emphatically belongs to the frail, inadequate type that has given the Teldec set a bad name.

Take the aria "Liebster Gott, erbarme dich" ("Dear God, have mercy"), for soprano solo and two accompanying oboes da caccia. The solo part is quite beyond the powers of the poor boy who is called upon to sing it, and who (in the witty words of Bach scholar John Butt) has "no strong views about rhythm or tempo."

Although the aria is in the key of A minor, the middle section modulates to, and ends in, the key of C minor. Not only is the juxtaposition intensely jarring, it also puts the music in a harmonic region where the instruments simply cannot play in tune, especially as Bach takes them down to their very lowest, least tractable range. At the middle cadence the boy, too, is asked to sing lower than his tonal support permits.

The whole performance sounds loathesome and disgraceful. And these are the words: "My sins sicken me like pus in my bones; help me, Jesus, Lamb of God, for I am sinking in deepest slime." Perform this aria with a hale and hearty mezzo-soprano full of strong musical views, accompany her with a pair of brand new English horns spiffily played, and only "the music itself" will gain, not the aria, which utterly depends on its performers' failings, and on the imperfections of their equipment to make its harrowing point.

This undermining of human agency is something Bach engineers time and again. If you want to witness a real assault by composer on performer, try the middle section of the bass aria in Cantata No. 104 (Volume 26). The text reads, "Here you taste of Jesus' goodness and look forward, as your reward for faith, to the sweet sleep of death." The vocal line extends for 18 measures in a stately 12/8 meter without a single rest, and with notes lasting as much as nine beats. It reduces the estimable Philippe Huttenlocher to a gasping, panting state in which, were the aria to continue another two minutes, he would surely receive his reward.

Nor could anyone possibly hear Frans Brüggen's incomparable enunciation of the obbligato to the great tenor aria in Cantata No. 114 (Volume 28)—*Wo wird in diesem Jammertale* ("Where, in this vale of woes, may I find refuge for my soul?")—and not realize that Bach was counting precisely on the fact, emphasized by Paul Henry Lang with asperity in 1972, that "the low region of the Baroque flute is breathy and weak."

It is for their refusal to flinch in the face of Bach's contempt for the world and all its creatures that Mr. Leonhardt and Mr. Harnoncourt deserve our admiration. Their achievement is unique and well-nigh unendurable. Unless one has experienced the full range of Bach cantatas in these sometimes all but unlistenable renditions, one simply does not know Bach. More than that, one does not know what music can do, or all that music can be. Such performances could never work in the concert hall, it goes without saying, and who has time for church? But that is why there are records.

POSTSCRIPT, 1994

Many were the readers who took this piece as an attack on Bach ("God help us, on Mozart's birthday," shrieked one), accusing me of taking "a kind of sadistic delight in denigrating every aspect of the works in extremely blunt not to say offensive language" (wrote another). The idea that great music can be ugly, or ugly great, is unthinkable to most music lovers, which shows how far we have strayed from the ancient esthetic of the sublime, and nicely supports my point about "the music itself."

Others had "theological" objections to my "charges" against Bach. "Did Bach really intend or think his music ugly?" wrote a thoughtful student. "If you say that Bach's music . . . implies a world of filth and horror, you suggest he conceived a world with a cruel and tyrannical God at its helm—*not* a Christian God. Considering Bach's devotion, such a conclusion does not make sense." But as the devoted know best of all, God is not a Christian. It is for us to be Christians.

Of course, Bach is bigger than any one view of him. One exceptionally well-informed correspondent contributed some interesting— to me, most welcome—qualification, which I am happy to pass along to my readers:

> At times Bach does set texts that smack of Lutheran polemics: against the Pope and Catholicism and, yes, against reason. But "the high-pitched German voice stridently shouting reason down" is, or should be, musical—albeit declamatory—and should, perhaps, be put beside the quieter, lower German voice referring to Christ as "the light of reason" in Cantata 76, which starts with two verses of Psalm 19: "The heavens declare the glory of God." Now I should say that the Bach who set Luther's translation of the Bible is more "essential" than the Bach

who set Lutheran polemics. Even when librettists present him with medical metaphors like "pus [or rottenness] in my bones" they are apt to have taken them from places like Habakkuk 3, 16.

And, she adds, "I like being harrowed by Bach—rather than Harnoncourt—and take Bach's words seriously. I doubt that he would object to some musical sublimation of the wild gestures and breathless gasps—provided the words are enunciated clearly and with conviction."

15

The Crooked Straight, and the Rough Places Plain

BACH: Trio Sonatas (4).

London Baroque. (Michel Bernard, prod.) HARMONIA MUNDI FRANCE CD, HMC 90.1173.

A Musical Offering, S. 1079: Sonata for Flute, Violin, and Continuo, in C minor. Sonatas: for Two Violins and Continuo in C, S. 1037; for Flute, Violin, and Continuo in G, S. 1038; for Two Flutes and Continuo in G, S. 1039.

COMPARISON: Cologne Musica Antiqua (S. 1036–39)
ARCHIV LP, 2533 448. OP: 413 084 (9)

One of the bonniest postconcert *mots* ever to reach my ears was uttered after a performance by a touring English early-music group, by the leader of one of its best-known American counterparts. "They're one of the best straight groups I've heard," he said. After his listeners had recovered from the apparent sexual innuendo, he continued: "It's like this: There are the straight players and the crooked players. I can respect the straight players, but my heart is with the crooked players." That is how I feel about this release, and for the same reason, I can (and do) respect it, but my heart is not with it.

Straight players have significant strengths and virtues. At their best (and they come, just like crooked players, both good and bad, and in various shapes and sizes), they display really solid and reliable all-purpose technique at the service of a very scrupulous musicianship,

Originally published in *Opus* (December 1986): 42–43. Reprinted by permission.

and they work very hard at ensemble. You can sit back and relax with them, confident that every jot and tittle will be perfectly executed and in place. They are not by any means necessarily conventional-minded musicians: The "one-on-a-part" Bach performers on both sides of the Atlantic have been straight players to a man. Nor are they necessarily lacking in spirit: Their fast movements rollick, their slow movements sigh, their *tempo ordinario* is as ordinary as can be. In short, they do what they're told (by a conductor, by a score, by "evidence"), and do it well.

What's wrong with that? Nothing at all, if what you want out of music is something to sit back and relax to, and if your idea of life or art is a mosaic of jots and tittles. The mind of a straight player is like a well-stocked and well-ordered musical emporium: The customer (conductor, score, evidence) places his order (for a tempo, an articulation, a dynamic), and the proper item is quickly found on the shelf or rack, just where it was the last time.

The crooked players, the ones who claim my heart, do not get their phrasings and tempos off the rack. Their responses are conditioned not by generic demands that can be easily classified, filed away, and retrieved, but by highly specific, unclassifiable, personal and intensely subjective imaginings, the sort of thing that makes logical positivists and their abundant musical progeny see red. They seek not to group and generalize, but to distinguish and differentiate. Every musical event ideally possesses a unique, never-to-be-repeated shape — even phrases in a sequence. The task the crooked players set themselves, and it's the hardest task in the world, is to find a way of realizing and rendering that exact shape in palpable, intelligible sound. They are the real artists among performers, in the sense of T. E. Hulme's wonderful metaphor—the one by which he sought, in his immortal essay on "Romanticism and Classicism," to convey what it is to be an artist, what an artist does, and why an artist is often misunderstood.

After first describing what are known as architect's curves, or templates—"flat pieces of wood with all different kinds of curvature, by a suitable selection from [which] you can draw approximately any curve you like"—Hulme went on: "The artist I take to be the man who simply can't bear the idea of that 'approximately.' He will get the exact curve of what he sees whether it be an object or an idea in the mind. I shall here have to change my metaphor a little to get the process in his mind. Suppose that instead of your curved pieces of wood you have a springy piece of steel of the same types of curvature as the wood. Now the state of tension or concentration of mind, if he is doing anything really good in this struggle against the ingrained habit of technique, may be represented by a man employing all his fingers to bend the steel out of its own curve and into the exact curve which you want. Something different to what it would assume naturally."

All that comes under the headings "period style" and "performance practice"—those are the templates. And most performances of early music—of any music—consist of matching the nearest template to the music at hand. But the crooked performers (and how apt the term in light of Hulme's metaphors!) are forever bending the templates out of shape, struggling against ingrained habit in quest of a really exact, and therefore authentic, rendering of what it is that makes this piece this piece and not that one.

Struggles do not make for relaxed listening. And listeners, who have their own ingrained habits of the ear, can find the poking and twisting to which crooked performers subject their mental templates as unbearable as they would busy fingers mauling and mashing at their brains. Hence the really big reputations in any field of musical endeavor are always likeliest to be made by straight musicians. Only an unchallenging approach can ever be popular. And an unchallenging approach coupled with the use of "original instruments," these days, can actually succeed in combining easy popularity with snob appeal. It was on this unlikely coalition of support that such a profoundly uninteresting straight performer as Christopher Hogwood, for example, could rise to his present position of preeminence in the Early Music field.

What prompts these thoughts is the interesting fact that, with the issue of this recording by London Baroque, the Bach trio sonatas—a very minor corner of the Master's output, but one that contains some delightful and affecting music—can be experienced in really classic straight and crooked renditions, the latter being those of the Cologne Musica Antiqua. Hearing them side by side is an education.

The very accomplished London performers give an immaculate representation in sound of what one sees on the page when one looks at the score. It is an ideal positivist job (if you'll pardon the oxymoron), and those who think of musical performance as "compliance" (as Nelson Goodman would say) with notation will get all they could ask for here. It follows, then, that a good score reader doesn't even have to hear these performances. A lay listener, on the other hand, will be very well served by them insofar as they will acquaint him, with a minimum of distortion, with the generic contents of the pieces performed. There is nothing in them that is not referable to the printed page, and hence "verifiable" in old-fashioned scientific terms.

(Still, there are always sharks in the water to threaten those who rely on the illusory comforts of literalism. The first movement of the "little" G major Trio [S. 1038] opens with a phrase in which the sixteenth notes are slurred in pairs. This sent the London performers scurrying off to the wrong rack: the French convention of *notes inégales*, the relevance of which to Bach was placed in serious doubt by Frederick Neumann over twenty years ago [see his "The French *Inégales*, Quantz, and Bach," *Journal of the American Musicological Society*, 18 (1965), 313–58], and which in any case is contradicted within the movement at hand by Bach's clear sectional delineation that alternates even sixteenths with dotted groups.]

By comparison, the Cologne performances are apt to seem at first like fun-house reflections. A score reader could form no idea of them a priori. Every moment brings a surprise. No articulation is taken for granted. Phrasings are asymmetric, arbitrary, "different to what [they] would assume naturally," that is, on the basis of the normal templates of antecedent/consequent or sequential patterning. Tempos tend toward the extreme, and are in any case extremely variable. None of this is "verifiable" by recourse to external norms. Its validation comes from within the players' minds as they confront the music on the page, and to make sense of these performances one must make an effort to penetrate those minds and through them to confront the music anew. A listener whose impression of the music has been formed on the basis of the score or on the basis of straight performances will be made at first uncomfortable by this defamiliarization of what he thought he knew, but (unless unwilling to make the effort of empathy) he will be quickly entranced by it. Fascinated and involved, one joins the artists in pursuit of the exact curve. One begins by wondering at every turn, "What will these jokers think of next?", and ends by asking, "What will Bach think of next?" Made attentive to Bach's argument as never before, one comes through the experience of the performance knowing the music more intimately than one has ever known it, regardless of whether one has "agreed" with every admittedly arbitrary twist and turn along the way.

There would be little point in trying to describe these performances, whether crooked or straight, in detail. We are dealing with essential musical matters that are lost in translation. I would simply urge readers to hear both performances in direct comparison. The better one knows the pieces (or thinks one knows them), the more one has to gain from hearing the crooked performances, so start with the straight (or, if you can, with the score). And be under no illusion that the crooked performance is automatically the "better" one, or that the straight performance is the more "faithful" one, or that either is the more "authentic" one. These points can be debated without end or profit unless the object of fidelity and the nature of authenticity are rigorously specified. Better to abandon all those loaded terms and concentrate on the music. And don't ask me whether I wouldn't rather hear a good straight performance than a bad crooked one. Would you rather be poor but healthy or rich but sick?

Finally, a number of prominent scholars and performers have been arguing vigorously that what I am calling "straight" performance was in fact the norm before 1800, and should therefore be the norm in modern performances of music of that vintage. In other words, it is held that composers and performers relied implicitly in pre-Romantic times on conventions and genres (what I've been calling templates), and that what it takes (if pressed, they will say *all* it takes) to perform the music of the eighteenth century authentically is mastery of these. But this is to convert a first step—the attainment of competence— into a limit. And in the second place it equates authenticity with historical verisimilitude (something about which I've said my piece before). If crooked performance is an anachronism—and I'm willing happily to concede that Bach (in Marie Leonhardt's well-known phrase) might sooner have recognized London Baroque's performances "without bewilderment" than Musica Antiqua's—it is no more so than textual criticism, analysis, or any of the other means we use to make the music of the past intelligible and meaningful to us today.

That is why I wish the crooked performers Godspeed, and why my heart is with them as they go about their risky business of empathy and hermeneutics. It would be in any case safer, and possibly more lucrative, to hide behind the score with the straights and trade in easily processed, easily assimilated templates that give a reassuring and unchallenging approximation of what Bach-the-Baroque-composer was like—a nicely restored portrait (to use the straights' favorite analogy) hanging up there on the wall. By taking the excruciating extra pains to fashion for themselves the exact image of *their* Bach, the crooked performers help us find *our* Bach—whom we can feel personally close to, and love.

ANTIQUARIAN
INNOCENCE

16

Report from Lincoln Center: The International Josquin Festival-Conference, 21–25 June 1971

Now that the International Josquin Festival-Conference has joined its protagonist in history, one is almost at a loss to fix on paper an adequate sense of the experience—engrossing, enlightening, exhausting, and ultimately ecstatic—which the participants and spectators underwent in the course of five days' total immersion in Josquiniana. The quality of the research papers and musical performances maintained a standard high enough to make the effort of sustained concentration a burden gladly borne. Moreover, the conference was provocative and challenging to the point of controversy, with constant discussion and argument filling the hours between sessions and concerts—making plain the ultimate wisdom of the decision to limit stringently partici-pation from the floor.

In his keynote address, Friedrich Blume summarized the state of Josquin research and called particular attention to lacunae in the composer's biography and to the need for a more certain establish-ment of authenticity and chronology in his works. Gratifyingly, many of the best papers addressed themselves to these problems. Among those dealing with biography, Edward Lowinsky, the festival's inde-fatigable director, gave a spectacular demonstration of the inspired speculation for which he is famous, in "Ascanio Sforza's Life: A Key to Josquin's Biography and an Aid to the Chronology of His Works." By assuming a far longer-lasting relationship between Josquin and As-canio than is documented, Professor Lowinsky putatively filled many

Originally published in *Current Musicology* 14 (1972): 47–64. Reprinted by permission of *Current Musicology*.

gaps in our knowledge of the composer's life. On the other hand, Herbert Kellman, in his virtuoso diplomatic study, "Josquin and the Courts of the Netherlands and France: The Evidence of the Sources," showed that virtually every date hitherto presumed certain in Josquin's post-Ferrarese biography is still open to more or less serious question. Thus, somewhat frustratingly, the two most "creative" biographical papers served in very different ways to increase the preponderance of hypothesis over fact in our knowledge of Josquin's life. Not until Lewis Lockwood's careful and detailed study, "Josquin at Ferrara: New Documents and Letters," were any positive additions to this knowledge offered.

It was thrilling to see the state of knowledge of Josquin's life and work change before one's very eyes. From the first day papers were hastily revised before delivery in the light of findings presented in others. For example, in his witty but impressively acute paper, "Problems of Authenticity in Josquin's Motets," Edgar Sparks challenged the attribution to Josquin of six motets which exhibit in common a curious "Satzfehler" (Osthoff): the simultaneous sounding of a suspension and its resolution. One of these motets, *In illo tempore stetit Jesus*, was to figure prominently in a later paper. But so convincing had Sparks's arguments been that it was deemed no longer possible to ascribe the work to Josquin, and the later report was modified so as to exclude it from consideration. Arthur Mendel's "Chronology and Authenticity: Some Attempts to Apply Objective Style Criteria" was a progress report on computer programs devised to reduce the labor and widen the possibilities of deductive inquiries such as the one Professor Sparks so painstakingly carried out.

Similarly challenging were the papers devoted to interpretive criticism. Saul Novack presented a Schenkerian analysis of several motets which succeeded in demonstrating "Tonal Tendencies in Josquin's Use of Harmony" without, for once, conjuring up the shade of Procrustes, even when Professor Novack was so bold as to refer to *Levavi oculos meos in montes* as an incipient chaconne. In Professor Novack's well-chosen examples (particularly in *Absalon fili mi*), where tonal analysis worked so much more efficiently than modal analysis in elucidating Josquin's plan, the paper's title seemed fully justified.

But over and above the excellent contributions to "pure" scholarship (and there were many—Professor Lowinsky promised that the proceedings of the conference would be published, and so I will pass over several which otherwise would have called for comment), the Josquin Festival will be most vividly remembered for its emphasis upon practical matters of vital interest. Six of the thirty papers dealt in some way with performance, and workshops on performance and editing occupied the afternoon sessions. Most important, the festival was graced by the presence of four distinguished performing groups: New York Pro Musica (NYPM), Prague Madrigal Singers (PMS), Schola Cantorum Stuttgart (SCS), and Capella Antiqua München (CAM). An unprecedented interaction between scholars and performers devoted to Josquin thus provided the real theme of the conference.

Opinion differed as widely among the scholars as among the performers as to what a performance of Renaissance music should be. Ludwig Finscher opened his address, "Historical Reconstruction versus Structural Interpretation in the Performance of Josquin's Motets," with the remark that he expected little agreement from his listeners. He went on to state that a performance for today's audience should strive above all for "idealization" and elucidation of structure regardless of what Renaissance performance practice may have been. Professor Finscher scorned the insistence upon historical instruments and voice production; he argued instead that such structural features as cantus firmus and canon be brought out in performance by whatever methods seem effective. In view of the overwhelmingly positive reaction to his paper, one surmises that his opening caveat was addressed primarily to Nanie Bridgman, who had preceded him on the session's agenda with a report "On the Discography of Josquin and the Interpretation of His Music in Recordings." Mme. Bridgman gave voice to a number of personal observations on the performance of Renaissance music, her major desideratum being, as she put it, "aesthetic asceticism." And she expressed her particular disapproval of "bringing out" cantus firmi. The weight of opinion at the conference was clearly on Finscher's side, but the exchange indicated that, even among distinguished musicologists, performance practice of Renaissance music, in sharp contrast to Baroque, is taken at present to be a matter of individual preference. That objective criteria are not generally acknowledged was amply demonstrated at the workshops and the concerts.

Frank D'Accone's paper, "The Performance of Sacred Music in Italy during Josquin's Time, ca. 1475–1525," attempted to establish some positive data about performance practices, but many problems raised by implication in the course of the report served only to point up the vexed nature of the question. Professor D'Accone traced the changing number of singers employed in various Italian churches and cathedrals over the fifty-year time span defined by his title. The information presented was impressive in sheer bulk, but of limited practical use, as the following example will illustrate. During Josquin's tenure as a singer at the Milan Cathedral, 1459–73, the choir averaged seven members. D'Accone did not make it clear whether all of these singers performed polyphony or if some were engaged solely

to perform chant, but let us assume that they all would have participated in a performance of a work like *Missa L'Amy Baudichon*, which
Josquin is assumed to have written there. The composer thus conceived his Mass for an ensemble that would probably have employed
about three "soprani" on the top line and soloists on the remaining
parts. But when the Mass was published by Petrucci in 1505, the
membership of the Cathedral's choir numbered eighteen, an increase of
more than 150 percent. And as early as 1492, St. Mark's in Venice, where
the Mass was published, employed no fewer than twenty-seven singers.
Since widespread performance of Josquin's works was presumably
spurred by their publication, does this mean that those performing
Missa L'Amy Baudichon from Petrucci's print were using "unauthen-
tically" large forces? Or, conversely, is a modern performance of this
Mass by a group consisting mainly of soloists more "authentic" than the
majority of performances the Mass received within the composer's
lifetime? If we argue that both are equally authentic, since "contemporary practice" admitted the adaptation of music to the forces at hand,
what is to prevent the Mormon Tabernacle Choir from claiming equal
authenticity upon the same grounds, in the perhaps not imminent
event that they should wish to perform the work?

However, an acknowledgement of the many quandaries into
which we are led in pursuing the question of Renaissance performance practice is a far cry from asseverating that in old music "anything goes." Yet, while no self-respecting musicologist or performer
would publicly quarrel with this, no one appeared willing to attempt
to set standards, not even at the workshops which seemed designed to
provide an excellent opportunity for just that.

Tuesday afternoon's "Workshop on the Performance and Interpretation of Josquin's Motets" brought the two German performing
groups face to face on the stage of the Juilliard Theater in a session
directed by Professors Finscher and Kirsch of the University of Frankfurt, with the additional participation of Professor Mendel as discus-
sant. The *modus operandi* adopted virtually assured the failure of the
workshop insofar as establishment of performance standards and
criteria were concerned: the two ensembles performed each piece in
immediate succession, giving the session the untoward atmosphere
of a contest. Apparently out of consideration for the feelings of the
performers and their understandably uncomfortable situation, the
directors of the workshop went out of their way to avoid comparative
evaluation of the musicians' work, or even a clear statement of their
own views. Nowhere was there evidence of the "argument and scholarly hair-pulling"[1] that the *New York Times* assumed would be part of

[1]26 June 1971, p. 20, col. 2.

any confrontation between musicologists and performers, although Professor Finscher had given strong expression to his viewpoint the day before and even seemed at that time to invite deliberately the controversy that failed to arise at the workshop.

Also most unfortunate was the ease with which the musicologists on stage allowed themselves to be sidetracked by petty and peripheral concerns, such as "If one verse of a hymn is set by Dufay and the other by Josquin, should the cadences of Dufay's verse be performed with doubled leading tones?"—an interesting point, to be sure. But was it really worth three-quarters of an hour's time, while more than thirty talented musicians sat silent upon the stage they had crossed an ocean to reach? It is sadly amusing that no voices were raised when CAM finally performed not only Dufay's verse with doubled leading-tone cadences, but Josquin's as well! Clearly, the directors of the workshop were content with mere theoretical argument, and actual performance mattered little to them. The presence of the performers was made to seem, infuriatingly, superfluous, and it took a vociferous interruption by one noticeably aroused member of the audience before the closing piece, *Paratum cor meum*, could be heard at all.

The first motet on the agenda was the newly discovered setting by Josquin of the second polyphonic verse ("Monstra te esse matrem") of the alternatim hymn *Ave maris stella*, preserved along with Dufay's three-part setting of the verse "Sumens illud ave" and two other polyphonic verses presumably by Josquin in Cappella Sistina, Ms. 15. Josquin's setting takes the form of a canon between superius and tenor on a slightly decorated paraphrase of the original chant, accompanied by a typically active and nonthematic altus and by a bassus that occupies a middle ground in style and function. I am aware that this description of the texture betrays a "structuralist" bias on my part in its assignment of subordinate roles to the nonparaphrasing parts. That this is by no means a self-evident interpretation of the meaning of Josquin's polyphony was demonstrated in the performance by SCS, which exactly reversed the perspective implied above. Dr. Clytus Gottwald, the group's conductor, explained that since the altus differed so radically in rhythmic activity from the other parts, he felt it should occupy the foreground. The resulting performance was a study in lyrical cantilena, which totally obscured the canonic writing in an admittedly beautiful blend of voices. This writer's opinion that this performance was wrong-headed and arbitrary was widely shared among the spectators, but CAM's performance, at the other extreme, also gave rise to controversy. The director, Konrad Ruhland, assigned voices only to the canonic parts and assured their prominence by relegating the altus and bassus lines to stringed instruments. At this point, one had to wonder whether structural clarity necessitated such a drastic imbalance of texture; the part with the greatest intrinsic musical interest was all but inaudible. Thus the rendition seemed more an analysis or a demonstration of Josquin's methods than a performance of the piece. An extreme structuralist view can, it appeared, falsify a composition just as thoroughly as an antistructuralist conception. Neither performance succeeded in illuminating the motet's texture; they merely spotlighted one or another aspect of it.

Absalon, fili mi was clearly chosen for the workshop because of its problems of range. The oldest source, British Museum, Royal 8, G VII, pitches it at a very low extreme, taking the bassus part down as far as Bb, while the other sources, German prints of the mid-sixteenth century, transpose the piece up a ninth, taking the superius up to *a″*. SCS attempted the motet at the low pitch. Throughout the performance one was uncomfortably aware of the strain to which the performers were submitting their voices in the execution of this tour de force. There was little linear clarity and a pinched, irritating tone color, showing that the performers cared only that the piece be done "as written," not that it be done well. Their literal interpretation of the notation assured them, at best, a Pyrrhic victory over the obstacles they thus had to face. Although Professor Lowinsky argued that optimal clarity and resonance were obviously not Josquin's intentions in writing this lament, there must be room for sufficient compromise so as to assure, at least, that the pitches themselves be minimally audible. CAM, on the other hand, opting for the later source, whose clefs they interpreted correctly as *chiavetti*, performed the motet a sixth higher, in G. However, the welcome improvement in tone quality and clarity of texture was achieved at the expense of the extraordinary somberness and atmosphere of the original low range. Clearly, the motet should, for best results, be performed by a male choir singing "as low as possible." Exactly how low this may be for a given performance must obviously be fixed by the director's practical, rather than theoretical, judgment of what is, to him, the minimum acceptable level of clarity and resonance. There was a certain reluctance to accept such a "subjective" yardstick on the part of some participants. Yet since pitch in the Renaissance was far from absolute, a literal interpretation is no less an arbitrary choice.

The major performance problem in the *prima pars* of *Stabat mater dolorosa* is the projection of the text. Professor Mendel pointed out the unusually high proportion of "bad" declamation in the motet, i.e., the setting of unaccented syllables to longer note values than accented ones, or their placement in strong metrical positions. To show that this was not simply due to carelessness on the composer's part, Professor Mendel played a tape of the text of the sequence as read by a Frenchman, in which the tonic stresses were smoothed out, or shifted to the ends of words. He then suggested that Josquin himself pronounced and set Latin in this way. In its performance, however, CAM easily succeeded in imposing the correct accentuation upon the musical setting. Their rendition, which may be heard on Telefunken SAWT-9480-A, is, to me, a model of enlightened and accomplished performance practice in this and many other respects.

But despite the high quality of much of the music-making at the workshop, it was an ultimately dispiriting affair. The extraordinary mismanagement of the proceedings by the discussants, coupled with their insensitivity to actual, sounding music, was a discredit to musicology and raised questions, even in the minds of the most committed among us, as to the credentials of the scholar as critic.

Fortunately, Thursday afternoon's workshop on the performance of Josquin's secular music was directed by Howard Mayer Brown with much greater efficiency. A selection of materials including scores and a long list of suggested topics of discussion and questions about performance practice was distributed to the audience. Three groups were brought face to face: CAM, NYPM, and PMS. Once again, however, the contest atmosphere inhibited evaluation and criticism, and the participation of three ensembles made for considerable redundance.

The performances of *Adieu mes amours* differed mainly in the matter of scoring. The tenor and bassus parts of this chanson present a *cantus prius factus* in not-quite-canonic imitation, beneath a pair of freely composed voices which quote phrases of the tune from time to time but elaborate filigree patterns for the most part. All three groups interpreted the altus line, rhythmically the most active, as an instrumental voice, but only PMS performed the superius vocally. NYPM and CAM both prepared two versions: a wholly instrumental one, and one with the lower imitative voices sung (with instrumental doubling) and the upper voices played. The latter groups justified their scoring by noting that the lower voices were "structural" and the upper ones "ornamental." This is undoubtedly true, and their performances were acceptable in terms of sound and balance. But again, the narrowly structural approach led to a misrepresentation of the music, in this case by distorting the composition's connection with the fifteenth-century chanson tradition. The version presented was an ahistorical anomaly, justifiable, it would seem, only when historical fidelity is impracticable. Needless to say, there is much room for argument in deciding when such is the case. The performers, even PMS, cited the superius line as being not only ornamental but also "instrumental" in character. This seemed to be a facile judgment, based upon a tacitly patronizing attitude toward the supposed technical limitations of Renaissance singers. Too often the mere appearance of eighth notes in a part is taken as a cue for instrumental rendition, and the result can be ludicrous. Witness the performances of Burgundian chansons, happily no longer so common as they once were, wherein a recorder or an organetto is called upon to play all the melismata. If we examine the altus part of Josquin's chanson, however, we *can* observe objective features of idiomatic instrumental writing. One is the extreme scarcity of rests (i.e., breaths); another, the ambitus of an eleventh (f-bb'), as opposed to an octave (d'-d") in the superius. The relatively disjunct quality of the writing may be taken as further supporting evidence of instrumental character. In fact, as Professor Joshua Rifkin pointed out from the floor, there is good historical evidence that *Adieu mes amours* was conceived as an instrumental piece, pure and simple. But if it is to be performed as a vocal chanson, it should be brought into line with what we know the contemporary French practice to have been in pieces of heterogeneous texture such as this one. It is perfectly easy to "bring out" the canonic writing in the lower parts by means of instrumentation, or even by articulation. At Professor Brown's suggestion, the soprano of PMS sang the superius with the strings of CAM. Most agreed that even on a sheer sonorous level, this scoring was the most effective.

Heterogeneous scoring, one might add, is too often used as an easy substitute for artful phrasing in the projection of the texture of Renaissance music. A case in point was the contrast between the instrumental versions of *Adieu mes amours* offered by NYPM and CAM. Whereas CAM employed a homogeneous consort of stringed instruments, NYPM scored the piece as follows: treble viol on the superius, vielle on the altus, regal on tenor, and lute and greatbass recorder doubling the bassus line. Leaving aside the historical impossibility, on many grounds, of such a consort, what was truly disturbing was the utter lack of inflection within the lines in NYPM's performance. CAM, on the other hand, differentiated the parts most satisfyingly by means of subtle contrasts of legato and staccato, and by underscoring the rise and fall of lines by a very supple employment of dynamic nuances.

A problem of a different sort was raised by PMS's scoring of the chanson for singers on all parts except the altus, and the assignment of two recorders, playing, respectively, one and two octaves higher than the notated pitch, to alternate phrases of the altus line. When questioned as to the reasons for this grotesque scoring, Miroslav Venhoda, the director of PMS, cited the ironic text, which he felt was best expressed by the high pipes. A director's subjective predilections, however, must never be used to justify a scoring which is objectively unresonant and obfuscating of texture. Venhoda's scoring failed simply as instrumentation, because of the disconcerting inversion of all the intervals between the two upper parts that resulted from the transposition of the altus above the range of the superius (to say nothing of the arbitrary register changes within that part). Even more serious was his disregard of what my experience has suggested to be a primary and all-but-inviolable rule in scoring for voices and instruments in textures of three or more parts: if voices and instruments are to be mixed, it is absolutely essential that an instrument play the lowest part, whether or not that voice is sung. If the lowest part is not played, instrumental colors on higher parts will sound unsupported and will adamantly refuse to mesh with the voices. An out-of-tune performance is virtually guaranteed, as well. And that is what we heard.

Plus nulz regrectz was performed by CAM first chorally, a practice which, although probably not "historical," was fully justified by the excellence of the rendition. Asked to give another version (why it was assumed that there *had* to be more than one equally valid way for each group to perform each piece was a mystery to me), CAM offered a version which matched their vocal rendition of *Adieu mes amours* — stringed instruments on all parts, voices on the lower two only. This approach, presumably a "structural interpretation" (since again the lower parts are largely imitative), was puzzling, for the upper parts of this work are just as imitative as the lower ones. In addition, the four parts are quite similar in rhythmic motion, and there is no *cantus prius factus*. CAM's second version was thus a "pseudostructural" interpretation, implying a structure that simply was not there. NYPM's performance by four vocal soloists convinced most listeners that this is the ideal medium for this late work, with its fairly homogeneous texture and predominantly syllabic prosody.

A few modestly decorated cadences in NYPM's instrumental version raised the question of ornamentation in Josquin's music. Professor Lowinsky vigorously opposed its application, on the grounds that Josquin's "fioritura," like Chopin's, is far more supple and inventive than the stereotyped patterns of conventional embellishment, and concluded with the old apocryphal story about Josquin's rage at a singer who dared tamper with his music. Paul Maynard, director of NYPM, defended the use of ornamentation, for his musicians at least, on the grounds that they were so proficient in its use. In their performance of *Je ne me puis tenir d'aimer* — with a typically outlandish instrumental ensemble consisting of regal, bass flute, vielle, lute, and bass viol, respectively, from top to bottom — the player of the superius proceeded to demonstrate NYPM's embellishing acumen in a rendition which convincingly supported Professor Lowinsky's contention that those who cannot enhance a piece by means of ornamentation had best leave it alone. What was most exasperating, however, was that this musician continued his wooden embellishments the next time around, when all the parts were joined by singers, in flagrant violation not only of the explicit injunction of every Renaissance (not to mention Baroque) writer on ornamental practice, but of simple good sense as well.

Finally, each group was asked to prepare *Fortuna d'un gran tempo* three different ways: first with no ficta, second with Professor Lowinsky's solution, still controversial after almost thirty years, and third with a new solution by Jaap van Benthem, as published in *Het Orgel*. Everyone acquainted with the piece has by now more or less made up his mind about its problems of musica ficta. Therefore, little controversy was generated, not only because a debate at the previous day's editing symposium had centered around *Fortuna* but also, most unfortunately, because a cavalier attitude toward ficta had been encouraged throughout the workshop by Professor Brown. Typical of his view was his remark, vis-à-vis the highly inconsistent, even illogical employment of ficta in NYPM's performance of *Plus nulz regrectz*, that "the world had not come to an end" because of it. If one of the most distinguished musicologists in the field of Renaissance performance practice upholds, however facetiously, the idea that musica ficta is a wholly arbitrary and subjective matter, then it is small wonder that hardly any performer has taken the trouble to master its rules, or even acknowledges that such rules exist. Needless to say, there are countless instances of ambiguity in the application of the rules of ficta, where more than one equally valid solution is indeed possible. And there are even cases where the rules of ficta contradict one another. But there are also many situations in which the hand of the performer is forced by the composer, and it is the performer's duty to be aware of them.

Friday's "Workshop on the Performance and Interpretation of Josquin's Masses," under the direction of Arthur Mendel, took an approach radically different from that adopted at the other workshops. Gone was the contest atmosphere. The three groups present— NYPM, PMS, and SCS—did not compete in the performance of the same pieces but rather were used to illustrate various specific problems of execution as represented by selected movements.

The famous triple mensuration canon which constitutes the second Agnus of the *Missa L'Homme Armé super voces musicales* was manfully attempted by PMS. The imprecision of the performance—the basses were unable to maintain their duple division of the beat against the triplets of the top part—certainly demonstrated the piece's difficulty. Professor Mendel called attention to two sixteenth-century solutions to the rhythmic problems of the music, which are both published in an appendix to the Smijers edition of the Mass. The first, from the

Dodekachordon of Glareanus, divides the note values of the superius part so that there is always a note beginning on the half-measure; thus the entire piece can be conducted "in two." The other solution, found in a Berlin manuscript (mus. theor. 1175), seeks to finesse the issue by rewriting the triple rhythms of the superius into duple meter. This solution effectively rids the piece of its difficulties but obviously throws the baby out with the bath water. At any rate, the investigation showed that "three against two" was a problem then as now. But that the problem is not an insurmountable one was demonstrated by SCS in their concert the night before in an almost flawless performance of the even more difficult *sesquitertia* passage at "Qui cum patre filioque" in the Credo of the *Missa de Beata Virgine*.

Another perplexing performance problem attacked at Friday's workshop involved the tempo implications of mensural signatures. Various inconsistencies in the notation of *Missa L'Homme Armé super voces musicales* were pointed out, and their ramifications were explored. The tenor, notated in augmentation, takes the minim as its beat throughout the Mass. The question was whether the absolute duration of this minim should be constant throughout. It was observed, both in the PMS performance of Agnus III and in NYPM's performance of the entire Kyrie, that this approach led to almost unmanageably fast tempos in those sections in which the other voices are notated in diminution. It appeared sensible to interpret signs of diminution, where they do not coexist with normal mensuration signatures within a movement, to mean simply (though vaguely) *più mosso*, and not to attempt a literal realization of their exact proportional significance.

Two ubiquitous and eminently practical problems—text placement and musica ficta—were approached strictly from the historian's point of view. Here the results were far from impressive. A comparison of all the sources for the Gloria of the *Missa de Beata Virgine* showed a fair consistency in the placement of ligatures, indicating that in most cases they perhaps ought not be broken when fitting text to music. But this is not a really helpful finding, since the rhythmic motion in Josquin's music is based upon a semibreve tactus, so that ligatures are too rare to be taken as a guide. And when a detailed comparison of the actual text placement in half a dozen sources for passages in the Masses *Fortuna Desperata* and *Pange Lingua* was presented, it proved only what most of us suspected anyway—that historical precedent is really of no assistance in the underlay of text. A more fruitful approach to the problem might have been found in investigating what makes for an effective solution, rather than in chasing the chimera of authenticity. Besides the general consideration of prosody and declamation and their changing significance in

Josquin's evolving style, such a discussion could have included the potential role of text placement in the clarification of texture. Most discussions of text placement seem tacitly to regard the text as a necessary evil in melismatic music, essentially at loggerheads with composer and performer alike. Yet I have never encountered an instance where a truly thoughtful and creative underlay could not function to the enhancement of the music, bringing it rhythmically to life. As Professor Lowinsky has pointed out in the introductory volume of his edition of the Medici Codex, otherwise obscure points of imitation can be illuminated by an apt matching of verbal to musical phrases. My own experience has shown that there is no more potent device for bringing out the cross rhythms, syncopations, and other textural intricacies which characterize the florid Flemish style of the fifteenth and early sixteenth centuries than canny deployment of the text in melismatic passages. Such an approach demands a thorough study of the rhythmic properties of each line on the part of the editor/performer, but it seems that such should be the true purpose behind the underlaying of the text for modern performance.

Finally, the question of musica ficta was addressed from a similar precedent-seeking standpoint. Eight sources of the Credo of the *Missa de Beata Virgine* were examined for explicitly notated flats arising from the realization of the chant-derived canon at the lower fifth. While it was interesting to observe that such explicitly notated accidentals were far more abundant in Northern than in Italian sources, the implications of this finding were not conclusive with regard to the application of ficta, for there is no reason to assume that flats not indicated in the Italian sources would not have been supplied in performance. The performances by SCS of four "historical" versions from these sources were not without interest, but the experiment was essentially unmusical. None of the versions constituted a convincing performance, because for demonstration purposes the singers were instructed to perform only those B♭'s which the various sources prescribed, leaving unflatted those B's which any performer, anywhere and anytime, would have adjusted as a matter of course. The results in each case were thus so riddled with obvious solecisms as to defeat the purpose of the demonstration, if in fact it had any purpose beyond the satisfaction of a purely academic curiosity. What made Friday's workshop ultimately unsuccessful, then, was over-reliance on historicism. The threshold of irritation was reached when, in conjunction with the underlay and ficta experiments, two of Professor Mendel's students read ostentatious and time-consuming reports on their collation projects. This scholastic busywork, unfinished scholarship at best, made no material contribution to the matters at hand. The research was inconclusive, and this could have been merely stated.

Yet despite such occasional lapses into pedantry, the festival-conference was structured first and foremost around Josquin's music as a living, aural experience, assuring the event a vitality and interest that greatly transcended the purely musicological. An excitement and enthusiasm which *The New York Times* found nothing short of "astounding" attended the four completely sold-out all-Josquin concerts at Tully Hall which made up the "festival" component of the Josquin week. Hearing interpretations embodying such widely varying approaches and virtues was a tremendously potent stimulus to the imagination, and the impact of these concerts will probably outlast anything else that transpired during the gathering.

The style and approach of the New York Pro Musica, which gave the first concert on Monday night, was certainly the most familiar to all. The group's personality has changed little since the death of Noah Greenberg and remains a reflection of his taste. Their performances thus tend toward lively tempos, colorful scoring, and great professionalism in stage deportment. The instrumentalists are all highly versatile, and the singers, assisted in the present concert by alumnus Arthur Burrows, are all highly cultivated soloists. These virtues were all welcome in the concert, which was of fairly inordinate length—two Masses, five motets, and eleven secular pieces. When the music suits their style, as in secular pieces like *Una musque de Buscgaya*, or the closing *El Grillo*, their renditions can certainly bring down the house.

But NYPM has an alarming tendency, also inherited from Greenberg, to turn their virtues into vices through exaggeration. Their tempos often exceed the feasible, as was evidenced in the Osanna of the *Missa L'Amy Baudichon*, where the final melisma of the superius was breathlessly bungled both times. Similarly, NYPM's scorings can be self-conscious and undiscriminating mixtures of sometimes inappropriate colors, as in their instrumentation of the same Mass, particularly in the use of the specifically courtly lute, which betrayed a fundamental insensitivity to sacred, as distinct from secular, style; or the assortment of strange bedfellows—rauschpfeife, shawm, viol, organetto, regal—which made the graceful and lyrical *Que vous madame* a raucous and ill-tuned mélange. Versatility, too, has its price. In many cases one was aware that a performer was playing his or her second or third instrument; and too often the problem of merely getting through the notes, particularly on sackbut, vielle (played "da braccio"), and shawm, precluded paying sufficient attention to articulation, phrasing, or intonation.

It was not surprising, then, that NYPM's best performances of sacred music were also among their most restrained. *Tribulatio et angustia invenerunt me* and *Benedicite omni opera Domini Domino*, both sung without instruments, were highly effective realizations of the vastly contrasting moods. The performance of *Missa D'ung aultre amer*, scored simply for four solo male voices, bass viol, organetto, and regal, possessed the dignity that *Missa L'Amy Baudichon* lacked, without losing the clarity and rhythmic verve that characterize NYPM's work at its best. This performance seemed to suggest that a historically possible rendition works much better, at least, than one which arbitrarily and naively flouts history. Ahistoricisms lacking concrete artistic or practical justification are indefensible. Performing Josquin's sacred music with English horns and cellos may be perfectly acceptable; performing it with lute can never be.

In view of the fact that NYPM's scoring can be by turns their finest asset and their most egregious liability, one listened with the greatest interest when Paul Maynard, the group's director, explained his philosophy of scoring at a discussion preceding Friday afternoon's performance workshop. Mr. Maynard offered three desiderata in the use of instruments. First, he cited the sheer augmentation of sound which instrumental doubling offers, which he claimed was necessary to a group of soloists like NYPM, a large part of whose repertoire is in fact choral. Second, he remarked that instruments, particularly winds, are capable of more incisive articulation than voices and hence help clarify texture. And last, Mr. Maynard mentioned the "emotional" properties of the various instruments, which aid in the projection of the music's "emotional content." This final point was admittedly vague and subjective, but still an objection may be raised. If, in fact, instrumental colors have "emotional" connotations, then does not mixing them all together in typical NYPM fashion effectively neutralize them? As for Mr. Maynard's first two points, they betray, it seems, a number of misunderstandings. First of all, the addition of instruments manifestly does not increase sonority in the way Mr. Maynard suggests, unless they be made to play so much louder than the singers as to drown them out. Volume increases logarithmically with doubling; that is to say, it takes about ten musicians doubling a line to actually double the volume of one. What instruments can do is to accentuate selectively one line over another, but this is due to the contrasting tone color, and not to the increment in volume. When the various lines of a polyphonic piece are each assigned to instruments of different families, as in many NYPM performances, the lines are thus *all* radically differentiated in timbre. Texture is thus clarified, but not in a structurally meaningful fashion; this practice also contributes a great deal to NYPM's pervasively secular sound in sacred choral music. Doubling solo voices with instruments does not, then, substitute for a chorus, but rather makes for an even less "choral" sound than unaccompanied solo voices could achieve. Finally, Mr. Maynard's contention as to the greater clarity of instrumental articulation over vocal seemed only a confession that the tempos adopted by NYPM are often essentially unsingable. The music in question *is* vocal, after all, and if NYPM's voices cannot negotiate it at the tempo selected, then the tempo, not the voices, is at fault.

Inappropriate use of instruments also marred the performance on Tuesday night by the Prague Madrigal Singers, under Miroslav Venhoda. The ensemble was oddly arranged on the stage: the instrumentalists sitting in a separate group across from the singers, giving a misleading suggestion of antiphony and creating acoustical problems for the audience. Problems were thus created for the instrumentalists, too, as Mr. Venhoda kept his back to them and devoted all of his attention to the singers, whom he conducted seated at a wonderful positive organ (which required an assistant to man the bellows), borrowed for the occasion from the National Museum of Prague. The ensemble was quite ragged in spots, and it seemed that a more conventional seating arrangement would have improved it considerably. But the major problem was one of conception rather than execution. The instruments were used in a kaleidoscopic, sometimes almost pointillistic manner. Apparently, their participation was viewed as a wholly extraneous veneer of color, with neither structural nor even volume-enhancing function. I was told that the instrumentalists—four versatile "doublers" on recorder, krummhorn, cornetto, vielle, etc., two sackbut players, and a young woman playing what Thurston Dart used to call the "cellamba" (a fretless viol fitted with an endpin, bowed palm downward, and fingered with a constant vibrato)—were not regular members of the group but had been hired especially to accompany the singers for this appearance. Clearly, Mr. Venhoda has little experience with instruments, but evidently he felt (rather naively, it seems) that he had to bring some along to give his ensemble credence in the light of current musicological fashion and, especially, the presence of NYPM and CAM.

Most of those who heard the concert, however, agreed that it would have been better had he left them at home. The vocal group is a superb one, possessing excellent individual voices, particularly an unforgettable countertenor (Jaroslav Tománek), yet capable of a truly "choral" blend and sonority. To the extent that one could ignore the dubious contribution of the instrumentalists, one was treated to extremely well-balanced and well-paced renditions of such motets as *Virgo salutiferi* or *Misericordias domini*. As he averred in the workshops, and as could be plainly observed in the performances, Mr. Venhoda is a director who responds first and foremost to the text and is capable of extremely moving and communicative interpretations of Josquin's more "humanistic" works. But even in these his lack of savoir faire in the use of instruments created a barrier between the music and the auditors. And in the earlier, more "scholastic" pieces like *Ut Phoebi radiis* or *Missa Fortuna Desperata*, where structural clarity is of paramount importance, the music was virtually deprived of its backbone.

In contrast to NYPM, PMS is at its best in the sacred repertoire. (They are even susceptible to an occasional overreverent mannerism. For example, every final cadence was executed pianissimo, even in the Osanna of the Mass, which otherwise was performed most energetically.) In the secular pieces which closed the first half of the concert, one was aware that this group was somewhat out of its element. Unsophisticated scorings reached a nadir in *En l'ombre d'ung buissonnet* and *Allégez moy*, which, for many, had the unfortunate effect of canceling out the real merits of the motet performances which preceded them. In these pieces four solo voices were accompanied by no instrument except a pair of bongo drums played with gusto but without much skill or precision. Percussion in an otherwise *a cappella* performance is equally a questionable affair on historical or acoustical grounds, but what was most distressing was that the drums' pitch, which was completely unrelated to that of the singers, was agonizingly audible. These performances degraded the entire concert, since they displayed a shocking tolerance for amateurish, unpleasant musical results arising from a misguided concept of "authentic" performance practice. No director should allow "musicological" considerations to take precedence over his musical judgment. To do so is to regard "Renaissance music" as something different in kind from "music."

The Schola Cantorum Stuttgart, directed by Clytus Gottwald, provided, on Thursday night, surely the most puzzling, even disconcerting interpretations of the week. As Dr. Gottwald was at pains to point out before Friday's workshop, Renaissance music is not the specialty of this strictly *a cappella* chorus, which is mainly known for their performances of contemporary music. Not surprisingly, SCS's performances are ahistorical, not to say antihistorical. Their primary intention, as Dr. Gottwald put it, is to elucidate the "utopian" qualities of Renaissance music. By this he seemed to mean that they endeavor to lift the music from its historical context and present it as purely abstract tonal pattern, likewise disembodied from its original function. In fact, when confronted by Professor Mendel on Friday, along with Messrs. Maynard and Venhoda, with the question "If we could tell you exactly how Josquin's music was performed in his time, would that in any way influence your performances?," Dr. Gottwald gave the only forthright answer ("No."), in refreshing contrast to the disingenuous and self-justifying circumlocutions of his colleagues. He thus impressed everyone with his intellectual honesty but left one nonetheless unconvinced that his was a valid approach to the performance of

Renaissance music. No positive stylistic orientation was projected at the concert; rather, one tended to describe Stuttgart's renditions in negative terms: unimaginative, unstylish, unexciting, uninteresting. In reevaluating the concert in terms of the revelations of the next day's roundtable, one was struck above all by the fact that a challenging "modern" concept of performance yielded tangible results that were indistinguishable from the efforts of the pious and pedestrian Early Music pioneers of a generation ago. In short, whatever their motivation, the performances of SCS are "old-fashioned" (but, one hastens to add, not old-fashioned enough) in actual, audible fact.

A detached, impersonal objectivity characterized SCS's performances, governed by an aesthetic point of view which Dr. Gottwald attributed to Stravinsky's influence—"expression by means of no expression." Specifically, this approach was revealed in matters of tempo and dynamics, which remained all but unvaried throughout the concert. But *senza espressione* is no less an "effect" than *molto espressivo*, and the doctrinaire "refinement" of SCS's performances rather quickly degenerated into caricature. The resolute refusal to "characterize" the music ultimately falsified it, almost comically so when *Basiez moy* was treated in precisely the same manner as "Kyrie eleison." This is no longer objectivity, but insensitivity. Renaissance musicians (viz., Tinctoris) distinguished between at least three "styles," or tones: high (Mass), middle (motet), and low (chanson), a distinction conditioned primarily by the degree to which the music was shaped by its text: the greater the bond, the lower the style. To adopt the lofty style arbitrarily as the only valid approach to Renaissance music, as SCS does, is at once snobbish and naive. Utopian detachment in their case seems but a mask for inability to make distinctions. And it is hard to see how Dr. Gottwald's reliance upon aesthetic analogies to Stravinsky, Monteverdi, or Schoenberg ensures idealization of Josquin's music, which is his professed method and aim, any more than reliance upon the aesthetic of Liszt, Busoni, or Reger is the key to the essence of Bach.

The pitfalls of the SCS approach were made plain in their performance of the acrostic motet *Illibata Dei Virgo*, which closed the concert. The next day Dr. Gottwald informed us that he had adopted a "serial" dynamic scheme for the work. While it is true that one was aware of rather more dynamic variation in this performance than in others on the program, the rationale remained a mystery until Dr. Gottwald's announcement, and it cannot be claimed that his performance elucidated either Josquin's plan or his own. Of course, it could be argued that in a work so full of "secret" meaning and structure, a "secret" performance practice is wholly appropriate. But any composer or performer who indulges in hidden meanings had better make sure that the surface of his work is also comprehensible, if he is interested in more than mere sterile hermeticism. Josquin was certainly sensitive to this need. It is questionable whether the same could be said of Dr. Gottwald, on the basis of this performance.

A fair amount of controversy was generated at Friday's roundtable by SCS's omission of the Gregorian intonations from its performance of the *Missa de Beata Virgine*. In light of their general approach, it would indeed have been surprising if they *had* included them. Yet, even a utopian performance of the *Missa de Beata Virgine* is in need of the intonations, because both the Gloria and the Credo are based on the chants of which the intonations are the beginnings. In a very real sense, this Mass is musically, not just liturgically, incomplete without the Gregorian incipits, whereas a Mass based, say, on a secular tune would not be. Strangely, none of the participants in the discussion advanced such an argument, and all were willing to accept the premise that all Gregorian intonations are dispensable in modern performances. Mr. Maynard of NYPM even went so far as to say that the only reason his ensemble employs them is to forestall suspicion of ignorance. However, SCS's failure to include the intonations raised not so much the question of their possible ignorance of the existence of the intonations as the question of their possible ignorance of the Gregorian basis of Josquin's polyphony, for the canonic treatment of the Gregorian tenor in the Credo was also obscured in their performance. The frequent and arresting Phyrygian progressions e-f-e in the *dux* voice were most noticeable, but the surrounding voices were allowed to bury the answering a-b(♭)-a in the *comes*. The result was a most disconcerting asymmetry—antecedent without consequent. Is such a structural feature also to be passed over in a "utopian" realization? Just what, then, does Dr. Gottwald consider important?

Yet, the performances of SCS did possess merit. In music of a lofty style, including much of the Mass, SCS was capable of fully convincing renditions, characterized by a very well-balanced choral sonority and a precise, if not exactly energetic, enunciation of the often difficult rhythmic writing. Dr. Gottwald should be given credit, above all, for absolutely just calculations of metric proportions, particularly in the Credo, a hurdle not often successfully cleared by modern performers. In view of the admirable musical abilities of the performers, then, it was all the more irritating and confounding to see their interpretations fatally shackled by so rigid, doctrinaire, and ultimately unenlightened an approach to the performance of Renaissance music as was offered.

That it is possible to be both scholarly and human in approaching Josquin's music was at last gratifyingly attested to by the concert of the Capella Antiqua München, under Konrad Ruhland's direction, which closed the festival-conference on Friday night. This amazing group of seventeen gifted and dedicated amateurs has achieved, in the course of fifteen years of association, an enviable reputation and, what is more important, a magnificent cohesion and unanimity of purpose in performance (not to be confused with superficial polish, for the timbre of the individual voices is somewhat harsh, and the sound of the chorus, therefore, has a rough edge). The ensemble is capable of astonishing subtlety of rhythmic nuance and elegance of dynamic gradation within a relatively restricted range. Thus, they are at their best in a cappella performances of works of comparatively homorhythmic texture; their performances of the motets *Qui velatus facie fuisti* and *Sanctus de Passione* were, to my ears, the musical highpoint of the festival. Impeccable precision and intonation, coupled with perfect textual declamation and "speaking" rhythm, produced something more than music: a rapt and eloquent ritual utterance, which transcended the immediate environment.

CAM's performances of "lofty" and "low" style works, however, did not reach the rarefied heights to which they brought the motets. The complex textures of *Missa La sol fa re mi* naturally tended to inhibit their freedom of rhythmic and dynamic nuance, and the group was not altogether successful in attaining the sturdy architectonic solidity with which they sought to replace it. Part of the problem was undoubtedly their use of instruments, which reduced the complement of singers by almost a quarter (the group contains a number of vocal-instrumental doublers) and gave them, at times, unequal competition. The use of a quartet of strings, two Baroque violins (one of which apparently started life as a *pardessus de viole*), viola, and bass viol, seemed a particular liability; their sound refused to blend with the voices on their parts and interfered with resonance without offering any compensatory clarity of texture. Their effect was to diminish, rather than augment, the sonority of the ensemble, and the performance sounded small-scale and even somewhat tentative. What did emerge, thanks to Ruhland's lively though unexaggerated tempos, was the sense of fantasy and whimsy in Josquin's virtuosically inventive treatment of the five-note "Grundmotif," for which this Mass is famous. Yet in terms of sheer sound, the performance was far from satisfactory, and a similar imbalance and lack of resonance marred CAM's performance, almost identically scored, of the great setting of Psalm 50, *Miserere mei, Deus*. In fact, all the larger-scale works on the program sounded constricted and constrained. CAM's forte is intimacy.

Curiously, however, the secular music on the program, which was, after all, the most intimate, was the least successful group. Again, the instruments were largely at fault, simply because the players were not in sufficient control of them. The magnificent tandem of freedom and precision which mark CAM's *a cappella* performances are beyond the reach of the same musicians when they play rather than sing. One suspects, too, that Ruhland's imagination is excited by words above all, perhaps another reason why the predominantly melismatic Mass was less effectively performed than the syllabic motets. The carnival song *Scaramella va alla guerra* was unaccountably treated as if it were a *Tenorlied*. Only the "tune" was sung, surrounded, again, by inexpertly played instruments and accompanied by a tambourine, which seems to be de rigueur in any modern performance of a Renaissance piece of even moderately dancelike character. The rudimentary technique of the amateur percussionists abounding in Renaissance groups and the naive use to which their instruments are put, conjuring up visions of elementary-school rhythm bands, are factors which contribute to the considerably patronizing attitude one often encounters toward Early Music among today's professional musicians. NYPM (and, one might add, New York's Waverly Consort), almost alone among professional Early Music ensembles, have generally approached percussion with the seriousness it deserves (this was nicely demonstrated by NYPM's total abstinence from its use at their festival concert).

About the performance of *Mille regretz* which closed the concert and the festival I have nothing to say. Its placement on the program was a bit of sentimental showmanship that disarmed criticism, for in fact it did give voice to our feelings on taking leave of Josquin after living intimately with him for five days. We can only hope that the International Josquin Festival-Conference will prove to be the last "astounding" success of its kind and that in the future such widespread and enthusiastic interest in the work of medieval and Renaissance masters, which so astonished the *New York Times*,[2] may be taken as a matter of course. The giant step in this direction happily provided by the festival was the finest fruit that the heroic efforts of Professor Lowinsky could possibly have borne, and for this alone he deserves the boundless gratitude and admiration of us all.

POSTSCRIPT, 1994

This essay, the earliest in the present collection, is included not only as a memento of what still seems an epoch-making event,[1] but as a period piece in its own right. It dates from what (in essay 7) I call Early

---

[2] 24 June 1971, p. 32, col. 3.

[1] The proceedings were indeed published after some delay, and they include edited—heavily edited—transcripts of the workshops on performance practice: see *Josquin des Prez*, ed. Edward E. Lowinsky in collaboration with Bonnie J. Blackburn (London: Oxford University Press, 1976).

Music's age of antiquarian innocence, when performance practice was mainly debated in the context of vanished repertories, and was hence an entirely "academic" issue, far removed (or so it seemed) from the reach of the culture industry.

The author was an enthusiastic graduate student then directing the Columbia University Collegium Musicum and therefore bubbling over with bright ideas about performing old music. Like many graduate students he saw himself as independent-minded, even rebellious: but his thinking, all the same and all too clearly, reflected the tacit assumptions of his training and can stand as a benchmark by which to measure change. I am amused to see myself so eagerly pursuing normative criteria (my own, yes, but still normative—that is, binding on you), so confidently distinguishing hypotheses from facts, and so full of faith that the collection of facts (provided they were the right sort of facts) was the path to the secure establishment of norms. Like any twentieth-century modernist, I sharply differentiated the "structural" from the "ornamental," wholly unaware that the privilege I pompously attached to the former was a prejudice that characterized my time, not an ecumenical value to which a Renaissance composer, no less than a Columbia graduate student, inevitably subscribed.

Like almost everyone else at the time (and surely like everyone else at the conference), I assumed that one could analyze internal evidence objectively—as witness my fantastic assurance in what has turned out to be the entirely erroneous matter of "instrumental" versus "vocal" style. I shared the general horror at the "merely" arbitrary or (worse) subjective, and saw progress in terms of its assiduous elimination ("where subjectivity was, objectivity shall be"). The funniest line of all is the one in which I took a performing group to task for implying "a structure that is not there"; the words now ring doubly bizarre in the ear of one who has come to realize that musical structure is never "there."

By the time of essay 1, a round decade after the Josquin fest, my thinking had changed more radically than I realized, as witness the unsympathetic reference there to Prof. Finscher's paper, with its call for "structural interpretation." In 1971 the only choice seemed to be the one Finscher proposed, between "structural analysis" and "historical reconstruction." Some of us thought the two might be reconciled— which in reality just meant prejudicially assimilating the notion of reconstruction to that of analysis on the assumption that structure was an undeniable transhistorical fact. Now Finscher's alternatives seem equally utopian and anachronistic, because both are reifications: that is, both conceive music in terms of things, not acts, objects to which performances approximate rather than experiences to which scores give access.

One might expect that, having characterized authentistic performance as a type of modernism, I would now be inclined to revise my negative assessment of the SCS performances, which advertised themselves as modernist. But of course that presupposed an opposition ("modern" versus historical) where I now see identity (and an exchange of scare quotes: modern *as* "historical"). The SCS performances were the ultimate, openly "utopian," statement of the reificationist position: works, in their view, had an ontological essence that could be revealed only by stripping away the incidental trappings of history.

The concluding predictions seem wishful. So far from a great growth in interest in antiquarian musics since the seventies, there has been a notable decline owing to the co-option of the "historical performance" movement by the recording companies. As seems so inescapably obvious in retrospect, Early Music and the record industry are natural allies, reification playing directly into commodification (and mini-forces saving megabucks). The claim of authenticity becomes an earnest of "objective" consumer value. Could there be a better marketing ploy? That Hogwood CD *is* Beethoven's Fifth (don't laugh; he said it himself—see essay 8), and it's yours for $12.98. And that is what has driven Early Music away from early music and into the standard rep.

17

The Price of Literacy, or, Why We Need Musicology

MONTEVERDI: Madrigals, Book 2 (18).
Cologne Collegium Vocale, Wolfgang Fromme, dir.
(Georges Kadar, prod.) CBS MASTERWORKS (d) LP, IM 42131.

Non si levav'ancor/E dicea l'una sospirando; Bevea Fillide mia; Dolcissimi legami di parole amorose; Non giacinti o narcisi; Intorno a due vermiglie; Non sono in questo rive fiori; Donna, nel mio ritorno; Quell'ombra esser vorrei; S'andassa amor a caccia; Mentre io miravo fiso; Ecco mormorar l'onde; Se tu mi lassi, perfida; La bocc'onde l'asprissime; Crudel, perchè mi fuggi; Questo specchio ti dono; Non m'e grav'l morire; Cantai un tempo, e se fu dolc'il canto.

The performances on this record are beautifully sung, with impeccable intonation and ravishing (if a bit too consistently *mezza voce*) production; and they are beautifully recorded. It's not enough.

Monteverdi's second book of madrigals (1590), "restless and heterogeneous," as Alfred Einstein aptly called it, contains some of his best works in the genre: *Ecco mormorar l'onde*, one of the great nature descriptions in music; the hotly erotic *Non si levav'ancor* at the beginning of the book; the grandly motetlike *Cantai un tempo* at the end. Unlike most of the other books, it seems for some reason never to have been recorded in its entirety. It would have been here except that three of the pieces (*Tutte le bocche belle in questo nero volta, Dolcemente*

Originally published in *Opus* (October 1986): 44. Reprinted by permission.

dormiva la mia Clori, Ti spontò l'ali amor, la donna mia) were found (to quote the liner notes) "not congenial to the vocal tessitura of the five virtuosi of Cologne." In other words, they were pitched too high. That the singers never thought to transpose them was my first inkling that a naive literalism might have hampered their approach to the music.

To oversimplify a little, in Monteverdi's time the modern system of keys and key signatures had not yet been introduced. Composers, especially when writing for voices unaccompanied, still adhered in theory to the older "modal" system that recognized only four notated "finals," that is, finishing notes: D, E, F, and G, corresponding to four different "white-key" scales. By Monteverdi's time the E-scale (the "Phrygian") had become virtually obsolete, and C was often used as a final. The C-scale (we call it major) was regarded theoretically as a transposed version of the F-scale (the "Lydian"). In such transpositions, in fact, the modern key system was born. In the latter there are only two scales, major and minor, but each can have any of twelve different finals (now called tonics), for they may be freely transposed to any pitch level one chooses. Under the system Monteverdi used, by contrast, the scales were identified with and by their notated finishing notes, and written transpositions were few and highly circumscribed. (Compare a situation in which all major pieces were written in C and all minor pieces in A, regardless of the key in which they would actually be performed.)

As long as the music was vocal, this presented no practical difficulty, for (unless cursed with perfect pitch, in which case they have to know their clefs) singers can transpose at will by ear. (It was the rise of an independent repertory of instrumental music in the seventeenth century, more than anything else, that conditioned the formulation of the modern key system.) So for a Monteverdi madrigal, the apparent "key" was just a convention of notation; it had little or nothing to do with actual pitch. To say a given piece lay too high or too low would have been meaningless to Monteverdi and his singers. Because the singers in the Collegium Vocale Köln didn't know this, but applied their ordinary assumptions about notation (and, one suspects with a shudder, about "authenticity") to a repertoire in which such assumptions are inoperative, we have in effect been cheated out of three wonderful madrigals.

Another ordinary assumption musicians make today is that you play or sing what you see. And what these singers saw before them as they sang was the second volume of Gian Francesco Malipiero's controversial Monteverdi edition of 1927. This recording has forced me to change my mind about that edition—in fact, about all editions. Malipiero is the perennial whipping boy of the musicology proseminar; generations of professors have used his work as an object lesson for their students in what an edition of old music should not be. Its chief sin is held to be its profusion of editorial expression marks, dynamics, and tempo indications. Except for the last, which are enclosed in parentheses, Malipiero's additions are not obviously distinguished from Monteverdi's notes and rests, and this, we are forever being told with stern looks and index fingers upraised, is an inexcusable deception.

Stuff and nonsense, I always thought. Singers are not so dumb. They know that expression marks were not explicitly prescribed by composers in Monteverdi's day, and can take Malipiero or leave him. And at least they will not be misled by the bare appearance of an "Urtext" into thinking that there *were* no variations of dynamics or tempo in the performances of yore. Malipiero's additions, I thought, being the work of an experienced, intelligent, and gifted musician, were far preferable to the nonperformances that might result from their absence. That must have been his rationale, and it was good enough for me.

I never predicted what I would encounter on this record. These singers are indeed sophisticated enough to distinguish Monteverdi from Malipiero when it comes to expression marks. They do ignore them—and not always to the benefit of these rather polite performances. How then do I know they used Malipiero? Because every mistake in the edition is right there on the record! The misinterpretation of the mensural relationships in *Bevea Fillide mia*, the wrong accidentals prescribed there and elsewhere, and even the obvious typos (e.g., p. 64, B-flat for C in the bass, thirteen bars from the end of *Mentre io miravo fiso*; p. 91, A for G in the alto, ten bars from the end of *Questo specchio ti dono*) are all dutifully reproduced. Anyone who has studied elementary counterpoint will immediately know how to correct these mistakes; anyone listening with half an ear will at least know there are mistakes to be corrected. Not our "virtuosi of Cologne," though, who have been thoroughly trained only to look, not to listen, and who may have picked up from someone's history book that Monteverdi was a daring harmonist. One can blame old Malipiero for the mensural misinterpretations, perhaps, but no edition will save such robot-minded performers from their play-it-as-written ways.

What a price we've paid for our literacy, we Western Art Musicians. And the thing that hurts the most is the way musicologists are always being blamed for the literalism that bedevils music-making (especially Early-Music-making) today. It's a bum rap. The first thing musicology teaches you is to be skeptical, to go back to the sources, to think for yourself. Or at least that's what it tries to teach. And that's why Monteverdi needs musicology—to save him not so much from Malipiero as from the virtuosi of Cologne and from the conservatory that turned them into what they are.

18

High, Sweet, and Loud

GOTHIC VOICES: The Castle of Fair Welcome (Fifteenth-Century Courtly Songs).

Gothic Voices, Christopher Page, harp and dir. (Martin Compton, prod.) HYPERION (d) CD, CDA 66194.

MORTON: Le Souvenir de vous me tue. REGIS: Puisque ma damme/Je m'en voy. ANON.: Las je ne puis plus nullement durer. MORTON: Que pourroit plus. BEDYNGHAM: Myn hertis lust. BINCHOIS: Dueil angoisseux. DUFAY: Ne je ne dors. ANON.: En amours n'a si non bien. VINCENET: La pena sin ser sabida. ANON.: Mi ut re ut. MORTON: Plus j'ay le monde regardé. FRYE: So ys emprinted. CHARLES THE BOLD (attrib.): Ma dame, trop vous mesprenés. ENRIQUE: Pues serviçio vos desplaze.

Can it really be ten years since Christopher Page first proposed what seemed the unbelievable notion that "late medieval" (i.e., fourteenth- and fifteenth-century) part songs (*chansons*, in the strictly construed musicological sense) were (hence are to be) performed by voices unassisted by instruments? It seems only yesterday, but there it is in the October 1977 *Early Music*, that innocuous little translation with commentary of a passage in a treatise of 1392 by the *rhétoriqueur* Eustache Deschamps, who, it was claimed, was the nephew and pupil of Guillaume de Machaut. Page's explication of the obscure phrase "*la triplicité des voix pour les teneurs et contreteneurs*" suggested that the untexted tenors and contratenors of courtly chansons were to be

Originally published in *Opus* (June 1987): 36–39. Reprinted by permission.

vocalized, and that this—though perhaps not the only way such songs might or could have been performed—was at the time considered the best way of doing so, since Deschamps speaks in the same sentence of *"la perfection dudit chant."*

Ten years ago it seemed easy enough to laugh this off. Page was a philologist, after all, not a musician. If the tenors and contratenors were supposed to be sung why were they untexted? Why did they jump around so "unmelodically"? Besides, much of what we loved about Early Music and Early Music performance, as exemplified, say, by the work of the New York Pro Musica, the Waverly Consort, or Musica Reservata, was due precisely to the multicolored, exotic instrumentarium (what Richard L. Crocker once called the "fourteenth-century French gamelan"). When we tried to imagine an a cappella rendering of a Machaut ballade, let us say, by Pro Musica or Waverly Consort voices, vintage c. 1970, what our mind's ears heard was such a wobbly, raucous, ill-tuned affair, rhythmically and harmonically so ill-defined, that we could only conclude that (1) Page had mistranslated his source, or (2) his source was defective, or (3) Deschamps had a tin ear, or (4) all of the above.

Meanwhile the pesky evidence continued to mount. In 1982 Page was back with another *explication de texte* in *Early Music*, this time of a prose romance from the middle of the fifteenth century (*Cleriadus et Meliadice*) that contained several references to vocal performances of chanson tenors—that is, if *"tenir teneur"* really meant to sing it, not play it. If it did, then Dufay and Binchois would bite the dust along with Machaut. (Of course the familiar account by Mathieu d'Escouchy of the Banquet of the Oath of the Pheasant, held in Lille on 17 February 1454, had referred to a performance of the famous chanson *Je ne vis oncques le pareille* with a boy on treble and an artificial stag he was riding singing tenor, but the unusual circumstances made it easy to ignore as evidence of performance practice.) A year later, David Fallows published a very informative lecture he had given in 1981 at New York University, in which, among many other goodies, he had listed no fewer than nine literary references to all-vocal performances of polyphonic chansons of the period 1389–c. 1490 (the two previously cited by Page among them; see "Ensembles for Composed Polyphony, 1400–1474," in Stanley Boorman, ed., *Studies in the Performance of Late Medieval Music* [Cambridge Univ. Press, 1983]). This was getting serious. But still there seemed to be an unbridgeable (or at least an unbridged) gap between the "internal evidence" of the music and the "external evidence" of all the facts Page and Fallows were marshalling around it.

The bridge was at last provided by Gothic Voices, a group of singers who, under Page's direction, managed to suspend their disbelief and evolve a performance style for this repertoire consistent with his ideas on performance practice and with a sophisticated understanding of the role of courtly chansons in the context of late-Medieval aristocratic art. Their magnificent, ear-opening recordings (beginning with "The Mirror of Narcissus: Songs by Guillaume de Machaut" in 1983) have shown the skeptics among us, to our astonishment, to what extent our conceptions of this repertoire had been formed by unwitting prejudice: a model of voice production and vocal expressivity dependent, let us say, on the performances of Dietrich Fischer-Dieskau or Elly Ameling, and a model of instrumentation founded, if you please, on that of Spike Jones and his City Slickers. (I well recall the director of one New York Early Music group telling me with a wink, one summer's day in 1973, of how another such group "actually played [I forget which piece] all the way through without changing the scoring once!")

To find the appropriate expressive tone for any repertoire, one must begin by inquiring what its creators and performers sought to express. As historians of culture (among musicologists, most notably Gary Tomlinson of the University of Pennsylvania) remind us, such knowledge depends on the broadest possible setting of the music within not only its artistic, but its social, political, and economic contexts. The lyric poets and composers of the nineteenth century who brought German Lieder to their peak operated within a bourgeois (domestic and essentially amateur) milieu that rewarded the vivid exploration and projection of private, personal sentiments. In this genre, the music follows closely the fugitive images and moods of the poem, and the singer of such music must be able to modulate the voice through an infinity of gradations in intensity and tone color, with special emphasis on the soft, confiding end of the dynamic scale. The sort of sensitivity to nuance, to color, and to pacing required of a good Lieder singer can all too easily come to seem a universal value, applicable to any kind of love song. But the kind of expressivity appropriate to songs rendered *en publicque* before an audience of princes may have been of a rather different order, as Page suggests in his fascinating liner notes to the present release:

> In these noble and royal milieux the tone and technique of anything written in French, whether for entertainment or for edification, was much the same, and it did not matter if the work in hand were a romance of King Arthur, a treatise on tourneying, or a love-song in rondeau form. All had the ceremonial quality of an official proclamation, the formality of a diplomatic letter and the hyperbole of a scrupulous speech by an ambassador newly arrived at court. The formal and grandiloquent tone of these poems, together with the degree of craftsmanship which the author had brought to his chosen poetic form, usually mattered more than what the words of the poem actually said.

Indeed most of the poems recorded here have no more "meaning" to them than the leafy sprays and branches painted in the margins of fifteenth-century manuscripts. Like those gilded flourishes, an amorous rondeau fills a space in a gracious and conventional way.

What is "expressed" in these chansons, in short, is the quality of *hauteur*, that is, "elevation" (from which, by the way, we get our word *haughty*): elevation in tone, in diction, in delivery, all reflecting the elevated social setting in which the performance took place. *Hauteur* had two specifically musical meanings, too, which related metaphorically to the more general concept: highness of pitch, and loudness of volume. And sure enough, late-Medieval musicians never fail to echo Isidore of Seville's classic definition of a good singing voice as one that is "high, sweet, and loud." The word "sweet" may connote to us a nuanced production suitable for the emotionally expressive music of recent centuries. The formal, conventionalized public rhetoric described by Page suggests a different sort of sweetness, that achieved by the euphony of clear, uncomplicated, well-matched timbres, true tuning assisted by straight white tone, and extreme sensitivity to flexibly shifting rhythmic groupings.

That, at any rate, is what Gothic Voices have achieved, and the stunning results of their achievement are now available for all to hear on records. As Fallows, Page's scholarly coconspirator, has exulted, it is "difficult to avoid concluding that the secular music of the French [late-Medieval] composers comes across more clearly, more directly and more eloquently with voices alone than with the accompaniment of instruments." Amen, say I, at least when the voices are the Gothic Voices. Page's experiments have been an object lesson in the molding of a truly "authentic" approach to the performance of old music—that is to say, an approach that seeks to reconcile all evidence, internal and external (rather than choosing by dim lights between the one and the other), to take into account what is known of past taste but not to neglect present-day standards of good execution, and to fill the gaps between the facts with bold and challenging imaginings of one's own. To meet the last requirement means facing and conquering one's own musical prejudices—which means first of all acknowledging that one has them (usually they are what masquerade as one's "musical instincts")—and forcing an accommodation between them and one's historical beliefs. The result, if the whole process is carried out with honesty and supported by the technical competence needed to realize one's intentions fully, carries immense conviction and authority. And that is what authenticity is (or should be) all about. It makes old music sound new.

I mean this last point literally, for such historical re-creations as that proposed by Page and the Gothic Voices remain creations of the twentieth century, and we'll never know how close they really come to what they purport to revive. The fact that they convince us does not prove any historical point. There are certain very specific ways in which they are highly speculative, and many music historians will have reason to doubt them. For one thing, Page elects to text all the parts, including those that carry no text in any source. This means not only breaking up the ligatures in the notation (which, in theory, can carry no more than a single syllable of text), but also breaking up the longer note values into shorter repeated notes to accommodate the words. Over and above niggling points like these, there is every likelihood that the Gothic Voices' approach to vocal production and tone color is as much the product of current prejudice as the Ameling manner it seeks to supplant, for there is much twentieth-century music that calls for all the same qualities as those I listed above when describing the quality of the Voices' "sweetness." Unnuanced dynamics and tempo, too, are at least as Stravinskian as they are putatively Dufayesque, and a straight white tone (by his own specific request) suits Hindemith's music for vocal ensemble as well as it suits that of Binchois, as Page and company understand the latter.

So maybe we've just exchanged an Elly Ameling/Spike Jones style for an Igor Stravinsky/Paul Hindemith one. But even if so, the latter is still the more authentic of the two for this repertory, because it arose out of a fundamental rethinking of the repertory in its specific details, and on as close to its own aesthetic and historical terms as human nature and human epistemics allow, rather than from the acceptance of a standard of beauty or of audience appeal imported unreflectingly from past experience.

The proof is in the hearing, needless to say, and I suggest starting with the magnum opus on the record, Gilles Binchois's great setting of Christine de Pisane's ballade *Deuil angoisseux*, a lament on the death of the poet's husband. This is a very personal poem by fifteenth-century standards. Even Page admits that its "ambitions go much further" than those of the rest of the songs recorded here, and that it is a genuinely "moving" piece, transcending the stilted court conventions of its day. It is just as "formal" as any, however, and therein lies the key to its interpretation here. Our present-day "musical instincts" demand that laments be set to extra slow, extra low music, harmonically dark ("minor") or dissonant, and that it be sung with covered timbre and a greater than ordinary range of dynamic and tempo fluctuation. Binchois's setting flatly contradicts these assumptions. The time signature tells us (as fifteenth-century signatures do) not only its meter but its tempo—and the tempo is extra fast. It is in a mode similar to what we would call the key of F major—not exactly Schubert's first choice for lamenting. The vocal tessituras are not exceptionally low. The vocal ranges are exceptionally wide, though, which is the first clue that exceptionally emotional expressions are to be conveyed by adopting a tone of even greater *hauteur* than usual, as additionally suggested by the statelier-than-ordinary harmonic rhythm and the extraordinary dwelling (by the standards of the period) on sonorous full triads. The Gothic Voices—the singers participating in this piece (in descending order of range) are Margaret Philpot, Rogers Covey-Crump, Leigh Nixon, and Peter Harvey—emphasize these unusual traits by singing in an even louder, straighter-toned, and more open-throated manner than usual, producing an effect more in keeping with "the ceremonial quality of an official proclamation" than anything else on the record. It must have given goose bumps in the 1450s, and gave them to me, too. Historical gooseflesh is "authenticity" at its best and (in existential terms) most authentic, and the Gothic Voices have revived my hopes for the movement even as the latest blast of Hogwood hype (now he's "discovering Beethoven") threatens to reduce me to despair.

19

Text and Act

It isn't fair. The closer we get to old music, the more it seems to elude us. The more we strive to get it right, the more we seem to distort it. The very bent that impels us toward "authenticity" prevents our ever achieving it. As a new, very welcome, very disquieting recording of sacred music by the Renaissance composer Antoine Busnoys proves, the historical deck is simply stacked against us. But that's the least of it. Our musical difficulties are but the prelude to a moral quagmire.

A swift genealogy of musical morals will begin to suggest why this is so. In the beginning, music was something you did (or that others did while you did something else), not something you gazed at or bought and sold. A lot of music (we call it "folk") is still like that. But some music has been objectified as "art." It happened in four stages.

Stage one was literacy, which in the West, for music, only goes back a thousand years (twelve hundred, tops—scholars are still fighting this one out). In written form, music had some sort of physical reality independent of the people who made it up and repeated it. It could outlive those who remembered it. It could be silently reproduced and transmitted from composer to performer, thus distinguishing their roles.

Stage two was printing, which for Western music goes back almost exactly five hundred years. Reproduction became easy and cheap. Music could take the form of books, for which there was a collectors'—a gazers' and a traders'—market. It could be all the more readily thought of as a thing (reified, as philosophers like to say). The durable music-thing could begin to seem more important than ephemeral music-makers. The idea of a classic was waiting to be born.

Originally published as "The Trouble with Classics: They are Only Human" in the Arts and Leisure section of the Sunday New York Times, 14 August 1994. Reprinted by permission of the New York Times.

Its birth had to await stage three, which was a change not of means but of mind. With Romanticism came the idea of transcendent and autonomous art — art that was primarily for gazing, not for doing, and for the ages, not for you or me. Makers of such art no longer functioned in real time, and were no longer thought of as inhabiting this world. They were not mere doers but creators, and became the object of the reverence that is an immortal's due.

The ultimate stage, of course, was recording. A whole new category of music-thing came into being, and with it came whole new categories of passive music-gazers who could consume music without any doers' skills whatever. Music could now be commercialized to an extent previously unimaginable, yet it could be more completely classicalized and sacralized than ever before, too.

The existence of permanent musical records made possible the idea of a definitive performance, one that is fully tantamout to the work performed. Such a performance (we are persuaded) fully reifies the work, placing it tangibly in our hands in exchange for money. It achieves its aura — its power of persuasion — by claiming a total grasp of the creator's intentions and a total submission to the creator's will. Selflessness becomes the ultimate selling point. And that's what "authenticity" was all about.

But such a view of art is very recent. There is a vast conceptual distance separating our current musical attitudes from those that reigned when much of the music we now perform was new. When it comes to music that is more than five hundred years old, there is virtually no congruence at all between our performing and listening habits, products of half a millennium of reification, and those of the era that produced the music.

So what? Critically speaking, what is inevitable is irrelevant. In itself, anachronism need never be a vice. Old music, whatever its creators' intentions or its original status as "art," richly rewards the modern gaze. What does it matter if, say, a piece of ancient service music is now approached "aesthetically"?

The medieval church fathers may have had a legitimate problem with aesthetics, even if they did not know the word. Saint Augustine felt that he had committed "a grievous sin" when he caught himself, in church, "finding the singing itself more moving than the truth which it conveys." But an objection made sixteen hundred years later by a mere secular music critic ought to have some musical, not just theological, justification. And it should point to something fixable.

Busnoys, who died just over five hundred years ago, in 1492, was "first singer" at the court of Charles the Bold, the Duke of Burgundy. The recording that has prompted all these ruminations is a Dorian

CD (DOR-90184) that offers a larger helping of his work (over seventy-two minutes) than has ever before appeared on disc: four motets, three chansons and a complete Mass, all sung by Pomerium, a thirteen-voice mixed choir conducted by Alexander Blachly, who doubles, when needed, as priestly intoner.

They serve up the sounds Busnoys imagined most effectively. Tone and blend are crystal clear. Intonation is exceptionally good. The most finicky polyrhythms (including one so difficult that the composer saw fit to provide a simpler option) are rendered with precision. Diction is superb, and the Latin texts are given an attractively atmospheric Gallic accent. And the music? Suffice it to say that Andrew Porter, the distinguished former critic of the *New Yorker*, neither a specialist in the Renaissance repertoire nor a special pleader for it, once pronounced a motet by Busnoys "one of the loveliest stretches of music ever written."

A Busnoys motet combines beautifully detailed textures with vaulting architectural designs. Two on this disc follow tradition by adopting old church melodies as their foundation tunes: the Easter anthem *Regina coeli laetare* ("Rejoice, O Queen of Heaven!") and the Easter sequence *Victimae paschali laudes* ("Praises to the Paschal Victim"). The other two are unique, playfully dazzling conceptions. *In hydraulis* ("On the Water Organ") compares Busnoys's older contemporary Johannes Ockeghem with Pythagoras, the legendary inventor of music. Its foundation is a three-note formula ("Oc-ke-ghem"?) that is put through a gamut of Pythagorean speed and pitch proportions. *Anthoni usque limina*, a prayer to Anthony the Abbot, the composer's patron saint, is built around a single periodically sustained tone ("Gonnnng! Gonnnng! Gonnnng!" as the Pomerium tenors delightfully vocalize it) representing a bell, one of Saint Anthony's attributes.

The half-hour Mass achieves its impressive length by alternating bold sections in motet style on the Gregorian hymn *O crux lignum triumphale* ("Cross, O Wood Triumphant!") with limpid settings in the then-new "imitative" (that is, fugal) style—sixteen sections in all, organized in five larger units corresponding to the five major parts of the standard Mass text. But here is where modern notions of music-as-thing come into direct collision with older concepts of music-as-act.

It is a cliché of music history to compare the Renaissance Mass setting, with its five "movements" and its status as top genre of its time, with the Classical symphony. The manuscript choirbooks that contain such works present the "movements" in direct sequence, like those of a symphony, and that is how they are usually performed today.

But Renaissance choirbooks are not at all like modern scores, really. They are service books that store music as economically as possible for active use. Each voice part is separately inscribed for the individual singer's convenience, rather than with all the parts space-wastingly aligned for a reader's perusal. Modern editions, both those published and those prepared by modern performers for concert use, "score" the works in accordance with modern practice, and make them look more like symphonies than ever.

So it is easy to forget that the "movements" of a Renaissance Mass, though grouped together in the service book, were actually spread out in performance over the whole length of the service. Only the first pair, the Kyrie and Gloria, were sung in immediate succession. The others were spaced as much as fifteen or twenty minutes apart, with a great deal of liturgical activity, including other music, intervening.

For precisely this reason, the "movements" of a typical Renais-sance Mass were deliberately made to resemble each other as much as possible. They all begin exactly alike, feature the same foundation melody, and—how unlike the movements of a symphony!—follow similar or identical formal schemes. In this way the polyphonic Mass setting could adorn and integrate a festal occasion with periodic, inspiring returns to familiar, significant sounds. But take away the intervening liturgical activity and the uplifting symbolic recurrences amount to mere redundancy. The music, even Busnoys's music, and even when sung as well as Pomerium sings it, inevitably palls.

Pomerium would have presented Busnoys's *Missa O Crux lignum triumphale* in a manner at once more faithful to historical practice and more satisfying to the modern gaze if they had interspersed the four motets on their program between the five "movements" of the Mass, to stand in for the missing liturgical action. That way the Mass's built-in repetitions might have refreshed rather than wearied the ear. A scholar as well informed as Mr. Blachly is certainly familiar with the historical practice. And yet his loyalty, it seems, is to the Mass as an object, tangibly preserved in ink and vellum, rather than the Mass as an unfolding or an enactment. The anachronistic, reifying gaze has in this case prevented the display of Busnoys's work in the best light.

The same modern allegiance to text rather than act is responsible for the exaggerated restraint with which most Early Music per-formers approach their task, a restraint that neither accords with what we know of historical practice nor necessarily serves the mod-ern listener. Matters of taste and temperament may not be subject to dispute (as the saying goes); but this is not simply a matter of taste. It can be illustrated by a technical point.

As Early Music aficionados know, medieval and Renaissance singers made many little pitch adjustments in the music they sang. They called the practice *musica ficta* ("false music"). We would now call it adding unwritten "accidentals," sharps or flats. Anyone who has studied the historical source material knows that actual Renaissance applications of musica ficta were far more pervasive and fanciful (even, some might be inclined to say, obtrusive) than most modern performers dare attempt. Modern performers, trained to feel a far greater, far more limiting sense of accountability to written notes than their predecessors felt, give performances that have far less variety in pitch content than contemporaneous performances had.

Yet as every scholar knows, *varietas* was the highest of all virtues for Renaissance musical theorists. There are still those who think it is the spice of life. Yet by and large, our "classical" musicians are more comfortable with logical consistency than with capricious variety, and our performances are the poorer for it. When the practical sources of early music do show accidentals, moreover, modern performers feel not only licensed but bound to include them, however outlandish (and however dubious their pedigree). And so most modern performances of fifteenth-century music are basically gray with a few inexplicable splashes of shocking pink (like the weird chromaticism, a diminished fourth, that comes out of nowhere about a minute before the end of Pomerium's reading of *Victimae paschali*).

There is something even more troubling, though, about modern reification and sacralization of texts. Pomerium's Busnoys CD poses the problem in the most pointed and pertinent, even painful, fashion. The sixth verse in the text of *Victimae paschali*, as set by Busnoys, reads as follows: *Credendum est magis soli Marie veraci / quam Judeorum turbe fallaci*, which means, "More trust is to be put in honest Mary [Magdalen] alone than in the lying crowd of Jews." Sensible to its nastiness, and aware of its bearing on a history of persecutions, Mr. Blachly writes: "This verse has long been abolished from the Catholic liturgy, but to excise it here would render the piece unperformable. Despite misgivings, we have left the text intact."

Excising the offensive verse from the text would certainly not have rendered Busnoys's motet unperformable. There are all kinds of things one can do. One can vocalize. One can bowdlerize. (How about *peccatorum*—"of sinners"—instead of *Judeorum*?) One might even announce in the program notes that one has expurgated the text, show how, and say why. That would not be bowdlerizing. Bowdlerizing, by definition, is "silent."

Or one could substitute another text altogether. That would be what Renaissance poets and musicians called *contrafactum*, and they did it every day. (Saint Thomas Aquinas's famous hymn *Lauda Sion Salvatorem*—"Praise ye the Savior, O Zion," still sung in traditional Roman Catholic churches on the feast of Corpus Christi—is a contrafactum of the hymn from which Busnoys took the cantus firmus for the very Mass Pomerium has recorded.) Mr. Blachly surely knows all about contrafactum. So why not do it? Because then the performance could not satisfy modern artistic and commercial criteria. It would no longer be "definitive."

Yet if the Catholic Church itself has seen fit to expurgate the *Victimae paschali*, removing from it the verse to which Mr. Blachly calls attention, what should prevent musicians from doing so? What artistic or scholarly scruple should outweigh doctrinal ones, to say nothing of mere humane concerns? Do we really need to be (in this case literally and somewhat farcically) more Catholic than the Pope?

Those who say yes, I believe, have a misplaced sense of obligation, born of the platitudes that we take in with our modern educations. We are taught to think that masterpieces of art are more important than people, because people die but art endures. We are taught to think that an artist's primary relationship is not to other people but to something T. S. Eliot called "much more valuable," namely art itself and its history. As already observed in essay 4, Lincoln Kirstein, the venerable founder of the New York City Ballet, borrows his artistic credo direct from Saint Augustine: "I understand with complete certainty that what is subject to decay is inferior to that which is not, and without hesitation I placed that which cannot be harmed above that which can, and I saw that what remains constant is better than that which is changeable."

The trouble is that Saint Augustine's subject was religion, and Mr. Kirstein's is only art. Religion gives its adherents a sense of defeating their mortality; putting art in that position is an idolatry that only defeats our humanity, leaving us defenseless against the inhumanity that may be embodied in the works we venerate. When I try to account for the persistence of anti-Semitism in our culture, even among the educated, I cannot shake the notion that one reason must be the reinforcement anti-Semitism receives in so much art that is the product of Christian doctrine, bearing traces of its darker as well as its radiant aspects. The list of musical "classics" that fall into this category is long, from Bach's St. John Passion to Stravinsky's *Cantata*.

To regard such works as inviolable, not for their status as doctrine, but merely for their status as art, is an antihumanitarian blasphemy. To sacralize works of art is to place them above the human plane—and ourselves below. Artistic integrity is precious. It matters. But there are things that should matter more, even to artists.

FULL CIRCLE

20

Stravinsky Lite (Even "The Rite")

Competing "Compleats"

Sony Classical's CD reissue of the CBS Stravinsky Edition (SX22K 46290; 22 CDs) differs from the original 1982 centennial release in several details. Some are of documentary interest. These include substituting Stravinsky's own recordings as pianist for the those of others.

The first volume in Robert Craft's planned Musicmasters recording of the complete Stravinsky (01612 67078; two CDs) includes an early warhorse, *The Rite of Spring*, and Stravinsky's last major composition, *Requiem Canticles*, in which Mr. Craft competes against his own prior recording, executed in Stravinsky's presence. There are three major Neoclassical scores, *Oedipus Rex*, the *Symphony of Psalms*, and the *Symphony in Three Movements*, and three lagniappes, *Fanfare for a New Theater* for two trumpets, a Fanfare for Three Trumpets originally intended as the opening of *Agon*, and the Pas de Deux somewhat inexplicably excerpted from *Apollo*. The orchestra, where there is one, is the Orchestra of St. Luke's.

As a theorist of musical performance, Igor Stravinsky gave early voice to ideas that achieved widespread currency only decades later with the advent of the "Early Music" movement and its peculiar etiquette.

In his autobiography he asserted that "music should be transmitted and not interpreted," and that "an executant's talent lies precisely

Originally published in the Arts and Leisure section of the Sunday *New York Times*, 22 December 1991, 25, 31. Reprinted by permission of the *New York Times*.

in his faculty for seeing what is actually in the score, and certainly not in a determination to find there what he would like to find." The last of his Harvard lectures of 1939, published under the title "Poetics of Music," was a snooty sermon on the distinction between execution— selfless submission to "an explicit will that contains nothing beyond what it specifically commands"—and interpretation, which lies "at the root of all the errors, all the sins, all the misunderstandings that interpose themselves between the musical work and the listener."

The chief command involved musical clock time, namely tempo, precisely because, being quantitative, it was most easily objectified. So as to "determine for the future the relationships of the tempi and the nuances in accordance with my wishes," Stravinsky sought means of casting his wishes in aural stone. Of all composers, he was the first to recognize the documentary value of recordings.

At first he made laborious transcriptions for mechanical pianos that amounted to virtual recompositions. (A couple have been released on records, most recently *The Rite of Spring*, on IMP Masters 25.) After electrical recording was introduced in the 1920s, he made conventional records as pianist and conductor, but did his best to turn himself into a walking pianola. The advent of the LP in the late 40s meant remaking them (though now as conductor only), and the arrival of stereo a decade later meant remaking them yet again, this time with an eye toward creating a complete documentation of his oeuvre. This final legacy, supplemented where necessary by earlier recordings, has now been released on twenty-two CDs by Sony.

The irony is that as the wholesale documentation of a lifetime of wishes and commands neared achievement, Stravinsky lost the impulse that had set the project in motion. The totalitarian control mania of the 20s and 30s (so typical of artists—and others—in the confusing decades after the Great War), and the happy positivism that saw eternal fixity in numbers and machines, gave way to fatalistic resignation as Stravinsky became the Oldest-and-Wisest of composers. On the eve of his eightieth birthday, with almost five years of recording still ahead, a more humane Stravinsky finally admitted that nothing in this life was stable.

"If the speeds of everything in the world and in ourselves have changed," he wrote, "our tempo feelings cannot remain unaffected." He gave up the dictator's dream, realizing that the composer's is only one voice—a good strong voice, but only one—in the chorus: "The metronome marks one wrote forty years ago were contemporary forty years ago. Time is not alone in affecting tempo—circumstances do too, and every performance is a different equation of them."

Again he was prescient. The world of "historical performance" is currently in the throes of a humanizing counterrevolution. It is beginning to show signs of relativism and a mature recognition that tradition—that messy engine of change—is what maintains works of performing art in living repertory. But where does that leave Stravinsky's recorded legacy? If he is just one "interpreter" among many, how does he stack up against the competition?

The question is especially timely, now that Robert Craft, the composer's former interlocutor, ghost-writer, musical assistant, and executor, has unexpectedly declared himself a rival. A new two-CD Musicmasters set represents the hefty down payment on a promised complete Stravinsky that will document everything, all the way down to alternative versions and arrangements. It is meant expressly to supersede the composer's records, which Mr. Craft writes off as "largely unsatisfactory," owing to the aged composer's limitations as a conductor, the harried conditions under which he had to work, and the newness of much of the music, resulting in precisely the kind of uncertainty of style the composer feared most from his "interpreters."

Mr. Craft is understandably ambivalent about his former closeness to Stravinsky. On one hand, it is his chief credential, and he does not hesitate to trade on it, quoting the composer's avowal, from 1959, that his then official deputy was the best conductor of his works. The endorsement was understood at the time to be an aspect of their business association, their quasi-familial relationship and Stravinsky's professed distrust of performers. (Mr. Craft himself once allowed that Stravinsky "would tolerate no interpreter he could not control—hence . . . in conducting, his preference for a mere craftsman over a Bernstein.")

Yet having by now passed Stravinsky's age at the time of their first meeting, the erstwhile junior partner feels entitled to recognition as an authority on a par with his former employer. "I do not claim that my performances represent his wishes," the notes surprisingly assert. "Rather, and at best, they represent my present feelings and ideas about the music." Can we overlook the contradiction? Do Mr. Craft's present feelings and ideas truly represent an advance over Stravinsky's? Perched on his mentor's shoulders, does he now see further?

Regrettably, he does not. His performances are a step forward only insofar as they represent the measurable progress of the generalizing, sterilizing trend that until recently characterized all truly modern performance. Faithful to the old objectivity, Mr. Craft is still inclined to value the generic over the specific, the type over the detail. Insight, being personal, is sacrificed to know-how.

What gives these otherwise dull renditions an interesting twist is that peculiar resonance with "Early Music," now widely recognized as the exemplary modern way of performing all classical music. Roger Norrington's Beethoven, as Alice might have said, is moderner than Toscanini's, which was moderner than Furtwängler's, which was moderner than Nikisch's. Which is to say: it is fleeter, lighter, drier, brittler, more uniform in every way. And it is therefore less individually characterized, less particularly memorable, less consequential—which is precisely the way it wants to be, and the way the passive, distracted contemporary audience evidently needs it to be. In this sense the newly Crafted Stravinsky is close kin to the Norringtonian Beethoven.

On the simplest level the trend may be measured by the clock. Virtually across the board, Mr. Craft's tempos are faster than Stravinsky's (which, by the last go-round, were themselves often faster than notated). One might imagine that increased speed would heighten excitement and produce exhilaration—and sometimes, as in the finale of the *Symphony in Three Movements*, it does. (Stravinsky's recording of that work was one of his least successful anyway, a thing of shreds and patches and dreadful splices, despite some strong details.)

Yet the opposite is far more often true, because the acceleration usually entails a loss of stress, or—even worse—because it frustrates the rapt stillness that was one of Stravinsky's greatest gifts. Two celebrated instances of trance music in the pieces under review—the "Ritual Action" in *The Rite of Spring* (in which a spell is cast on the hypnotized "adolescent" to compel her fatal dance) and the transcendent coda to the *Symphony of Psalms* (where we are the ones hypnotized)—are ruined by Mr. Craft's kinetic tempos, between 20 and 30 percent faster than those indicated in the score.

Also pushed outlandishly is the famously brusque "Augurs of Spring" ostinato in "The Rite," where Mr. Craft is far more speedy—and correspondingly unbrusque—than any of the performances Stravinsky reviewed in 1964 and 1970, including one (Zubin Mehta's) he then pronounced "vitiatingly fast."

But how remote the esthetic of "The Rite" has become. Stravinsky's neoprimitivist ballet was written against a background of furious debate between proponents of European culture and advocates of primeval Slav immediacy. Debussy, for one, resisted it. To Stravinsky's face he praised "The Rite" as "a beautiful nightmare," but behind the composer's back he mocked it as "primitive music with all modern conveniences."

Little did he know! By now, its demon thoroughly exorcised, Stravinsky's masterpiece has become the very touchstone of assembly-line efficiency and well-schooled orchestral precision. It receives readings, even from student or semiprofessional ensembles—like Benjamin Zander's Boston Philharmonic, on the same IMP Masters CD as the piano roll—that are more accurate than Debussy (for Stravinsky) could ever have imagined at the time of the stormy premiere. But of course it threatens no one.

Mr. Craft's rendition of the culminating "Danse sacrale" is a triumph of know-how. Far faster than Stravinsky specified, it is probably faster than any orchestra could have managed the piece during Stravinsky's performing days, and faster than any on record except Mr. Zander's John Henry-ish effort to outpace the piano roll.

But was Stravinsky's holy dance meant to be dispatched with Nijinskian élan? Or should it represent a crushing, lethal strain the athletic young Orchestra of St. Luke's is obviously not feeling? And if the players don't feel it, will we? These strictures are not prompted by the mere authority of the composer's notation on his performances, to say nothing of his presumed opinion. They arise from the evident loss of contact (not Mr. Craft's alone) with the music's imagic sources and its expressive potential.

Sometimes it seems we may never get over Stravinsky's absurd half-century-old battle cry that music is "powerless to *express* anything at all." The joyless hand of the formalist still lurks behind Mr. Craft's ideal of extraordinary execution, exposing yet another link between routine modern and routine "historical" performance style.

The congruence is particularly intriguing here, since Mr. Craft conducts an ensemble known for its Early Music affinities (it is Mr. Norrington's orchestra, after all), and echoes of "historical" playing often surface unexpectedly in the sounds it makes. The exaggerated parsing of the string phrases in the Andante from the *Symphony in Three Movements* is just the sort of thing we get in Mozart these days; and the vibratoless string halo around Jocasta's recitative at the beginning of act 2 in *Oedipus Rex* might have come straight out of a period-instrument *St. Matthew Passion*.

Not that these touches are inappropriate; indeed, in a bizarre way they bring Stravinsky's "Neoclassicism" full circle. One would like to know, though, whether Mr. Craft called for them, or whether they arose serendipitously from the band.

What is most inappropriate and unfortunate is the flattening of the drama in *Oedipus*, a powerful "opera-oratorio," despite an excellent vocal cast and chorus, headed by John Humphrey (best known, it happens, for impersonating Bach's evangelists). Mr. Craft's tempos, conspiring with—at times producing—a lamentable absence of instrumental detail, rob the music of its force, if not its volume. One simply does not hear the individual pitches in the kettledrum tattoo accompanying the protagonist's fatal realization of his crime. One simply does not hear the searing reprise of the messenger's trumpet fanfares accompanying his third attempt to describe Jocasta's suicide.

These shortcomings could be the fault of the microphone placement (as is, one trusts, the horrible imbalance at the beginning of the *Symphony of Psalms*, where one of the most distinctive chords Stravinsky ever wrote is reduced to the thwap of the bass drum). Yet there are other indications that Mr. Craft is uneasy with the work's high—yes, down-right stilted—rhetorical style.

Those coy pseudo-explanatory interpolations by "Le Speaker" are a notorious irritant (though anyone who has heard Jean Cocteau himself summon the attention of the "Spectateurrrrrs" in Stravinsky's old monaural recording has surely never forgotten it). The solution, however, is not to amplify them in the interests of an unwanted colloquial "clarity" and assign them to a listener-friendly, slightly slurring, overdubbed but underrehearsed movie star, in this case Paul Newman. If, as Mr. Craft says, the postintermission reprise of the chorus in praise of Jocasta can be dispensed with in a recording, then so can the whole Speaker's role, especially if one is unconcerned to adjust its single musically notated moment—"the assassin of the *king-is-a-king!*"—to the tempo of the orchestra.

Mr. Craft appears more concerned with the proper pronunciation of the classical Latin text ("Oydipus!") than with projecting the full intensity of its meaning, though he is ready to discuss that meaning in copious irrelevant detail in his notes. True enough, Stravinsky often declared himself, as a composer, more interested in "syllables" than in "words"—but as a performer he did not slight them. *Oedipus Rex* was very well served by the composer's high-flown—yes, downright stilted—recording (complete with the frostiest Speaker you'll ever love to hate, John Westbrook), now back in circulation on Sony.

For what Stravinsky never did as a performer was undercharacterize, and that is why his recordings remain indispensable and often thrilling, whatever their status as documents. At particularly doctrinaire periods of his life he could be awe-inspiringly graceless and unyielding, as in the despotic reading of the *Concerto for Two Solo Pianos* he recorded with his son Soulima just before World War 2, now reissued for the first time. That inexpressive pose was as vivid a characterization as anyone's maudlin caterwauling, and, anything but bland, it transfixes.

Mr. Craft is bland. The blandness he radiates has become as emblematic of classical performance in our time as Stravinsky's hauteur had been in its very different day. It is therefore an authentic cultural expression and the truest, most painful symptom of regression from Stravinsky. Now that we have had Beethoven lite from

Christopher Hogwood and Brahms lite from John Eliot Gardiner, and even Wagner lite from Mr. Norrington, it was inevitable that someone would bring us Stravinsky lite, even a lite "Rite." It is just too ironic that that person should have been one who used to speak in Stravinsky's own voice.

POSTSCRIPT, 1994

The *Times* would not let me review Benjamin Zander's *Rite* alongside Robert Craft's, since one of its staff reviewers had already given it a wild welcome. Exactly reproducing the claims "historical" performers have made for Early Music repertories, Mr. Zander maintained that by submitting to the authority of Stravinsky's piano roll performance in the matter of tempo, he had produced a definitive orchestral realization of the score. (He even ventured to call his performance of the *"Danse sacrale"* " 'the truth,' " though the scare quotes betrayed residual discomfort with the claim.) And just like the other historical performers whose claims have been evaluated in this book, Mr. Zander submitted selectively. Stravinsky's authority (or, to put it another way, the doctrine of *Werktreue*) was invoked exactly insofar as it served the performer's needs.

Mr. Zander's agenda, like that of Robert Craft and many other latter-day performers of the early modernist repertory, was mainly one of increasing speed. Where Stravinsky's tempo on the piano roll was faster than the customary tempo or the one prescribed in the score, as was most conspicuously the case in the "Danse sacrale," that tempo was touted as "the truth." But where the piano roll tempo agreed with the published or traditional tempo (as in the "Danse de la Terre"), Mr. Zander still went faster if he could. Where the piano roll was significantly slower than the published or traditional tempo (and from Mr. Zander's description of it you would not guess that there were such places), it was simply ignored.

A remarkable case in point is the "Jeu du Rapt," where the score carries the metronome setting dotted-quarter = 132, where the piano roll varies between 109 and 116, and where Mr. Zander is out in front of all competitors at 152. (All competitors, that is, except Stravinsky himself, in his 1960 stereo recording. Mr. Zander might again wish to argue for his tempo on the strength of Stravinsky's authority, but the authority would then simply be the fastest tempo Stravinsky ever set over the course of his career, and again it would seem that authority was being sought to validate the conductor's speeds ex post facto.) At the "Glorification de l'Élue," the piano roll speed (two eighths = 123) is much slower than the score's prescription (144). Stravinsky, in 1929, conducted the piece at the piano roll tempo; in 1960 he was a little faster, at 132. Mr. Zander, at a steady 152, is the fastest ever recorded except for Pierre Monteux, who in his 1929 recording sets an initial 154 but failed to hold it. (The orchestra kept slipping back to around 134 after each return of the opening theme.) At the beginning of the Introduction to part 2, where the piano roll is slower than anyone's performance, Mr. Zander matches the old Monteux recording, in which the tempo is slower than any that Stravinsky either set down on paper or produced as conductor.

There are actually a couple of unadvertised instances where Mr. Zander's tempo is slower than the field. In the preface to the "Rondes printanières" (fig. 48), the score sets the quarter note at 108, the piano roll at 102, and Mr. Zander at 84. (Stravinsky's own recordings are consistently faster than what the score prescribes.) In the little "Kiss of the Earth" ("Le Sage") at fig. 42, the score puts the quarter note at 42, the piano roll has 46, and Mr. Zander takes it at 38, a very significant deviation when the tempo is so slow.

As to the "Danse sacrale" itself, on which Mr. Zander staked his main claim of fidelity, it turns out that his tempo is far faster than that of the piano roll (eighth = 172 vs. 147, with a spurt to 154 at the end). Pierre Monteux had equaled the piano roll tempo as early as 1929, and (as implied in essay 20), Robert Craft, though nowhere near as fast as Mr. Zander, also exceeded it.

What is the upshot of all these facts and figures? Only that Mr. Zander's exciting performance is his performance, not Stravinsky's, that it represents the "modernist" trend for this music, and that his claim of fidelity, not to say "truth," is as specious a claim of privilege as anyone else's. Like everyone else, he respects authority (the composer's "intention") only insofar as he agrees with it. And, as always, that only makes his performance the more authentic and respectable, not less. Performers can leave the quest for truth to scholars. What they need, and what Mr. Zander clearly has, is certainty.

Index

Abstraction, 17, 110; and withdrawal, 111
Academy of Ancient Music, 30, 99, 112, 144, 218–19, 293
Accountability, 16, 21–22, 24–25, 28, 30–31, 38, 57, 59, 94–95, 357; misplaced sense of, 212
Adorno, Theodor W., 37, 107, 138
Aesthetic response vs. historical response, 219
Affektenlehre, 247
Alberich, 11, 17–18, 37
Albrechtsberger, Johann Georg, 287, 289
Allanbrook, Wye J., 271–72
Allen, Woody, 67–68
Allgemeine musikalische Zeitung, 214–16
Alsop, Joseph, 219
Amadeus, 268
Ameling, Elly, 349, 351
American Musicological Society, 3, 92
Analysis, musical, 22, 24, 53, 74, 85, 250
Anthropology, 176–77, 182, 195
Anti-Semitism, 357–58
Antonyms, invidious, 90–91, 93
Appropriation, 31
Argerich, Martha, 305
Aristotle, 137n
Art, why it is not to be confused with religion, 358
Art restoration, 150, 152, 219
Articulation, 279–80
Asafiev, Boris, 133–34
Ashkenazy, Vladimir, 206
Astaire, Fred, 54
Astrology, 26
Atlas, Allan, 157, 160
Auden, W. H., 302–3
Audience, contempt for, 72–73
Auer, Leopold, 169
Augustine, Saint, 104, 354, 358

"Aura," 205, 354
Authentication, 68, 90
Authenticity, 9, 36–37, 46, 55, 68, 151, 166, 303, 318; ambiguity of term, 69; and conviction, 58, 81, 350; cultural, of authentistic performance, 102; defined in terms of moral philosophy, 67; defined in terms of musical performance, 77; desirability of an authentic understanding of, 175; and novelty, 140; process of acquisition of, 177–78; role of period instruments in achieving, 79; and skepticism, 77–78; Trilling on, 72; and what we like, 192
"Authenticity," 4–5, 11, 16, 30, 44, 46, 60, 63, 68, 70, 74, 149, 234, 319; anachronistic application of the term, 91; appeals by virtue of novelty (not antiquity), 231; as commercial propaganda, 90, 165, 354; characterized by Joseph Kerman, 92; defined by Gary Tomlinson, 92; dodging interpretive problems in name of, 228; early use of term by Donald Grout, 92; euphemisms for, 92–93; of first performance, 162; and historical verisimilitude, 94–95, 113; and intentions, 98; as movement, 68, 76, 95, 143; paradox of, 36–37, 295; and performance practice, 90; and sound-materialism, 207; spurious assumption of moral authority in name of, 77; and Urtext ideology, 72; and *Werktreue*, 278, 366; Walter Benjamin on, 204–5
Authentistic performance, 286; ahistoricity of, 164–72, 295; articles of faith of, 130; art restoration as metaphor for, 150, 152, 219; and

Printed in Great Britain
by Amazon.co.uk, Ltd.,
Marston Gate.